£13-95

PROGRAM
CONSTRUCTION
AND
VERIFICATION

Prentice-Hall International
Series in Computer Science

C.A.R. Hoare, Series Editor

Published

BACKHOUSE, R. C., *Program Construction and Verification*
BACKHOUSE, R. C., *Syntax of Programming Languages, Theory and Practice*
de BAKKER, J. W., *Mathematical Theory of Program Correctness*
BJORNER, D. and JONES, C., *Formal Specification and Software Development*
CLARK, K. L. and McCABE, F. G., *micro-PROLOG: Programming in Logic*
DROMEY, R. G., *How to Solve it by Computer*
DUNCAN, F., *Microprocessor Programming and Software Development*
ELDER, J., *Construction of Data Processing Software*
GOLDSCHLAGER, L. and LISTER, A., *Computer Science: A Modern Introduction*
HEHNER, E. C. R., *The Logic of Programming*
HENDERSON, P., *Functional Programming: Application and Implementation*
HOARE, C. A. R., *Communicating Sequential Processes*
HOARE, C. A. R., and SHEPHERDSON, J. C., (eds) *Mathematical Logic and Programming Languages*
INMOS, LTD., *The Occam Programming Manual*
JACKSON, M. A., *System Development*
JOHNSTON, H., *Learning to Program*
JONES, C. B., *Software Development: A Rigorous Approach*
JOSEPH, M., PRASAD, V. R. and NATARAJAN, N., *A Multiprocessor Operating System*
LEW, A., *Computer Science: A Mathematical Introduction*
MacCALLUM, I., *Pascal for the Apple*
MacCALLUM, I., *UCSD Pascal for the IBM PC*
MARTIN, J. J., *Data Types and Data Structures*
REYNOLDS, J. C., *The Craft of Programming*
TENNENT, R. D., *Principles of Programming Languages*
WELSH, J. and ELDER, J., *Introduction to Pascal, 2nd Edition*
WELSH, J., ELDER, J., and BUSTARD, D., *Sequential Program Structures*
WELSH, J. and McKEAG, M., *Structured System Programming*

Program Construction and Verification

ROLAND C. BACKHOUSE

*Department of Computer Science,
University of Essex*

Prentice/Hall PHI International

Englewood Cliffs, NJ   London   Mexico   New Delhi   Rio de Janeiro
Singapore   Sydney   Tokyo   Toronto   Wellington

Library of Congress Cataloging in Publication Data

Backhouse, Roland, C., 1948–
    Program construction and verification.

    Bibliography: p.
    Includes index.
    1. Electronic digital computers—Programming.
I. Title.
QA76.7.B28   1986   005   85-16883
ISBN 0-13-729153-1

British Library Cataloguing in Publication Data

Backhouse, Roland Carl
    Program construction and verification.

    1. Computer programs   2. Computer programs
    —Validation
    I. Title
    001.64′2   QA76.754
ISBN 0-13-729153-1
ISBN 0-13-729146-9 Pbk

© 1986 Prentice-Hall International (UK) Ltd

Prentice-Hall Inc., *Englewood Cliffs, New Jersey*
Prentice-Hall International (UK) Ltd, *London*
Prentice-Hall of Australia Pty Ltd, *Sydney*
Prentice-Hall Canada Inc., *Toronto*
Prentice-Hall Hispanoamericana S.A., *Mexico*
Prentice-Hall of India Private Ltd, *New Delhi*
Prentice-Hall of Japan Inc., *Tokyo*
Prentice-Hall of Southeast Asia Pte Ltd, *Singapore*
Editora Prentice-Hall do Brasil Ltda, *Rio de Janeiro*
Whitehall Books Ltd, *Wellington, New Zealand*

Printed and bound in Great Britain for
Prentice-Hall International (UK) Ltd,
66 Wood Lane End, Hemel Hempstead, Herts. HP2 4RG,
by A. Wheaton and Co Ltd, Exeter

1   2   3   4   5   90   89   88   87   86

ISBN 0-13-729153-1
ISBN 0-13-729146-9 PBK

CONTENTS

PREFACE

Programming has been variously described as an Art, a Craft, a Discipline, a Logic, and a Science. Indeed, all of these epithets are appropriate, and none on its own can completely characterize the subject. Programming is one of our most demanding intellectual activities, requiring great clarity and economy, of thought and of expression. Programming is, also, a very creative and rewarding activity; it is, therefore, not surprising that skilled programmers are scarce and highly-valued.

The objective of this book is to introduce the reader to the principles of developing programs that provably achieve a given, mathematical specification. The book is intended to appeal both to novice programmers who wish to start on the right track, and to experienced programmers who wish to increase their pride in their programming ability. My approach is to show how the process of *verifying* that a program achieves its specification should also dictate the process whereby programs are *constructed*. For those unfamiliar with the ideas of program verification, chapter 0 presents an illustrative example, but without the mathematical rigor of subsequent chapters.

Complete familiarity with the techniques of program verification is essential if one is to use those techniques effectively for program construction. Enabling the reader to gain such familiarity is the purpose of chapters 1, 2 and 3. Chapter 1 is an introduction to the propositional calculus. The emphasis in these chapters is on acquiring skill in the mathematical manipulation of logical formulae; in order to integrate this material with the method of program development, the examples used, particularly in chapter 2, are selected from programming problems in later sections of the book.

Given its aims, an inevitable decision on the book's presentation was to restrict discussion to a very small and simple programming language, so

ix

as to exclude extraneous issues about controversial language features. Chapter 3, therefore, describes Hoare's and Dijkstra's program verification techniques for a language consisting only of assignment statements, conditional statements, **while** statements and the sequential composition of statements. An advantage of so restricting the language is that the text is not tied to a particular programming language; the features described are present in one form or another in all languages likely to be encountered in the career of a professional programmer. In addition, I have occasionally used Pascal notation to describe and refer to some simple data structures.

The final chapter, chapter 4, draws together the threads of the earlier chapters. It shows by example how the programmer's craft is in doing creative mathematics, in the sense that even the most mundane assignment requires the discovery and verification of a (perhaps quite shallow) constructive theorem about some data space. The topics in this chapter are largely independent of each other and may be studied in a different order according to individual needs.

In common with all crafts, the skill involved in programming cannot be acquired by passive study. It must be practiced diligently. To this end, I have supplied a large number of exercises, together with solutions. However, complete understanding can only be achieved by consciously and actively exploiting the suggested techniques away from the classroom, on all programming problems that are encountered. One should also avoid reliance on a computer to rectify careless mistakes—the aim should be for complete confidence in the program text *before* it is first submitted for execution.

I have lectured on this material for several years to groups containing both experienced and novice student programmers. The novices were students from other disciplines who were being 'converted' to Computing Science, and the experienced programmers were drawn from industry. Inevitably, it is the experienced programmers who are quicker to appreciate the merits of a mathematical approach to their work. But, it is the novice programmers who, in the long run, will derive most benefit from such an approach. I hope, therefore, that this, or similar, material will increasingly find a place in the earliest stages of a Computing Science curriculum.

I have received a very great deal of help in the preparation of this text, far more than I could ever have hoped for. My warm thanks go firstly to Tony Hoare for his continuing patience, encouragement and advice. David Gries, Eric Hehner and Maurice Clint have all read the typescript at various stages in its preparation, far surpassing their duty in the wealth of expert comments, criticism and corrections they have provided. I have also received many comments and ideas from colleagues and students, in particular from Stuart Anderson and Aziz Khamiss. In addition, I am extremely grateful to those scientists who, though never directly involved in the book's production, have contributed its source material through their publications. In particular, I am indebted to E. W. Dijkstra, who has led the way in changing programming into a science and whose imprint is evident on almost every page. At a more mundane, but nevertheless vital, level I am grateful to Marisa Bostock, Christine Barker and Ann Cook for their expert assistance in typing the manuscript. Finally, my warmest thanks go to my wife, Hilary.

R. C. B.

PROGRAM
CONSTRUCTION
AND
VERIFICATION

0 A SCIENCE OF COMPUTING

0.1 THE FALLACY OF DEBUGGING

The subject matter of this book is a mathematical approach to correct program development. The need for such an approach was first recognized in the late sixties when the large computer manufacturers began to realize that the costs of producing computer software were outstripping by far the costs of producing computer hardware. They spoke, and still do speak, of a 'software crisis'. The problems of producing reliable computer software were aired at a conference on Software Engineering held in 1969. Typical of the sort of facts laid bare at that conference was the following statement by M. E. Hopkins, from IBM Corporation.

> We face a fantastic problem in big systems. For instance, in OS/360[†] we have about 1000 errors per release.

In spite of considerable advances in the design of programming languages, the gulf between the cost and the reliability of hardware and software has widened. This is due to the intrinsic difficulty of software design. But the problems of software design are made worse by the continued reliance of most programmers on the process euphemistically known as 'debugging' to ensure the correctness of their programs. Debugging consists essentially of an iterative process of testing, followed by correcting, and is *not* a scientific method of ensuring a program's correctness. As M. E. Hopkins has said,

> Programmers call their errors 'bugs' to preserve their sanity; that number of 'mistakes' would not be psychologically acceptable.

[†] OS/360 is an operating system for IBM computers.

1

It comes as a surprise to many programmers to be told that debugging is unsound and unreliable and I should therefore like to spend some time explaining why.

The process of debugging has two major drawbacks. The first is that it is useless as a methodology for program design; the second is that it can never be used to establish the correctness of a correct program or, equally, it cannot be relied upon to establish the incorrectness of an incorrect program.

Let us look in detail at the second of these drawbacks. Here are two examples, each illustrating a different aspect.

0.1.1 Testing a Correct Program

One well-known method of computing n^2, for some positive integer n, without performing a multiplication is to sum the first n odd numbers. This is based on the property that

$$1 + 3 + 5 + \ldots + (2n - 1) = n^2$$

and is expressed by the following algorithm:

```
i := 0;   s := 0;
while i ≠ n do
   begin i := i + 1;   s := s + 2*i − 1
   end
```

Not so well known is that a similar algorithm can be used to compute n^3, n^4, n^5, etc. To see how to do this let us re-express the computation of n^2 as follows.

First write down all the positive integers up to $2n - 1$, so:

$$1 \quad 2 \quad 3 \quad 4 \quad 5 \quad 6 \quad 7 \quad 8 \quad 9 \quad 10 \quad 11$$

Now cross out every second integer:

$$1 \quad\quad 3 \quad\quad 5 \quad\quad 7 \quad\quad 9 \quad\quad\quad 11$$

Finally, add these together to form a running total:

$$1 \quad\quad 4 \quad\quad 9 \quad\quad 16 \quad\quad 25 \quad\quad 36$$

To compute n^3 we begin as before by writing down all the positive integers, but this time up to $3n - 2$, so:

$$1 \quad 2 \quad 3 \quad 4 \quad 5 \quad 6 \quad 7 \quad 8 \quad 9 \quad 10 \quad 11 \quad 12 \quad 13 \quad 14 \quad 15 \quad 16$$

Now cross out every third integer:

$$1 \quad 2 \quad\quad 4 \quad 5 \quad\quad 7 \quad 8 \quad\quad 10 \quad 11 \quad\quad 13 \quad 14 \quad\quad 16$$

Then form a running total:

| 1 | 3 | | 7 | 12 | | 19 | 27 | | 37 | 48 | | 61 | 75 | | 91 |

Now cross out every second value:

| 1 | | 7 | | 19 | | 37 | | 61 | | 91 |

Finally, from a running total:

| 1 | | 8 | | 27 | | 64 | | 125 | | 216 |

Now we can test this algorithm in two ways. We can extend one of the existing tables to the right, for example the table for n^2 can be extended to calculate 7^2 and 8^2.

1	2	3	4	5	6	7	8	9	10	11	12	13	14	15
1		3		5		7		9		11		13		15
1		4		9		16		25		36		49		64

or we can add new tables to the ones we already have, for example the table for 3^4,

1	2	3	4	5	6	7	8	9
1	2	3		5	6	7		9
1	3	6		11	17	24		33
1	3			11	17			33
1	4			15	32			65
1				15				65
1				16				81

We can continue this testing as much as we like (indeed for ever and a day). Each time we add more entries and verify the correct result our confidence in the algorithm grows. But this process will never make us *totally* confident in the algorithm. Can we be sure that it will correctly compute 21^5 or 6^{12}? On the evidence presented so far would you be willing to gamble on its correctness?

Edsger Dijkstra, an eminent computer scientist, has summarized this flaw in debugging in a now-famous quotation.

Program testing can be used to show the presence of bugs, but never to show their absence.

0.1.2 Testing an Incorrect Program

A consequence of this is that testing cannot even be relied on to show the presence of bugs. I once had a very graphic illustration of this when I had to mark a first-year student's assignment. The problem the students had been set was to write in Pascal a program that would compare two strings for equality. One student's solution was to assign the value **true** or **false** to a Boolean quantity *equal* as follows:

$equal := (string1 \cdot length = string2 \cdot length)$;
if *equal*
then for $i := 1$ **to** $string1 \cdot length$ **do**
   $equal := string1 \cdot character[i] = string2 \cdot character[i]$

The problem with this code is that it returns the value **true** if and only if the two strings have equal length and their *last* characters are identical. For example, the two strings 'cat' and 'mat' would be declared equal because they both have length 3 and end in 't'.

When I demonstrated this to the student (without explaining what was wrong) he shrieked at me 'But it worked last Tuesday!' as if it were the computer's fault. Indeed his testing of the program had been quite systematic. He had first tested the program on several pairs of identical strings and then on several pairs of strings of unequal length. Both these tests had produced satisfactory results as one might expect. His final test had been to input several pairs consisting of equal length but unequal strings, such as 'cat' and 'dog', or 'house' and 'ships'.

Now this final test is interesting because it is possible to use simple probability theory to make a very rough estimate of the chances of his having

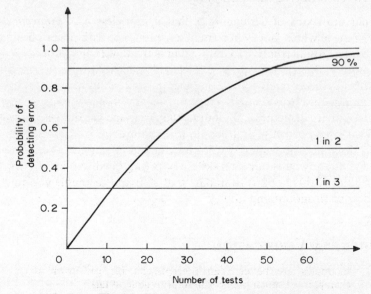

Fig. 0.1 'Buggy' string comparison.

discovered the programming error. Suppose, to make the analysis easy, that letter frequencies are equal and that words of length n occur one-tenth of the time for lengths up to ten, and not at all for longer lengths. Then the probability that any two randomly generated strings of equal length have unequal last characters is 25/26. Thus the probability that the input of just one pair of strings in the final test would reveal the error is at most 1/26 (since the probability that two *unequal* strings differ in their last character is higher than 25/26). Similarly, one can argue that the probability of n such pairs showing up the error is less than $1 - (25/26)^n$. The latter formula has been plotted in Fig. 0.1 for values of n between 0 and 60.

The results of this analysis reveal quite startlingly just how unreliable debugging is for discovering errors. With this probability distribution there is only a 1 in 3 chance of discovering the error after ten tests; increasing the number of tests to 20 would still only yield a 1 in 2 chance, and one would need to perform over 50 tests to achieve a 90 percent chance of discovering the error. Finally, and most importantly, there is no certainty that one would ever discover the error no matter how many tests are performed.

So you see that program testing is never-ending. We can never be sure that all avenues have been tried; we can never be sure that there is not one more error lurking unseen, just waiting for the most crucial opportunity to show itself.

0.1.3 An Alternative to Debugging

The other drawback of debugging is that it is useless as a *program design methodology*, of which fact even a small acquaintance with programming will convince you. An alternative to debugging is the development of a *science* of programming. Such a science would provide the techniques to enable the *verification* of the correctness of computer programs. But it would do more than that; it would provide a *discipline* for the development of programs that guarantees their correctness. Of course, the discipline guarantees correctness only if it is used correctly, and people will continue to make mistakes, even with our discipline. So testing is still wise, and debugging will occasionally be necessary. But now, it is our own skill in applying the discipline on which we rely. The aim of this book is to impart that skill and to enable you to take a pride in your programming ability.

0.2 PROGRAM VERIFICATION

> Examples are better than precepts; let me get down to examples—I much prefer examples to general talk.
>
> G. Polya

0.2.1 A Searching Problem and Its Solution

Problem Statement

To give you the flavor of the subject this section is about the systematic development of a searching algorithm and its proof of correctness. The problem we consider is this. Suppose you are presented with a deck of cards as shown in Fig. 0.2. On each card is printed the name of a student together with personal details (date of birth, address, examination record, etc.). The cards are all in alphabetic order (according to surname). Suppose you are also presented with one additional card on which is printed the name of a student X. The task is to describe a general procedure for splitting the deck of cards into two parts in such a way that (a) all of the cards in the first part precede X and (b) none of the cards in the second part precedes X in alphabetic order. Otherwise, the original deck should be left intact. (We call this a searching problem because we are effectively looking for the position in the deck at which to insert the new card.)

When presented with a problem like this, the first step should always be to ensure that you have a clear understanding of the problem. For programming purposes, the demands on clarity and unambiguity of the problem specification are much higher than if the task is to be carried out manually by a

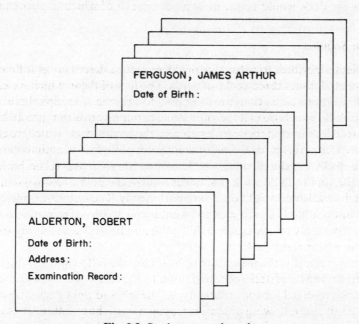

Fig. 0.2 Student record cards.

colleague, when one can rely on common sense and intelligence. We discuss program specification in detail in chapter 2, but for the purposes of this exposition we rely on your good will in making sense of some of the actions to be described.

One point needing clarification is that the process of splitting the original deck may result in one (or indeed both) of the parts being empty. For example, if the deck contains the student surnames

Einstein
Newton
Russell

and the name X is Galileo then the deck should be split into the two parts consisting of, first, the card belonging to Einstein and, second, the two cards belonging to Newton and Russell. However, if the name X is Turing then the first part consists of all three cards in the original deck and the second part is empty.

The mathematical abstraction of regarding no cards as being nonetheless a deck of cards is a useful one with the very practical effect of reducing the number of cases one has to consider from three (X is at the beginning, X is in the middle, and X is at the end) to one. As a bonus, the original problem statement now applies to an empty deck of cards, in which case the process of splitting the deck would result in two parts, each of which is also empty.

Problem Solution

An efficient algorithm to solve this problem can be described as follows. We maintain at all times three decks of cards. The first of these, which we call the *left deck*, contains cards that are all known to precede X in alphabetic order; the third deck, which we call the *right deck*, contains cards that are all known not to precede X in alphabetic order; finally, the second deck, which we call the *middle deck*, contains cards that may or may not precede X in alphabetic order. All three decks are alphabetically ordered and are such that recombining the left, middle, and right decks in that order returns the deck to its original form.

Initially the left and right decks are both empty. The task is complete when the middle deck has been reduced to an empty deck. We make progress to this state by repeatedly removing cards from the middle deck and adding them to either the left or right deck.

More specifically, the procedure to be used is the following. Arrange space on a table for the three decks of cards. Initially, the entire deck is placed face up in the space reserved for the middle deck. The left and right decks are empty. Subsequently, the following process is repeated until the middle deck is empty.

Pick up the middle deck and split it in two. This splitting may take place in an arbitrary fashion except that the deck containing the cards that are last in alphabetic order should be nonempty. Call the two decks the lower and upper decks, where the lower deck contains the cards that are first in alphabetic order. Then, depending on the student name now revealed at the start of the upper deck, do one of two things.

(1) If the name precedes X then place the entire lower deck and the first card of the upper deck face down on the left deck and put the remainder of the upper deck back onto the middle space. (Thus the remainder of the upper deck becomes the new middle deck.)
(2) If the name does not precede X then place the entire upper deck face up on the right deck and return the lower deck to the middle space. (Thus the lower deck becomes the new middle deck.)

When the middle deck is empty the original goal will have been achieved.

This completes the description of the algorithm. Let us now see what would constitute a proof of its correctness.

0.2.2 Proof of Correctness

The first thing to be completely clear about is that 'correctness' is a relative notion. The world 'correct' sounds absolute—and that may be the way you use it in everyday conversation—but it is being used here as a technical term. When we refer to a program being correct we mean relative to some given *specification*. Generally, the specification of a programming problem consists of a *precondition* describing the properties of the supplied data and a *postcondition* describing the desired effect of the computation. In our searching problem the precondition comprises a description of the given deck of cards and the information it contains, together with the important requirement that the names on the cards be alphabetically ordered. The postcondition states that the given deck of cards is to be split into two and details the properties required of the two parts. In terms of the solution we have presented these properties are:

(P1) All of the cards in the left deck and none of the cards in the right deck precede X in alphabetic order.
(P2) The original deck can be retrieved by recombining the left and right decks in that order.

The crux of our proof of correctness consists of the invention of two things called the *variant* and *invariant* of the repeated process. The variant is an integer-valued quantity that is altered on each repetition. We use it to prove that the process will always terminate, i.e. that it will not 'get into a loop' and repeat the same sequence of actions indefinitely. The *invariant* is a property of the decks of cards that holds whenever the search process is about to be repeated, irrespective of the number of repetitions that have been executed.

(a) Proof of Termination

For the variant we take the number of cards in the middle deck. To use it to prove that the repetition will always terminate, it suffices to make two observations.

(T1) There is a lower bound on the size of the middle deck. In this case the lower bound, zero, is dictated by the physical characteristics of a deck of cards, but usually we look to the termination condition to provide such a bound.

(T2) Every time the repeated part of the search process is executed the number of cards in the middle deck always decreases since the card that is inspected is always removed from it.

Together, these two observations make it quite obvious that the number of times the repeated part is executed is at most equal to the number of cards in the original deck.

(b) Conditional Correctness

The second part of the proof of correctness is given the name *conditional correctness*. A proof of conditional correctness assumes that the execution of a process terminates and concentrates on establishing that its specification is met.

The properties we use to establish the conditional correctness of the algorithm have already been stated. They are:

(I1) All the cards in the left deck and none of the cards in the right deck precede X in alphabetic order.

(I2) The original deck may be retrieved by recombining the left, middle, and right decks in that order.

Note that these properties hold no matter how often the splitting process has been executed, and so we refer to them as *invariants*.

We use the *principle of mathematical induction* to prove that properties (I1) and (I2) really are invariant. Generally, the principle of mathematical induction is used to prove that some property $P(n)$ is true for all natural numbers (nonnegative integers) n. In our case n refers to the number of times the middle deck has been split and property P is property (I1) **and** property (I2). In other words, what we wish to prove is that, for any natural number n, conditions (I1) and (I2) hold after n iterations.

The first step is therefore to show that properties (I1) and (I2) hold after 0 iterations—i.e. initially. This is true of (I1) since initially the left and right decks are empty. Property (I2) is also true because the combination of the left, middle, and right decks is just the middle deck which is identical to the original deck.

The next step is to make the inductive hypothesis that (I1) and (I2) hold just before execution of the repeated part. Then we examine in turn the two cases considered within the splitting process and show that in each case properties (I1) and (I2) remain true after its execution. Let us examine just one of these cases to see how the argument goes.

We are assuming that the original deck has been split into three decks— the left, middle, and right decks—and that all of the cards in the left deck and none of the cards in the right deck precede X in alphabetic order. Let us suppose that cutting the middle deck reveals a name that precedes X in alphabetic order. Then, since the original deck was sorted, the name on every card in the lower part of the middle deck must also precede X. Thus removing the lower deck and the revealed card from the middle deck and appending them to the left deck preserves property (I1). Clearly, also, we leave the deck intact in the sense of property (I2) by adding the removed cards to the end of the left deck.

The final step in our use of mathematical induction is to argue that since properties (I1) and (I2) hold initially, they must, by the above argument, also hold after one iteration of the loop body and therefore after two and three and so on. We conclude that properties (I1) and (I2) are invariants, i.e. their truth is independent of the number of iterations that have been executed.

There is one more step remaining before our proof is complete. This is to show that the postcondition of the algorithm is a logical consequence of the condition for terminating the repetition and the two invariant properties. This is clearly true because on termination the middle deck is empty, which is equivalent to saying that the original deck has been split in two. More formally, invariant (I1) is identical to property (P1) of the postcondition and invariant (I2) reduces to property (P2) when we take account of the fact that the middle deck is empty. This completes the proof.

0.2.3 Summary

The argument we have given in section 0.2.2 can be criticized for not being a proof in the mathematical sense. The problem lies in the use of an imprecise language (English) to describe the algorithm; on occasion you have been expected to interpret the statements generously. (For example, the way in which the left and lower decks, or the right and upper decks, are combined into one was never precisely stated although it is crucial to keeping the original deck intact.) The main objective, however, has been to summarize the main elements in a proof of correctness.

One important feature of this example, which we shall stress continually later on, is the manner in which the algorithm was presented. To remind you let us quote the first paragraph in the description of the algorithm.

We maintain at all times three decks of cards. The first of these, which we call the *left deck*, contains cards that are all known to precede X in alphabetic order; the third deck, which we call the *right deck*, contains cards that are all known not to precede X in alphabetic order; finally, the second deck, which we call the *middle deck*, contains cards that may or may not precede X in alphabetic order. All three decks are alphabetically ordered and are such that recombining the left, middle, and right decks in that order returns the deck to its original form.

Note that this part of the description says little about *how* the algorithm works; it is much more an explanation of *why* the algorithm works. We call it a *functional* description because it describes the function or purpose of each of the three decks. Essentially it is a summary of the proof of conditional correctness of the algorithm.

Equally, the second part of the algorithm's description is more concerned with *why* rather than *how* the algorithm works. It forms a summary of the proof of termination.

Initially the left and right decks are both empty. The task is complete when the middle deck has been reduced to an empty deck. We make progress to this state by repeatedly removing cards from the middle deck and adding them to either the left or right deck.

We shall not quote the third part of the algorithm's description because it is likely to be the sort of description with which you are most familiar. Unlike the first two parts it is very much concerned with *how* the algorithm works and not *why* it works. We call it an *operational* description because it describes the operations to be performed on the supplied data.

A conventional computer program written in a language like Pascal provides an operational description of a problem's solution. The problem statement or specification says *what* the program is intended to compute. These, together with the program's proof, provide the what, the how, and the why of the problem and its solution. Each part complements the others and is essential to true understanding. Unfortunately, too often the what and the why—the specification and proof—are completely omitted (and sometimes nonexistent). It is time to redress the balance.

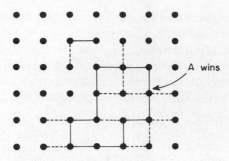

Fig. 0.3 The grid game.

Exercises

These exercises are intended to encourage you to think in terms of invariants. They all involve two-person games and for each there is some way in which one of the players can always guarantee to win. You have to discover the winner's strategy: the clue is to always endeavor to establish an appropriate invariant property.

0.1 The two players are given a daisy having 16 petals arranged symmetrically around the center. A move involves removing one petal or two adjacent petals from the daisy and the winner is the one removing the last petal. Who should win and what is the winning strategy?

0.2 The two players sit at a large rectangular table and are provided with an unlimited supply of coins. The coins may be of varying size so long as they are all circular and there is an unlimited supply of each type of coin. A move is to place a coin on the table so that it does not touch any other nor overlap the edge of the table. The winner is the one to place the last coin on the table (and, of course, the winner pockets all the money!). Who should win and what is the winning strategy?

0.3 In this game players A and B are provided with a grid of any size (see Fig. 0.3). Player A draws a solid horizontal line (———) or a solid vertical line (|) between two adjacent points on his turn. Player B draws a dashed horizontal line (----) or a dashed vertical line (¦) between two adjacent points on his turn. One player cannot play in a place that another has played. Player A wins if he gets a closed curve of solid lines (see Fig. 0.3); B wins if he *prevents* A from getting a closed curve. Who should win and what is the winning strategy?

0.3 OVERVIEW

The remainder of the book has been divided into four chapters. The next chapter is about logical reasoning. In it we discuss what is a 'valid' or 'logical' argument and what is meant by the word 'proof'. The predicate calculus forms the basis of all formal specification languages, and its use in specifying simple computational problems is exemplified in chapter 2.

Chapter 3 introduces a simple programming language consisting only of assignments, conditional statements, **while** statements, and the sequential composition of statements. Such constructs appear in one form or another in almost all conventional programming languages. It is assumed that you have a basic knowledge of programming; if so you should have no difficulty in mastering these few constructs. The notation used is that of Pascal, on which there are many introductory texts. In chapter 3, rules for arguing about the correctness of programs with respect to given pre- and postconditions are formulated and applied to simple programs.

Chapter 4 inverts the process begun in chapter 3. Instead of proving a given program we use the principles of proof to guide the design of a correct program from the given pre- and postconditions. This chapter is the *raison d'être* of the earlier chapters.

It is not easy to write a scientific text starting at page one and ending at the last page, and that is certainly not the way this one was written. Equally, the best way to read it is not necessarily to begin at the beginning and read through to the end. Many of the examples and exercises in the earlier chapters arise from problems discussed in the last chapter so that the motivation for them may not be immediately apparent. When teaching this material it is my practice to present students with problems from the final chapter in discussion sessions while the material in chapters 1, 2 and 3 is being presented in formal lectures. In this way I hope that they gain insight into the major principles even though they have not yet acquired the apparatus required to apply them formally. It may be valuable therefore if you skim through chapter 4 at this stage and refer to it whenever the earlier material seems to lack motivation.

1 THE PROPOSITIONAL CALCULUS

1.1 FORMAL AND INFORMAL PROOFS

When the word 'proof' is used it can generally be understood in two different ways. An *informal proof*, the sort most commonly used by mathematicians, consists of an outline of, or a strategy for constructing, a *formal proof*. A *formal proof* is a sequence of statements, each of which is a well-established fact or which follows from earlier statements by a process so simple that it is deemed to be self-evident. A formal proof is conducted in an artificial (or 'formal') language consisting entirely of signs and symbols; a mathematician's proof, on the other hand, will make significant use of natural language (such as English) as well as signs and symbols where they are considered appropriate. Figures 1.1 and 1.2 illustrate both types of proof.

Both types of proof have their own characteristic type of complexity. In the case of the mathematician's proof it is the complexity of hidden details and assumed knowledge; in the case of formal proofs it is the complexity of size, since such proofs are usually quite long. The mathematician's art in constructing convincing proofs is one of presenting the right level of detail, i.e. striking a balance between formality and informality. Being able to strike this balance is a fundamental part of our mathematical training, and it is an ability that takes many years to acquire.

It is well accepted that to be a good programmer one must have a particular aptitude for logical reasoning. Unfortunately, it is not always recognized that the art of logical reasoning implies an ability to strike a balance between formality and informality. An ability for informal reasoning seems to be innate in all of us, but formal reasoning is a skill that is less natural and must be practised. In order to be able to strike the right balance it is therefore necessary that we tip the scales towards formality for a little while.

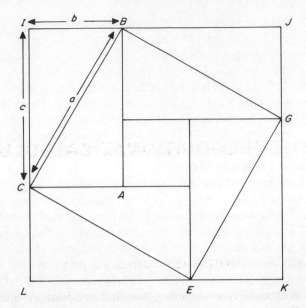

Let ABC be a triangle with $B\hat{A}C = 90°$. Let the lengths of sides BC, AC, and AB be respectively a, b, and c. Then we wish to prove that $a^2 = b^2 + c^2$. Construct a square $IJKL$ of side $b + c$ as shown in the figure.

Clearly, $\text{area}(IJKL) = (b + c)^2 = b^2 + c^2 + 2bc$
but also, $\text{area}(IJKL) = \text{area}(CBGE) + 4 \cdot \text{area}(ABC)$
$$= a^2 + 2bc$$
thus, $a^2 + 2bc = b^2 + c^2 + 2bc$
i.e. $a^2 = b^2 + c^2.$

Fig. 1.1 A mathematician's proof of Pythagoras' theorem.

0.   if $a > 0$ and $b > c > 0$ then $a + b > a + c > 0$
1.   if $a > b > 0$ then $\sqrt{a} > \sqrt{b} > 0$
2. $224 > 9 > 0$
3. $\sqrt{224} > \sqrt{9} > 0$ (1 and 2)
4. $4\sqrt{14} > 3 > 0$
5. $57 + 4\sqrt{14} > 57 + 3 > 0$ (0 and 4)
6. $\sqrt{(57 + 4\sqrt{14})} > \sqrt{(57 + 3)} > 0$ (1 and 5)
7. $1 + 2\sqrt{14} > 2\sqrt{15} > 0$
8. $8 + 1 + 2\sqrt{14} > 8 + 2\sqrt{15} > 0$ (0 and 7)
9. $\sqrt{(8 + 1 + 2\sqrt{14})} > \sqrt{(8 + 2\sqrt{15})} > 0$ (1 and 8)
10. $\sqrt{2} + \sqrt{7} > \sqrt{3} + \sqrt{5} > 0$
Hence $\sqrt{2} + \sqrt{7} > \sqrt{3} + \sqrt{5}$

Fig. 1.2 Formal proof of $\sqrt{2} + \sqrt{7} > \sqrt{3} + \sqrt{5}$.

In a proof, whether formal or informal, we may distinguish two types of reasoning. There is reasoning that involves properties of the data and is therefore problem dependent, and there is reasoning that is independent of the problem domain. The latter form of reasoning we call *logical reasoning*. For instance, lines 4, 7, and 10 of Fig. 1.2 are deduced by simplifying the preceding line, and thus are dependent on properties of the integers. However, lines 3, 5, 6, 8, and 9 of Fig. 1.2 are deduced by a logical process. It is very important that one be able to distinguish both forms. In this chapter our concern is with formalizing logical reasoning; the next chapter provides a mechanism for reasoning about properties of the data.

This chapter is about the *propositional calculus*; chapter 2 is about the *predicate calculus*. The propositional calculus concerns absolute truths and is essentially a formalization of the logical operators such as **and, or**, and **if...then...**. The predicate calculus concerns relative truths, i.e. propositions that depend on the value(s) of one or more variables. For example, the precondition and postcondition that make up a program specification are predicates that depend on the values of the program variables. The word 'calculus' in both these terms signifies that they are manipulative systems.

Exercises

1.1 The proof in Fig. 1.1 assumes quite a lot of knowledge about geometric figures. Can you fill in some of the details in the proof by stating these properties?

1.2 Below is an algorithm to determine whether $\sqrt{a} + \sqrt{b} > \sqrt{c} + \sqrt{d}$ for given natural numbers $a, b, c,$ and d. What is wrong with it? (*Hint*: examine each step in the algorithm to see whether it makes a valid use of the properties stated in lines 0 and 1 of Fig. 1.2.) Construct an example to demonstrate the error.

We refer to $\sqrt{a} + \sqrt{b}$ and $\sqrt{c} + \sqrt{d}$ as the *left* and *right sides* of the inequality, respectively.

Step 1. Square the left side and simplify it to the form $u + \sqrt{v}$. (For example $(\sqrt{3} + \sqrt{11})^2$ is simplified to $14 + \sqrt{132}$.) Similarly, square and simplify the right side to the form $x + \sqrt{y}$.

Step 2. Subtract u from both sides and simplify. The left side is now in the form $\sqrt{v}$ and the right side is in the form $z + \sqrt{y}$.

Step 3. Square both sides again. Simplify the right side to the form $p + \sqrt{q}$. The left side will of course just be v.

Step 4. Subtract p from both sides and then square again.

$\sqrt{a} + \sqrt{b}$ is greater than $\sqrt{c} + \sqrt{d}$ if and only if the left side is now greater than the right side. (Note that Fig. 1.2 was derived by reversing the steps in a correct version of this algorithm.)

1.2 PROPOSITIONS

> He thought he saw an Argument
> That proved he was the Pope:
> He looked again, and found it was
> A Bar of Mottled Soap.
> *Lewis Carroll*

Let us begin our discussion of logical reasoning by considering the following argument:

> If Superman were able and willing to prevent evil, he would do so. If Superman were unable to prevent evil, he would be impotent; if he were unwilling to prevent evil, he would be malevolent. Superman does not prevent evil. If Superman exists, he is neither impotent nor malevolent. Therefore Superman does not exist.

This argument, which exemplifies the general form of an argument, consists of the *premises*:

(a) if Superman were able and willing to prevent evil, he would do so;
(b) if Superman were unable to prevent evil, he would be impotent;
(c) if Superman were unwilling to prevent evil, he would be malevolent;
(d) Superman does not prevent evil;
(e) if Superman exists, he is neither impotent nor malevolent,

and the conclusion

> Superman does not exist.

Now you may agree or disagree with any combination of the five premises, but that is not our concern nor the concern of logical reasoning. What will concern us is whether the conclusion *logically follows* from the premises. If so, we say that the argument is *logical* or *valid*.

The premises and conclusion in the above argument can be further broken down into *propositions* which have been combined by *logical connectives*. The propositions are as follows:

> Superman exists.
> Superman is willing to prevent evil.
> Superman is able to prevent evil.
> Superman is malevolent.
> Superman is impotent.
> Superman prevents evil.

A *proposition* is simply *a statement that is true or false*.

Whilst the propositions in an English argument are usually straightforward to identify, the connectives and, more particularly, their precise meaning are not always. The connectives above are implied by the use of 'if' and 'therefore'. Other commonly used connectives are 'but', 'so', 'hence', 'consequently', 'thus', 'accordingly', 'because', 'since' and 'for'.

Exercises

1.3 For each of the following say whether or not the sentence expresses a proposition.

(a) I think, therefore I am.
(b) Do as I say, not as I do.
(c) Whenever the assignment $x := y$ is executed the value of y remains unchanged.
(d) Write clearly and legibly.
(e) How do you know your answers are correct?

1.4 Several sets of sentences follow, each of which constitutes an argument. For each identify the premises and the conclusion. Which of them would you regard as being logical?

(a) The knowledge in universities grows and grows. Each new student brings a little knowledge in, and the graduates do not take any away.
(b) There are five marks for each of four projects, making a total of 20 marks. There are also 20 marks for each examination question, and students are asked to answer four questions. If a student fails to submit an item of project work the mark given for that item is − 5. The pass mark is 40. Therefore, if a student submits no project work whatsoever he/she must achieve a mark of at least 60 in the examination questions in order to pass.
(c) Only an elephant or a whale gives birth to a creature whose weight is 70 kilograms or more. The President's weight is 75 kilograms. Therefore the President's mother is either an elephant or a whale.

1.3 INTRODUCING SYMBOLS

Many arguments take the same form; to the logician they are identical, although their subject matter may be different. For instance, take the following arguments:

(1) If k eventually equals x the algorithm will terminate.
    k is eventually equal to x.
    Therefore the algorithm will terminate.

(2) If the book is a recommended text a copy will be held in the library.

The book is a recommended text.
Therefore a copy will be held in the library.

If arbitrary letters of the alphabet are chosen to represent the propositions in the arguments, both will be seen to exhibit the form:

If A then B
A
Therefore B

We would all recognize the above as a valid form. However, not all arguments are valid. A concrete example would be:

(3) If the book is a recommended text a copy will be held in the library.
The book is not a recommended text.
Therefore a copy will not be held in the library.

Argument (3) takes the form:

If A then B
Not A
Therefore, not B

Intuitively, it is false because the initial premise provides no information about nonrecommended texts. Presumably the library will hold books that have not been recommended or were at one time but are no longer. We cannot, therefore, conclude logically that the book will not be held in the library.

Simple though these examples may be, they capture the essential ingredient of all valid arguments, namely:

An argument is valid if it is impossible for the premises to be true and the conclusion to be false.

Thus, argument (3) is invalid because it is possible for nonrecommended books to be held in the library.

Usually, arguments are not so simple as (1), (2), and (3); the first argument (Superman does not exist) is more representative. The feature that makes it seem much more complex is that the premises involve *compound propositions*. Generally, a *simple proposition* is a proposition that contains no other proposition as a part. A *compound proposition* is a proposition formed from two or more simple propositions. Its truth or falsity will (usually) depend on the truth or falsity of its constituent propositions and the manner in which they are combined. Examples of compound propositions are:

If you are good at Mathematics then you will be good at Computer Science.
You do not need to be good at Mathematics to be good at Computer Science.

Each of these is a proposition since each may be true or false. Each is a compound proposition formed from the two simple propositions:

You are good at Mathematics
You are good at Computer Science

Now in arithmetic we are used to combining expressions using operators such as $+$ and $*$. For example, if i and j are integers, then

$$i*j + i$$

is a function of i and j. Equally, in symbolic logic propositions are combined using logical connectives. Thus,

$$p \textbf{ and } q \textbf{ or } p$$

is a function of the propositions p and q. In computer programs, propositions are represented by *Boolean variables* and the above function is said to be *Boolean-valued*.

To conform with conventional usage in programming languages we will use **and, or**, and **not** to denote the three most common logical connectives. Two other logical connectives we use are **if... then...**, which we denote by $\Rightarrow$, and **...if and only if...**, which we denote by $\Leftrightarrow$. You may find that other authors use different signs. Table 1.1 shows a number of common conventions. In each row the sign we use is the leftmost; all other signs in the row have the same meaning.

Table 1.1 Common notations for the logical connectives

and	$\wedge$	.
or	$\vee$	$+$
not	$-$	$\sim$
$\Rightarrow$	$\supset$	$\rightarrow$
$\Leftrightarrow$	$=$	$\equiv$

At this point it is worthwhile pausing to rewrite symbolically the very first argument in this section. To do so we abbreviate its constituent propositions as follows:

Superman exists	X
Superman is willing to prevent evil	W
Superman is able to prevent evil	A
Superman is malevolent	M
Superman is impotent	I
Superman prevents evil	E

The argument then becomes:

{[(W and A)⇒E]   If Superman were willing and able to prevent evil, he would do so.

and

[(not A)⇒I]   If he were unable to prevent evil, he would be impotent;

and

[(not W)⇒M]   If he were unwilling to prevent evil, he would be malevolent.

and

(not E)   Superman does not prevent evil.

and

[X ⇒ not (I or M)]}   If Superman exists, he is neither impotent nor malevolent.

⇒(not X)   Therefore, Superman does not exist.

Or, in a single compound proposition:

{[(W and A)⇒E] and [(not A)⇒I] and [(not W)⇒M] and (not E)
  and [X ⇒ not (I or M)]}
  ⇒(not X)

Before proceeding you should satisfy yourself that you understand the process of transcribing the English argument into a symbolic formula. Basically, the form taken by the argument is an implication:

{premise (a) and premise (b) and premise (c) and premise (d) and premise (e)}
  ⇒ conclusion

which can be read either as:
if premise (a) and premise (b) and premise (c) and premise (d) and premise (e) then the conclusion
or as:
premise (a) and premise (b) and premise (c) and premise (d) and premise (e) imply the conclusion.

Next, each premise has been rewritten as a logical combination of the simple propositions, replacing 'if...then...' by ⇒, and 'un...' and 'not...' by **not**. Note, particularly, that in the final premise 'neither impotent nor malevolent' has been replaced by **not** (I **or** M) rather than (**not** I) **or** (**not** M), which means something quite different. Negations such as this are often difficult to understand and you must take care with them.

Exercises
Rewrite the following arguments symbolically as a single implication using the suggested abbreviations.

1.5 Either the program never terminates or the value of n is eventually zero. If the value of n is eventually zero than the value of m will also eventually be zero. The program does terminate. Therefore the value of m will eventually be zero. (T: the program terminates; N: the value of n is eventually zero; M: the value of m is eventually zero.)

1.6 x, y, and z can not all be positive. However, if they were then x would be greater than both y and z. So x is not greater than one of y or z. (A: x, y, and z are all positive; B: x is greater than y; C: x is greater than z.)

1.4   LOGICAL CONNECTIVES AND TRUTH TABLES

In this section we look at five logical connectives—**not**, **and**, **or**, implies ($\Rightarrow$), and if and only if ($\Leftrightarrow$). We use a *truth table* to give precise meaning to these connectives.

1.4.1   Negation

A negation is obtained when a proposition is prefixed by the word 'not'. For example, the proposition

$$\text{not (the value of } i \text{ is zero)} \tag{1.1}$$

is the negation of

$$\text{the value of } i \text{ is zero.} \tag{1.2}$$

If proposition (1.2) is true then proposition (1.1) is false. Conversely, if proposition (1.1) is true, then proposition (1.2) is false. These results are represented by a truth table as follows:

p	**not** p
T	F
F	T

In the above table T denotes true and F denotes false.

Negation is a *unary* operator because it has only one operand. The remaining operators are *binary*, i.e. they operate on two propositions.

1.4.2   Conjunction

A conjunction is obtained when two or more propositions are linked together by the word 'and', for example:

John is at home and Jane is at school.

The truth or falsity of this statement depends on whether 'John is at home' and 'Jane is at school' are true statements. If either is false or both are false then their conjunction is false; only when both are true is the conjunction true. Again, this is neatly captured by a truth table.

p q	p **and** q
T T	T
F T	F
T F	F
F F	F

This table *defines* conjunction. Each row specifies a combination of true and false values for p and q and the associated value of p **and** q. Moreover, *every* combination of true and false values for p and q appears within the table.

Many English words other than 'and' can be interpreted by conjunction— for instance, 'but', 'however', 'moreover', 'also', and 'yet'. Equally, writing two or more consecutive statements implies a conjunction. For example,

> Kevin plays piano,
> Andrew rides his bike,
> And David loves to wear his gloves
> When going for a hike.

is the conjunction of three propositions although there is only one explicit 'and'.

1.4.3 Disjunction

'Books can be bought in a book shop or through a book club' is a disjunction of the two propositions 'books can be bought in a book shop' and 'books can be bought through a book club'. The defining truth table for disjunction is the following

p q	p **or** q
T T	T
F T	T
T F	T
F F	F

From this table we can see that p **or** q is false only when both p and q are false. It is true when at least one of p or q is true.

Disjunction is often called *inclusive or* to distinguish it from *exclusive or* as used, for example, in this sentence:

Either spiders have six legs or they have eight legs.

The implication in this statement is that 'spiders have six legs' is a true statement or 'spiders have eight legs' is a true statement *but not both*. Thus, the truth table for **xor** (exclusive or) shown below differs from the table above in its first line — when p is true and q is true, p **or** q is true while p **xor** q is false.

p	q	p **xor** q
T	T	F
F	T	T
T	F	T
F	F	F

It is not always easy to distinguish between inclusive or and exclusive or in English. Taken out of context,

Either I am wrong or you are wrong

could be either. To ensure clarity, for example in legal documents, and/or is sometimes written when inclusive or is intended.

1.4.4 Implication

An *implication* is commonly introduced by 'if' in English sentences. For example,

$$\text{if } x \text{ is positive then it is even} \qquad (1.3)$$

may appear as part of some mathematical argument. A statement of the form 'if A then B' is symbolized by

$$A \Rightarrow B$$

A is called the *antecedent* and B the *consequent* of the implication.

Working out the truth table for $A \Rightarrow B$ is not as easy as for the earlier tables. Let us therefore make use of statement (1.3) as a concrete example. Here, A is 'x is positive' and B is 'x is even'. Either proposition may be true or false as may the proposition 'if x is positive then x is even'. Consider the easy cases first.

Suppose x is indeed positive (A is true) but is not even (B is false). Clearly then, x positive cannot imply that x is even. In other words, if A is true and B is false, then $A \Rightarrow B$ is false. This is the third line of the truth table below.

Now suppose x is positive (A is true) and is also even (B is true). In this case we would recognize (1.3) as a valid statement. Thus $A \Rightarrow B$ is true when both A and B are themselves true. This is the first line of the truth table.

In the two cases above it was assumed that x is positive (A is true). What happens when x is not positive? Well, strictly, the statement 'if x is positive then x is even' tells us nothing and whether it is true or not is undefined. However, logicians have agreed on the convention that $A \Rightarrow B$ is defined to be true when A is false. This gives us the second and fourth lines of the truth table:

A B	$A \Rightarrow B$
T T	T
F T	T
T F	F
F F	T

(There are various arguments why $A \Rightarrow B$ should be true when A is false, none of which is wholly convincing. The argument I like the most is this one which is attributed to a dinner conversation involving Bertrand Russell. Apparently, Russell made the claim that he could prove anything given a false statement from which to begin. 'OK, then' came the immediate challenge, 'if $1 = 0$ prove that you are the pope'. 'That's easy' said Russell, '$1 = 0$. Hence, $1 + 1 = 0 + 1$, i.e. $2 = 1$. The pope and I are two, therefore the pope and I are one.')

1.4.5 If and Only If

The phrase 'if and only if' is cumbrous and, consequently, is not often encountered in ordinary English. It does, however, appear frequently in mathematical arguments, the mathematician's 'if and only if' being hidden within a single 'if' in English. For example, the statement

'If X wins then I'll eat my hat'

can invariably be understood to mean 'I'll eat my hat if X wins and I won't eat my hat if X doesn't win'. In contrast

'If John is guilty then his wife is guilty'

may mean in one context 'If John is guilty his wife is guilty and if John is innocent his wife is also innocent' or it may mean 'If John is guilty then his wife *must* be guilty, but if John is innocent it isn't clear whether his wife is guilty or not'. Thus, the mathematician's use of if and only if (which you will often find abbreviated to iff) may be clumsy but it is a lot clearer.

A B	$A \Leftrightarrow B$
T T	T
F T	F
T F	F
F F	T

The difference between $A \Leftrightarrow B$ and $A \Rightarrow B$ is that the former is false in two cases whereas the latter is false in only one. Specifically, $A \Leftrightarrow B$ is false when B is true and A is false, unlike $A \Rightarrow B$. The explanation is that $A \Leftrightarrow B$ is a double-barreled implication—it means if A is true then B is true *and* if B is true then A is true. The two-way nature of $\Leftrightarrow$ is suggested by the two arrows on the symbol: $A \Leftrightarrow B$ means $A \Rightarrow B$ and $B \Rightarrow A$.

'If and only if' appears frequently in the specification of programs. An example might be a program for stock control. Suppose that a computer is being used to store a list C of car components. With each item c is stored its part number, which we denote by $c \cdot n$, and the quantity of that item left in stock, which we denote by $c \cdot q$. Consider a procedure to list the part numbers of all items for which the quantity has fallen below some threshold s. Letting the list be denoted by L, its precise specification is

$$c \cdot n \text{ is in } L \text{ if and only if } c \cdot n \text{ is in } C \text{ and } c \cdot q < s.$$

The use of if and only if is vital to this specification because there are two distinct requirements on the list L:

(a) if $c \cdot n$ is in C and $c \cdot q < s$ then $c \cdot n$ is to be included in L;
(b) if $c \cdot n$ is included in L then $c \cdot n$ must be in C and $c \cdot q$ must be less than s.

Exercises
1.7 If A and B are *true* propositions and X and Y are *false* propositions, which of the following compound propositions are true?

(a) **not** $(A$ **or** $X)$
(b) $(\textbf{not } A)$ **or** $(\textbf{not } X)$
(c) $(\textbf{not } B)$ **and** $(\textbf{not } Y)$
(d) **not** $(B$ **and** $Y)$
(e) A **or** $(X$ **and** $Y)$
(f) $(A$ **or** $X)$ **and** Y
(g) $(A$ **or** $X)$ **and** $(B$ **or** $Y)$
(h) **not** $(A$ **or** $X)$ **and not** $(A$ **or** $Y)$
(i) **not** $(A \Rightarrow B)$
(j) $(A \Rightarrow B) \Rightarrow Y$
(k) $[(\textbf{not } (A \Rightarrow X))$ **and** $B] \Rightarrow Y$
(l) $[\textbf{not } (A$ **or** $B)] \Leftrightarrow [(\textbf{not } A)$ **and** $(\textbf{not } B)]$
(m) $(A \Leftrightarrow B) \Leftrightarrow [(A \Rightarrow B)$ **and** $(B \Rightarrow A)]$
(n) $(A \Rightarrow X) \Rightarrow [(\textbf{not } A)$ **and** $X]$
(o) $(A \Rightarrow B) \Rightarrow [\textbf{not } (A$ **and** $(\textbf{not } B))]$
(p) $(Y \Rightarrow B) \Rightarrow [(\textbf{not } Y)$ **or** $B]$
(q) $(X \Rightarrow Y) \Leftrightarrow \textbf{not } (X$ **or** $Y)$

1.8 Below are some propositions each of which is composed of two simple propositions and a single connective. Construct a truth table for each compound proposition in terms of its constituent propositions and then use the truth table to express the connective in terms of the connectives **not, and, or,** ⇒, and ⇔.

For example, suppose the proposition is 'At most one of A and B is lying'. This consists of the two propositions 'A is lying' and 'B is lying' connected by 'at most one of'. The truth table for 'at most one of' is shown below, and by comparing it with the truth table of **and** we deduce that 'at most one of p and q' is equivalent to '**not** (p **and** q)'.

A is lying	B is lying	At most one of A and B is lying
T	T	F
F	T	T
T	F	T
F	F	T

(a) At least one of A and B is lying.
(b) Exactly one of A and B is lying.
(c) Either both A and B are lying or both are telling the truth.
(d) The value of x is positive unless y is zero.
(e) From the fact that x is positive one can infer that y is also positive.
(f) The middle deck is initially nonempty provided that $n > 0$.
(g) Were x positive we would know that y is also positive.
(h) The value of i always decreases because the increment is greater than zero.
(i) $a < b$ contradicts the assumption that $n > 0$.

1.9 The table below is a list of part numbers and quantities. Let us suppose the threshold s is 10.

Part no.	Quantity
A10	5
B12	12
F9	20
F21	25
G2	8
H61	9

Consider the following three lists of parts:

$$L_1 = \text{A10, B12, G2, H61}$$
$$L_2 = \text{G2, H61}$$
$$L_3 = \text{A10, G2, H61}$$

State which of L_1, L_2, and L_3 satisfy the requirement (a) and which satisfy the requirement (b) (see page 26).

1.5 OPERATOR PRECEDENCE

In mathematics we are all accustomed to the notion of *precedence* of arithmetic operators. For instance the expression

$$2 + 3 * 5$$

conventionally means $2 + (3 * 5)$ and not $(2 + 3) * 5$. In ordinary language there is often ambiguity in the way sentences are parenthesized.

> The best programmers are young men and women trained in
> program proving   (1.4)

can be interpreted as

> The best programmers are young men trained in program
> proving and young women trained in program proving   (1.5)

or

> The best programmers are women trained in program proving
> and young men.   (1.6)

Commas are used in written English to avoid some of these ambiguities. Thus placing a comma after men in (1.4) would imply the meaning (1.6), otherwise one would normally assume (1.5).

In logical formulae we adopt a precedence convention, just as in arithmetic. Specifically, the precedence of the connectives is as follows:

What this table means is this. To evaluate a logical formula begin by evaluating the **not**s, next evaluate the **and**s, then **or**s, and finally implications and iff s (except where parentheses dictate otherwise). For example,

$$\textbf{not } p \textbf{ or } q \textbf{ and } r \Rightarrow s \textbf{ and not } t$$

means

$$[(\text{not } p) \text{ or } (q \text{ and } r)] \Rightarrow [s \text{ and } (\text{not } t)].$$

Exercises

1.10 Fully parenthesize the following compound propositions.

(a) X **and not** Y **or** $Z \Rightarrow X$
(b) $X \Leftrightarrow$ **not** Y **and** Z
(c) X **and** $Y \Rightarrow$ **not** Z
(d) X **or** Y **and** Z **or not** $Z \Leftrightarrow X$
(e) $X \Leftrightarrow (Y$ **and** $Z \Leftrightarrow X)$

1.11 Assuming that X has the value T, Y has the value T and Z has the value F evaluate the following compound propositions:

(a) X **and not** (**not** Y **or** $Z) \Rightarrow X$ **and** Z
(b) $(X \Rightarrow Y$ **or not** $X) \Rightarrow Z$
(c) X **or** Y **and** $Z \Rightarrow$ **not** X
(d) $X \Leftrightarrow$ **not** Y **or** X **and** Z
(e) Y **and not not** Y **or** Z

1.6   TAUTOLOGIES AND COUNTEREXAMPLES

1.6.1   A Valid Argument

Consider the following argument:

> If an algorithm is proven then it is reliable. Therefore, an algorithm cannot be both proven and unreliable.

We would all recognize that the conclusion of this argument 'an algorithm cannot be both proven and unreliable' logically follows from its premise 'if an algorithm is proven then it is reliable', and would therefore describe the argument as valid. If asked for further justification of its validity we might reason as follows.

The argument concerns two propositions about an arbitrary algorithm:

(a) the algorithm is reliable;
(b) the algorithm is proven.

Consider, therefore, any algorithm A, say and let us consider the four combinations of A is reliable/unreliable and A is proven/unproven.

(i) A is proven and is reliable. This case clearly confirms the conclusion.

 (ii) *A* is unproven and is reliable. This case again confirms the conclusion.
(iii) *A* is proven and is unreliable. This case contradicts the premise and so can
       be discounted.
(iv)   *A* is unproven and is unreliable. Once more the conclusion is true.

We can summarize this case analysis in the form of a truth table. Specifically,
letting *P* denote '*A* is proven' and *R* denote '*A* is reliable', what we have done,
in effect, is to evaluate the formula

$$(P \Rightarrow R) \Rightarrow \textbf{not}\ (P\ \textbf{and not}\ R)$$

for each of the four true/false values of *P* and *R*.

P R	$(P \Rightarrow R)$	$\Rightarrow$	**not**	$(P$ **and not** $R)$	
T T	T	T	T	F	F
F T	T	T	T	F	F
T F	F	T	F	T	T
F F	T	T	T	F	T

   Let us look closely at the above truth table and compare it with our English
argument. Firstly, we have expressed the argument in the form of an
implication—the premise, if an algorithm is proven then it is reliable $(P \Rightarrow R)$,
implies the conclusion, an algorithm cannot be both proven and unreliable—
not $(P$ **and not** $R)$. Lines of the truth table correspond in order to the four cases
(i) to (iv). The correspondence beyond this point is not so obvious simply
because the truth table entry is much more detailed. Nevertheless the
construction of a truth table may be regarded as a rather laborious case
analysis.
   However, we have yet to make the most important observation. Look at
the boxed column of the above truth table. It contains *only* the value true. In
other words, the implication in the argument is true whatever the values of *P*
and *R*, i.e. irrespective of whether a given algorithm is proven/unproven,
reliable/unreliable. We say that the formula $(P \Rightarrow R) \Rightarrow \textbf{not}\ (P\ \textbf{and not}\ R)$ is a
tautology and the general rule that this formula exemplifies is the following:

Definition A *tautology* is a propositional form that is true whatever assignment
of true or false values is given to each of its constituent simple propositions.
   An *argument* is an implication in which the premises form the antecedent
and the conclusion forms the consequent.
   An argument is *valid* iff it is a tautology.

The implication of lowest precedence in the propositional form of an argument
is called the *principal connective*. The validity of an argument may thus be
verified by examining the entries in the *principal column* of its truth table.

1.6.2 An Invalid Argument

Consider another argument.

If an algorithm is proven then it is reliable. Therefore, an algorithm is proven or it is not reliable.

Examination of the truth table soon reveals that this argument is invalid.

P R	$(P \Rightarrow R) \Rightarrow (P$	**or**	**not** $R)$
T T	T T	T	F
F T	T F	F	F
T F	F T	T	T
F F	T T	T	T

Note that there is a false entry in the principal column corresponding to the case in which P is false and R is true. Specifically, we would say the argument is invalid because it is possible for an algorithm to be reliable but unproven without violating the premise but contradicting the conclusion.

Exercise

1.12 Consider the following argument.

If an algorithm is reliable then it is proven. Therefore, either an algorithm is proven or it is unreliable.

Show that this argument is valid if 'or' in the conclusion is interpreted as inclusive or, i.e. and/or, and is invalid if 'or' is interpreted as exclusive or, i.e. the conclusion is that an algorithm is proven or unreliable but not both.

1.6.3 Constructing a Truth Table

So far we have considered only truth tables involving one or two variables. We now want to give the rule for constructing a truth table involving an arbitrary number of variables. Suppose, for example, that we wish to construct the truth table for

$$[p \textbf{ and } q \Rightarrow r] \Leftrightarrow [(\textbf{not } p \textbf{ and not } q) \textbf{ or } r].$$

We begin by writing down each variable and the expression separated by a vertical line.

p q r	$[p \textbf{ and } q \Rightarrow r] \Leftrightarrow [(\textbf{not } p \textbf{ and not } q) \textbf{ or } r]$

Next we include a row in the table for every combination of true/false values of the variables. If there are n variables there will be 2^n rows in the table. Thus, in our example we will need $2^3 = 8$ rows. A simple, systematic way of ensuring that all combinations are included is as follows. Begin by writing, alternately, T and F in the first column until you have 2^n rows. In the second column write, alternately, T T (on consecutive lines) followed by F F (again on consecutive lines) until all rows are complete. Next write, alternately, T T T T followed by F F F F. Continue this process of doubling the number of consecutive T and F entries until all of the columns to the left of the vertical line have been completed.

The truth table for our example now looks like this.

p q r	$[p$ **and** $q \Rightarrow r] \Leftrightarrow [($**not** p **and not** $q)$ **or** $r]$
T T T	
F T T	
T F T	
F F T	
T T F	
F T F	
T F F	
F F F	

Now evaluate the expression for each row of the table. Below each operator in the table write the truth value of the subexpression to which it relates. Start, of course, with the innermost expressions and work outwards, remembering the rules of precedence given earlier.

Below is the truth table for our example, together with an indication of the order in which subexpressions were evaluated.

p q r	$[p$ **and** $q \Rightarrow r] \Leftrightarrow [($**not** p **and not** $q)$ **or** $r]$						
T T T	T	T	T	F	F	F	T
F T T	F	T	T	T	F	F	T
T F T	F	T	T	F	F	T	T
F F T	F	T	T	T	T	T	T
T T F	T	F	T	F	F	F	F
F T F	F	T	F	T	F	F	F
T F F	F	T	F	F	F	T	F
F F F	F	T	T	T	T	T	T
	↑	↑	↑	↑	↑	↑	↑
	5th	6th	7th	1st	3rd	2nd	4th

Note that the appearance of two 'F' entries in the principal column of this table signifies that the two formulae $(p$ **and** $q) \Rightarrow r$ and (**not** $p)$ **and** (**not** $q)$ **or** r are not equivalent. The assignments to p, q, and r that they specify are called *counterexamples*. Thus, taking the first such row, we say that **(not p) and q and (not r)** is a *counterexample* to the proposition $[(p$ **and** $q) \Rightarrow r] \Leftrightarrow [((\text{not } p) \text{ and } (\text{not } q)) \text{ or } r]$.

Example
1.1 If a student fails to submit a project report he cannot pass Computer Science. If a student fails Computer Science he cannot proceed to the following year. Thus, if a student proceeds to the following year he must have submitted a project report.

To formalize this argument we begin by abbreviating its constituent propositions as follows:

S = the student submits a project report
C = the student passes Computer Science
P = the student proceeds to the following year

With this notation the two premises are

$$\text{not } S \Rightarrow \text{not } C \qquad \text{and} \qquad \text{not } C \Rightarrow \text{not } P$$

and the conclusion is

$$P \Rightarrow S.$$

The complete argument is therefore expressed by the implication

$$[(\text{not } S \Rightarrow \text{not } C) \text{ and } (\text{not } C \Rightarrow \text{not } P)] \Rightarrow (P \Rightarrow S)$$

which has the following truth table.

S	C	P	$[(\text{not } S$	$\Rightarrow \text{not } C)$	**and**	$(\text{not } C$	$\Rightarrow \text{not } P)]$	$\Rightarrow$	$(P \Rightarrow S)$
T	T	T	F	T F	T	F	T F	T	T
F	T	T	T	F F	F	F	T F	T	F
T	F	T	F	T T	F	T	F F	T	T
F	F	T	T	T T	F	T	F F	T	F
T	T	F	F	T F	T	F	T T	T	T
F	T	F	T	F F	F	F	T T	T	T
T	F	F	F	T T	T	T	T T	T	T
F	F	F	T	T T	T	T	T T	T	T

Since all the entries in the principal column are true we have verified that the argument is valid.

Exercises
1.13 Use truth tables to determine the validity or invalidity of each of the following arguments:

(a) If x equals 0 then either y is positive or z is negative. z is negative. Therefore if y is positive then x is not equal to 0. (X: x equals 0; Y: y is positive; Z: z is negative.)

(b) If x equals 0 then if y is positive then z is negative. y is positive. Therefore either x equals 0 or z is negative. (Same abbreviations as for (a).)

(c) If the initialization is correct and if the loop terminates then the required postcondition is guaranteed. The required postcondition is guaranteed. Therefore if the initialization is correct then the loop terminates. (I: the initialization is correct; T: the loop terminates; P: the required postcondition is guaranteed.)

(d) If there is a man on the Moon then the Moon is made of cheese, and if the Moon is made of cheese then I am a monkey. Either there is not a man on the Moon or the Moon is not made of cheese. Therefore either the Moon is not made of cheese or I am a monkey. (A: there is a man on the Moon; B: the Moon is made of cheese; C: I am a monkey.)

1.7 EQUIVALENCES

The use of truth tables is straightforward for a small number of variables but the number of cases we have to consider rapidly becomes very large as the number of variables increases. This is a major drawback, making it impractical in normal circumstances. We now begin a development of alternative techniques for manipulating logical formulae. In this section we present a number of *equivalences* between propositional formulae; later we discuss the use of *rules of inference*. The combination of these two provides us with a very powerful system, called *natural deduction*, for verifying formal arguments. However, in the meantime we must rely on truth tables for their verification.

1.7.1 The Notion of Equivalence

Already in this text we have described a valid argument in two different ways. An argument is valid if and only if

(a) it is impossible for the premises to be true and the conclusion to be false.

An argument is valid if and only if

(b) its associated implication is a tautology.

Informally we would say that the two statements (a) and (b) are equivalent. To obtain a formal definition of equivalence let us inspect the truth table of both statements. Letting p denote the premises and q denote the conclusion of an

argument, statement (a) is formalized as **not** (*p* **and not** *q*) and statement (b) is
formalized as $p \Rightarrow q$. Below we show the truth table for both expressions. Note
that the principal columns in both are identical.

p *q*	**not** (*p* **and not** *q*)				*p* *q*	$p \Rightarrow q$
T T	T	F	F		T T	T
F T	T	F	F		F T	T
T F	F	T	T		T F	F
F F	T	F	T		F F	T

Equally, we can express this observation in terms of if and only if: The
formula

$$(p \Rightarrow q) \Leftrightarrow \textbf{not } (p \textbf{ and not } q) \tag{1.7}$$

is a tautology.

This provides us with a formal definition of equivalence.

Definition A tautology of the form $p \Leftrightarrow q$ is called an *equivalence* and is written
$p \equiv q$.

Since $\equiv$ is a new operator we must define its place in the table of precedence.
Specifically, $\equiv$ has the lowest precedence so that, for example,

$$p \textbf{ and } q \equiv \textbf{not } (\textbf{not } p \textbf{ or not } q)$$

means

$$\{p \textbf{ and } q\} \equiv \{\textbf{not } (\textbf{not } p \textbf{ or not } q)\}.$$

As a second example of an equivalence, consider the following way of
describing a valid argument:

An argument is valid if and only if

(c) it is always the case that the conclusion is true or the premise is false.

The implied equivalence here is

$$(p \Rightarrow q) \equiv (q \textbf{ or not } p) \tag{1.8}$$

which can be verified by the following truth table:

p *q*	$(p \Rightarrow q) \Leftrightarrow q$ **or not** *p*			
T T	T	T	T	F
F T	T	T	T	T
T F	F	T	F	F
F F	T	T	T	T

A good way of remembering the truth table of $\Rightarrow$ is that the only false value is the combination of p true and q false. Thus the latter combination is the only *true* value of **not** $(p \Rightarrow q)$. This is captured by the following claim, which you should verify using a truth table:

$$\textbf{not } (p \Rightarrow q) \equiv p \textbf{ and not } q. \tag{1.9}$$

1.7.2 Substitutivity, Transitivity, and Symmetry

A knowledge of equivalences such as (1.7), (1.8), and (1.9) is extremely valuable in logical arguments because we can use them to simplify complex expressions. When two propositions p and q are equivalent, one may be substituted for the other in any proposition, yielding an equivalent result. For example, if p is equivalent to q then **not** p is equivalent to **not** q, p **and** r is equivalent to q **and** r, and $p \Rightarrow r$ is equivalent to $q \Rightarrow r$, for any proposition r. Thus it is possible to derive (1.7) from (1.9) using one additional equivalence, viz.

$$\textbf{not not } p \equiv p. \tag{1.10}$$

For, by considering the negation of the two equivalent propositions in (1.9) we have

$$\textbf{not } (\textbf{not } (p \Rightarrow q)) \equiv \textbf{not } (p \textbf{ and } (\textbf{not } q)). \tag{1.11}$$

Simplifying (1.11) using (1.10) we obtain

$$(p \Rightarrow q) \equiv \textbf{not } (p \textbf{ and } (\textbf{not } q))$$

which is identical to (1.7)

Two other rules which are valid for equivalences are rules of *symmetry* and *transitivity*. The rule of symmetry states that if $p \equiv q$ then $q \equiv p$. The rule of transitivity states that if $p \equiv q$ and $q \equiv r$ then $p \equiv r$.

Using symmetry and transitivity we can infer from (1.8) and (1.11) that

$$q \textbf{ or not } p \equiv \textbf{not } (p \textbf{ and } (\textbf{not } q)). \tag{1.12}$$

For, by symmetry, we can rewrite (1.8) as

$$q \textbf{ or not } p \equiv p \Rightarrow q. \tag{1.13}$$

The equivalence (1.12) therefore follows by applying the rule of transitivity to (1.13) and (1.11).

Note that, if $\equiv$ were used to mean equality of arithmetic expressions, we would take these three rules for granted. The rule of transitivity motivates a convention that we already use in arithmetic and which we also adopt for logical expressions. The convention is that equality is used 'conjunctively' in the form $a = b = \ldots = z$. This means simply that $x = y = z$ is a shorthand for $x = y$

and $y = z$. Applying this convention to equivalence of logical expressions we can summarize (1.8), (1.11), and (1.12) as follows:

$$p \Rightarrow q \equiv q \text{ or not } p \equiv \text{not } (p \text{ and } (\text{not } q)).$$

1.7.3 Some Useful Equivalences

There are lots of equivalences, but only a few are really useful. For reference purposes, we list some useful ones.

(a)   *Constants*

p **or true** $\equiv$ **true**	p **or false** $\equiv p$
p **and true** $\equiv p$	p **and false** $\equiv$ **false**
true $\Rightarrow p \equiv p$	**false** $\Rightarrow p \equiv$ **true**
$p \Rightarrow$ **true** $\equiv$ **true**	$p \Rightarrow$ **false** $\equiv$ **not** p

(b)   *Law of Excluded Middle*

p **or not** $p \equiv$ **true**

(c)   *Law of Contradiction*

p **and not** $p \equiv$ **false**

(d)   *Negation*

not not $p \equiv p$

(e)   *Associativity*

p **or** $(q$ **or** $r) \equiv (p$ **or** $q)$ **or** r
p **and** $(q$ **and** $r) \equiv (p$ **and** $q)$ **and** r
$p \Leftrightarrow (q \Leftrightarrow r) \equiv (p \Leftrightarrow q) \Leftrightarrow r$

(f)   *Commutativity*

p **and** $q \equiv q$ **and** p
p **or** $q \equiv q$ **or** p
$(p \Leftrightarrow q) \equiv (q \Leftrightarrow p)$

(g)   Distributivity

$$p \text{ and } (q \text{ or } r) \equiv (p \text{ and } q) \text{ or } (p \text{ and } r)$$
$$p \text{ or } (q \text{ and } r) \equiv (p \text{ or } q) \text{ and } (p \text{ or } r)$$

$$p \text{ or } (q \Rightarrow r) \equiv (p \text{ or } q) \Rightarrow (p \text{ or } r)$$
$$p \text{ or } (q \Leftrightarrow r) \equiv (p \text{ or } q) \Leftrightarrow (p \text{ or } r)$$

$$p \Rightarrow (q \text{ and } r) \equiv (p \Rightarrow q) \text{ and } (p \Rightarrow r)$$
$$p \Rightarrow (q \text{ or } r) \equiv (p \Rightarrow q) \text{ or } (p \Rightarrow r)$$
$$p \Rightarrow (q \Rightarrow r) \equiv (p \Rightarrow q) \Rightarrow (p \Rightarrow r)$$
$$p \Rightarrow (q \Leftrightarrow r) \equiv (p \Rightarrow q) \Leftrightarrow (p \Rightarrow r)$$

(h)   Idempotency

$$p \text{ or } p \equiv p$$
$$p \text{ and } p \equiv p$$

(i)   De Morgan's Laws

$$\text{not } (p \text{ or } q) \equiv \text{not } p \text{ and not } q$$
$$\text{not } (p \text{ and } q) \equiv \text{not } p \text{ or not } q$$

(j)   Implication

$$(p \Rightarrow q) \equiv (\text{not } p \text{ or } q)$$
$$(p \Rightarrow q) \equiv (\text{not } q \Rightarrow \text{not } p)$$
$$[(p \text{ and } q) \Rightarrow r] \equiv [p \Rightarrow (q \Rightarrow r)]$$

(k)   If and Only If

$$(p \Leftrightarrow q) \equiv [(p \Rightarrow q) \text{ and } (q \Rightarrow p)]$$
$$(p \Leftrightarrow q) \equiv [(p \text{ and } q) \text{ or } (\text{not } p \text{ and not } q)]$$
$$(p \Leftrightarrow q) \equiv [(p \Rightarrow q) \text{ and } (\text{not } p \Rightarrow \text{not } q)]$$

You should verify a number of these equivalences using the method of truth tables.

Equivalences (a)–(f) are trivial in the sense that we would not bother to mention them in an informal argument. Even in a strict formal argument it would be considered pedantic to make explicit reference to them. Accordingly, we will not.

There is an analogy between **and** and $*$, and between **or** and $+$. Evidence of this comes from the distributive law p **and** $(q$ **or** $r) \equiv (p$ **and** $q)$ **or** $(p$ **and** $r)$. When rewritten, with $*$ replacing **and** and $+$ replacing **or** we get the familiar rule:

$$p*(q+r) = (p*q)+(p*r)$$

Note, however, that the second distributive law does not hold in arithmetic. For $p + q*r \neq (p+q)*(p+r)$. Perhaps because of this the second distributive law may seem strange and is easy to forget. But do not forget it for it can be very useful.

De Morgan's laws are also very useful. Indeed, the first is reflected in the English expression 'neither p nor q' meaning 'both not p and not q'. ('Nor' may also be regarded as another Boolean connective with the property that p 'nor' $q \equiv (\textbf{not } p)$ **and** $(\textbf{not } q)$.)

The third implication rule is also embodied in everyday English, for it is as equally common to say 'if p *and* if q then r' (i.e. p **and** $q \Rightarrow r$) as it is to say 'if p *then* if q then r' (i.e. $p \Rightarrow (q \Rightarrow r)$).

The first of the iff laws explains the use of a double-headed arrow to mean if and only if. For, it is common to prove $p \Leftrightarrow q$ by proving, firstly, that $p \Rightarrow q$ and, secondly, $p \Leftarrow q$ (i.e. $q \Rightarrow p$).

Example

1.2 As an example of the use of these equivalences let us prove that the expression $(p$ **and** $(p \Rightarrow q)) \Rightarrow q$ is a tautology.

$(p$ **and** $(p \Rightarrow q)) \Rightarrow q \equiv (p$ **and** $(\textbf{not } p$ **or** $q)) \Rightarrow q$	(implication)
$\equiv ((p$ **and not** $p)$ **or** $(p$ **and** $q)) \Rightarrow q$	(distributivity)
$\equiv (\textbf{false or } (p$ **and** $q)) \Rightarrow q$	(contradiction)
$\equiv (p$ **and** $q) \Rightarrow q$	(constants)
$\equiv \textbf{not } (p$ **and** $q)$ **or** q	(implication)
$\equiv (\textbf{not } p$ **or not** $q)$ **or** q	(De Morgan)
$\equiv \textbf{not } p$ **or** $(\textbf{not } q$ **or** $q)$	(associativity)
$\equiv \textbf{not } p$ **or** $(q$ **or not** $q)$	(commutativity)
$\equiv \textbf{not } p$ **or true**	(excluded middle)
$\equiv \textbf{true}$	(constants)

Exercises

1.14 Exploit the equivalences given in this section to verify the following. Look out for the opportunity to use earlier exercises.

(a) p **or** $(q$ **and** $p) \equiv p$

(b) $(p$ **or** $q)$ **and** $q \equiv q$

(c) $[(p$ and $q)$ or $($not p and $q)$ or $(p$ and not $q)] \equiv p$ or q

(d) $[(p \Rightarrow q)$ and $(p \Rightarrow$ not $q)] \equiv$ not p

(e) $[(p$ and $q) \Leftrightarrow p] \equiv [p \Rightarrow q]$

(f) not $(p \Leftrightarrow q) \equiv (p \Leftrightarrow$ not $q)$

(g) $[(p$ and $q \Rightarrow r)$ and $(p$ and not $q \Rightarrow$ not $r)] \equiv [p \Rightarrow (q \Leftrightarrow r)]$

(h) $($not p and $q)$ or $(p$ and not $q) \equiv (p$ or $q)$ and not $(p$ and $q)$

(i) $[(p$ and $q \Rightarrow r)$ and $(p$ and not $q \Rightarrow s)]$
$\equiv [p \Rightarrow (q \Rightarrow r)$ and $($not $q \Rightarrow s)]$

(j) $[(p \Rightarrow q)$ and $($not $p \Rightarrow r)] \equiv [(p$ and $q)$ or $($not p and $r)]$

1.15 Which of the following are true?

(a) $[(p \Rightarrow q) \Rightarrow r] \equiv [p \Rightarrow (q \Rightarrow r)]$

(b) $[(p \Leftrightarrow q) \Leftrightarrow r] \equiv p \Leftrightarrow (q \Leftrightarrow r)]$

(c) $[(p \Leftrightarrow q) \Leftrightarrow r] \equiv [(p \Leftrightarrow q)$ and $(q \Leftrightarrow r)]$

What is the significance of (b) and (c)?

1.8 LOGIC PUZZLES: AN INTRODUCTION TO LOGICAL DEDUCTION

This section provides an interlude to the rather formal development of the propositional calculus. It is devoted almost entirely to the statement of a variety of problems concerning a mythical island of knights and knaves. You should be able to solve all the problems using your own common sense, but it is also possible to solve them using the formal apparatus developed so far. Such a solution is presented immediately after the first problem and hints towards formal solutions of subsequent problems are supplied. The way to derive most benefit from these problems is perhaps to tackle them both formally and informally and then to try to see the relation between the two methods.

On the island of knights and knaves there are two types of inhabitants, 'knights' who always tell the truth and 'knaves' who always lie. It is assumed that every inhabitant is either a knight or a knave unless the problem states otherwise.

Here is the first question. Immediately following it we indicate how to formalize its solution. However, you may like to tackle the problem first before reading the solution.

Exercise

1.16 Someone asks person A (who is either a knight or a knave), 'Are you a knight?' He replies, 'If I am a knight then I'll eat my hat'.
Prove that A has to eat his hat.

In all of these questions the information needed to solve them is contained in the statements of the inhabitants. This first question, for example, can be solved by examining the implications of the proposition 'A said, if I am a knight then I'll eat my hat.' By now you should immediately think of introducing symbols. Accordingly, we shall introduce the following abbreviations:

X X is a knight (where X is $A, B, C...$).
H A eats his hat.

A's statement is therefore

$$A \Rightarrow H.$$

The next step is to pose the question 'What does it mean when person X makes a statement S?' Well, if X is a knight we know that S is true (i.e. $X \Rightarrow S$) and, conversely, if X is a knave we know that S is false (i.e. **not** $X \Rightarrow$ **not** S). Moreover, these are the only two possibilities. In other words, we have the *premise*

$$(X \Rightarrow S) \textbf{ and } (\textbf{not } X \Rightarrow \textbf{not } S) \tag{1.14}$$

There is another, neater, way of writing proposition (1.14). Refer back to section 1.7.3 and you will find that $(p \Rightarrow q)$ **and** $(\textbf{not } p \Rightarrow \textbf{not } q)$ is equivalent to $p \Leftrightarrow q$. Applying this to (1.14), we obtain the premise

$$X \Leftrightarrow S. \tag{1.15}$$

We shall refer to (1.15) as the *basic rule* for problems involving knights and knaves.

Let us pause to check (1.15) from a different angle. In English it says:

X is a knight if and only if X's statement is true.

This is just what the conditions of the problem tell us.

Returning to question 1.16, we know that A's statement is $A \Rightarrow H$ (if I am a knight then I'll eat my hat). Thus we begin with the premise

$$A \Leftrightarrow (A \Rightarrow H)$$

and our objective is to deduce logically from it that

$$H$$

(i.e. A eats his hat).

There are two ways we can proceed. The first is simply to construct a truth table for the premise and examine its consequences. The truth table is shown below. From it we can immediately deduce A **and** H because the only true entry in the principal column (the boxed entry) is in that row.

A H	A	$\Leftrightarrow$	$(A \Rightarrow H)$
T T	T	T	T
F T	F	F	T
T F	F	F	F
F F	F	F	T

The second is to use our knowledge of equivalences to simplify the premise.

$A \Leftrightarrow (A \Rightarrow H) \equiv A \Leftrightarrow (\text{not } A \text{ or } H)$

$\equiv [A \text{ and } (\text{not } A \text{ or } H] \text{ or } [\text{not } A \text{ and not } (\text{not } A \text{ or } H)]$

Now, A **and** $(\text{not } A \text{ or } H) \equiv (A \text{ and not } A) \text{ or } (A \text{ and } H)$

$\equiv \text{false or } (A \text{ and } H)$

$\equiv A \text{ and } H.$

Also, **not** A **and not** $(\text{not } A \text{ or } H) \equiv \text{not } A \text{ and } (\text{not not } A \text{ and not } H)$

$\equiv \text{not } A \text{ and } (A \text{ and not } H)$

$\equiv (\text{not } A \text{ and } A) \text{ and not } H$

$\equiv \text{false and not } H$

$\equiv \text{false}.$

Hence $A \Leftrightarrow (A \Rightarrow H) \equiv (A \text{ and } H) \text{ or false}$

$\equiv A \text{ and } H.$

For problems involving only two simple propositions as in this example the truth table method is clearly much simpler. But you should try to persevere with the method of equivalences because its practical application is much greater.

Exercises

1.17 In this question there are two people, A and B. Now, A says, 'If B is a knight then I am a knave'. What are A and B?

(*Hint*: using the abbreviation A for 'A is a knight', the proposition 'A is a knave' is abbreviated **not** A. Also, be careful to interpret A's statement as an implication and not as an equivalence.)

1.18 It is rumored that there is buried gold on the island. You ask one of the natives, A, whether there is gold on the island. He makes the following response: 'There is gold on this island if and only if I am a knight.'

(a) Can it be determined whether A is a knight or a knave?

(b) Can it be determined whether there is gold on the island?

1.19 According to this problem, three of the inhabitants—A, B, and C—were standing together in a garden. A stranger passed by and asked A, 'Are you a knight or a knave?' A answered, but rather indistinctly, so the stranger could not make out what he said. The stranger then asked B, 'What did A say?' B replied, 'A said that he is a knave.' At this point the third man, C, said, 'Don't believe B; he's lying!' The question is, what are B and C?

   (*Hint*: the two statements made by B and C are all that is relevant to this problem. Also C's statement that B is lying is equivalent to C saying that B is a knave.)

1.20 Suppose the stranger, instead of asking A what he is, asked A, 'How many knights are among you?' Again A answers indistinctly. So the stranger asks B, 'What did A say?' B replies, 'A said there is one knight among us.' Then C says, 'Don't believe B; he's lying'. Now what are B and C?

1.21 A and B make the following statements:

A: All of us are knaves.

B: Exactly one of us is a knight.

What are A, B and C?

The next and final question is, appropriately enough, the most difficult. Treat it as a challenge to your intellect.

1.22 In this question a 'normal' person is one who sometimes tells the truth and sometimes lies.

   Suppose that there are three neighboring islands A, B, and C and that there is gold buried on at least one of the islands. Islands B and C are uninhabited; island A is inhabited by knights and knaves, and there is also the possibility that there are some normals on the island.

   By good fortune, you find a coded message left by Captain Marston, the pirate who buried the gold, containing clues as to its location. The decoded message contains two sentences:

(a) There is no gold on island A.
(b) If there are any normals on island A, then there is gold on two of the islands.

Now, given this information and supposing that the natives on island A know all about the gold, you are allowed to ask one question of one native chosen at random. What question would you ask?

   (*Hint*: firstly, it is obvious from sentence (a) that your question must enable you to decide whether the gold is on island B or on island C.

Equally, your question must enable you to decide whether or not there is gold on island *B* (for if there is not there must be gold on *C*). Secondly, the possibility of there being normals on island *A* is just a red herring. For, we are told in sentence (b) that, if there are, then there is gold on both islands *B* and *C*. If you assume, therefore, that there are no normals you can not go wrong.

Thus the question you pose should take the form 'Is *Q* true?' such that if it is asked of a knight or a knave and the response is 'Yes' then there is gold on island *B* and if the response is 'No' then there is gold on island *C*.)

1.9   RULES OF INFERENCE AND LOGICAL DEDUCTION

1.9.1   Rules of Inference

An informal argument will generally consist of three parts. Firstly there is a statement of the premises on which the argument is based, lastly is the conclusion, and, in between, is the justification for the conclusion. We would accept the argument as valid if each step follows 'logically' from earlier steps.

Likewise, a *formal proof* of an argument consists of a sequence of propositions beginning with the premises and ending with the conclusion. In between is another sequence of propositions comprising the justification. The proof is valid if each of the propositions following the premises follows from its predecessors by the application of one of a number of simple rules called *rules of inference*. Table 1.2 is a list of rules of inference developed by a German mathematician called Gerhard Gentzen and intended to model 'natural' processes of logical deduction.

The rules are divided into two sets called the *introduction rules* and the *elimination rules*. The introduction rules are so called because each introduces a logical operator; similarly, the elimination rules eliminate a logical operator. Each rule consists of one or more premises separated by a dividing line from a single conclusion or *inference*. A premise in square brackets denotes an assumption. Let us go through the meaning of each of the rules.

The **and**-introduction rule (**and**-I) states that if it is possible to prove proposition *p* and proposition *q* then it is valid to infer the conjunction *p* **and** *q*. Conversely the two **and**-elimination rules (**and**-E) state that if it is possible to prove the conjunction *p* **and** *q* then it is valid to infer *p* and it is also valid to infer *q*. The two **or**-introduction rules state that it is valid to infer *p* **or** *q* if either *p* is proved (the first rule) or *q* is proved (the second rule).

The **or**-elimination rule models case analysis in informal arguments. It has three premises which may be read as '*p* **or** *q*', '*r* assuming *p*', and '*r* assuming *q*'.

Table 1.2 Rules of logical deduction.

Introduction rules	Elimination rules
and-I	**and**-E
$$\frac{p \quad q}{p \text{ and } q}$$	$$\frac{p \text{ and } q}{p} \qquad \frac{p \text{ and } q}{q}$$
or-I	**or**-E
	$$[p] \quad [q]$$
$$\frac{p}{p \text{ or } q} \qquad \frac{q}{p \text{ or } q}$$	$$\frac{p \text{ or } q \quad r \quad r}{r}$$
$\Rightarrow$-I	$\Rightarrow$-E
$$[p]$$	
$$\frac{q}{p \Rightarrow q}$$	$$\frac{p \quad p \Rightarrow q}{q}$$
not-I	**not**-E
$$[p]$$	
$$\frac{\text{false}}{\text{not } p}$$	$$\frac{p \quad \text{not } p}{\text{false}} \qquad \frac{\text{false}}{p}$$

In words, the complete rule may be paraphrased as follows. Suppose it has been shown that only two cases p and q need be considered, and suppose r is true assuming p, and r is also true assuming q. Then it is valid to infer r in all cases. Note that, as here, where one or more assumption appears in the list of premises we say that the assumptions are *discharged* by the rule.

The $\Rightarrow$-introduction rule also discharges an assumption. It states that if q follows from the assumption p then $p \Rightarrow q$ is true. A name commonly given to $\Rightarrow$-elimination is *modus ponens*. It states that q follows from a proof of p and a proof of $p \Rightarrow q$.

The final two rules occupy a special position in logic texts. The first **not**-elimination rule states that it is possible to infer a contradiction (**false**) from the proof of a proposition p and its negation **not** p. The **not**-introduction rule states that if a contradiction follows from the assumption p then it is valid to infer **not** p. A proof making use of this rule is called a *proof-by-contradiction*. The second **not**-elimination rule states that any proposition p may be inferred from a contradiction.

To these rules the law of the excluded middle is added as an axiom (that is as an inference rule with no premises). If it is not added one obtains 'intuitionistic' logic; the logic we are discussing is called 'classical' logic. Typically, the law of the excluded middle is used in conjunction with **or**-elimination when two cases of the form 'suppose p is true' and 'suppose p is false' are considered.

As an example of the use of these rules let us return to the very first argument presented in section 1.2. Recall the statement of the argument.

> If Superman were able and willing to prevent evil, he would do so. If Superman were unable to prevent evil, he would be impotent; if he were unwilling to prevent evil, he would be malevolent. Superman does not prevent evil. If Superman exists, he is neither impotent nor malevolent. Therefore Superman does not exist.

and the abbreviations

Superman exists	X
Superman is willing to prevent evil	W
Superman is able to prevent evil	A
Superman is malevolent	M
Superman is impotent	I
Superman prevents evil	E

Our objective is therefore to prove the proposition:

$\{[(W$ **and** $A) \Rightarrow E]$
and $[(\text{not } A) \Rightarrow I]$
and $[(\text{not } W) \Rightarrow M]$
and $(\text{not } E)$
and $[X \Rightarrow \text{not } (I \text{ or } M)]\}$
$\Rightarrow \text{not } X$

Note that the form of this argument is $p \Rightarrow (\text{not } X)$. This suggests that the last step of the proof will use $\Rightarrow$-introduction. Since the latter rule involves discharging the assumption p we begin by making that assumption.

Assume 1. $\{[(W$ **and** $A) \Rightarrow E]$
and $[(\text{not } A) \Rightarrow I]$
and $[(\text{not } W) \Rightarrow M]$
and $(\text{not } E)$
and $[X \Rightarrow \text{not } (I \text{ or } M)]\}$

The objective is now to prove **not** X. Were **not** X to appear as a term in assumption 1 the strategy would be to try to prove it directly. But it does not, and we therefore try to prove it by contradiction. The **not**-introduction rule suggests that we assume X and try to prove a contradiction (i.e. **false**).

  Assume 2. X

The strategy now is to see what can be inferred from assumption 1 by using the elimination rules to break it down. By **and**-elimination it is trivial to derive the five premises.

    3. W **and** $A \Rightarrow E$
    4. **not** $A \Rightarrow I$
    5. **not** $W \Rightarrow M$
    6. **not** E
    7. $X \Rightarrow$ **not** (I **or** M)

An application of $\Rightarrow$-elimination derives another simple proposition.

    8. **not** (I **or** M)   (2 and 7, $\Rightarrow$-E)

  Now the objective is to prove I **or** M because, by doing so, a contradiction with 8 is obtained. The only way to proceed is to perform a case analysis on the truth of W or on the truth of A. We choose to begin with a case analysis on the truth of W. The case in which W is **false** is easier.

  Assume 9. **not** W
    10. M (5 and 9, $\Rightarrow$-E)
    11. I **or** M (10, **or**-I)

The case in which W is **true** obliges us to perform a case analysis on A.

  Assume 12. W
    Assume 13. A
      14. W **and** A (12 and 13, **and**-I)
      15. E (3 and 14, $\Rightarrow$-E)
      16. **false**   (6 and 15, **not**-E)
      17. I **or** M (16, **not**-E)
    Assume 18. **not** A
      19. I (4 and 18, $\Rightarrow$-E)
      20. I **or** M (19, **or**-I)
    21. I **or** M (excluded middle, 17 and 20, **or**-E)

Since it has now been established that I **or** M is true whether or not W is true or false we can proceed to the desired contradiction.

22. *I* or *M*   (excluded middle, 11 and 21, **or**-E)

23. **false**   (8 and 22, **not**-E)

The last two steps are the ones that guided the initial assumptions.

24. **not** *X*   (2 and 23, **not**-I)

25. $\{[(W$ **and** $A) \Rightarrow E]$

   and $[(\text{not } A) \Rightarrow I]$

   and $[(\text{not } W) \Rightarrow M]$

   and not E

   and $[X \Rightarrow \text{not } (I \text{ or } M)]\} \Rightarrow \text{not } X$ (1 and 24, $\Rightarrow$-I)

Note how indention has been used to indicate the dependence of one step on an earlier assumption, and how 'outdention' indicates the discharge of one or more assumptions.

Exercises

1.23 Add explanations to the following proofs.

  (a) Assume 1. (**not** *A* **or** *B*) **and** *A*
               2. **not** *A* **or** *B*
               3. *A*
           Assume 4. *B*
           Assume 5. **not** *A*
                  6. **false**
                  7. *B*
               8. *B*
             9. $[(\text{not } A \text{ or } B) \text{ and } A] \Rightarrow B$

  (b) Assume 1. (*A* **or** *B*) **and** $(A \Rightarrow C)$ **and** $(B \Rightarrow D)$
               2. *A* **or** *B*
               3. $A \Rightarrow C$
               4. $B \Rightarrow D$
           Assume 5. *A*
                  6. *C*
                  7. *C* **or** *D*
           Assume 8. *B*
                  9. *D*
               10. *C* **or** *D*
             11. *C* **or** *D*
           12. $[(A \text{ or } B) \text{ and } (A \Rightarrow C) \text{ and } (B \Rightarrow D)] \Rightarrow (C \text{ or } D)$

  (c) Assume 1. $A \Rightarrow (B \text{ and } C)$
          Assume 2. *A*

    3. B **and** C

    4. B

  5. $A \Rightarrow B$

Assume 6. A

    7. B **and** C

    8. C

  9. $A \Rightarrow C$

  10. $(A \Rightarrow B)$ **and** $(A \Rightarrow C)$

11. $[A \Rightarrow (B$ **and** $C)] \Rightarrow [(A \Rightarrow B)$ **and** $(A \Rightarrow C)]$

1.24 Use the inference rules to prove the following.

(a) $[(A \Rightarrow B)$ **and** $(A \Rightarrow C)] \Rightarrow [A \Rightarrow (B$ **and** $C)]$

(b) $[(A \Rightarrow B)$ **and** $(C \Rightarrow D)$ **and** $(\textbf{not } B \textbf{ or not } D)] \Rightarrow (\textbf{not } A \textbf{ or not } C)$

(c) $[(\textbf{not } A \Rightarrow (B \Rightarrow C))$ **and** $(\textbf{not } D \Rightarrow (C \Rightarrow E))$

    and $(A \Rightarrow D)$ **and** $(\textbf{not } D)] \Rightarrow (B \Rightarrow E)$

1.9.2 Natural Deduction?

In Shakespeare's *Merchant of Venice* Portia had three caskets: gold, silver, and lead. Inside one of these caskets Portia had put her portrait and on each was an inscription. Now Portia explained to her suitor that each inscription could be either true or false but on the basis of the inscriptions he was to choose the casket containing the portrait. If he succeeded he could marry her.

    There is a multitude of possible inscriptions each giving rise to an intriguing logical puzzle. Our purpose here is to illustrate formal versus informal reasoning and, as an example, we take a simpler version of the problem in which there are just two caskets. The exercises are a little harder.

    Suppose then that Portia had two caskets, gold and silver, into one of which she placed her portrait and on which she wrote the inscriptions.

  Gold: The portrait is not in here.

  Silver: Exactly one of these inscriptions is true.

Here is an informal proof that the portrait is in the gold casket.

A. If the portrait is not in the gold casket then the inscription on the gold casket is true.

B. If the inscription on the silver casket is true then the inscription on the gold casket must be false.

C. Also, if the inscription on the silver casket is false then the inscription on the gold casket must be false.

D. By B and C the inscription on the gold casket must be false.

E. Now, suppose the portrait is not in the gold casket.

F. By A and E the inscription on the gold casket must be true.

G. So by D and F the inscription on the gold casket must be true and false which is a contradiction.

H. We conclude therefore that the portrait is in the gold casket.

Let us now consider how to formalize the argument. We begin by introducing the abbreviations 'G' for 'the portrait is in the gold casket', 'S' for 'the portrait is in the silver casket', 'g' for 'the inscription on the gold casket is true', and 's' for 'the inscription on the silver casket is true'. Since the portrait is in one of the caskets we begin with the premise

    1. *G* **and not** *S* **or** *S* **and not** *G*

(In fact we never use this premise.)

Next we formalize the two inscriptions. The inscription on the gold casket is true if and only if the portrait is not in the gold casket, i.e. $g \Leftrightarrow$ **not** G. Since there is no rule of logical deduction involving $\Leftrightarrow$ we express this as two implications.

    2. $g \Rightarrow$ **not** G

    3. **not** $G \Rightarrow g$

Note that premise 3 is step A of the informal proof.

Similarly, the inscription on the silver casket is true if and only if exactly one of g and s is true, i.e.

    4. $s \Rightarrow g$ **and not** s **or** s **and not** g

    5. g **and not** s **or** s **and not** $g \Rightarrow s$

Step B of the informal proof takes several lines.

Assume 6. s	
7. g **and not** s **or** s **and not** g	(4 and 6, $\Rightarrow$-E)
Assume 8. g **and not** s	
9. **not** s	(8, **and**-E)
10. **false**	(6 and 9, **not**-E)
11. **not** g	(10, **not**-I)
Assume 12. s **and not** g	
13. **not** g	(12, **and**-E)
14. **not** g	(7, 11 and 13, **or**-E)
15. $s \Rightarrow$ **not** g	(6 and 14, $\Rightarrow$-I)

Step C also takes several lines.

Assume 16. **not** s	
Assume 17. g	
18. g **and not** s	(16 and 17, **and**-I)
19. g **and not** s **or** s **and not** g	(18, **or**-I)

20. *s*	(5 and 19, $\Rightarrow$-E)
21. **false**	(16 and 20, **not**-E)
22. **not** *g*	(17 and 21, **not**-I)
23. **not** *s* $\Rightarrow$ **not** *g*	(16 and 22, $\Rightarrow$-I)

Now, however, step D follows immediately by **or**-elimination from 15, 23, and the law of the excluded middle.

24. **not** *g*

and the remainder of the formal proof closely matches the informal version.

Assume 26. **not** *G*	
27. *g*	(3 and 26, $\Rightarrow$-E)
28. **false**	(24 and 27, **not**-E)
29. *G*	(26 and 28, **not**-I)

It is clear from this example that a large amount of detail is required in a completely formal proof; on the other hand such a proof leaves nothing to chance. If you have worked through most of the exercises in this chapter the detail should now be 'mental arithmetic' to you (and if you have cause to doubt your 'arithmetic' you have the knowledge to check your calculations). In succeeding chapters we do not go into this level of detail, at least where the manipulations involve propositional formulae.

Exercises

1.25 Suppose that Portia put the following inscriptions on the three caskets.

Gold: The portrait is in here.
Silver: The portrait is in here.
Lead: At least two of these caskets bear a false inscription.

Which casket should the suitor choose? Give a convincing, informal argument supporting your answer. Using the following abbreviations, state formally the premises on which your argument is based:

G: the portrait is in the gold casket.
S: the portrait is in the silver casket.
L: the portrait is in the lead casket.
g: the inscription on the gold casket is true.
s: the inscription on the silver casket is true.
l: the inscription on the lead casket is true.

1.26 In this version of the problem Portia puts a dagger into one of the caskets. This time the suitor must choose a casket *not* containing the dagger. The inscriptions on the caskets are as follows.

Gold: The dagger is in this casket.
Silver: The dagger is not in this casket.
Lead: At most one of these three caskets bears a true inscription.

Again give a convincing, informal argument for the right choice of casket. State formally the premises on which your argument is based. This time use $G(S, L)$ to mean the dagger is in the gold (silver, lead) casket.

2 THE PREDICATE CALCULUS

2.1 PREDICATES, STATES, AND SATISFIABILITY

Whereas the propositional calculus is concerned with absolute truths, the predicate calculus deals with relative truths. A simple example is the statement

$$i < j$$

which is a property of the two integers i and j that is either true or false depending on the values assigned to i and j. It is true, for example, when $i = 0$ and $j = 1$ but false when $i = 2$ and $j = 1$. We say that $i < j$ is *predicated on i and j* or, more simply, the relation $i < j$ is a *predicate*.

Predicates are built by combining primitive relations (such as ' $<$ ') with the propositional connectives. For instance, the predicate *is_a_day_in_January* may defined by the statement that applying it to the integer d is equivalent to the proposition $1 \leqslant d$ **and** $d \leqslant 31$, i.e.

$$is\_a\_day\_in\_January(d) \equiv 1 \leqslant d \textbf{ and } d \leqslant 31.$$

The predicates we write typically involve constants like '0' and '1', function symbols like ' $+$ ' and '$*$', and one or more variables, as well as the logical operators **and, or**, etc. The variables are classified into two types called the *free* and *bound* variables. We explain the distinction in section 2.3.3; for the moment all predicates use only free variables and you may ignore the adjective 'free'.

To assign a truth value to a predicate it is necessary to know the interpretation of each of the constant and function symbols, and to know the value associated with each of its free variables. You should recognize and immediately know the interpretation of all of the constant and most of the function symbols we use. (For example, ' $+$ ' is interpreted as addition, '1' is the integer 'one', etc.) We introduce and explain some more unusual ones as we go along.

The value associated with a variable s is called the *state* of s. The set of all possible values that s may assume is called the *state space* of s. If a program employs variables $a, b, c, \ldots$ with state spaces $A, B, C, \ldots$ then the *state space* of the program is the *Cartesian product* of $A, B, C, \ldots$ which is the set of all tuples $(x, y, z, \ldots)$ where x is a value in the set A, y is a value in the set B and so on. The name Cartesian product is derived from the name of René Descartes, the inventor of Cartesian coordinates. It is called a 'product' because the number of elements in the product space is the product of the number of elements in each of the spaces $A, B, C, \ldots$.

Example

2.1 A program employs two variables, i: *integer*, and *present: Boolean*. The state space of i is therefore the set of all integers, i.e. $\{\ldots -, -2, -1, 0, 1, 2, 3, \ldots\}$, and the state space of *present* is $\{$**true, false**$\}$. Thus the state space of the program consists of the set of pairs $\{\ldots(-2, \textbf{true}), (-1, \textbf{true}), (0, \textbf{true}), (1, \textbf{true}), (2, \textbf{true}), \ldots, (-2, \textbf{false}), (-1, \textbf{false}), (0, \textbf{false}), (1, \textbf{false}), (2, \textbf{false}), \ldots\}$.

In order to avoid any ambiguity in the ordering of tuple-values we use a notation exemplified by $(i = 3, present = \textbf{false})$ to specify program states. When a predicate is true in a given state we say that the state *satisfies* the predicate. Thus $(i = 2, j = 3)$ satisfies the predicate $i < j$. When there is *no* state satisfying a given predicate the predicate is said to be *unsatisfiable*. When *all* states satisfy a given predicate the predicate is *valid*. For example, the predicate $(i < j)$ **and** $(j < i)$ is unsatisfiable and the predicate $(i < j) \Rightarrow (i \leqslant j)$ is valid.

Exercise

2.1 Which of the following propositions are unsatisfiable and which are valid? For each of the remainder specify a state that satisfies the predicate and one that does not satisfy the predicate.

(a) $(n = 0 \text{ and } m = 1) \Rightarrow m = 1$
(b) $m = 1 \Rightarrow (n = 0 \text{ and } m = 1)$
(c) $(n = k * (k - 1)/2 + j \text{ and } j = k) \Rightarrow n = k * (k + 1)/2$
(d) $n = k * (k + 1)/2 \Rightarrow (n = k * (k - 1)/2 + j \text{ and } j = k)$
(e) $(n = k - 1 \text{ and } j = k + 1) \Rightarrow j - n = -2$
(f) $i + j = 0 \text{ and } i - j = 0$

2.2 SIMPLE SPECIFICATIONS

2.2.1 Inequalities

Many of the predicates we write involve inequalities. The purpose of this section is partly to document some of their less obvious properties but mainly to give you some practice in manipulations involving a combination of inequalities and the logical operators.

Two characteristic properties of $\leqslant$ are that it is *transitive*,

$$i \leqslant j \text{ and } j \leqslant k \Rightarrow i \leqslant k,$$

and *asymmetric*,

$$i \leqslant j \text{ and } j \leqslant i \Rightarrow i = j.$$

The transitivity property is of course also true for $<$, so that

$$i < j \text{ and } j < k \Rightarrow i < k.$$

However, asymmetry is not true for $<$, since

$$i < j \text{ and } j < i \equiv \textbf{false}.$$

In combination with the common arithmetic operations, inequalities have the property that they are preserved by the addition of an arbitrary quantity,

$$i < j \Rightarrow i + k < j + k$$
$$i \leqslant j \Rightarrow i + k \leqslant j + k,$$

and by multiplication by an arbitrary positive value,

$$k > 0 \Rightarrow [i < j \Rightarrow k*i < k*j]$$
$$k > 0 \Rightarrow [i \leqslant j \Rightarrow k*i \leqslant k*j],$$

but inequalities are reversed when the multiplication is by a negative value,

$$k < 0 \Rightarrow [i < j \Rightarrow k*i > k*j]$$
$$k < 0 \Rightarrow [i \leqslant j \Rightarrow k*i \geqslant k*j].$$

Exercise

2.2 Fill in the relations indicated by question marks in the following.

(a) $k \geqslant 0 \Rightarrow [i < j \Rightarrow k*i \ ? \ k*j]$
(b) $k \geqslant 0 \Rightarrow [i \leqslant j \Rightarrow k*i \ ? \ k*j]$
(c) $k \leqslant 0 \Rightarrow [i < j \Rightarrow k*i \ ? \ k*j]$
(d) $k \leqslant 0 \Rightarrow [i < j \Rightarrow k*i \ ? \ k*j]$

When i and j are integers (which is the case in all our programs) we have that

$$i < j \equiv i + 1 \leqslant j$$

and

$$i < j + 1 \equiv i \leqslant j.$$

A less familiar arithmetic operation, which is nevertheless commonly available in programming languages, is the operation of integer division denoted by **div**. For positive integers i and j, i **div** j is the largest integer k which when multiplied by j is less than or equal to i.

Thus 6 **div** 2 = 3 since $3*2 \leqslant 6$ and $4*2 > 6$.

Also 37 **div** 5 = 7 since $7*5 \leqslant 37$ and $8*5 > 37$.

Division by zero is of course undefined. When i and j are of opposite signs the result of i **div** j is not obvious except in the case that i is an exact multiple of j. Thus (-4) **div** 2 is -2 but is (-5) **div** 2 equal to -3 or -2? We shall not answer this question because none of our programs relies on it. Instead we assume the following properties of **div**. First, division by j of an exact multiple of j results in that multiple:

$$(k*j) \textbf{ div } j = k.$$

Second, **div** is a *monotonic* operator, i.e. it preserves inequalities of the form $i \leqslant k$ when the divisor j is positive:

$$j > 0 \textbf{ and } i \leqslant k \Rightarrow (i \textbf{ div } j) \leqslant (k \textbf{ div } j).$$

Exercises

2.3 Use **div** to define the predicates $i|j$ (i 'divides' j), meaning j is an integral multiple of i, and $even(i)$, meaning that i is divisible by 2.

2.4 Simplify the following expressions:

(a) $i \leqslant j < i + 1$

(b) $(z*z)^{k \textbf{ div } 2}$

(c) $[even(k) \textbf{ and } 2*(k \textbf{ div } 2) = n] \Rightarrow k = n$

2.2.2 Sets

Sets are ubiquitous in mathematics and programming is no exception. Here we use simple arithmetic operations and inequalities to define subsets of array indices.

The notation used for sets is a conventional one. Curly brackets { } indicate that a set is being defined. Within the brackets we write one or more variables separated by a colon from a predicate, for example

$$\{i: i \geqslant 0\}$$

and

$$\{i, j: i < j\}.$$

When reading such a set description the curly brackets are verbalized as 'the set of' and the colon as 'such that'. Thus the two sets above would be read as

'the set of all integers i such that i is at least zero'

and   'the set of pairs of integers i, j such that i is less than j'.

Such a set definition identifies a subset of a *universe* of values. We assume throughout that all variables are integers unless specified otherwise. Thus the universe for the two sets defined above is, respectively, the set of all integers and the set of all pairs of integers.

Two familiar operations on sets are set union (denoted by $\cup$) and set intersection (denoted by $\cap$). For the most part, we avoid using these operators since they can be expressed equally well using the logical operators **or** and **and**. Specifically,

$$\{i: P(i) \text{ or } Q(i)\} = \{i: P(i)\} \cup \{i: Q(i)\}$$

and

$$\{i: P(i) \text{ and } Q(i)\} = \{i: P(i)\} \cap \{i: Q(i)\}.$$

Exercise

2.5 The symmetric difference, $A \div B$, of two sets A and B is the set of all elements of A that are not in B together with the set of all elements of B that are not in A. Express the symmetric difference $\{i: P(i)\} \div \{i: Q(i)\}$ using logical operations.

The empty set, the set containing no elements and denoted by $\emptyset$, can also be so expressed. Specifically,

$$\emptyset = \{i: \textbf{false}\}.$$

Here the traditional notation $\emptyset$ is shorter, but we often wish to show that a set defined in the form $\{i: P(i)\}$ is empty by showing that $P(i)$ is unsatisfiable, i.e. $P(i)$ is equivalent to **false**. An example which will appear frequently later is

$$\{i: 0 \leqslant i < 0\}.$$

Since the predicate $0 \leqslant i < 0$ requires i to be both positive ($0 \leqslant i$) and negative ($i < 0$) it is unsatisfiable and the set is empty.

Finally the universe can be written as

$$\{i: \textbf{true}\}.$$

Note that the implicit nature of the type of i becomes very clear here. In this case the set defined is the set of all integers.

Subsets of Cartesian Space

The set, $\{i, j: i \geqslant 0 \text{ and } j \geqslant 0\}$, of all pairs of positive integers, can be represented diagrammatically as a set of grid points in two-dimensional Cartesian space (Fig. 2.1(a)). Other subsets of two-dimensional Cartesian space are shown in Figs. 2.1(b)–(g).

Figure 2.1(b) shows a rectangle containing a total of $m * n$ points with bottom left corner (p, q). It is defined as

$$\{i, j: p \leqslant i < p + m \text{ and } q \leqslant j < q + n\}.$$

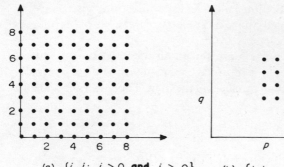

(a) $\{i, j: i \geq 0 \text{ and } j \geq 0\}$

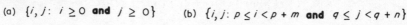

(b) $\{i, j: p \leq i < p + m \text{ and } q \leq j < q + n\}$

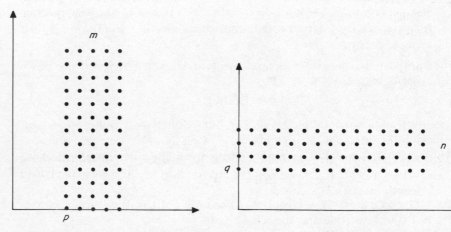

(c) $\{i, j: p \leq i < p + m \text{ and } j \geq 0\}$

(d) $\{i, j: i \geq 0 \text{ and } q \leq j < q + n\}$

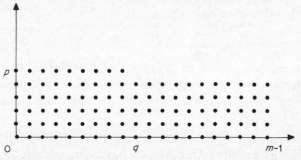

(e) $\{i, j: (0 \leq i < m \text{ and } 0 \leq j < p) \text{ or } (0 \leq i < q \text{ and } j = p)\}$

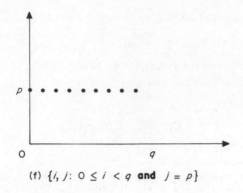

(f) $\{i, j: 0 \le i < q$ **and** $j = p\}$

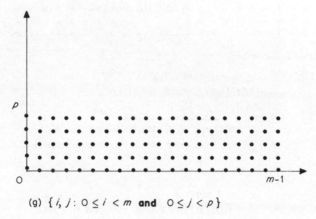

(g) $\{i, j: 0 \le i < m$ **and** $0 \le j < p\}$

Fig. 2.1 Examples of sets.

Note that this rectangle is the intersection of the two strips shown in Figs. 2.1(c) and (d), namely

$$\{i, j: p \le i < p + m \text{ and } j \ge 0\}$$

and

$$\{i, j: i \ge 0 \text{ and } q \le j < q + n\}$$

Note also that, when $m = 0$, the definition of the set illustrated in Fig. 2.1(b) becomes

$$\{i, j: p \le i < p \text{ and } q \le j < q + n\}$$

which, since $p \le i < p$ is unsatisfiable, simplifies to

$$\{i, j: \textbf{false}\}$$

i.e. the empty set. This provides a good check on the correctness of the definition since when $m = 0$ we do indeed expect the set to contain $0*n = 0$

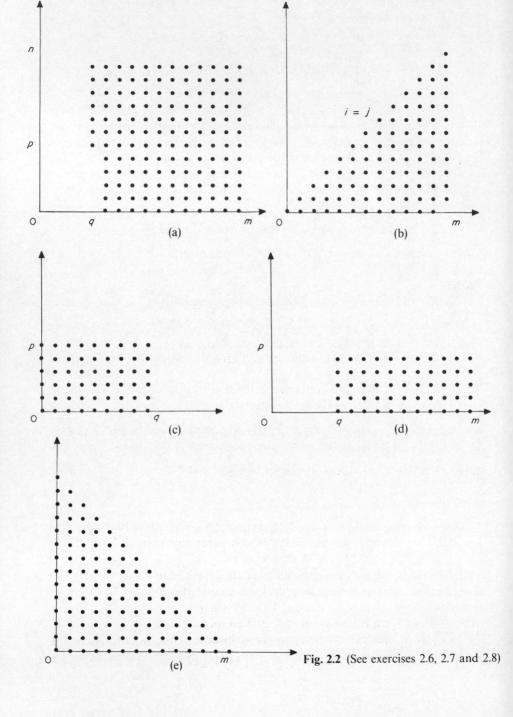

Fig. 2.2 (See exercises 2.6, 2.7 and 2.8)

points. Similarly, one can check that the empty set is defined when $n = 0$. Also, when $m = n = 1$ the defined set is

$$\{i, j: p \leq i < p + 1 \text{ and } q \leq j < q + 1\}$$

which equals $\quad \{i, j: p \leq i \leq p \text{ and } q \leq j \leq q\}$

i.e. $\quad \{i, j: i = p \text{ and } j = q\}$.

Thus we obtain a set containing exactly one element.

The set illustrated in Fig. 2.1(e) is a common feature of algorithms that search a two-dimensional array. Imagine an algorithm that searches an array a indexed by i and j in the ranges $0 .. m - 1$ and $0 .. n - 1$. If the searching process begins at the index $[0, 0]$ and searches the array elements in the order $[0, 0]$, $[1, 0], ..., [m - 1, 0]$, $[0, 1]$, $[1, 1], ...$ then at some stage all of the elements in the shaded area will have been searched. There are various ways to describe this set, one of which is

$$\{i, j: (0 \leq i < m \text{ and } 0 \leq j < p) \text{ or } (0 \leq i < q \text{ and } j = p)\}.$$

This corresponds to the union of the two sets shown in Figs. 2.1(f) and 2.1(g).

Exercises

2.6 Specify the following sets of points in two-dimensional Cartesian space.

(a) The set of all points contained in a square of side m (and thus having m^2 elements) and with top right corner (p, q).

(b) The set of all points contained in a square of side m and with top left corner (p, q).

(c) The set of all points contained in the shaded area shown in Fig. 2.2(a).

(d) The set of all points contained in the shaded area shown in Fig. 2.2(b).

2.7 Construct a definition of the set of all points shown in Fig. 2.1(e) by regarding it as the union of the two sets shown in Figs. 2.2(c) and (d).

2.8 Define the set of all points shown in Fig. 2.2(e).

2.2.3 Trees

To conclude this section we consider the specification of simple tree structures since such structures occur frequently in computer applications. Some of the exercises here are used again in chapter 4.

In a so-called *binary heap* the integers are arranged in a tree structure as shown below. Further nodes can be added to this tree line by line. The next line would therefore contain the integers 15 to 30 where 15 and 16 are the children of 7, 17 and 18 are the children of 8, and so on.

In a binary heap the children and grandchildren of integer i are defined by

$$children(i) = \{j: 2*i + 1 \leq j \leq 2*i + 2\}$$

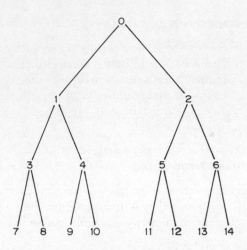

and

$$grandchildren(i) = \{j : 4*i + 3 \leqslant j \leqslant 4*i + 6\}.$$

Exercises

2.9 Define the set *greatgrandchildren(i)* in a binary heap.

    (*Note*: as yet we have no way of defining the set of all descendants (i.e. children, grandchildren, greatgrandchildren, and so on) of integer *i*. We shall return to this exercise when we consider quantifiers in the next section.)

2.10 A 3-ary heap has the structure shown below:

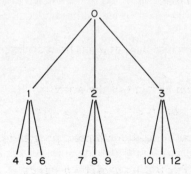

    Give definitions of the children and grandchildren of node *i* in a 3-ary heap.

    Generalize your definitions to a *k*-ary heap in which each node has *k* children.

2.11 What is the parent of node *i* (> 0) in a binary heap?
What is the parent of node *i* in a *k*-ary heap?

2.3 LOGICAL QUANTIFIERS

We want to make statements about the elements of a set such as 'every element in the set has the property that...' or 'there is some element in the set having the property that...'. We also want a notation for the number of elements in a set with a given property, or the maximum value of a function defined on a set. These and other operators defined on sets are called *quantifiers* and are discussed in this section and the next.

2.3.1 Universal Quantification (A)

To specify that every element of a set has a certain property we use the so-called *universal quantifier*, denoted by **A** and pronounced 'for all'. For example, to state that every element of an array a is nonnegative we might write

$$\mathbf{A}(i: 0 \leqslant i < n: a[i] \geqslant 0).$$

This expression is read as follows:

$\mathbf{A}(i$	for all (integers) i
$:$	such that
$0 \leqslant i < n$	i is between 0 and $n-1$
$: a[i] \geqslant 0)$	$a[i]$ is nonnegative

Omitting the quantifier, the bracketed expression describes a set and a predicate on that set. In this case the set is $\{i: 0 \leqslant i < n\}$ and the predicate is $a[i] \geqslant 0$. The identifier is called a *bound variable* and the defined set is called the *range* of the bound variable.

Examples

In examples 2.2 to 2.4 we assume that a has been declared to be of type **array** $[0..n-1]$ **of** *integer*.

2.2 $a[k]$ is the maximum element of the array:

$$\mathbf{A}(i: 0 \leqslant i < n: a[k] \geqslant a[i]).$$

2.3 The elements of a are in the arithmetic progression b, $b+d$, $b+2*d$, $b+3*d,...$

$$\mathbf{A}(i: 0 \leqslant i < n: a[i] = b + i*d).$$

2.4 The fact that the elements of a are stored in increasing order can be expressed in a number of ways, the simplest being:

(a) $\mathbf{A}(i: 0 < i < n: a[i-1] \leqslant a[i]).$

Note that the range of i begins at 1.   (Why?)
More complex ways of saying the same thing are as follows:

(b) $\mathbf{A}(i: 0 \leqslant i < n: \mathbf{A}(j: 0 \leqslant j < n: i \leqslant j \Rightarrow a[i] \leqslant a[j]))$

meaning 'For all i and for all j in the range 0 to $n-1$, if i is less than or equal to j then $a[i]$ is less than or equal to $a[j]$'.

(c) $\mathbf{A}(i: 0 \leqslant i < n: \mathbf{A}(j: i \leqslant j < n: a[i] \leqslant a[j]))$

meaning 'For all i in the range 0 to $n-1$ and all j in the range i to $n-1$, $a[i] \leqslant a[j]$'.

The predicates in examples (b) and (c) are predicates on the set of integers in the range $0 .. n-1$ defined in terms of predicates on the set of integers in the same range. They may also be regarded as predicates on the Cartesian product of the two ranges. In this way (b) may be rewritten more succinctly as

(d) $\mathbf{A}(i, j: 0 \leqslant i < n \text{ and } 0 \leqslant j < n: i \leqslant j \Rightarrow a[i] \leqslant a[j])$

and (c) may be rewritten as

(e) $\mathbf{A}(i, j: 0 \leqslant i < n \text{ and } i \leqslant j < n: a[i] \leqslant a[j])$.

The range is omitted if it is **true**. An example is

$$\mathbf{A}(d:: 0 = d*0)$$

which states that multiplication of an arbitrary value by 0 always yields 0. Note the implicit nature of the type of d (integer) in this predicate.

Exercises

2.12 Suppose $n = 10$ and the elements of the array a (in the order $a[0]$, $a[1], \ldots, a[9]$) are 12, 15, 8, 10, 20, 25, 29, 53, 53, 99. Which of the following states satisfy the proposition

$$\mathbf{A}(i, j: 0 \leqslant i < j \text{ and } q \leqslant j < n: a[i] \leqslant a[j])?$$

(a) $q = 5$
(b) $q = 0$
(c) $q = 9$
(d) $q = 10$

What is the minimum value of q satisfying the predicate? What is the maximum value of q satisfying the predicate?

2.13 Translate the following sentences into predicates. Assume that a and b have both been declared to be of type **array** $[0 .. n-1]$ **of** *integer*.

(a) a is an exact copy of b (i.e. for all i, $a[i]$ equals $b[i]$).
(b) For all i, the ith element of a is less than the ith element of b.
(c) Every element of a is less than every element of b.

(d) If the elements of a are sorted in ascending order then so are the elements of b.

(e) For every pair of indices i, j if $a[i] \leqslant a[j]$ then $b[i] \leqslant b[j]$.

(f) All of the elements of a are distinct.

(g) Every element of a is different from every element of b.

2.3.2 Existential Quantification (E)

Sometimes we wish to make a statement like 'There is an element of the array a which has the value x'. To do this we use the existential quantifier **E** meaning 'there exists'.

$$\mathbf{E}(i: 0 \leqslant i < n: a[i] = x)$$

The meaning of this predicate can be expressed in English as follows:

$\mathbf{E}(i$	there exists an (integer) i
:	such that
$0 \leqslant i < n$	i is between 0 and $n-1$
:	and the following holds
$a[i] = x)$	$a[i]$ equals x.

As with the universal quantifier we use **E** in predicates having two forms.

The predicate

$$\mathbf{E}(v: R: P)$$

is read as 'there exists a v in the range R such that P', whilst

$$\mathbf{E}(v:: P)$$

is read as 'there exists a v such that P'. In the latter case the range of v is implicitly the type of v.

Note that 'there is a v in the range R such that P' means the same thing as 'it is not true that for all v in the range R the predicate P is false'. In other words

$$\mathbf{E}(v: R: P) \equiv \mathbf{not}\ \mathbf{A}(v: R: \mathbf{not}\ P).$$

Exercise

2.14 Which of the following is equivalent to $\mathbf{E}(v: R: P)$?

    (a) $\mathbf{E}(v:: R \Rightarrow P)$

    (b) $\mathbf{E}(v:: R\ \mathbf{and}\ P)$

    (c) $\mathbf{E}(v:: R\ \mathbf{or}\ P)$

Which of the following is equivalent to $\mathbf{A}(v: R: P)$?

    (d) $\mathbf{A}(v:: R \Rightarrow P)$

(e) **A**(*v*:: *R* **and** *P*)

(f) **A**(*v*:: *R* **or** *P*)

Examples

Again assume that *a* and *b* are of type **array** [0..*n* − 1] **of** *integer*.

2.5 Some elements of *a* are nonzero:

$$\mathbf{E}(i: 0 \leqslant i < n: a[i] \neq 0)$$

or

$$\mathbf{E}(i:: a[i] \neq 0).$$

2.6 The array *a* is not sorted in ascending order:

$$\mathbf{E}(i:: a[i] > a[i + 1]).$$

2.7 At least one element of *a* is greater than all elements of *b*:

$$\mathbf{E}(i:: \mathbf{A}(j:: a[i] > b[j])).$$

2.8 Every element of *b* is a copy of some element of *a*:

$$\mathbf{A}(j:: \mathbf{E}(i:: a[i] = b[j])).$$

2.9 *n* is even:

$$\mathbf{E}(m:: n = 2*m).$$

2.10 Given any strictly positive integer *i*, either *i* is odd or successive division of *i* by 2 will always result in an odd value.

$$\mathbf{A}(i: 0 < i: \mathbf{E}(k: 0 \leqslant k: \text{odd}(i \text{ div } 2^k))).$$

Exercises

2.15 Suppose *a*: **array** [0..*m*−1] **of** *integer* and *b*: **array** [0..*n*−1] **of** *integer*. We say that *b* is a *nonredundant copy* of *a* if *b* is a copy of *a* with duplicates removed. For example if *a*[0] = 1, *a*[1] = 2, *a*[2] = 2, *a*[3] = 5, *a*[4] = 5 then a nonredundant copy of *a* is the array *b* where *b*[0] = 1, *b*[1] = 2 and *b*[2] = 5.

Write a predicate that formalizes the statement '*b* is a nonredundant copy of *a*'.

2.16 Which of the following is the negation of the statement 'All British cars are badly made'?

(a) All non-British cars are well made.

(b) All British cars are well made.

(c) Some British cars are well made.

(d) Some British cars are badly made.

(e) Some non-British cars are badly made.

(f) Some non-British cars are well made.

2.17 Given a: **array** $[0..n-1]$ **of** *integer*, say $(5, 3, 8, 4, 1)$, a second array $b[0..n-1]$ can be used to indicate the numerical ordering of the values in a. For the array a above we would have $b = (4, 1, 3, 0, 2)$ because $a[4]$ is the smallest, $a[1]$ the next smallest, $a[3]$ the next smallest and so on. When two array elements have the same value the ordering on them is arbitrary. Describe such arrays a and b in a predicate.

2.18 Which of the following are valid?

(a) $\mathbf{A}(i: 0 \leqslant i: \mathbf{E}(j: 0 \leqslant j: i < j))$

(b) $\mathbf{A}(i: 0 \leqslant i: \mathbf{E}(j: 0 \leqslant j: j < i))$

(c) $\mathbf{E}(i: 0 \leqslant i: \mathbf{A}(j: 0 \leqslant j: j \leqslant i))$

(d) $\mathbf{E}(j:: i \geqslant j \text{ and } i \geqslant -j) \Leftrightarrow i \geqslant 0$

(e) $\mathbf{A}(j:: i \geqslant j \text{ and } i \geqslant -j) \Leftrightarrow i \geqslant 0$

(f) $\mathbf{A}(j:: i \geqslant j \text{ or } i \geqslant -j) \Leftrightarrow i \geqslant 0$

(g) $\mathbf{E}(j:: i \geqslant j \text{ or } i \geqslant -j) \Leftrightarrow i < 0$

(h) $\mathbf{A}(j:: i < j \text{ or } i < -j) \Leftrightarrow i < 0$

2.3.3 Free and Bound Variables, Substitution

In an expression $\mathbf{Q}(i: r(i): p(i))$ (where, for the moment, $\mathbf{Q}$ is either $\mathbf{A}$ or $\mathbf{E}$) the variable i is said to be *bound* to the quantifier $\mathbf{Q}$. Occurrences of a variable i that are not bound to a quantifier in some expression R, say, are said to be *free* in R. For example, in the expression

$$\mathbf{E}(d:: p = q*d) \tag{2.1}$$

the variables p and q are free, and the variable d is bound.

The bound variables act only as 'place-holders' and can be renamed at will so long as the renaming does not bind, or *capture*, an already free variable. Thus, replacing d by m in (2.1), we obtain the equivalent expression

$$\mathbf{E}(m:: p = q*m).$$

However, the replacement of d by p captures the free variable p and the resulting expression

$$\mathbf{E}(p:: p = q*p)$$

means something totally different!

In principle, it is possible for a variable to be both free and bound in the same expression, for example i in

$$0 < i \text{ and } \mathbf{E}(i: 0 \leqslant i < n: a[i] = 0). \tag{2.2}$$

In (2.2) the occurrence of i in the first conjunct is free, but all its occurrences in the second conjunct are bound. Although the meaning of such expressions is perfectly well defined it is a practice that can be confusing and which, therefore, will be avoided. In particular, we will always keep program variables and bound variables quite distinct from each other. However, this does not preclude us from writing expressions in which a variable i, say, is bound to more than one quantifier. For example, in the expression

$$\mathbf{A}(i\colon 0 \leqslant i < n\colon a[i] = 0) \Rightarrow \mathbf{E}(i\colon 0 \leqslant i < n\colon a[i] = 0)$$

the six occurrences of i split into three that are bound to $\mathbf{A}$ and three that are bound to $\mathbf{E}$.

Substitution of a free variable by an expression plays an important role in the semantics of assignment discussed in the next chapter. To indicate an intention to replace one or more free variables, $i, j,$ and k, say, in a predicate R, say, we introduce the predicate by a statement of the form

$$R(i, j, k) \equiv \ldots$$

For example, the predicate (2.1) might be introduced as

$$is\_divisor(q) \equiv \mathbf{E}(d\colon\colon p = q * d).$$

Then the expression obtained by substituting, say, $2 * q$ for q is denoted by $is\_divisor(2 * q)$ which is equivalent to

$$\mathbf{E}(d\colon\colon p = (2 * q) * d).$$

Note that it is not our practice to include every free variable as a parameter in the definition of a predicate—p is free in $\mathbf{E}(d\colon\colon p = q * d)$ but is absent from $is\_divisor(q)$, for example. This has the advantage of reducing the amount of unnecessary detail in our explanations.

A final word of caution. When substituting a variable by an expression you should make liberal use of parentheses to avoid mistakes resulting from failure to observe operator precedence. For example, if $R(i)$ is defined by

$$R(i) \equiv 2 * i = 10$$

then $R(i + 1)$ is $2 * (i + 1) = 10$ and *not* $2 * i + 1 = 10$.

2.4   ARITHMETIC QUANTIFIERS

Two familiar quantifiers are summation ($\mathbf{S}$) and product ($\mathbf{P}$). The formula

$$\mathbf{S}(i\colon r(i)\colon f(i))$$

is defined to be the sum of values of $f(i)$ taken over all i satisfying $r(i)$. Thus $\mathbf{S}(i\colon 0 \leqslant i < n\colon i)$ denotes $0 + 1 + 2 + \cdots + n - 1$. Similarly, $\mathbf{P}(i\colon 1 \leqslant i \leqslant n\colon i)$ denotes $1 * 2 * 3 * \ldots * n$. Note that summation over an empty set yields the value zero, i.e.

$$\mathbf{S}(i: \text{false}: f(i)) = 0$$

and product over an empty set yields the value 1, i.e.

$$\mathbf{P}(i: \text{false}: f(i)) = 1.$$

Two further arithmetic quantifiers are **MIN** and **MAX** which generalize the binary operators min and max, respectively. Thus $\mathbf{MIN}(i: r(i): f(i))$ denotes the minimum value of $f(i)$ and $\mathbf{MAX}(i: r(i): f(i)$ denotes the maximum value of $f(i)$, where i ranges over values satisfying $r(i)$. Examples are

$$\mathbf{MIN}(i: 0 \leqslant i < n: i + 1) = 1$$

and

$$\mathbf{MAX}(i: 0 \leqslant i < n: i*i) = (n-1)*(n-1).$$

The minimum of an empty set is ∞(infinity) and the maximum of an empty set is $-\infty$.

One final quantifier that is sometimes useful is denoted by **N** and means 'the number of'. Thus

$$\mathbf{N}(i: 0 \leqslant i < n: a[i] = x)$$

denotes the number of occurrences of the element x in the array segment $a[0 .. n-1]$.

The quantifier **N** is different from all the earlier quantifiers since it does not generalize a binary operator to a set of arguments. Indeed **N** is derived from summation by the formula

$$\mathbf{N}(i: r(i): p(i)) = \mathbf{S}(i: r(i) \text{ and } p(i): 1).$$

This may be read as 'the number of i in the range $r(i)$ satisfying $p(i)$ is calculated by counting 1 for each i in the range $r(i)$ **and** $p(i)$.'

Examples
Several problems making use of these quantifiers will be discussed in chapter 4. Here is a selection from them.

2.11 (Minsum problem) Given a: **array** $[0 .. n-1]$ **of** *integer*, the problem is to find the minimum sum of a sequence of consecutive elements of a. For example, given the array displayed below

i	0	1	2	3	4	5	6	7	8	9	10
$a[i]$	1	-2	3	-1	-5	-4	1	0	-2	5	-1

the minimum sum is $(-1)+(-5)+(-4)+1+0+(-2)$.
The sum of elements $a[i], a[i+1], \ldots, a[j-1]$ is defined by

$$sum(i, j) = \mathbf{S}(k: i \leqslant k < j: a[k])$$

and the minimum sum in the array segment $a[0..n-1]$ is defined by

$$minsum(n) = \textbf{MIN}(i, j: 0 \leqslant i \leqslant j \leqslant n: sum(i, j)).$$

2.12 (Largest **true** square problem) Given b: **array** $[0..m-1, 0..n-1]$ **of** *Boolean*, the problem is to find the size of the largest square subarray of b all of whose elements are **true**. In the array below (in which **true** has been abbreviated to T and **false** to F) the largest **true** square has been outlined. It has size 3.

T	F	T	F	T	F	T	F	T	F
T	T	T	T	F	T	T	T	T	F
F	T	T	T	T	T	T	T	F	T
T	T	T	T	F	T	F	T	T	T
T	T	T	T	T	T	T	T	T	T

The property that there is a **true** square in b of size d with bottom left corner (p, q) can be defined as

true_square(p, q, d)
$\equiv 0 \leqslant d \leqslant min(m - p, n - q)$ **and** *alltrue*(p, q, d)

where

alltrue$(p, q, d) \equiv \textbf{A}(i, j: p \leqslant i < p + d$ **and** $q \leqslant j < q + d: b[i, j]).$

Then the size of the largest **true** square in b can be defined as

$$size = \textbf{MAX}(d: \textbf{E}(p, q: 0 \leqslant p < m \text{ and } 0 \leqslant q < n: true\_square(p, q, d)):d)$$

You should read the latter formula as 'size is the maximum value of d for which there are array indices p and q such that there is a **true** square of size d with bottom left corner (p, q).' Note that the range of d is nonempty since it always includes $d = 0$.

2.13 (Sorting) Given a: **array** $[0..m-1]$ **of** *integer*, the 'unsortedness' of a is measured by the number of *inversions* in a, i.e. the number of pairs (i, j) such that $i < j$ and $a[i] > a[j]$. For example, an array of size 5 containing the elements

$$a[0] = 5, \ a[1] = 3, \ a[2] = 4, \ a[3] = 6, \ a[4] = 1$$

has six inversions because

$$a[0] > a[1]$$
$$a[0] > a[2]$$
$$a[0] > a[4]$$
$$a[1] > a[4]$$
$$a[2] > a[4]$$
$$a[3] > a[4].$$

Formally the number of inversions in the array a is defined as

$$\mathbf{N}(i, j: 0 \leqslant i < j < m: a[i] > a[j]).$$

Exercises

2.19 Another quantifier that is sometimes useful is **LEAST** defined by **LEAST**(i: $r(i)$: $p(i)$) is the least value of i satisfying the predicate p. Define **LEAST** in terms of **MIN**.

2.20 Given an array $a[0..n-1]$, an array $b[0..n-1]$ can be used to indicate the rank of each element of a. For example if a is $(19, 4, 17, 16, 21, 13, 5, 19)$ the array b is $(5, 0, 4, 3, 7, 2, 1, 5)$ because $a[1]$ is the smallest element and so has rank 0; $a[6]$ is the next smallest and so has rank 1, and so on. Construct a predicate *is_rank* formalizing this property.

2.21 A *plateau* of an array $a[0..n-1]$ is a segment $a[i..j-1]$ all of whose values are equal. Such a plateau has length $j - i$. Define formally the predicate *allequal*(j, *len*) to mean that all the elements $a[j-len]$, $a[j-len+1], \ldots, a[j-1]$ are equal. Use this predicate to define *plateau*(*len*, n), meaning there is a plateau of length *len* in the segment $a[0..n-1]$, and *longest_plateau_length*(n), the length of the longest plateau in the segment $a[0..n-1]$.

2.22 A plateau $a[i..j-1]$ of $a[0..n-1]$ is *maximal* if it cannot be extended into a plateau of longer length. The maximal plateaus in the array segment below are $a[0..0]$, $a[1..3]$, and $a[4..5]$.

i	0	1	2	3	4	5
$a[i]$	0	3	3	3	2	2

Define the predicate *maximal_plateau*(i, *len*, n) meaning $a[i-len..i-1]$ is a maximal plateau of $a[0..n-1]$. Use the quantifier **N** to define the number of maximal plateaus in $a[0..n-1]$.

2.23 In an array $a[0..n-1]$ we say that 'all equal values are adjacent' if and only if no two equal array values $a[i]$ and $a[k]$ are separated by an unequal value $a[j]$. The array displayed in the first line below satisfies the predicate but that in the second line does not (since two occurrences of 2 are separated by the value 5).

```
1   1   7   7   2   4   9   3   3   3   6
2   5   2
```

Define formally the predicate *adjacent_equal_values*(n).

2.5 PROPERTIES OF QUANTIFIERS

With the exception of **N**, all of the quantifiers so far discussed have involved the generalization to an arbitrary set of an associative and commutative binary operator. (Thus S is the generalization of $+$, A is the generalization of **and** and MIN is the generalization of *min*.) A consistent notation has been deliberately adopted so that we may collate properties common to all quantifiers. In general terms the notation we use is that, if q is an associative and commutative binary operator (i.e. $(a\ \mathbf{q}\ b)\ \mathbf{q}\ c = a\ \mathbf{q}\ (b\ \mathbf{q}\ c)$ and $a\ \mathbf{q}\ b = b\ \mathbf{q}\ a$ for a, b and c of the appropriate type), then $\mathbf{Q}$ denotes the application of $\mathbf{q}$ to arbitrary sets. We write

$$\mathbf{Q}(i\colon r(i)\colon f(i))$$

to mean 'the quantity of $f(i)$ where i ranges over $r(i)$'.

There are three parts to such an expression, the bound variable i, the range $r(i)$ and the function $f(i)$. The following is a list of rules for manipulating each of the parts. *Care should be taken with their use since they are not always valid.* Nevertheless their use is always valid when the range denotes a finite set, and in the few instances of infinite ranges in this text. The bibliography points you to texts in which the complications are discussed. If you are already familiar with manipulating summations (S) then most of the rules should be self-evident. Except for the most elementary, each rule is followed by an example of its usage. (The longer examples make use of the elementary rules.)

It should be emphasized that these properties apply only where q is both associative and commutative and so do not apply to N. Properties of N can, however, be derived from its definition as $\mathbf{N}(i\colon r(i)\colon p(i)) = \mathbf{S}(i\colon r(i)$ **and** $p(i)\colon 1)$ and the properties of S.

2.5.1   Bound Variable Part

(a)   Change of Variable

$$\mathbf{Q}(i\colon r(i)\colon f(i)) = \mathbf{Q}(k\colon r(k)\colon f(k))$$

provided k is not free in $r(i)$ or $f(i)$.

(b)   Cartesian Product

$$\mathbf{Q}(i,j\colon r(i)\ \textbf{and}\ s(i,j)\colon f(i,j))$$
$$= \mathbf{Q}(i\colon r(i)\colon \mathbf{Q}(j\colon s(i,j)\colon f(i,j)))$$

where j denotes any nonempty set of bound variables.

Examples
2.14 *minsum*(n)
$$= \mathbf{MIN}(i,j\colon 0 \leqslant i \leqslant j \leqslant n\colon sum(i,j))$$
$$= \mathbf{MIN}(j\colon 0 \leqslant j \leqslant n\colon \mathbf{MIN}(i\colon 0 \leqslant i \leqslant j\colon sum(i,j)))$$
$$= \mathbf{MIN}(i\colon 0 \leqslant i \leqslant n\colon \mathbf{MIN}(j\colon i \leqslant j \leqslant n\colon sum(i,j)))$$

2.15 *no_of_inversions*
$$= \mathbf{N}(i, j : 0 \leqslant i < j < m : a[i] > a[j])$$
$$= \mathbf{S}(i, j : 0 \leqslant i < j < m \text{ and } a[i] > a[j] : 1)$$
$$= \mathbf{S}(i : 0 \leqslant i < m : \mathbf{S}(j : i < j < m \text{ and } a[i] > a[j] : 1))$$
$$= \mathbf{S}(i : 0 \leqslant i < m : \mathbf{N}(j : i < j < m : a[i] > a[j]))$$

Exercises

2.24 The sum of all the elements in the lower triangular portion of the array a can be expressed as

$$\mathbf{S}(i : 0 \leqslant i < n : \mathbf{S}(j : 0 \leqslant j < i : a[i, j]))$$
or as $\qquad \mathbf{S}(j : 0 \leqslant j < n : \mathbf{S}(i : j < i < n : a[i, j]))$

Prove that these are equal.

2.25 Make use of the fact that

$$r(i) \text{ and } s(i, j) \equiv r(i) \text{ and } s(i, j) \text{ and } \mathbf{E}(k :: r(k) \text{ and } s(k, j))$$

(see exercise 2.27) to show that

$$\mathbf{Q}(i : r(i) : \mathbf{Q}(j : s(i, j) : f(i, j)))$$
$$= \mathbf{Q}(j : \mathbf{E}(i : r(i) : s(i, j)) : \mathbf{Q}(i : r(i) \text{ and } s(i, j) : f(i, j))).$$

2.5.2 Range Part

(a)   Range Translation

A function g is said to be $(1-1)$ if $i \neq j$ implies that $g(i) \neq g(j)$. Suppose g is $(1-1)$. Then

$$\mathbf{Q}(i : r(i) : f(i)) = \mathbf{Q}(i : r(g(i)) : f(g(i)))$$

Examples

2.16 $\mathbf{S}(i : 1 \leqslant i \leqslant n : i) = \mathbf{S}(i : 0 \leqslant i < n : i + 1)$
Take $g(i) = i + 1$. The function g is a $(1-1)$ mapping from $\{i : 0 \leqslant i < n\}$ to $\{i : 1 \leqslant i \leqslant n\}$.

2.17 $\mathbf{E}(d :: p = q * d + r) \equiv \mathbf{E}(d :: p = q * d + r - q)$
Take $g(d) = d - 1$. The function g is a $(1-1)$ mapping from integers to integers, so by range translation:

$$\mathbf{E}(d : integer(d) : p = q * d + r)$$
$$\equiv \mathbf{E}(d : integer(d) : p = q * (d - 1) + r)$$
$$\equiv \mathbf{E}(d : integer(d) : p = q * d + r - q)$$

Exercise

2.26 Suppose $minsum = \mathbf{MIN}(i, j : 0 \leqslant i < j \leqslant n : sum(i, j))$
where $sum(i, j) = \mathbf{S}(k : i \leqslant k < j : b[k])$

Show that $minsum = \mathbf{MIN}(i, j: 0 \leqslant i \leqslant j < n: s(i, j))$

where $s(i, j) = \mathbf{S}(k: i \leqslant k \leqslant j: b[k])$.

(The differences in these definitions are in the inequalities involving j.)

(b) Singleton Range

$$\mathbf{Q}(i: i = k: f(i)) = f(k)$$

(c) Range Splitting

$$\mathbf{Q}(i: r(i): f(i)) = \mathbf{Q}(i: r(i) \text{ and } b(i): f(i))$$
$$\mathbf{q}\ \mathbf{Q}(i: r(i) \text{ and not } b(i): f(i))$$

Example
2.18 Suppose $i \leqslant k$. Then

$$\mathbf{MIN}(j: i \leqslant j \leqslant k + 1: sum(i, j))$$
$$= min(\mathbf{MIN}(j: i \leqslant j \leqslant k: sum(i, j)),$$
$$\mathbf{MIN}(j: i \leqslant j = k + 1: sum(i, j)))$$

(range splitting with the predicate $b(j) \equiv j = k + 1$)
$$= min(\mathbf{MIN}(j: i \leqslant j \leqslant k: sum(i, j)), sum(i, k + 1)).$$

(singleton range)

Exercises
2.27 Show that $r(i) \text{ and } \mathbf{E}(k::r(k)) \equiv r(i)$

2.28 Show that

$$\mathbf{Q}(i: [r(i) \text{ and } s(i)] \text{ or } [\text{not } r(i) \text{ and } t(i)]: f(i))$$
$$= \mathbf{Q}(i:r(i) \text{ and } s(i): f(i))\mathbf{q}\ \mathbf{Q}(i: \text{ not } r(i) \text{ and } t(i): f(i)))$$

2.29 Show that

$$\mathbf{Q}(i: r(i): f(i))\mathbf{q}\ \mathbf{Q}(i: s(i): f(i))$$
$$= \mathbf{Q}(i:r(i) \text{ or } s(i): f(i))\mathbf{q}\ \mathbf{Q}(i:r(i) \text{ and } s(i): f(i)$$

(d) Identity Element

$$\mathbf{Q}(i: \textbf{false}: f(i)) \text{ is an identity of } \mathbf{q}, \text{ i.e.}$$
$$\mathbf{Q}(i: r(i): f(i)) = \mathbf{Q}(i: r(i): f(i))\mathbf{q}\ \mathbf{Q}(i: \textbf{false}: f(i)).$$

(This is a special case of range splitting.)

Examples
2.19 $\mathbf{S}(i: 0 \leqslant i < 0: f(i)) = 0$

2.20 $A(i: 0 \leqslant i < 0: f(i)) \equiv$ **true**

2.21 $E(i: 0 \leqslant i < 0: f(i)) \equiv$ **false**

(e) (Generalized) Range Splitting

$$Q(i: E(j: r(j): p(i,j)): f(i))$$
$$= Q(j: r(j): Q(i: p(i,j): f(i)))$$

provided that for each *i*, there is at most one *j* satisfying $p(i,j)$, i.e.

$$A(j, j': r(j) \text{ and } r(j'): j = j' \text{ or not } (p(i,j) \text{ and } p(i,j'))).$$

Examples

2.22 Exercise 4.11 asks you to design an algorithm to determine all positive integer solutions *i*, *j* to the equation $i^2 + j^2 = r$, where *r* is a given positive integer. The number of such solutions is

$$N(i: i \geqslant 0: E(j: j \geqslant 0: i^2 + j^2 = r)).$$

Using (e) and the definition of **N**, this can be re-expressed as

$$S(i: i \geqslant 0 \text{ and } E(j: j \geqslant 0: i^2 + j^2 = r): 1)$$
$$= S(j: j \geqslant 0: S(i: i \geqslant 0 \text{ and } i^2 + j^2 = r: 1))$$
$$= S(j: j \geqslant 0: N(i: i \geqslant 0: i^2 + j^2 = r)).$$

2.23 A *plateau* of an array $a[0..n-1]$ is a segment $a[i..j-1]$ of *a* all of whose values are equal. Such a plateau has length $j - i$. The *longest* plateau length in *a* can be defined as

MAX(*len: plateau(len): len*)

where $plateau(len) \equiv E(j: 0 < j \leqslant n: 0 < len \leqslant j$

and $allequal(j, len))$

and $allequal(j, len) \equiv A(k: 0 < k < len: a[j-1] = a[j-k])$

Using (e) with $i = len$, $p(len, j) \equiv 0 < len \leqslant j$ and $allequal(j, len)$ and $r(j) \equiv 0 < j \leqslant n$ we get

MAX(*len: plateau(len): len*)
$= $ MAX($j: 0 < j \leqslant n$: MAX(*len*: $0 < len \leqslant j$ and $allequal(j, len): len$))
$= $ MAX($j: 0 < j \leqslant n$: *longest_plateau_length*(j))
where *longest_plateau_length*(j)
$= $ MAX(*len*: $0 < len \leqslant j$ and $allequal(j, len): len$)

2.24 Note the importance of the restriction on the predicates $p(i, j)$ in generalized range splitting. An example illustrating an invalid use of range splitting would be the following.

Suppose b: **array**$[0..m-1, 0..n-1]$ of *Boolean*. The number of rows of b containing a **true** value is denoted by

$$\mathbf{N}(i: 0 \leqslant i < m: \mathbf{E}(j: 0 \leqslant j < n: b[i,j])).$$

If **N** is rewritten using **S**, and (e) applied, then we obtain:

$$\mathbf{S}(j: 0 \leqslant j < n: \mathbf{N}(i: 0 \leqslant i < m: b[i,j]))$$

which equals the number of **true** elements in the array. The reason that the two summations are unequal is straightforward. In the first case each row number i is counted just once if there is a column j with $b[i,j]$ equal to **true**; in the second case each row number is counted once for *each j* such that $b[i,j]$ is **true**.

Range disjunction (property (f)) and its generalization ((g)) enable the range to be split into nondisjoint sets whenever **q** is idempotent, i.e. $a \mathbf{q} a = a$ for all a. Of the operators we have seen only $+$ and $*$ are not idempotent—all of **and, or,** *min,* and *max are* idempotent.

(f)   Range Disjunction

If **q** is idempotent then

$$\mathbf{Q}(i: r(i) \text{ or } s(i): f(i))$$
$$= \mathbf{Q}(i: r(i): f(i)) \mathbf{q} \mathbf{Q}(i: s(i): f(i))$$

This is again a special case of range splitting and is proved as follows. Assume **q** is idempotent. Then

$\mathbf{Q}(i: r(i): f(i)) \mathbf{q} \mathbf{Q}(i: s(i): f(i))$

$\quad = \mathbf{Q}(i: r(i) \text{ and } s(i): f(i)) \mathbf{q} \mathbf{Q}(i: r(i) \text{ and not } s(i): f(i))$

$\quad \mathbf{q} \mathbf{Q}(i: s(i) \text{ and } r(i): f(i)) \mathbf{q} \mathbf{Q}(i: s(i) \text{ and not } r(i): f(i))$ \qquad (range splitting)

$\quad = \mathbf{Q}(i: r(i) \text{ and not } s(i): f(i)) \mathbf{q} \mathbf{Q}(i: r(i) \text{ and } s(i): f(i))$

$\quad \mathbf{q} \mathbf{Q}(i: \text{not } r(i) \text{ and } s(i): f(i))$ \qquad (commutativity and idempotence of **q**)

$\quad = \mathbf{Q}(i: r(i) \text{ and not } s(i): f(i)) \mathbf{q} \mathbf{Q}(i: s(i): f(i))$ \qquad (range splitting)

$\quad = \mathbf{Q}(i: r(i) \text{ or } s(i): f(i))$ \qquad (range splitting and propositional calculus)

Example
2.25 Define *alltrue*(p, q, d)

$$\equiv \mathbf{A}(i, j: p \leqslant i < p + d \text{ and } q \leqslant j < q + d: b[i, j])$$

and suppose $d > 0$.

Then, since

$p \leqslant i < p + d$ and $q \leqslant j < q + d$
$\equiv (p + 1 \leqslant i < p + d$ and $q \leqslant j < q + d - 1)$
     or $(p \leqslant i < p + d - 1)$ and $q + 1 \leqslant j < q + d)$
     or $(p = i$ and $q = j)$
     or $(i = p + d - 1$ and $j = q + d - 1)$,

$alltrue(p, q, d)$
$\equiv \mathbf{A}(i, j: p + 1 \leqslant i < p + d$ and $q \leqslant j < q + d - 1: b[i, j])$
     and $\mathbf{A}(i, j: p \leqslant i < p + d - 1$ and $q + 1 \leqslant j < q + d: b[i, j])$
     and $\mathbf{A}(i, j: p = i$ and $q = j: b[i, j])$
     and $\mathbf{A}(i, j: i = p + d - 1$ and $j = q + d - 1: b[i, j])$
$\equiv alltrue(p + 1, q, d - 1)$
     and $alltrue(p, q + 1, d - 1)$
     and $b[p, q]$ and $b[p + d - 1, q + d - 1]$.

Exercise

2.30 Show that if $\mathbf{q}$ is associative, commutative, and idempotent then the relation $\leqslant_q$ defined by

$$a \leqslant_q b \equiv a \mathbf{\ q\ } b = a$$

is reflexive, transitive, and antisymmetric.

Show also that

$$\mathbf{Q}(i: r(i): f(i)) \leqslant_q \mathbf{Q}(i: r(i) \text{ and } s(i): f(i)).$$

(*Note*: $\leqslant_{MIN}$ is the conventional inequality '$\leqslant$'; $\leqslant_{MAX}$ is the conventional inequality '$\geqslant$'.)

(g)   (Generalized) Range Disjunction

If $\mathbf{q}$ is idempotent then

$$\mathbf{Q}(k: \mathbf{E}(j: r(j): p(j, k)): f(k))$$
$$= \mathbf{Q}(j: r(j): \mathbf{Q}(k: p(j, k): f(k))).$$

Note that, unlike generalized range splitting, there is no restriction on the predicates $p(j, k)$, on account of the idempotency of $\mathbf{q}$.

Examples

2.26 $\mathbf{MAX}(d: \mathbf{E}(p, q: 0 \leqslant p < m$ and $0 \leqslant q < n: true\_square(p, q, d)): d)$

$$= \textbf{MAX}(p, q: 0 \leqslant p < m \text{ and } 0 \leqslant q < n:$$
$$\textbf{MAX}(d: true\_square(p, q, d): d)).$$

2.27 It is a property of inequalities that

$$p \leqslant i < p + d \text{ and } q \leqslant j < q + d$$
$$\equiv \textbf{E}(d': 0 \leqslant d' \leqslant d: p \leqslant i < p + d' \text{ and } q \leqslant j < q + d').$$

Hence *alltrue*(p, q, d)

$$\equiv \textbf{A}(i, j: \textbf{E}(d': 0 \leqslant d' \leqslant d: p \leqslant i < p + d' \text{ and } q \leqslant j < q + d'): b[i, j])$$
$$\equiv \textbf{A}(d': 0 \leqslant d' \leqslant d: \textbf{A}(i, j: p \leqslant i < p + d' \text{ and } q \leqslant j < q + d'): b[i, j])$$
$$\equiv \textbf{A}(d': 0 \leqslant d' \leqslant d: alltrue(p, q, d')).$$

In other words, there is a **true** square of size d with bottom left corner (p, q) if and only if there is a **true** square of size d' with bottom left corner (p, q) for all d' such that $0 \leqslant d' \leqslant d$.

2.5.3 Function Part

(a) (Generalized) Associativity and Commutativity

(i) $\textbf{Q}(i: r(i): f(i) \textbf{ q } g(i)) = \textbf{Q}(i: r(i): f(i)) \textbf{ q } \textbf{Q}(i: r(i): g(i)).$
(ii) $\textbf{Q}(i: r(i): \textbf{Q}(j: s(j): f(i, j))) = \textbf{Q}(j: s(j): \textbf{Q}(i: r(i): f(i, j))).$

Examples
2.28 We use (i) to prove that $0 + 1 + 2 + \cdots + n - 1 = n*(n - 1)/2$ as follows:

$$2 * \textbf{S}(i: 0 \leqslant i < n: i)$$
$$= \textbf{S}(i: 0 \leqslant i < n: i) + \textbf{S}(i: 0 \leqslant i < n: n - i - 1)$$

                                     (range translation with $g: i \mapsto n - i - 1$)

$$= \textbf{S}(i: 0 \leqslant i < n: i + (n - i - 1)) \qquad\qquad\qquad\qquad \text{(by (i))}$$
$$= \textbf{S}(i: 0 \leqslant i < n: n - 1)$$
$$= n * (n - 1).$$

Thus $\textbf{S}(i: 0 \leqslant i < n: i) = n*(n - 1)/2.$
2.29 The sum of the elements in a two-dimensional array a is expressed as

$$\textbf{S}(i: 0 \leqslant i < m: \textbf{S}(j: 0 \leqslant j < n: a[i, j]))$$

or equally as

$$\textbf{S}(j: 0 \leqslant j < n: \textbf{S}(i: 0 \leqslant i < m: a[i, j]))$$

(b)   (Generalized) Distributivity

When an algebraic relationship exists between certain operators, such as the relation $a*(b+c) = a*b + a*c$ between multiplication and addition, that relation can be extended to the corresponding quantifiers. Two instances of distributivity relations are generalized in this section.

(i)   We say that the operator $\oplus$ *distributes* over **q** if

$$(a \; \mathbf{q} \; b) \oplus c = (a \oplus c) \; \mathbf{q} \; (b \oplus c)$$

and $1_q \oplus c = 1_q$

where 1_q denotes the identity of **q**.

Then if $\oplus$ distributes over **q** we have

$$\mathbf{Q}(i \colon r(i) \colon g \oplus f(i)) = g \oplus \mathbf{Q}(i \colon r(i) \colon f(i))$$

provided i is not free in g.

(The requirement that $1_q \oplus c = 1_q$ is unusual. Without it generalized distributivity would be invalid when the range is **false**.)

Examples

2.30 $\mathbf{S}(i \colon r(i) \colon 2*f(i)) = 2*\mathbf{S}(i \colon r(i) \colon f(i))$.

2.31 $\mathbf{A}(i \colon r(i) \colon p \text{ or } f(i)) \equiv p \text{ or } \mathbf{A}(i \colon r(i) \colon f(i))$.

2.32 $\mathbf{E}(i \colon r(i) \colon p \text{ and } f(i)) \equiv p \text{ and } \mathbf{E}(i \colon r(i) \colon f(i))$.

2.33 $\mathbf{MIN}(i \colon r(i) \colon c + f(i)) = c + \mathbf{MIN}(i \colon r(i) \colon f(i))$.

2.34   Suppose $ms(j) = \mathbf{MIN}(i \colon 0 \leqslant i < j \colon \mathbf{S}(k \colon i \leqslant k < j \colon a[k]))$.

Then $ms(j+1) = \mathbf{MIN}(i \colon 0 \leqslant i < j+1 \colon \mathbf{S}(k \colon i \leqslant k < j+1 \colon a[k]))$

$= \mathbf{MIN}(i \colon 0 \leqslant i < j+1 \colon \mathbf{S}(k \colon i \leqslant k < j \colon a[k]) + a[j])$

$= \mathbf{MIN}(i \colon 0 \leqslant i < j+1 \colon \mathbf{S}(k \colon i \leqslant k < j \colon a[k]) + a[j]$

(generalized distributivity)

$= min(\mathbf{MIN}(i \colon 0 \leqslant i < j \colon sum(i, j)), 0) + a[j]$

(range splitting and singleton range)

$= min(ms[j] + a[j], a[j])$.

(distributivity of $+$ over min)

Note: $\mathbf{MIN}(i \colon r(i) \colon c*f(i)) = c*\mathbf{MIN}(i \colon r(i) \colon f(i))$ is true only for positive values c.

Exercises

2.31   What is $\mathbf{MIN}(i \colon r(i) \colon c*f(i))$ when c is negative?

2.32 Use distributivity of **or** over **and** to show that

$$\mathbf{A}(i: r(i): \textbf{true}) \equiv \textbf{true}.$$

2.33 Suppose that $x \neq 1$ and $n \geqslant 0$. Show that

$$\mathbf{S}(i: 0 \leqslant i < n: x^i) = (1 - x^n)/(1 - x).$$

(ii) Suppose the function g and the operators $\mathbf{q}$ and $\oplus$ satisfy the relation

$$g(a \ \mathbf{q} \ b) = g(a) \oplus g(b)$$
$$g(1_\mathbf{q}) = 1_\oplus$$

for all a and b of the appropriate type where $1_\mathbf{q}$ and $1_\oplus$ denote, respectively, the identities of $\mathbf{q}$ and $\oplus$. Then

$$g(\mathbf{Q}(i: r(i): f(i)) = \bigoplus (i: r(i): g(f(i)))$$

where $\bigoplus$ is the quantifier corresponding to the operator $\oplus$.

Examples

2.35 De Morgan's laws state that $\textbf{not}(a \ \textbf{and} \ b) \equiv (\textbf{not} \ a) \ \textbf{or} \ (\textbf{not} \ b)$ and $\textbf{not}(a \ \textbf{or} \ b) \equiv (\textbf{not} \ a) \ \textbf{and} \ (\textbf{not} \ b)$.

Also $\textbf{not true} \equiv \textbf{false}$ and $\textbf{not false} \equiv \textbf{true}$. Thus we obtain

$$\textbf{not}(\mathbf{A}(i: r(i): f(i))) \equiv \mathbf{E}(i: r(i): \textbf{not} \ (f(i)))$$

and

$$\textbf{not}(\mathbf{E}(i: r(i): f(i))) \equiv \mathbf{A}(i: r(i): \textbf{not}(f(i))).$$

2.36 Minimum and maximum obey the property

$$min(-a, -b) = -max(a, b).$$

Thus

$$\mathbf{MIN}(i: r(i): -f(i)) = -\mathbf{MAX}(i: r(i): f(i)).$$

Exercises

2.34 Use De Morgan's law and exercise 2.32 to show that

$$\mathbf{E}(i: r(i): \textbf{false}) \equiv \textbf{false}.$$

2.35 Show that

$$\mathbf{E}(i: r(i): p(i)) \Rightarrow \mathbf{E}(j: s(j): q(j))$$
$$\equiv \mathbf{A}(i: r(i): p(i) \Rightarrow \mathbf{E}(j: s(j): q(j))).$$

2.5.4 Range and Function Interchange

When $\mathbf{Q}$ is an arithmetic quantifier the range and function part have different types: the range is always a predicate but the function part may have arbitrary type. Thus it is not possible in general to relate the two parts. However, for the logical quantifiers **A** and **E** the two parts do have the same type and it is possible to interchange predicates between the two. The rules governing such an interchange are as follows.

(*a*)   **A**-*rule*

$$\mathbf{A}(i\colon r(i) \text{ and } s(i)\colon p(i)) \equiv \mathbf{A}(i\colon r(i)\colon s(i) \Rightarrow p(i))$$

(*b*)   **E**-*rule*

$$\mathbf{E}(i\colon r(i) \text{ and } s(i)\colon p(i)) \equiv \mathbf{E}(i\colon r(i)\colon s(i) \text{ and } p(i))$$

Example
2.37 An alternative proof of exercise 2.32 is the following.

$\mathbf{A}(i\colon r(i)\colon \text{true}) \equiv \mathbf{A}(i\colon r(i)\colon \text{false} \Rightarrow \text{true})$	(propositional calculus)
$\equiv \mathbf{A}(i\colon r(i) \text{ and false}\colon \text{true})$	(**A**-rule)
$\equiv \mathbf{A}(i\colon \text{false}\colon \text{true})$	(propositional calculus)
$\equiv \text{true}$	(identity)

Exercises

2.36 Show that $\mathbf{A}(i\colon r(i)\colon \text{false}) \equiv \text{not } \mathbf{E}(i\colon \text{true}\colon r(i))$.

2.37 Show that $\mathbf{A}(i\colon p \leqslant i < q\colon r(i) \Rightarrow (s(i) \text{ or } i = p))$

$$\equiv \mathbf{A}(i\colon p < i < q\colon r(i) \Rightarrow s(i)).$$

2.38 Show that $\mathbf{E}(i\colon 0 \leqslant i\colon m = 2^i * q) \text{ and } \mathbf{E}(d\colon\colon p = q*d + r - m)$

$$\equiv \mathbf{E}(i\colon 0 \leqslant i\colon m = 2^i * q) \text{ and } \mathbf{E}(d\colon\colon p = q*d + r).$$

(*Hint*: use distributivity of **and** over **or**.)

3 VERIFICATION

The purpose of this chapter is to discuss program verification techniques for a very simple programming language consisting solely of assignments to simple variables, conditional statements, **while** statements, and the sequential composition of statements.

There are two basic approaches to program verification, one using inference rules originally developed by C. A. R. Hoare and the other using so-called 'predicate transformers' developed by E. W. Dijkstra. The two approaches are related, although different. We consider them in parallel. In section 3.1 our programming language is made explicit and the basic concepts and terminology of the two methods are discussed. Section 3.2 then considers proof techniques for programs without loops. At this stage the differences between Hoare's proof rules and Dijkstra's predicate transformers are not readily apparent. The construction of loops is intimately related to inductive proof, and section 3.3 on invariants and induction prepares the ground for the discussion of **while** statements in section 3.4. It is in the latter section that we first see the true relationship between the two proof techniques. The final section considers proof summaries. Such summaries provide all the information necessary for the reconstruction of a formal proof without confusing the reader with copious amounts of unnecessary detail. Proof summaries therefore offer a very effective way to document the function of a program.

3.1 NOTATION AND TERMINOLOGY

3.1.1 The Language

Our programming language consists only of simple assignments, conditional statements, **while** statements, and the sequential composition of statements. In

BNF its syntax is defined as follows.

$\langle$ *statement* $\rangle$ :: = **'begin'** $\langle$ *statement* $\rangle$ **'end'**|
$\langle$ *assignment statement* $\rangle$|
$\langle$ *conditional statement* $\rangle$|
$\langle$ **while** *statement* $\rangle$|
$\langle$ *statement* $\rangle$ ';' $\langle$ *statement* $\rangle$
$\langle$ *assignment statement* $\rangle$ :: = $\langle$ *simple variable* $\rangle$ ':=' $\langle$ *expression* $\rangle$
$\langle$ *conditional statement* $\rangle$ :: = **'if'** $\langle$ *expression* $\rangle$
'then' $\langle$ *statement* $\rangle$ **'else'** $\langle$ *statement* $\rangle$|
'if' $\langle$ *expression* $\rangle$ **'then'** $\langle$ *statement* $\rangle$
$\langle$ **while** *statement* $\rangle$ :: = **'while'** $\langle$ *expression* $\rangle$ **'do'** $\langle$ *statement* $\rangle$

Note that only simple variables like x and y are allowed on the left side of assignments. This is a severe restriction, which in theory limits us to the verification of programs which merely search rather than update arrays. In practice, the next chapter does indeed discuss the design of several programs that alter array values using the *principles* expounded in this chapter.

The purpose of exhibiting this syntax is so that the structure of any

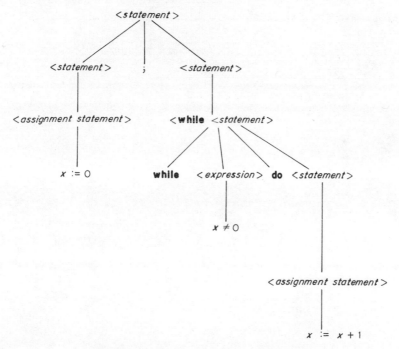

Fig. 3.1 Structure of a simple statement.

statement in the language may be identified. An example is the statement

$$x := 0;$$
$$\textbf{while } x \neq 0 \textbf{ do}$$
$$x := x + 1$$

which has the structure shown in Fig. 3.1.

Unfortunately, there is considerable ambiguity in the structure assigned to statements by this definition. One source of ambiguity, which turns out to be of no consequence, is in sequences of statements as illustrated by Fig. 3.2. Basically the problem here is whether to group the composition of three statements S_1, S_2, and S_3 in the form $(S_1; S_2); S_3$ or in the form $S_1;(S_2; S_3)$. A more serious source of ambiguity would arise were we to write statements like

$$x := 0; \textbf{ while } x \neq 0 \textbf{ do } x := x + 1; x := x - 1$$

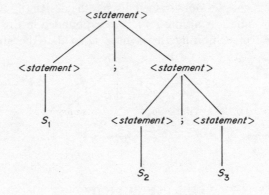

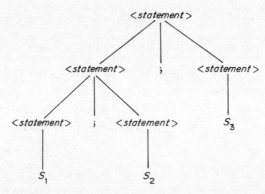

Fig. 3.2 Two possible structures for $S_1; S_2; S_3$.

which could be interpreted as

$$x := 0;$$
$$\textbf{while } x \neq 0 \textbf{ do } x := x + 1;$$
$$x := x - 1$$

or as

$$x := 0;$$
$$\textbf{while } x \neq 0 \textbf{ do}$$
$$\quad \textbf{begin } x := x + 1; x := x - 1$$
$$\quad \textbf{end}$$

Figure 3.3 illustrates the two structures given to this statement. In this case, of course, the chosen structure is of vital importance.

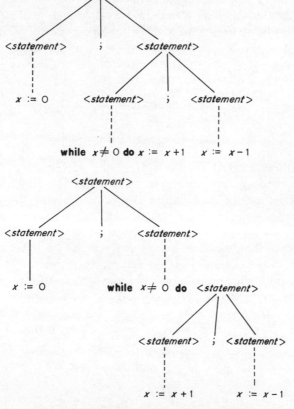

Fig. 3.3 Ambiguity of statement structure.

To avoid the problems that this causes we use **begin–end** pairs as in Pascal to group statements wherever necessary. Thus, the use of **begin–end** has no semantic content (we do not give any proof rules for **begin** ⟨ *statement* ⟩ **end**); it serves only to disambiguate the statement structure.

3.1.2   The Notation {P} S {Q}

Consider the following sequential composition of three statements:

$$t := x;\ x := y;\ y := t.$$

Its purpose is to interchange the values of x and y, the variable t being a scratch variable. We can see this by the following chain of reasoning. After the first assignment both x and t have the original value of x, and y has its original value. After the second assignment t has the original value of x, and x and y have the original value of y. Finally after the third assignment x has the original value of y and y the original value of x.

To document this argument effectively we need to adopt some notational conventions. Firstly, we need some mechanism for expressing predicates like 't has the original value of x' and, secondly, we need a notation for saying that 'if the program segment is executed then, afterwards, x will have the original value of y'. The notation we use is the following:

$$\{x = x_0 \text{ and } y = y_0\}$$
$$t := x;\ x := y;\ y := t \qquad\qquad (3.1)$$
$$\{x = y_0 \text{ and } y = x_0\}.$$

In (3.1) x_0 and y_0 are called *ghost variables*; they are variables which do not appear in the program, but simply serve to relate the final values of the program variables to their initial values. The form of (3.1) is $\{P\}\ S\ \{Q\}$ where P is the predicate $x = x_0$ **and** $y = y_0$, S is the statement $t := x;\ x := y;\ y := t$, and Q is the predicate $x = y_0$ **and** $y = x_0$. Generally, when we write $\{P\}\ S\ \{Q\}$ we are making a claim to the effect that, if the initial state of the program variables satisfies P, and S is executed, then the final state of the program variables satisfies Q. We call P the *precondition* and Q the *postcondition* for execution of S. Thus (3.1) means that if initially $x = x_0$ and $y = y_0$ and $t := x;\ x := y;\ y := t$ is executed then finally $x = y_0$ and $y = x_0$.

Using the same notation we can expand (3.1), giving details of its justification:

$$\{x = x_0 \text{ and } y = y_0\}$$
$$t := x;$$
$$\{t = x = x_0 \text{ and } y = y_0\}$$
$$x := y; \qquad\qquad (3.2)$$

$$\{t = x_0 \text{ and } x = y = y_0\}$$
$$y := t$$
$$\{x = y_0 \text{ and } y = x_0\}$$

(3.2) is called a *tableau* and is a shorthand for the three steps in our justification of (3.1):

1. $\{x = x_0 \text{ and } y = y_0\}$ If $x = x_0$ and $y = y_0$ when
   $t := x$ $t := x$ is executed then afterwards
   $\{t = x = x_0 \text{ and } y = y_0\}$ $t = x = x_0$ and $y = y_0$.
2. $\{t = x = x_0 \text{ and } y = y_0\}$ If $t = x = x_0$ and $y = y_0$ when
   $x := y$ $x := y$ is executed then afterwards
   $\{t = x_0 \text{ and } x = y = y_0\}$ $t = x_0$ and $x = y = y_0$.
3. $\{t = x_0 \text{ and } x = y = y_0\}$ If $t = x_0$ and $x = y = y_0$ when
   $y := t$ $y := t$ is executed then afterwards
   $\{x = y_0 \text{ and } y = x_0\}$ $x = y_0$ and $y = x_0$.

The notation $\{P\} S \{Q\}$ is so important that it is worth repeating its meaning and making it stand out.

$\{P\} S \{Q\}$ means if, initially, the state of the program variables satisfies the predicate P and the statement S is executed, then, on termination of S, the final state of the program variables will satisfy the predicate Q.

The notation $\{P\} S \{Q\}$ expresses the *conditional correctness* of S—its correctness with respect to pre- and postconditions P and Q *assuming* that the precondition P guarantees termination of S. We have more to say about this in the next few subsections but more particularly in section 3.4 when we consider **while** statements.

3.1.3   Weakest Preconditions

Consider the problem of finding the maximum of two integers x and y. More specifically we are to construct a program segment that will assign to the variable z one of the values x and y such that $z \geqslant x$ and $z \geqslant y$. One way of tackling this problem is to consider the requirement $z \geqslant x$ and $z \geqslant y$ in conjunction with, firstly, the assignment $z := x$ and, secondly, the assignment $z := y$. Suppose we were to execute $z := x$. What condition would need to be satisfied in order to guarantee that $z \geqslant x$ and $z \geqslant y$? The answer is: $x \geqslant y$. Similarly if we were to execute $z := y$ we must have $y \geqslant x$ in order to guarantee that $z \geqslant x$ and $z \geqslant y$. Obviously, if $x \geqslant y$ is not satisfied then $y \geqslant x$. (In fact $y > x$.) So we conclude that the statement

$$\textbf{if } x \geqslant y \textbf{ then } z := x \textbf{ else } z := y$$

will always satisfy our requirement.

The above reasoning is typical of a line of reasoning that is fundamental to *program synthesis*. First we formulate a predicate, Q, describing the final state we require of the program variables. (In the above, Q is $z \geqslant x$ **and** $z \geqslant y$.) Then we postulate a statment S (e.g. $z := x$) and ask what condition, P, must be satisfied in order that $\{P\}\ S\ \{Q\}$. Thus program synthesis works backwards from the required *postcondition* Q to the *precondition P*.

Usually there are many candidates for the precondition P. For example, the precondition $x < y$ will guarantee the postcondition $z \geqslant x$ **and** $z \geqslant y$ after executing $z := y$. However, given postcondition Q and statement S, we seek the *weakest* precondition P satisfying $\{P\}\ S\ \{Q\}$. The condition $x < y$, for example, is *stronger* than the condition $x \leqslant y$ in the sense that fewer states will satisfy it.

Definition If Q is a predicate and S a statement then *the weakest precondition of S with respect to Q*, denoted $wp(S, Q)$, is a predicate describing the set of all initial states such that execution of S begun in any one of the states is guaranteed to terminate in a state satisfying Q.

Examples

3.1 $wp(z := x, z \geqslant x$ **and** $z \geqslant y) \equiv x \geqslant y$.

3.2 Let S be the assignment $t := x$ and let Q be the condition $t = x_0$, then

$$wp(t := x, t = x_0) \equiv x = x_0$$

for after execution of $t := x$ the values of t and x will be equal.

3.3 Let S be the assignment $i := i + 1$ and let Q be the condition $i \leqslant n$, then

$$wp(i := i + 1, i \leqslant n) \equiv i < n$$

for if we increase i by 1 and its value remains less than or equal to n then it must have been less than n beforehand.

Two properties describe succinctly the meaning of $wp(S, Q)$. The first is that $wp(S, Q)$ is a precondition guaranteeing Q after execution of S, i.e.

$$\{wp(S, Q)\}\ S\ \{Q\}. \tag{3.3}$$

The second is that $wp(S, Q)$ is the weakest such condition, i.e.

if P guarantees termination of S and $\{P\}\ S\ \{Q\}$ then $P \Rightarrow wp(S, Q)$ (3.4)

Let us use these two facts to sort out two slightly confusing cases.

Examples

3.4 Let S be the assignment $i := 0$ and Q be $i = 0$. Clearly, Q will always be true after the assignment whatever the value of i beforehand. So what is $wp(S, Q)$? Well, since $P \Rightarrow$ **true** for all predicates P, it is certainly the case that $wp(S, Q) \Rightarrow$ **true**. But **true** also satisfies the two premises of (3.4), and so **true** $\Rightarrow wp(S, Q)$. We conclude that

$$wp(i: = 0, i = 0) \equiv \textbf{true}.$$

In other words, **true** is a predicate describing all states.

3.5 Let S be the assignment $i: = 0$ and Q be $i = 1$. This is the converse situation to that in example 3.4. No matter what the value of i beforehand the assignment $i: = 0$ will not guarantee that $i = 1$. Thus, by analogy with example 3.4,

$$wp(i: = 0, i = 1) \equiv \textbf{false}.$$

In other words, **false** describes no states.

Exercise

3.1 Determine $wp(S, Q)$ for the following S and Q based on your knowledge of how S is executed.

S	Q
(a) $\quad i: = i + 1$	$i > 0$
(b) $\quad i: = i + 1; j: = j - 1$	$i + j = 0$
(c) $\quad i: = i + 1; \ j: = j - 1$	$i * j = 0$
(d) $\quad i: = i - 1; \ z: = z * j$	$z * j^i = c$
(e) $\quad a[a[i]]: = i$	$a[i] = i$

3.1.4 Logical Properties

In later sections we present inference rules that enable us to make specific inferences of the form $\{P\} \ S \ \{Q\}$. We also present rules for calculating specific instances of $wp(S, Q)$. These rules describe the properties of the statement types in our language but they do not embody any properties of the data that we use. All programs will, however, exploit many algebraic and logical properties even if those properties may be very simple like $1 - 1 = 0$ or $0 \neq j \Rightarrow j/j = 1$. In order to introduce such properties into proofs about programs, a mechanism for relating proofs about the program structure and proofs about the data is essential.

There is another compelling reason for wishing to investigate the logical properties of $\{P\} \ S \ \{Q\}$ and $wp(S, Q)$ at the outset. Since programming languages are man-made objects, the laws that they obey (or do not obey) are entirely our responsibility. It is well, therefore, that we endeavor to anticipate desirable properties and then verify their validity rather than trust to luck!

Consequence Rules

In Hoare's proof system logical and algebraic properties of the data are related to properties arising from the program structure by use of the so-called *consequence rules*. The consequence rules can be readily understood from the intended meaning of $\{P\}\ S\ \{Q\}$. Assume that $\{P\}\ S\ \{Q\}$ is valid and consider first a postcondition Q' that is *weaker* than postcondition Q. Thus Q' describes more states than Q. Then if P guarantees that, upon termination of S, the state s satisfies Q, it clearly guarantees that, upon termination of S, the state s satisfies Q'.

Now consider a precondition P' that is *stronger* than precondition P. Thus P' describes fewer states than P, and any state that satisfies P' also satisfies P. Thus any state s that satisfies P' will guarantee the postcondition Q by virtue of the fact that s also satisfies P. These two observations are formalized as inference rules as follows.

$$\frac{\begin{array}{c} P \Rightarrow Q \\ \{Q\}\ S\ \{R\} \end{array}}{\{P\}\ S\ \{R\}} \qquad \frac{\begin{array}{c} Q \Rightarrow R \\ \{P\}\ S\ \{Q\} \end{array}}{\{P\}\ S\ \{R\}}$$

Dijkstra's Healthiness Conditions

The sort of properties of wp of interest concern the way in which it behaves in combination with the logical constants **true** and **false**, and the logical operators **and**, **or**, etc. For instance, which of the following are true and which are false?

$$wp(S, Q \text{ and } R) \equiv wp(S, Q) \text{ and } wp(S, R)$$
$$wp(S, Q \text{ or } R) \equiv wp(S, Q) \text{ or } wp(S, R)$$
$$wp(S, \text{not } Q) \equiv \text{not } wp(S, Q)$$

In addition, is it possible to make a general statement about $wp(S, \textbf{true})$ and/or $wp(S, \textbf{false})$? Let us consider each in turn, beginning with the constants.

(a) To understand the meaning of $wp(S, \textbf{false})$ it is vital to recall that the postcondition **false** describes *no* states. Thus the precondition $wp(S, \textbf{false})$ is one that guarantees that execution of S results in an impossible state. Thus we obtain *the law of the excluded miracle*:

$$wp(S, \textbf{false}) \equiv \textbf{false}. \tag{3.5}$$

Dijkstra has called this the law of the excluded miracle because it would be a miracle if there were some statement S and some state s such that execution of S begun in state s were to terminate, but in no state.

(b) Recalling that **true** describes all states one might be excused for supposing that $wp(S, \textbf{true}) \equiv \textbf{true}$, since beginning in an arbitrary state will guarantee termination of S in an arbitrary state. But this is not true! The important words here are 'guarantee termination of'. We all know the phenomenon of a program that is 'stuck in a loop'. The correct interpretation of $wp(S, \textbf{true})$ is therefore the predicate describing all states that guarantee termination of S.

Example

3.6 $wp(\textbf{while } 0 \neq n \textbf{ do } n := n - 1, \textbf{true}) \equiv 0 \leqslant n$

The process of repeatedly decrementing n by 1 will terminate with $0 = n$ if and only if, initially, $0 \leqslant n$.

(c) Consider $wp(S, Q \textbf{ and } R)$. This describes the set of all states that guarantee termination of S in a state satisfying both Q and R. Any such state, s, therefore guarantees that S terminates in a state satisfying Q, i.e.

$$wp(S, Q \textbf{ and } R) \Rightarrow wp(S, Q). \tag{3.6}$$

Additionally, any such state, s, guarantees that S terminates in a state satisfying R, i.e.

$$wp(S, Q \textbf{ and } R) \Rightarrow wp(S, R). \tag{3.7}$$

Thus (by the propositional calculus) we obtain

$$wp(S, Q \textbf{ and } R) \Rightarrow wp(S, Q) \textbf{ and } wp(S, R). \tag{3.8}$$

Considering the converse case in which the state, s, satisfies $wp(S, Q)$ **and** $wp(S, R)$, it is clear that s guarantees termination of S in a state satisfying both Q and R. Thus

$$wp(S, Q) \textbf{ and } wp(S, R) \Rightarrow wp(S, Q \textbf{ and } R). \tag{3.9}$$

Hence we obtain **and**-*distributivity*:

$$wp(S, Q) \textbf{ and } wp(S, R) \equiv wp(S, Q \textbf{ and } R). \tag{3.10}$$

(d) It is a consequence of (3.10) that if $Q \Rightarrow R$ then $wp(S, Q) \Rightarrow wp(S, R)$. For if $Q \Rightarrow R$ it is also true that $Q \textbf{ and } R \equiv Q$. So $wp(S, Q \textbf{ and } R) \equiv wp(S, Q)$.

Therefore, by (3.10), $wp(S, Q) \textbf{ and } wp(S, R) \equiv wp(S, Q)$, i.e. $wp(S, Q) \Rightarrow wp(S, R)$.

(e) The relationship between $wp(S, Q \textbf{ or } R)$ and $wp(S, Q) \textbf{ or } wp(S, R)$ is a little more complex. We can argue that

$$wp(S, Q) \textbf{ or } wp(S, R) \Rightarrow wp(S, Q \textbf{ or } R) \tag{3.11}$$

since a state, s, that satisfies $wp(S, Q)$ **or** $wp(S, R)$ will either guarantee termination of S in a state satisfying Q, and hence Q **or** R, or in a state satisfying R, and hence also Q **or** R. Thus in either case s guarantees termination of S in a state satisfying Q or R. However, the converse case

$$wp(S, Q \text{ or } R) \Rightarrow wp(S, Q) \text{ or } wp(S, R) \qquad (3.12)$$

requires the assumption that if state s guarantees termination of statement S then it does so in a unique state s'. (This means that we consider only *deterministic* programs. *Nondeterministic programs*, ones whose outcome may vary from one execution to the next, even with the same initial state, will not be considered in this text.) With this assumption, let us suppose that state s satisfies $wp(S, Q \text{ or } R)$ and s' is the state after execution of S. Then s' satisfies Q or s' satisfies R. In the former case, s satisfies $wp(S, Q)$, and in the latter case, s satisfies $wp(S, R)$. We conclude that (3.12) is valid and hence **or**-*distributivity* *(for deterministic programs)*:

$$wp(S, Q \text{ or } R) \equiv wp(S, Q) \text{ or } wp(S, R). \qquad (3.13)$$

Exercises

3.2 Which (if any) of the following do you expect to be valid?

  (a) $wp(S, \textbf{not } Q) \Rightarrow \textbf{not } wp(S, Q)$
  (b) $\textbf{not } wp(S, Q) \Rightarrow wp(S, \textbf{not } Q)$
  (c) $wp(S, Q \Rightarrow R) \Rightarrow [wp(S, Q) \Rightarrow wp(S, R)]$
  (d) $[wp(S, Q \Rightarrow R) \Rightarrow wp(S, Q)] \Rightarrow wp(S, R)$

For those that are, you should be able to derive their validity from the properties already stated.

3.3 Suppose that $\{P\}\ S\ \{\textbf{false}\}$ is valid. What can you say about P and /or S? Similarly, what can you say about P and/or S in the case that $\{P\}\ S\ \{\textbf{true}\}$ is valid?

3.2 NONLOOPING PROGRAMS

3.2.1 The Assignment Axiom

Let us now look in more detail at assignment statements. Consider an assignment $x := e$ and a postcondition Q. To emphasize the fact that Q is a (Boolean-valued) function of x (and possibly other program variables) let us write it as $Q(x)$. Now, suppose we want to guarantee $Q(x)$ immediately after executing $x := e$. What can one say about the program state beforehand? Well, afterwards x will have the value that e had before executing the assignment. So, the weakest precondition guaranteeing $Q(x)$ after executing $x := e$ is $Q(e)$, i.e. the condition obtained by substituting e for x in the predicate Q. Thus

$$wp(x := e, Q(x)) \equiv Q(e).$$

Examples

3.7 $wp(i: = i - 1, i = 0) \equiv i - 1 = 0.$
If $i = 0$ after subtracting 1 from i then beforehand $i - 1$ must be zero
(i.e. $i = 1$).

3.8 $wp(i: = (l + u)$ **div** $2, l \leqslant i \leqslant u) \equiv l \leqslant (l + u)$ **div** $2 \leqslant u.$
If i lies between l and u after being assigned the value $(l + u)$ **div** 2 then
$(l + u)$ **div** 2 must lie between l and u.

3.9 $wp(i: = 1, i = 0) \equiv 1 = 0.$
If $i = 0$ after executing $i: = 1$ then 1 must equal 0. Note that $1 = 0$ is **false**
which describes no states as discussed in the last section.

3.10 $wp(i: = 1, i = 1) \equiv 1 = 1.$
If i equals 1 after executing $i: = 1$ then 1 must equal 1. Note that $1 = 1$ is
true which describes all states as discussed in the last section.

3.11 $wp(x: = y, z = y) \equiv z = y.$
The assignment $x: = y$ has no effect on the predicate $z = y$ so for $z = y$ to
hold after the assignment it must hold beforehand.

Now that we know how to construct the weakest precondition of any
assignment statement we also have our first rule of inference for proofs which
specifically concern programs. The rule is called the *assignment axiom*:

$$\{Q(e)\} \ x: = e \ \{Q(x)\}$$

where $Q(e)$ denotes the predicate obtained by substituting e for all free
occurrences of x in the predicate Q.

Unlike earlier rules of inference the assignment axiom has no premises. It is
invoked directly without first having to establish any auxiliary results. This is
the reason for calling it an 'axiom'.

Examples

3.12 $\{x = x\} \ y: = x \ \{x = y\}$ $wp(\ y:=x,\ x=y) \ = \ (x=x)$
3.13 $\{0 \leqslant s + t - 1\} \ s: = s + t - 1 \ \{0 \leqslant s\}$
3.14 $\{i = 10\} \ j: = 25 \ \{i = 10\}$

Two provisos ought to be included in the assignment axiom. The first is
that the precondition should guarantee that the expression e is well defined. For
example, i/j is not well defined if $j = 0$; nor is $a[i]$ if the index i is outside the
declared bounds of the array a. Secondly, the types of x and e should agree—it
is not permissible to assign an integer to a Boolean variable, for example. Such
provisos are very important but their formalization would entail much greater
detail in the description of our programming language than we care to go into.
Instead we provide informal arguments regarding such problems when the
need arises.

3.2.2 Rule of Sequential Composition

The proof we outlined in section 3.1.2 of the correctness of interchanging x and y using the three assignments $t := x$; $x := y$; $y := t$ made implicit use of the assignment axiom. It also made use of the properties of sequential composition which we now make explicit.

Weakest Precondition

Consider the circumstances in which a state s will guarantee termination of the sequence of statements S_1; S_2 in a state satisfying Q. Noting that the weakest precondition guaranteeing termination of S_2 in a state satisfying Q is $wp(S_2, Q)$, it is a requirement on s that it cause termination of S_1 in a state satisfying that condition. In other words $wp(S_2, Q)$ is the requisite *post*condition for statement S_1. Thus s must satisfy $wp(S_1, wp(S_2, Q))$ and we have

$$wp(S_1; S_2, Q) \equiv wp(S_1, wp(S_2, Q)).$$

Examples

3.15 $wp((x := x + 1; y := y + 1), x = y)$

$\equiv wp(x := x + 1, wp(y := y + 1, x = y))$

$\equiv wp(x := x + 1, x = y + 1)$

$\equiv x + 1 = y + 1$

$\equiv x = y$

3.16 $wp((x := 2*x + 1; y := y - 1), y = 3*x)$

$\equiv wp(x := 2*x + 1, wp(y := y - 1, y = 3*x))$

$\equiv wp(x := 2*x + 1, y - 1 = 3*x)$

$\equiv y - 1 = 3*(2*x + 1)$

$\equiv y = 6*x + 4$

It is important to note that this rule implies that sequential composition is associative, that is $(S_1; S_2); S_3$ has the same meaning as $S_1;(S_2; S_3)$. For, if Q is an arbitrary predicate,

$wp((S_1; S_2); S_3, Q)$

$\equiv wp(S_1; S_2, wp(S_3, Q))$

$\equiv wp(S_1, wp(S_2, wp(S_3, Q)))$

$\equiv wp(S_1, wp(S_2; S_3, Q))$

$\equiv wp(S_1;(S_2; S_3), Q)$

Hoare's Rule

The corresponding rule in Hoare's system is called the *rule of sequential composition:*

$$\{P\} \ S_1 \ \{R\}$$
$$\{R\} \ S_2 \ \{Q\}$$

$$\overline{\{P\}S_1;S_2\{Q\}}$$

Omitting provisos on the termination of S_1 and S_2, this rule can be paraphrased as follows:

Suppose   (i) executing S_1 with precondition P guarantees the postcondition R

and   (ii) executing S_2 with precondition R guarantees the postcondition Q

then   (iii) executing S_1; S_2 with precondition P guarantees the postcondition Q.

Let us now provide a formal proof of the correctness of our interchange routine.

Example
3.17 $\{x = x_0 \text{ and } y = y_0\}$
     $t := x;$
     $x := y;$
     $y := t$
     $\{x = y_0 \text{ and } y = x_0\}$

Proof   1. $\{t = x_0 \text{ and } x = y_0\} \ y := t \ \{y = x_0 \text{ and } x = y_0\}$
                                                  (assignment axiom)

         2. $\{t = x_0 \text{ and } y = y_0\} \ x := y \ \{t = x_0 \text{ and } x = y_0\}$
                                                  (assignment axiom)

         3. $\{t = x_0 \text{ and } y = y_0\}$
            $x := y; \ y := t$
            $\{y = x_0 \text{ and } x = y_0\}$ (1 and 2, rule of sequential composition)

         4. $\{x = x_0 \text{ and } y = y_0\} \ t := x \ \{t = x_0 \text{ and } y = y_0\}$
                                                  (assignment axiom)

         5. $\{x = x_0 \text{ and } y = y_0\}$
            $t := x; \ x := y; \ y := t$
            $\{y = x_0 \text{ and } x = y_0\}$ (3 and 4, rule of sequential composition)

It is much more straightforward to apply these proof rules than the rules of inference in chapter 1 because there is a definite order in which to proceed. You should always work backwards from the last assignment to the first applying the assignment axiom as you come to each assignment. The use of the rule of sequential composition allows the last assignment to be combined with the second last, then the last two assignments to be combined with the third last, and so on. In this way one eventually obtains a proposition of the form $\{P\}\ S_1;\ S_2;\ldots;\ S_r\ \{Q\}$ as required.

The next two examples illustrate the use of the consequence rules given in section 3.1.4.

Example
3.18 The objective is to prove

$$\{\mathbf{E}(m::\ k = 2*m)\ \textbf{and}\ y*z^k = c\}\ k := k\ \textbf{div}\ 2;\ z := z*z\ \{y*z^k = c\}.$$

We begin by applying the assignment axiom twice followed by the rule of sequential composition as in example 3.17.

1. $\{y*(z*z)^k = c\}\ z := z*z\ \{y*z^k = c\}$ (assignment axiom)
2. $\{y*(z*z)^{k\,\textbf{div}\,2} = c\}\ k := k\ \textbf{div}\ 2\ \{y*(z*z)^k = c\}$ (assignment axiom)
3. $\{y*(z*z)^{k\,\textbf{div}\,2} = c\}\ k := k\ \textbf{div}\ 2;\ z := z*z\ \{y*z^k = c\}$
                      (1 and 2, rule of sequential composition)

Since the precondition in step 3 is not equivalent to the supplied precondition it is necessary to show that the latter implies the former so that the appropriate consequence rule may be used. This we do using the properties established in chapter 2.

4. $\mathbf{E}(m:: k = 2*m)\ \textbf{and}\ y*z^k = c$
   $\equiv \mathbf{E}(m:: k = 2*m\ \textbf{and}\ y*z^k = c)$ (distributivity)
   $\equiv \mathbf{E}(m:: k = 2*m\ \textbf{and}\ y*z^{(2*m)} = c)$ (substitutivity)
   $\equiv \mathbf{E}(m:: k = 2*m\ \textbf{and}\ y*(z*z)^m = c)$ (property of exponentiation)
   $\equiv \mathbf{E}(m:: k = 2*m\ \textbf{and}\ y*(z*z)^{k\,\textbf{div}\,2} = c)$ (property of **div**)
   $\equiv \mathbf{E}(m:: k = 2*m)\ \textbf{and}\ y*(z*z)^{k\,\textbf{div}\,2} = c$ (distributivity)
   $\Rightarrow y*(z*z)^{k\,\textbf{div}\,2} = c$ (propositional calculus)

Finally we apply the consequence rule.

5. $\{\mathbf{E}(m:: k = 2*m)\ \textbf{and}\ y*z^k = c\}$
   $k := k\ \textbf{div}\ 2;\ z := z*z$
   $\{y*z^k = c\}$ (3 and 4, consequence rule)

The examples and exercises in this chapter have been chosen so that the arithmetic and logical properties they presume are rather trivial, like the property proven in step 4 of example 3.18. This is atypical. As you gain familiarity with them you will begin to realize that the proof rules in this section and the next are all very straightforward, and it is the use of the consequence rules that is the most significant part of any proof. However, it means that we are often able simply to state that one predicate implies another and confidently leave you to fill in the details. Here is an example.

Example

3.19 The objective is to prove

$$\{s = i*(i + 1)/2\}$$
$$i := i + 1;$$
$$s := s + i$$
$$\{s = i*(i + 1)/2\}$$

and the proof, this time using weakest preconditions, is as follows.

1. $wp(s := s + i, s = i*(i + 1)/2) \equiv s + i = i*(i + 1)/2$

   (assignment axiom)

2. $wp(i := i + 1, s + i = i*(i + 1)/2)$
   $\equiv s + i + 1 = (i + 1)*(i + 1 + 1)/2$

   (assignment axiom)

3. $wp((i := i + 1; s := s + i), s = i*(i + 1)/2)$
   $\equiv s + i + 1 = (i + 1)*(i + 1 + 1)/2$

   (1 and 2, sequential composition)

4. $s = i*(i + 1)/2 \equiv s + i + 1 = (i + 1)*(i + 1 + 1)/2$

   (simple algebra)

5. $\{s = i*(i + 1)/2\} i := i + 1; s := s + i \{s = i*(i + 1)/2\}$

   (3 and 4, definition of wp)

Exercises

Use Hoare's rules to give formal proofs of the following:

3.4 $\{i = j^k\}$

$$k := k + 1;$$
$$i := i*j$$
$$\{i = j^k\}$$

3.5 $\{s = i*(i + 1)*(2*i + 1)/6 \text{ and } j = i^2\}$

$$i := i + 1;$$
$$j := j + 2*i - 1;$$

$s + i + 1 = (i + 1) * (i + 1 + 1)/2$

$2s + 2i + 2 = i^2 + 3i + 2$

$2s = i^2 + i$

$s = i * (1 + i)/2$

$$s := s + j$$
$$\{s = i*(i + 1)*(2*i + 1)/6 \text{ and } j = i^2\}$$

3.6 $\{j = i^n \text{ and } k = (i^{n+1} - 1)/(i - 1)\}$

$$j := j*i;$$
$$k := k + j;$$
$$n := n + 1$$
$$\{j = i^n \text{ and } k = (i^{n+1} - 1)/(i - 1)\}$$

Use the *wp* rules to give formal proofs of the following.

3.7 $\{s = n^3 \text{ and } i = 2*n \text{ and } k = n*(n + 1) + 1\}$

$$i := i + 2;$$
$$s := s + n*i + k;$$
$$k := k + i;$$
$$n := n + 1$$
$$\{s = n^3 \text{ and } i = 2*n \text{ and } k = n*(n + 1) + 1\}$$

3.8 $\{c^2 - c - 1 = 0 \text{ and } c^n = a*c + b\}$

$$n := n + 1;$$
$$t := a + b;$$
$$b := a;$$
$$a := t$$
$$\{c^n = a*c + b\}$$

3.9 $\{0 \leqslant s < n\}$

$$q := s \text{ div } (n - 1);$$
$$p := q + 1;$$
$$t := s + 1 - q*(n - 1)$$
$$\{1 \leqslant t \leqslant n \text{ and } q \geqslant 0 \text{ and } p = q + 1 \text{ and } s = p*(t - 1) + q*(n - t)\}$$

3.2.3 Conditional Statements

In this section we introduce the proof rules for conditional statements. As always, we begin by formulating a weakest precondition rule and use it to derive the corresponding inference rule.

Weakest Preconditions

As a first example consider the statement

if $i = 1$ **then** $j := i$ **else** $j := i + 1$.

Suppose we require this statement to guarantee the postcondition $j = 1$. What precondition must be satisfied?

The answer is fairly easy to see. If $i = 1$ the postcondition will be satisfied, but if $i \neq 1$ we require that $i = 0$ for it to be satisfied. Thus we write

$wp(\text{if } i = 1 \text{ then } j := i \text{ else } j := i + 1, j = 1)$

$\equiv (i = 1) \text{ or } [(i \neq 1) \Rightarrow (i = 0)]$

$\equiv (i = 1) \text{ or } (i = 0)$.

Let us look at some more examples, using our intuition to identify the weakest preconditions.

Examples

3.20 $wp(\text{if } i = j \text{ then } m := k \text{ else } j := k, k = j = m)$

$\equiv [(i = j) \Rightarrow (k = j)] \text{ and } [(i \neq j) \Rightarrow k = m].$

The postcondition here is that all three of k, j, and m are equal. Now if $m := k$ is executed we certainly know that m will equal k afterwards, but we cannot guarantee that k equals j unless, of course, it is a precondition of the assignment. Thus the first part of the precondition is if $i = j$ (i.e. $m := k$ is executed) then $k = j$. Similarly, if $j := k$ is executed we will certainly know that $j = k$ afterwards but we can only guarantee that $k = m$ if we know that it is also a precondition. Thus the second part of the precondition is if $i \neq j$ (i.e. $j := k$ is executed) then $k = m$.

3.21 $wp(\text{if } i > 1 \text{ then begin } i := i + 1; j := j + i \text{ end}, j \leqslant i + 1)$

$\equiv [(i > 1) \Rightarrow j \leqslant 1] \text{ and } [(i \leqslant 1) \Rightarrow j \leqslant i + 1].$

In this example it is easier to consider the case $i \leqslant 1$ first. Suppose $i \leqslant 1$. Then the statement makes no change whatsoever to j or i. Thus if $i \leqslant 1$ we must already have that $j \leqslant i + 1$. This is the second part of the weakest precondition. Now suppose $i > 1$. In this case the two assignments $i := i + 1$ and $j := j + i$ are executed. From our earlier discussion we know that $wp(i := i + 1; j := j + i, j \leqslant i + 1) \equiv j \leqslant 1$. Thus the condition for executing these assignments, $i > 1$, must guarantee this weakest precondition. In other words we require that $i > 1 \Rightarrow j \leqslant 1$. This is the first part of the weakest precondition of the **if** statement.

Let us now look at the problem in more abstract terms. Suppose Q is a postcondition of the statement **if** B **then** S_1 **else** S_2 where B is a Boolean expression and S_1 and S_2 are statements. What is the weakest precondition that will guarantee Q after execution of such a statement?

Well, we can identify two distinct requirements corresponding to the possibilities of (i) executing S_1 and (ii) executing S_2. Suppose firstly that S_1 is executed. Then its execution must guarantee Q. But for S_1 to guarantee Q the state of the program variables beforehand must be described by $wp(S_1, Q)$, the weakest precondition that will guarantee Q after execution of S_1. Thus if S_1 is executed $wp(S_1,\cdot Q)$ must be satisfied beforehand. In other words our requirement is

$$B \Rightarrow wp(S_1, Q). \tag{3.14}$$

Now suppose that S_2 is executed. Again, its execution must guarantee Q and so, beforehand, the state of the program variables must satisfy $wp(S_2, Q)$. Thus our requirement is

$$\textbf{not } B \Rightarrow wp(S_2, Q). \tag{3.15}$$

The conjunction of (3.14) and (3.15) is the condition we are after:

$wp(\textbf{if } B \textbf{ then } S_1 \textbf{ else } S_2, Q)$
$$\equiv (B \Rightarrow wp(S_1, Q)) \textbf{ and } (\textbf{not } B \Rightarrow wp(S_2, Q)). \tag{3.16}$$

Examples
3.22 Suppose B is $i = 0$, S_1 is $j = 0$, S_2 is $j := 1$ and Q is $j = 1$.
Then

$wp(S_1, Q) \equiv 1 = 0 \equiv \textbf{false},$
$wp(S_2, Q) \equiv 1 = 1 \equiv \textbf{true}.$

Thus

$wp(\textbf{if } i = 0 \textbf{ then } j := 0 \textbf{ else } j := 1, j = 1)$
$\equiv [(i = 0) \Rightarrow \textbf{false}] \textbf{ and } [(i \neq 0) \Rightarrow \textbf{true}]$
$\equiv i \neq 0.$

3.23 Suppose B is $i > j$, S_1 is $j := j + 1$, S_2 is $i := i + 1$ and Q is $i \geqslant j$.
Then

$wp(S_1, Q) \equiv i \geqslant j + 1 \equiv i > j,$
$wp(S_2, Q) \equiv i + 1 \geqslant j \equiv i \geqslant j - 1.$

Thus

$wp(\textbf{if } i > j \textbf{ then } j := j + 1 \textbf{ else } i := i + 1, i \geqslant j)$
$\equiv (i > j \Rightarrow i > j) \textbf{ and } (i \leqslant j \Rightarrow i \geqslant j - 1)$
$\equiv \textbf{true and} (i > j \textbf{ or } i \geqslant j - 1)$
$\equiv i \geqslant j - 1.$

3.24 In this example we make use of a procedure *interchange*(x, y) which interchanges the values of x and y. The body of the procedure is in fact the three statements $t := x; x := y; y := t$ discussed in an earlier section, but this is irrelevant to the present discussion. What is relevant is a rule for computing $wp(interchange(x, y), Q)$. Specifically

$$wp(interchange(x, y), Q) \equiv Q_{y,x}^{x,y}$$

where $Q_{y,x}^{x,y}$ is the predicate obtained by replacing x by y and y by x everywhere in Q. For example,

$$wp(interchange(x, y), x = 10 \text{ and } y = 20) \equiv y = 10 \text{ and } x = 20.$$

Now suppose B is $y \geqslant z$, S_1 is $interchange(x, y)$, S_2 is $interchange$ (x, z), and Q is $(x \geqslant y)$ **and** $(x \geqslant z)$.
Then

$$wp(S_1, Q) \equiv (y \geqslant x) \text{ and } (y \geqslant z),$$
$$wp(S_2, Q) \equiv (z \geqslant y) \text{ and } (z \geqslant x).$$

Hence

$$wp(\textbf{if } y \geqslant z \textbf{ then } interchange(x, y) \textbf{ else } interchange(x, z),$$
$$(x \geqslant y) \text{ and } (x \geqslant z))$$
$$\equiv [(y \geqslant z) \Rightarrow (y \geqslant x) \text{ and } (y \geqslant z)]$$
$$\textbf{and } [(y < z) \Rightarrow (z \geqslant y) \text{ and } (z \geqslant x)]$$
$$\equiv [(y \geqslant z) \Rightarrow (y \geqslant x)] \text{ and } [(y < z) \Rightarrow (z \geqslant x)].$$

Exercise
3.10 Another argument on its form might lead to the conclusion that

$$wp(\textbf{if } B \textbf{ then } S_1 \textbf{ else } S_2, Q)$$
$$\equiv (B \text{ and } wp(S_1, Q)) \text{ or } ((\text{not } B) \text{ and } wp(S_2, Q)). \tag{3.17}$$

Check that this is equivalent to the expression (3.16).

We can use the same form of argument to deduce a method for evaluating the weakest precondition of a statement of the form **if** B **then** S with respect to a postcondition Q. Again there are two requirements. The simpler requirement is that if **not** B then Q must already be true (because no change occurs in the program state). This is formalized as

$$\textbf{not } B \Rightarrow Q. \tag{3.18}$$

The second requirement is that if S is executed then $wp(S, Q)$ must hold beforehand, i.e.

$$B \Rightarrow wp(S, Q). \tag{3.19}$$

Thus from (3.18) and (3.19) we have

$$wp(\textbf{if } B \textbf{ then } S, Q) \equiv [B \Rightarrow wp(S, Q)] \text{ and } [\textbf{not } B \Rightarrow Q]. \tag{3.20}$$

Examples

3.25 $wp($ **if** $i \neq 0$ **then** $i:=0, i=0)$

$\equiv [(i \neq 0) \Rightarrow 0 = 0]$ **and** $[(i=0) \Rightarrow (i=0)]$

$\equiv$ **true.**

As discussed earlier, **true** describes all states. Thus the statement **if** $i \neq 0$ **then** $i:=0$ always guarantees the postcondition $i=0$.

3.26 Consider the weakest precondition of the statement S

> **if** $(x \leqslant y)$ **or** $(x \leqslant z)$
> **then begin**
>   **if** $y \geqslant z$ **then** $interchange(x, y)$
>   **else** $interchange(x, z)$
> **end**

with respect to the postcondition Q

> $(x \geqslant y)$ **and** $(x \geqslant z)$.

Let S_1 be the statement

> **if** $y \geqslant z$ **then** $interchange(x, y)$
>   **else** $interchange(x, z)$

Then, using the result of example 3.24, we have

$$wp(S_1, Q) \equiv [(y \geqslant z) \Rightarrow (y \geqslant x)] \text{ and } [(y < z) \Rightarrow (z \geqslant x)].$$

Hence

$wp(S, Q)$

$\equiv \{(x \leqslant y) \text{ or } (x \leqslant z) \Rightarrow wp(S_1, Q)\}$

 and $\{($**not** $[(x \leqslant y) \text{ or } (x \leqslant z)]) \Rightarrow [(x \geqslant y) \text{ and } (x \geqslant z)]\}$

$\equiv \{(x \leqslant y) \text{ or } (x \leqslant z)$

  $\Rightarrow \{[(y \geqslant z) \Rightarrow (y \geqslant x)] \text{ and } [(y < z) \Rightarrow (z \geqslant x)]\}$

 and $\{(x > y) \text{ and } (x > z) \Rightarrow (x \geqslant y) \text{ and } (x \geqslant z)\}$

$\equiv$ **true and true**

$\equiv$ **true**

Thus execution of S will always guarantee Q.

Exercise

3.11 Construct and simplify $wp(S, Q)$ for the following statements and postconditions.

S	Q
(a) **if** $odd(x)$ **then** $x := x + 1$	$even(x)$
(b) **if** $even(i)$ **then begin**	$y^i = c$
$\quad\quad i := i$ **div** $2;$	
$\quad\quad y := y * y$	
$\quad$ **end**	
(c) **if** $x > y$ **then** $x := x - y$ **else** $y := y - x$	$y \geqslant 0$ **and** $x \geqslant 0$
(d) **if** $x = y$ **then** $equal := $ **true**	$equal \Leftrightarrow x = y$
(e) **if** $(i + k)^2 \leqslant n$ **then** $i := i + k$	$(i^2 \leqslant n)$ **and** $(j^2 > n)$
$\quad\quad$ **else if** $(j - k)^2 > n$	
$\quad\quad\quad$ **then** $j := j - k$	
(f) **if** $j = k + 1$ **then begin**	$m = i * j + k$
$\quad\quad i := i + 1;$	
$\quad\quad k := 0$	
$\quad$ **end**	
$\quad$ **else** $k := k + 1$	

3.12 Derive an alternative form of $wp(\textbf{if } B \textbf{ then } S, Q)$ similar to (3.17).

Proof Rules for Conditionals

As with assignment statements and sequential composition we can express the foregoing results in the form of proof rules. The two rules describing conditional statements are as follows.

$$\frac{\{P \textbf{ and } B\}\ S_1\ \{Q\}}{\{P\}\ \textbf{if } B \textbf{ then } S_1 \textbf{ else } S_2\ \{Q\}}$$

and

$$\frac{\{P \textbf{ and } B\}\ S\ \{Q\}}{\{P\}\ \textbf{if } B \textbf{ then } S\ \{Q\}}$$

The first rule can be paraphrased as follows:

	If one can prove that
$\{P \text{ and } B\}$	(a) if P **and** B describes the state before
S_1	S_1 is executed
$\{Q\}$	then Q will describe the state afterwards
	and also that
$\{P \text{ and (not } B)\}$	(b) if P **and (not** B**)** describes the state before
S_2	S_2 is executed
$\{Q\}$	then Q will describe the state afterwards
———	then one can infer that
$\{P\}$	if P describes the state before
if B **then** S_1 **else** S_2	**if** B **then** S_1 **else** S_2 is executed
$\{Q\}$	then Q will describe the state afterwards.

Exercise
3.13 Paraphrase the second rule in the same way.

To see how these rules are related to the respective weakest preconditions we need to adopt a slightly roundabout argument. The justification we gave earlier for equation (3.16) was somewhat informal but, using the first conditional rule, we can verify it formally. What we need to show is that the right hand side of (3.16) is (a) a *precondition* of the **if** statement and also that (b) it is the weakest such condition. In other words we claim the following.

Theorem Let P denote $[B \Rightarrow wp(S_1, Q)]$ **and** $[\text{not } B \Rightarrow wp(S_2, Q)]$.

Then (a) $\{P\}$ **if** B **then** S_1 **else** S_2 $\{Q\}$
and (b) if S_1 and S_2 always terminate then
$\{R\}$ **if** B **then** S_1 **else** S_2 $\{Q\}$ implies $R \Rightarrow P$.

Proof

(a) By definition of wp, if $R \Rightarrow wp(S_1, Q)$ then $\{R\}$ S_1 $\{Q\}$
and, if $R \Rightarrow wp(S_2, Q)$ then $\{R\}$ S_2 $\{Q\}$.
But P **and** $B \equiv B$ **and** $wp(S_1, Q)$
$\Rightarrow wp(S_1, Q)$.
Therefore $\{P \text{ and } B\}$ S_1 $\{Q\}$.
Similarly, $\{P \text{ and (not } B)\}$ S_2 $\{Q\}$.
Hence, by the conditional rule,
$\{P\}$ **if** B **then** S_1 **else** S_2 $\{Q\}$.
(b) Suppose S_1 and S_2 always terminate and $\{R\}$ **if** B **then** S_1 **else** S_2 $\{Q\}$.
Then $\{R \text{ and } B\}$ S_1 $\{Q\}$
$\{R \text{ and (not } B)\}$ S_2 $\{Q\}$
and **if** B **then** S_1 **else** S_2 always terminates.

Hence, by definition of *wp*,
$$R \text{ and } B \Rightarrow wp(S_1, Q)$$
and R **and (not** $B) \Rightarrow wp(S_2, Q)$,
i.e. $R \Rightarrow (B \Rightarrow wp(S_1, Q))$
and $R \Rightarrow$ (**not** $B \Rightarrow wp(S_2, Q))$.
Thus $R \Rightarrow (B \Rightarrow wp(S_1, Q))$ **and (not** $B \Rightarrow wp(S_2, Q))$.

Exercise

3.14 Verify (3.20) using the second conditional rule.
You should prove

(a) $\{(B \Rightarrow wp(S, Q))$ **and (not** $B \Rightarrow Q)\}$ **if** B **then** S $\{Q\}$, and
(b) if S always terminates and $\{R\}$ **if** B **then** S $\{Q\}$ then
$R \Rightarrow (B \Rightarrow wp(S, Q))$ **and (not** $B \Rightarrow Q)$.

Examples

3.27   {**true**}

if $i \leqslant j$

then if $j < k$ **then** $m := k$

                   else $m := j$

else if $i < k$ **then** $m := k$

                   else $m := i$

{$m \geqslant i$ **and** $m \geqslant j$ **and** $m \geqslant k$}

To prove this assertion we need to work from the innermost statements
(the assignments) outwards. Again it is convenient for us to introduce
some notation. Specifically, let S_1 denote the statement

if $j < k$ **then** $m := k$ **else** $m := j$

and S_2 denote the statement

if $i < k$ **then** $m := k$ **else** $m := i$.

Now consider S_1. Clearly it is only executed when $i \leqslant j$. Thus we
begin by proving

$$\{i \leqslant j\} \, S_1 \, \{m \geqslant i \text{ and } m \geqslant j \text{ and } m \geqslant k\}.$$

1. $\{k \geqslant i$ **and** $k \geqslant j\} m := k \{m \geqslant i$ **and** $m \geqslant j$ **and** $m \geqslant k\}$
                                                        (assignment axiom)

2. $\{j \geqslant i$ **and** $j \geqslant k\} m := j \{m \geqslant i$ **and** $m \geqslant j$ **and** $m \geqslant k\}$
                                                        (assignment axiom)

3. $i \leqslant j$ and $j < k \Rightarrow k \geqslant i$ and $k \geqslant j$ (inequalities)
4. $i \leqslant j$ and $j \geqslant k \Rightarrow j \geqslant i$ and $j \geqslant k$ (inequalities)
5. $\{i \leqslant j$ and $j < k\} m := k \{m \geqslant i$ and $m \geqslant j$ and $m \geqslant k\}$
    (1 and 3, consequence rule)
6. $\{i \leqslant j$ and $j \geqslant k\} m := j \{m \geqslant i$ and $m \geqslant j$ and $m \geqslant k\}$
    (2 and 4, consequence rule)
7. $\{i \leqslant j\} S_1 \{m \geqslant i$ and $m \geqslant j$ and $m \geqslant k\}$ (5 and 6, conditional rule)

The following step is proved similarly to step 7. Equally, 8 is 7 with the roles of i and j reversed.

8. $\{j \leqslant i\} S_2 \{m \geqslant i$ and $m \geqslant j$ and $m \geqslant k\}$
9. $j < i \Rightarrow j \leqslant i$ (inequalities)
10. $\{j < i\} S_2 \{m \geqslant i$ and $m \geqslant j$ and $m \geqslant k\}$ (8 and 9, consequence rule)
11. $\{$**true**$\}$ **if** $i \leqslant j$ **then** S_1 **else** $S_2 \{m \geqslant i$ and $m \geqslant j$ and $m \geqslant k\}$
    (7 and 10, conditional rule)

3.28 $\{$**true**$\}$
    if $i < j$ **then** *interchange*(i,j);
    if $j < k$ **then** *interchange*(j,k);
    if $i < j$ **then** *interchange*(i,j);
    $\{i \geqslant j \geqslant k\}$

The assertions added to this statement sequence claim that, whatever the initial state, after its execution i, j, and k will be sorted, i.e. $i \geqslant j \geqslant k$. As with the use of the assignment axiom we work backwards from the postcondition to the precondition. For brevity we use S_1, S_2, and S_3 to denote the three statements. The basis for our argument is to determine in turn $wp(S_3, i \geqslant j \geqslant k)$, $wp(S_2, wp(S_3, i \geqslant j \geqslant k))$, and $wp(S_1, wp(S_2, wp(S_3, i \geqslant j \geqslant k)))$.

Specifically, by (3.20) we have

$$wp(S_3, i \geqslant j \geqslant k) \equiv (i < j \Rightarrow j \geqslant i \geqslant k) \text{ and } (i \geqslant j \Rightarrow i \geqslant j \geqslant k)$$
$$\equiv i \geqslant k \text{ and } j \geqslant k$$

$$wp(S_2, i \geqslant k \text{ and } j \geqslant k) \equiv (j < k \Rightarrow i \geqslant j \text{ and } k \geqslant j)$$
$$\text{and } (j \geqslant k \Rightarrow i \geqslant k \text{ and } j \geqslant k)$$
$$\equiv i \geqslant j \geqslant k \text{ or } i \geqslant k > j$$

$$wp(S_1, i \geqslant j \geqslant k \text{ or } i \geqslant k > j)$$
$$\equiv [i < j \Rightarrow (j \geqslant i \geqslant k \text{ or } j \geqslant k > i)]$$
$$\text{and } [i \geqslant j \Rightarrow (i \geqslant j \geqslant k \text{ or } i \geqslant k > j)]$$
$$\equiv \text{**true**}$$

Exercises

3.15 Repeat example 3.27 using weakest preconditions and example 3.28 using Hoare's proof rules.

3.16 Prove the following

$$\{p = m * n\}$$

if $odd(m)$ **then** $x := 1$ **else** $x := 0$;

if $odd(n)$ **then** $y := 1$ **else** $y := 0$;

if $odd(p)$ **then** $z := 1$ **else** $z := 0$

$$\{z = x * y\}$$

(*Hint*: let P denote $[odd(p) \Rightarrow x = y = 1]$ **and** $[$**not** $odd(p) \Rightarrow x = 0$ **or** $y = 0]$. Prove that

$$\{p = m * n\}$$

if $odd(m)$ **then** $x := 1$ **else** $x := 0$;

if $odd(n)$ **then** $y := 1$ **else** $y := 0$

$$\{P\}$$

and $\{P\}$ **if** $odd(p)$ **then** $z := 1$ **else** $z := 0 \{z = x * y\}$.)

3.3 INVARIANTS AND INDUCTION

In this section we explore the process of inductive reasoning and the concept of an invariant. Inductive reasoning lies at the heart of problem-solving; it is the process by which one makes informed guesses or conjectures from a limited number of experimental observations and then subjects those guesses to the rigors of proof. 'Invariants' are the subject matter of the guesses.

3.3.1 Invariants

> It is an inherent property of intelligence that it can jump out of the task which it is performing, and survey what it has done; it is always looking for, and often finding, patterns.
>
> *Douglas R. Hofstadter*

An invariant is something which is unchanging and, paradoxically in a world which seems to be changing faster than ever, invariants can be said to dominate our lives. Some of the first that a child learns (in an English-speaking country) are the formation of plurals:

dogs, cats, hands, arms, legs

and the past tense:

kick*ed*, jump*ed*, walk*ed*.

Later come the rules for forming numbers:

six*ty*, seven*ty*, eigh*ty*

one *hundred and* twenty, two *hundred and* forty.

The fact that these 'invariants' are not truly so can be perplexing to the child and frustrating to the parents; it can take many years to dissuade a child from saying 'sheeps', 'foots', and 'buyed'.

The human brain seems to have a particular aptitude for recognizing invariants—or 'patterns' as they are more commonly called—and many intelligence tests involve just that. Consider, for example, the following tests which ask you to find the next two shapes in a sequence.

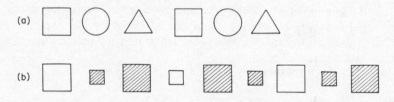

The questions seem to ask you for the next *change* but, in fact, are solved by recognizing what *does not* change. In (a) it is easy to see that the sequence square, circle, triangle is repeated and hence the next two are a square and a circle. Question (b) is more difficult (but only just) since it exploits *two* invariants, the first being that there is always a large square followed by a small square and the second that there is one white square followed by two striped squares. We conclude that the next two are a small white square followed by a large striped square.

Recognition of invariants often provides a simple solution to a seemingly difficult problem. The following problem is a well-known example. Suppose the top left and bottom right squares of a chessboard are removed leaving a board with 62 black and white squares. Now suppose you are supplied with a box of dominoes each of which has been made to cover exactly two of the squares on the chessboard. The problem is: can you completely cover the chessboard with the dominoes? If so, how, and, if not, prove that you cannot.

The answer is that it is impossible. The two squares removed are the same color leaving more black squares than white and no matter how many dominoes we place on the board *the number of black squares that have been covered will always be the same as the number of white squares*. The invariant here, the property that does not change despite changing the number of dominoes, is the italicized statement. It and the initial configuration of the board together imply that the number of uncovered black squares is always two more than the number of uncovered white squares.

The word 'invariant' is synonymous with 'pattern', 'rule', or 'law'. Recognition of an invariant is synonymous with understanding. When a scientist formulates a law, for example the law of motion, then he believes he has increased his understanding of the subject of his study. But the understanding associated with recognition of invariants is much more fundamental than this. Whenever we use a word—eye, arm, cup, saucer—we are naming an invariant, the property that is common to all the objects which go by that name. Sometimes it is very difficult, if not impossible, for us to define what is unchanging—what, for instance, is meant by 'living' and 'nonliving'— nevertheless, we are naming something that is unchanging. The fact that the 'something' is imprecise merely signifies that our understanding is incomplete.

And so it is with computer programs. We shall find in section 3.4 that the way to understand loops, statements that repeatedly *change* the program variables, is to examine what is left *unchanged* by the loop—the so called *loop-invariant*. A simple example is the following statement which sums the *n* elements in the array *a*:

$s := 0;$

for $i := 1$ **to** n **do** $s := s + a[i]$

The invariant of the **for** statement is that, whatever the value of i, s is the sum of the elements $a[1]$, $a[2]$, ..., $a[i]$ immediately before i is incremented.

Exercises

3.17 What are the next two elements in the following sequences? Rationalize your answer by listing as many invariants of the sequences as possible.

(a) ƎSNИЕSИNE ƨ∾∧

(b) SSN ƎƧSNE Ƨ∂NEᶜS

(c) EmƎwAMƎwEⱯ ƎШEmⱯ

3.18 Which is the odd one out in the following groups of figures? Again, rationalize your answer by specifying the property or properties common to the remainder.

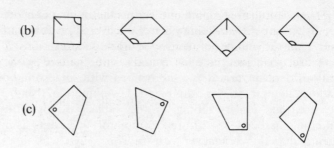

3.19 Four beetles—A, B, C, and D—occupy the corners of a square 10 cm along a side (Fig. 3.4). A and C are male, B and D are female. Simultaneously A crawls directly towards B, B towards C, C towards D, and D towards A. If all four beetles crawl at the same constant rate, they will describe four congruent logarithmic spirals which meet at the center of the square.

How far does each beetle travel before they meet? The problem can be solved without calculus.

3.20 Consider an urn filled with a number of black and white balls. There are also enough balls outside the urn to play the following game. We want to reduce the number of balls in the urn to one by repeating the following process as often as necessary.

Pick any two balls in the urn. If both have the same color then throw them away, but put another black ball into the urn; if they have different colors then return the white one to the urn and throw the black one away.

Each execution of the above process reduces the number of balls in the urn by one; when only one ball is left the game is over. Now, what, if anything, can be said about the color of the final ball in the urn in relation to the original number of black balls and white balls?

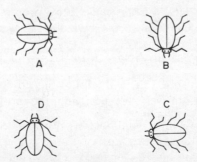

Fig. 3.4 The amorous beetles.

Hint: denote the original number of black balls and white balls in the urn by b_0 and w_0, respectively. Let b and w be the numbers of black balls and white balls after an arbitrary number of executions. Then on the next execution the values of b and w are changed according to the following rules:

$$b := b - 2; b := b + 1 \quad \text{if both balls are black}$$
$$w := w - 2; b := b + 1 \quad \text{if both balls are white}$$
$$b := b - 1; \qquad\qquad\quad \text{if the balls are different colors}$$

Can you see what is *invariant* about b and/or w?

3.3.2 Inductive Reasoning

The logician, the mathematician, the physicist, and the engineer. 'Look at this mathematician', said the logician. 'He observes that the first ninety-nine numbers are less than a hundred and infers hence, by what he calls induction, that all numbers are less than a hundred.'

'A physicist believes', said the mathematician, 'that 60 is divisible by all numbers. He observes that 60 is divisible by 1, 2, 3, 4, 5, and 6. He examines a few more cases, as 10, 20, and 30, taken at random as he says. Since 60 is divisible also by these, he considers the experimental evidence sufficient.'

'Yes, but look at the engineer', said the physicist. 'An engineer suspected that all odd numbers are prime numbers. At any rate, 1 can be considered as a prime number, he argued. Then there come 3, 5, and 7, all indubitably primes. Then there comes 9; an awkward case, it does not seem to be a prime number. Yet 11 and 13 are certainly primes. "Coming back to 9", he said, "I conclude that 9 must be an experimental error".'

G. Polya

The process by which one infers an invariant property from a set of observations is called *inductive reasoning*. It is a process with which you are probably already familiar, because it is so vital to all scientific study, although you may not know it by that name.

Inductive reasoning proceeds from observation to conjectures to proof. Conjectures that are proved become laws. For example, we may observe that $1 + 3 = 4$, $1 + 3 + 5 = 9$ and $1 + 3 + 5 + 7 = 16$. We recognize a pattern and so make the conjecture that $1 + 3 + \cdots + (2*m - 1) = m^2$. We test the conjecture—for the case $m = 5$ and possibly others—and then we prove the conjecture. Figure 3.5 shows such a proof—note that as the squares increase in size, the number of dots added is an odd integer which itself increases by two at each stage.

Fig. 3.5 An inductive proof.

Typically, inductive reasoning is not so straightforward. More often than not the conjectures we make are unfounded. They do not stand up to proof and have to be either discarded or, at best, modified in some way. As a consequence, inductive reasoning is most valuable in the early stages of algorithm design, the stage when one is trying to gain familiarity with the problem in hand, when one is still groping for the most appropriate invariants.

We can illustrate the process of inductive reasoning by applying it to the Tower of Hanoi problem. This problem is a favorite of Computer Science textbooks, where it is usually used to illustrate recursion as a programming technique. Our presentation of it, however, is rather unorthodox!

In the problem there are n disks of unequal size which can be stacked on three posts. Initially, the disks are all stacked in order of decreasing size on the first post. Figure 3.6 depicts the initial state when $n = 5$. The problem is to move all the disks from the first post to the second. Each move involves only one disk and this disk must be placed on a larger disk than itself or on an empty post.

Recursion is the ideal technique for *programming* a solution to this problem and if you have not already seen a recursive solution you are bound to come across one before long. However, a human being would find it very difficult to recover the correct sequence of moves, unaided, from a recursive solution and, indeed, it is not too difficult to deduce a nonrecursive solution, as we shall soon see.

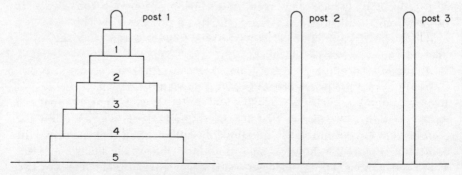

Fig. 3.6 The Tower of Hanoi problem.

Table 3.1 Solution for $n = 1$, 2, and 3 disks.

$n = 1$ Move disk from to			$n = 2$ Move disk from to			$n = 3$ Move disk from to		
1	1	2	1	1	3	1	1	2
			2	1	2	2	1	3
			1	3	2	1	2	3
						3	1	2
						1	3	1
						2	3	2
						1	1	2

Suppose we proceed inductively. That is, let us compute a solution for the cases $n = 1$, $n = 2$, $n = 3$, and so on, and see if we can see a pattern emerging.

The case $n = 1$ is trivial, and the case $n = 2$ hardly less so. The sequence of moves in each case is recorded in Table 3.1; you should have no difficulty in deriving these moves for yourself. The case $n = 3$ is a little more difficult, and may require some experimentation. Even so, it is possible to derive a suitable sequence of moves by simple trial and error. If the disks and posts are numbered as shown in Fig. 3.6, the first move offers the choice between moving disk 1 to post 2 or to post 3. Suppose we arbitrarily make the first choice. Then subsequent moves are almost inevitable given the desire to get into a position in which disk 3 can be moved, and the simple observation that no two consecutive moves should involve the same disk.

On the second move, disk 2 should be moved to post 3, then on the third move the only sensible possibility is to move disk 1 onto disk 2. (Try it yourself and see.) This leaves both disks 1 and 2 on post 3 and disk 3 on post 1 as shown in Fig. 3.7(c). We now realize that disk 3 can be moved onto post 2 and— eureka!—it is only a short step to move disks 1 and 2 back onto disk 3 as shown in Figs. 3.7(e)–(g). This sequence of moves has also been included in Table 3.1.

The case $n = 4$, on the other hand, is rather daunting to solve by trial and error, and so, let us turn to Table 3.1 to see if there is any pattern emerging in the solution.

Study Table 3.1 for yourself and see if you can see a pattern. Look for an invariant property, but do not imagine that it is complicated—if you can not find at least one invariant it is because you are overlooking the obvious.

If you have now studied Table 3.1 and have not deduced some pattern then try asking yourself the following questions. For some of them your answer may be no, or that there is insufficient evidence, but for some you should be able to conjecture the answer yes.

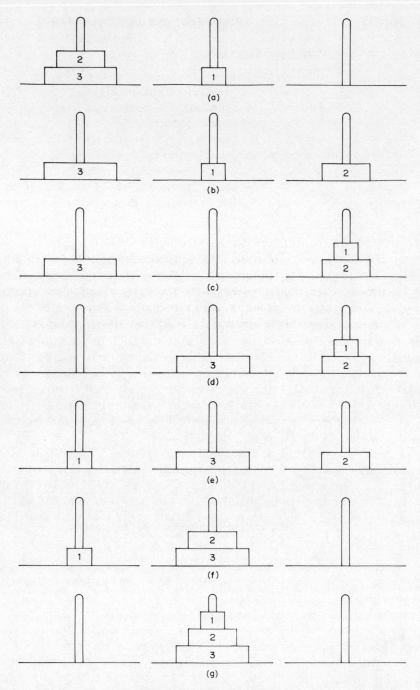

Fig. 3.7 Solution for $n = 3$.

(a) Is there a pattern in the disk being moved at each stage (the first column in each table)?
(b) Is there a pattern in the post from which the disk is taken at each stage (the second column in each table), or the post to which the disk is moved at each stage (the third column in each table)?
(c) Is there a pattern in the successive positions of disk 1, in the successive positions of disk 2, or in the successive positions of disk 3?
(d) Is there a pattern in the number of moves taken?

Your answer to (a) should have been, Yes. There is a pattern—every odd move involves disk 1, the smallest disk. However, there is not sufficient evidence to warrant a conjecture about the form that the even moves take.

Your answer to (b) is, most likely, No.

Your answer to (c) is Yes for disk 1, but No for disk 2. If we examine the successive positions of disk 1 for the case $n = 3$ we find that they are posts

$$1, \ 2, \ 3, \ 1, \ 2.$$

This sequence looks very much like the beginning of the infinite sequence

$$1, \ 2, \ 3, \ 1, \ 2, \ 3, \ 1, \ 2, \ 3, \ 1, \ 2, \ 3, \dots .$$

Let us take a bold step, and conjecture that it is. The significance of this conjecture can be seen if we imagine the posts arranged to form a triangle as shown in Fig. 3.8. In this configuration, the conjecture takes the form that disk 1 is always moved clockwise around the posts.

Unfortunately, this does not hold for the case $n = 2$ where the successive positions of disk 1 are posts 1, 3, and 2, i.e. disk 1 is moved anticlockwise around the disks. This leaves us with two possibilities: either we abandon the conjecture or we take the very bold step and conjecture that, for a given number n of disks, either disk 1 is always moved clockwise or it is always moved anticlockwise.

To summarize our progress so far, we have a quite firm belief that an algorithm will involve moving the smallest disk on every odd move, and we have a more tenuous belief that the direction in which this disk is moved (clockwise or anticlockwise) remains constant.

Post 1
O

O   O
Post 2   Post 3

Fig. 3.8 Triangular arrangement of the posts.

At this point you should have a go at computing the sequence of moves for the case $n = 4$ using pencil and paper to record the state of play (as in Fig. 3.7), or the real thing if you have one at your disposal. Try moving disk 1 always in a clockwise direction first (i.e. from post 1 to post 2 to post 3 to post 1 to post 2 to post 3, etc.) Then begin again, this time always moving disk 1 in an anticlockwise direction. What do you find?

Finished? Then what you should have observed is that on every even move, if one does not move the smallest disk, there is only one move that can be made. This is quite obvious when you think about it. On one post—call it i—there will be a stack of disks on the top of which is the smallest disk. Now, no disk may be moved onto this post since the rule that no disk may be placed on one smaller than itself would be violated. This leaves two posts—call them j and k—to be considered. One of them, say k, may be empty, in which case the only possibility is to take the top disk from post j and move it across to k. Alternatively, there are disks on both posts j and k. But the top disk on one of them, say j, must be larger than the top disk on the other and so the only option is to move the top disk from post k to post j.

You should also have observed that moving disk 1 continuously in a *clockwise* direction eventually moves all four disks from the first to the third post; moving disk 1 continuously in an *anticlockwise* direction accomplishes the given task of moving all four disks from the first to the second post. Table 3.2 shows this sequence of moves.

The pieces of the jigsaw are now beginning to fall into place. The success in

Table 3.2 Solution for $n = 4$ disks.

Disk	Move from	Move to
1	1	3
2	1	2
1	3	2
3	1	3
1	2	1
2	2	3
1	1	3
4	1	2
1	3	2
2	3	1
1	2	1
3	3	2
1	1	3
2	1	2
1	3	2

applying our earlier, sometimes tenuous, conjectures gives us a great deal more confidence in their validity. Indeed we are just a small step away from proposing an algorithm.

You may well have already seen a pattern in the number of moves required. For $n = 1$, 2, 3, and 4 there are, respectively 1, 3, 7, and 15 moves. We conjecture, therefore, that for the general case $2^n - 1$ moves are required. Other patterns are also beginning to emerge. For instance, disk n, the largest disk, is moved just once, disk $n - 1$ is moved twice, disk $n - 2$ is moved four times, and so on. In particular, disk 1 is moved 2^{n-1} times. Consequently it should be moved in a clockwise direction if (2^{n-1}) **mod** $3 = 1$, and in an anticlockwise direction if (2^{n-1}) **mod** $3 = 2$. Using the fact that (2^{n-1}) **mod** $3 = 1$ implies that 2^n **mod** $3 = 2$, (2^{n+1}) **mod** $3 = 1$, and that 2^0 **mod** $3 = 1$, we conclude that disk 1 is moved clockwise when n is odd and anticlockwise when n is even. This is all that remains in our search for an algorithm, which is presented below.

```
const NoMoves = 2ⁿ − 1;
var   k: integer;
      d: (clockwise, anticlockwise);
begin
if odd(n) then d := clockwise else d := anticlockwise;
k := 0;
while k < NoMoves do
      begin k := k + 1;
      if odd(k)
      then move the smallest disk from its current position to the next
              in the direction d
      else begin Consider the two posts from which the smallest
                  disk is absent.
                  if one is empty
                  then move the topmost disk from the other post to the
                          empty post
                  else pick the post whose topmost disk is the smaller and
                          move that disk onto the other post
            end
      end
end
```

Algorithm 3.1 Solution to Tower of Hanoi problem.

Exercises

3.21 Construct the truth tables for p_0, $p_0 \Rightarrow p_1$, and $p_0 \Rightarrow (p_1 \Rightarrow p_2)$.

How many **true** entries are there in each table? Conjecture how many **true** entries there are in the truth table for

$$p_0 \Rightarrow (p_1 \Rightarrow (p_2 \Rightarrow \cdots (p_{n-2} \Rightarrow p_{n-1}) \cdots)).$$

3.22 Construct the truth tables for $a \Leftrightarrow b$, $(a \Leftrightarrow b) \Leftrightarrow c$, and $((a \Leftrightarrow b) \Leftrightarrow c) \Leftrightarrow d$. Do you see a pattern in the **true** entries? Use your observation to make a conjecture relating the truth of $((\cdots((a_0 \Leftrightarrow a_1) \Leftrightarrow a_2) \cdots) \Leftrightarrow a_{n-1})$ to the number of indices i for which a_i is **true**.

3.3.3 Proof by Induction

> You should not put too much trust in any unproved conjecture, even if it has been propounded by a great authority, even if it has been propounded by yourself. You should try to prove it or disprove it....
>
> *G. Polya*

The Principle of Mathematical Induction

Proofs by induction normally involve proving some predicate $P(n)$ involving a natural number n. An example, which we use in the following discussion, is the predicate

$$P(n) \equiv 0 + 1 + 2 + \cdots + n = n*(n+1)/2. \tag{3.21}$$

The essence of the principle of (simple) mathematical induction is that $P(n)$ is provably true for all natural numbers, n, if it is possible to prove

(i) $P(0)$ is true

and   (ii) if $P(n)$ is true then $P(n+1)$ is true.

To illustrate this principle let us apply it to the predicate (3.21) above. We begin by proving $P(0)$. This is obviously true since

$$P(0) \equiv 0 = 0*(0+1)/2. \tag{3.22}$$

This first step is called the *basis* of the inductive proof.

The next step, called the *inductive step*, is to assume $P(n)$ and prove $P(n+1)$. Thus, in our example, we assume that

$$0 + 1 + 2 + \cdots + n = n*(n+1)/2 \tag{3.23}$$

and we wish to prove that

$$0 + 1 + 2 + \cdots + (n+1) = (n+1)*[(n+1)+1]/2 \tag{3.24}$$

Equation (3.24) is, of course, just equation (3.23) with $(n+1)$ replacing n throughout. Now, examining the left-hand side of (3.24) we note that

$$0 + 1 + 2 + \cdots + (n+1) = 0 + 1 + 2 + \cdots + n + (n+1).$$

So, applying our assumption (3.23),

$$0 + 1 + 2 + \cdots + (n + 1) = n*(n + 1)/2 + (n + 1)$$
$$= (n + 1)*(n + 2)/2$$
$$= (n + 1)*(n + 1 + 1)/2 \qquad (3.25)$$

We have thus proved that if (3.23) is true then (3.24) is also true.

The final step is to cite the principle of mathematical induction to combine the basis and the inductive step in the conclusion that the predicate $P(n)$ is true for all natural numbers, n. For our example, we state the following. 'By equations (3.22) and (3.25) and the principle of mathematical induction we conclude that $0 + 1 + 2 + \cdots + n = n*(n + 1)/2$ for all natural numbers, n'.

Let us summarize the steps in a proof by induction.

Principle of Simple Mathematical Induction
We are given a predicate $P(n)$ on the natural number n. We then prove two things about $P(n)$.

(i) $P(0)$ is true.
(ii) If $P(n)$ is assumed to be true then $P(n + 1)$ is also true.

The statement (i) is called the *basis* of the proof and (ii) the *inductive step*. From (i) and (ii) we may conclude by the *principle of mathematical induction* that $P(n)$ is true of all natural numbers.

Intuitively, the reasoning behind the principle of mathematical induction is very clear. After having established the inductive step we know in particular that

$P(0) \Rightarrow P(1)$.

This combined with the basis

$P(0)$

enables us to infer (by *modus ponens*)

$P(1)$.

But we also know from the inductive step that

$P(1) \Rightarrow P(2)$.

So we may again conclude by *modus ponens* that

$P(2)$.

In this way one can see intuitively that all of $P(0), P(1), P(2), P(3), \ldots$ are true, i.e. $P(n)$ is true for all $n \geqslant 0$.

Example

3.29 In this example we prove that, for all natural numbers, n,

$$2^0 + 2^1 + 2^2 + \cdots + 2^n = 2^{n+1} - 1.$$

(a) Basis. When $n = 0$

$$2^0 + 2^1 + 2^2 + \cdots + 2^n = 2^0 = 1 = 2 - 1 = 2^{0+1} - 1.$$

Thus $2^0 + 2^1 + 2^2 + \cdots + 2^n = 2^{n+1} - 1$.

(b) Inductive step. Assume $n \geqslant 0$ and

$$2^0 + 2^1 + 2^2 + \cdots + 2^n = 2^{n+1} - 1.$$

Then $2^0 + 2^1 + 2^2 + \cdots + 2^{n+1} = 2^0 + 2^1 + 2^2 + \cdots + 2^n + 2^{n+1}$

$$= 2^{n+1} - 1 + 2^{n+1}$$

$$= 2 * 2^{n+1} - 1$$

$$= 2^{n+2} - 1$$

i.e. $2^0 + 2^1 + 2^2 + \cdots + 2^{n+1} = 2^{(n+1)+1} - 1$.

We conclude, by the principle of mathematical induction, that

$$2^0 + 2^1 + 2^2 + \cdots + 2^n = 2^{n+1} - 1.$$

The principle of mathematical induction is often used in slightly different ways from the form stated above. One instance is when we wish to prove a property of all integers $n \geqslant m$, where m is some given constant different from 0. In this case the *basis* of the inductive proof must be the proof of $P(m)$ (rather than $P(0)$).

When one wishes to prove a property $P(n)$ of a range of integers, say for n such that $m \leqslant n \leqslant p$ it is still possible to use the principle of mathematical induction, but the basis must be $P(m)$ and the inductive step must include the hypothesis that $m \leqslant n < p$. In other words, we prove

(a) $P(m)$

(b) if $m \leqslant n < p$ and $P(n)$ is true then $P(n + 1)$ is true

and then conclude that $P(n)$ is true for all $m \leqslant n \leqslant p$.

Exercises

Prove the following by induction on n.

3.23 $1^2 + 2^2 + 3^2 + \cdots + n^2 = n*(n+1)*(2*n+1)/6$ for all $n \geqslant 1$.

3.24 $1^3 + 2^3 + 3^3 + \cdots + n^3 = n^2*(n+1)^2/4$ for all $n \geqslant 1$

3.25 $x^0 + x^1 + x^2 + \cdots + x^n = (x^{n+1} - 1)/(x - 1)$ for all $x \neq 1$
and all $n \geqslant 0$.

3.26 $(1 + p)^n \geqslant 1 + n*p$ for all numbers $p > -1$ and all $n \geqslant 1$.

3.27 $1/(1*2) + (1/(2*3) + \cdots + 1/n*(n+1) = n/(n+1)$ for all $n \geqslant 1$.

3.28 $1/2 + 2/2^2 + 3/2^3 + \cdots + n/2^n = 2 - (n+2)/2^n$ for all $n \geqslant 1$.

3.29 $1 + 2*q + 3*q^2 + \cdots + n*q^{n-1} = [1 - (n+1)*q^n + n*q^{n+1}]/(1-q)^2$
$$\text{for all } n \geqslant 1 \text{ and } q \neq 1.$$

3.30   Prove the conjectures you made in exercises 3.21 and 3.22 by induction on n.

Strong Induction

A more significant variation on the principle of mathematical induction is the so-called *strong induction principle*. When using strong induction the inductive step assumes $P(k)$ *for all* $k \leqslant n$, rather than just $P(n)$, in order to infer $P(n+1)$. In full, the strong induction principle is as follows.

Suppose we are given a predicate $P(n)$ defined on the natural number, n. Now suppose we prove the following statements about P.

(a) $P(0)$ is true.
(b) If it is assumed that $P(0), P(1), \ldots, P(n)$ are all true then $P(n+1)$ is also true.

Then we may conclude that $P(n)$ is true for all $n \geqslant 0$.

The primary difference between simple induction and strong induction is the *inductive hypothesis*. In the former the inductive hypothesis is just $P(n)$; in the latter it is $\mathbf{A}(i: 0 \leqslant i \leqslant n: P(i))$. (Equally, one can take $Q(n) \equiv \mathbf{A}(i: 0 \leqslant i < n: P(i))$ as the inductive hypothesis. The basis $Q(0)$ is then vacuously true and only the inductive step requires a proof. This apparent gain may be illusory, however, since it is often necessary to give special treatment to the case when $n = 0$ in the inductive step.)

As for simple induction, by altering the basis of the proof it is possible to apply strong induction to the proof of a property $P(n)$ for all integers $n \geqslant m$. Also, by adding the proviso $n < p$ to the inductive hypothesis it is possible to restrict the range of n to $m \leqslant n \leqslant p$.

Example

3.30 Very often in the analysis of algorithms we are faced with a *recurrence relation* whose solution expresses, for example, the worst-case running time of the algorithm. An example might be the following.

$$T(1) = 1$$
$$T(n) = 1 + T(1) + T(2) + \cdots + T(n-1) \text{ when } n > 1.$$

The problem is to find a closed formula for $T(n)$. In this case by writing down a few values

$$T(1) = 1, \quad T(2) = 2, \quad T(3) = 4, \quad T(4) = 8$$

it is plausible to guess that $T(n) = 2^{n-1}$ for all $n \geq 1$.
Let us first use strong induction to verify this guess.

(a) Basis. $T(1) = 1 = 2^{1-1}$.
(b) Inductive step. Suppose $n \geq 1$, $T(1) = 2^{1-1}$, $T(2) = 2^{2-1}$, $T(3) = 2^{3-1}, \ldots, T(n) = 2^{n-1}$. Then $T(n+1) = 1 + 2^0 + 2^1 + \cdots + 2^{n-1}$
But we know from the last example that

$$2^0 + 2^1 + \cdots + 2^{n-1} = 2^n - 1$$

Hence $T(n+1) = 2^n = 2^{(n+1)-1}$.

We conclude by strong induction that $T(n) = 2^{n-1}$ for all $n \geq 1$.

Exercise
3.31 Prove the latter result using simple induction.
(*Hint*: begin by rewriting the definition of $T(n)$.)

Example
(Fibonacci Numbers)
3.31 The recurrence relation

$$F_0 = 0, \tag{3.26}$$

$$F_1 = 1, \tag{3.27}$$

$$F_{n+2} = F_{n+1} + F_n, \; n \geq 0 \tag{3.28}$$

defines the Fibonacci numbers. The first few elements in this sequence are

$$0, \quad 1, \quad 1, \quad 2, \quad 3, \quad 5, \quad 8, \quad 13, \quad 21, \ldots.$$

The Fibonacci sequence has a number of remarkable properties which are discussed in depth in many textbooks. Many involve its relationship to the *golden ratio*, *G*, where

$$G = (1 + \sqrt{5})/2$$

G is one of the roots of the equation

$$c^2 - c - 1 = 0.$$

(In other words, $G^2 - G - 1 = 0$.) The other root is

$$G' = (1 - \sqrt{5})/2.$$

Here we use strong induction to prove that

$$G^{n-2} \leq F_n \leq G^{n-1} \text{ when } n \geq 1 \tag{3.29}$$

The exercises ask you to prove further properties of F_n.

(a) Basis. It is important to be careful in the proof of any theorem about F_n because the formula (3.28) only applies when $n \geq 0$. It is very easy to quote it when, in fact, it is not applicable. In addition, in this particular case, our claim (3.29) is made for $n \geq 1$ and not for $n = 0$ (it is false in the latter case), yet F_2 is defined in terms of F_0. This obliges us to make F_1 and F_2 the basis of our proof.
Now $\sqrt{5} > 1$. So $G = (1 + \sqrt{5})/2 > 1$ and $G^{-1} < 1$. Also $G^0 = 1$.
Therefore $\qquad\qquad G^{-1} \leq F_1 = 1 \leq G^0$
and $\qquad\qquad\qquad G^0 \leq F_2 = 1 \leq G^1$.

(b) Inductive step. Suppose $n \geq 2$ and, for all k, $1 \leq k \leq n$, $G^{k-2} \leq F_k \leq G^{k-1}$ (inductive hypothesis).
Then $n + 1 > 2$ and so

$$F_{n+1} = F_n + F_{n-1}. \tag{3.30}$$

So, by the inductive hypothesis,

$$G^{n-2} \leq F_n \leq G^{n-1}, \tag{3.31}$$

$$G^{n-3} \leq F_{n-1} \leq G^{n-2} \tag{3.32}$$

and $\qquad\qquad G^{n-2} + G^{n-3} \leq F_{n+1} \leq G^{n-1} + G^{n-2}$.
But $\qquad\qquad\qquad\qquad G^2 = 1 + G$.
Therefore $\qquad G^{n-2} + G^{n-3} = G^{n-3}(1 + G) = G^{n-1}$
and $\qquad\qquad\qquad G^{n-1} + G^{n-2} = G^n$.
Consequently $\qquad\qquad G^{n-1} \leq F_{n+1} \leq G^n$,
i.e. $\qquad\qquad G^{(n+1)-2} \leq F_{n+1} \leq G^{(n+1)-1}$.

We conclude by strong induction that $G^{n-2} \leq F_n \leq G^{n-1}$ for all $n \geq 1$.

Look again at this proof to ensure that you have understood the use of strong induction. Its use, rather than simple induction, was necessary when we made statements (3.31) and (3.32).

It is also worth looking again at the warnings we made before establishing the basis of the proof. The real significance of these warnings only became apparent when we quoted equations (3.30), (3.31), and (particularly) (3.32). Satisfy yourself that they are correct and then determine why they would have been incorrect had the basis excluded the case $n = 2$.

Exercises

3.32 Prove that $F_{n+1} * F_{n-1} - (F_n)^2 = (-1)^n$ for all $n \geq 1$.

3.33 Here is a proof that $F_n = 0$ for all $n \geq 0$.
What is wrong with it?

(a) Basis $F_0 = 0$ by definition.
(b) Inductive step. Suppose $n \geqslant 0$ and $F_k = 0$ for all k, $0 \leqslant k \leqslant n$.
Then $F_{n+1} = F_n + F_{n-1}$

$$= 0 + 0$$
$$= 0$$

We conclude by strong induction that $F_n = 0$ for all $n \geqslant 0$.

3.34 There are three combinations of **true/false** values of p_0 and p_1 for which $p_0 \Rightarrow p_1$ is **true**. There are five combinations of **true/false** values of p_0, p_1 and p_2 for which $(p_0 \Rightarrow p_1) \Rightarrow p_2$ is **true**.

Let Q_n denote $(\ldots(p_0 \Rightarrow p_1) \Rightarrow \ldots) \Rightarrow p_{n-1})$ and T_n denote the number of combinations of **true/false** values for which Q_n is **true**. Prove that $T_{n+1} + T_n = 2^{n+1}(n \geqslant 2)$ and hence prove that $T_n = (2^{n+1} + 1)/3$ if n is even and $T_n = (2^{n+1} - 1)/3$ if n is odd.

3.4 WHILE STATEMENTS

3.4.1 Weakest Preconditions

When we discussed weakest preconditions in section 3.1 we deliberately glossed over the issue of termination—we were, after all, discussing nonrepetitive statements and so termination was always guaranteed. For looping constructs, however, termination is an important issue and we need to be much more careful about its role in our definition. Let us therefore recall the two most important definitions in section 3.1, the definition of $\{P\}\,S\,\{Q\}$ and $wp(S, Q)$.

$\{P\}\,S\,\{Q\}$ means that if the computation of S begins in a state satisfying P *and if S terminates* then the state will satisfy Q after execution of S.

$wp(S, Q)$ is the set of all initial states that *will guarantee termination of S* in a state satisfying Q.

Note the difference in these definitions: $\{P\}\,S\,\{Q\}$ *assumes* that S will terminate while $wp(S, Q)$ *guarantees* that S will terminate. This is an important difference and some terminology has been invented to stress its importance. Specifically, we say that a proof of $\{P\}\,S\,\{Q\}$ is a proof of the <u>conditional correctness</u> of S, i.e. a proof that S meets its specification *assuming* it terminates, while a proof that $P \Rightarrow wp(S, Q)$ is a proof of the *correctness* of S, i.e. a proof that S meets its specification *and* always terminates.

The criterion of termination is the basis for an inductive formulation of the weakest precondition of a **while** statement. Firstly we formulate the rule using a concrete example and then we derive it in more general terms. Consider the statement

$$\textbf{while } i \neq n \textbf{ do begin } i := i + 1; \quad s := s + i \textbf{ end}$$

with respect to the postcondition

$$Q \equiv s = n*(n + 1)/2.$$

We shall call the **while** statement W; the loop body, which consists of the two statements

$$i := i + 1; \quad s := s + i$$

will be called S.

Now if W is to terminate then S must be executed a finite number of times—either zero times, once, twice, three times, etc. Let us use k to refer to the number of iterations of the loop body before it terminates. We reason inductively:

(0) If $k = 0$ then $i = n$ and the postcondition Q must be automatically satisfied. In other words, the precondition is

$$P_0 \equiv (i = n) \textbf{ and } (s = n*(n + 1)/2).$$

(1) If $k = 1$ then executing W is equivalent to executing S from a state in which $i \neq n$. The postcondition is the conjunction of Q and $i = n$ (the condition that S is never executed again) which we observe to be P_0. Thus the required precondition is

$$P_1 \equiv (i \neq n) \textbf{ and } wp(S, P_0)$$
$$\equiv (i \neq n) \textbf{ and } (i = n - 1) \textbf{ and } (s + i + 1 = n*(n + 1)/2)$$
$$\equiv (i = n - 1) \textbf{ and } (s = (n - 1)*n/2).$$

$$s + n = n + (n+1)/2$$
$$s = \frac{n*n + n}{2} - \frac{2n}{2}$$
$$= \frac{n+n}{2} - n$$
$$= \frac{n*(n-1)}{2}$$

(2) If $k = 2$ then executing W is equivalent to executing S twice. The initial state must satisfy three conditions:

(a) $i \neq n$;
(b) after one execution of S, i is still different from n;
(c) after two executions of S, i equals n and $s = n*(n + 1)/2$.

Now looking carefully at (1) one sees that (b) and (c) can be combined into the condition that after one execution of S the condition P_1 holds. Thus

$$P_2 \equiv (i \neq n) \textbf{ and } wp(S, P_1)$$
$$\equiv (i \neq n) \textbf{ and } (i = n - 2) \textbf{ and } (s = (n - 2)*(n - 1)/2)$$
$$\equiv (i = n - 2) \textbf{ and } (s = (n - 2)*(n - 1)/2).$$

$$s + i + 1 = \frac{(n-1)*n}{2}$$
$$s + n - 1 = \frac{n^2 - n}{2}$$
$$s = \frac{n^2 - n - 2n + 2}{2}$$
$$= \frac{(n-2)(n-1)}{2}$$

A pattern is now emerging in the conditions P_k. To be precise

$$P_k \equiv (i = n - k) \text{ and } (s = (n - k)*(n - k + 1)/2)$$
$$\equiv (i = n - k) \text{ and } (s = i*(i + 1)/2).$$

But P_k is the condition which will guarantee Q after exactly k executions of S. The condition we want is that Q is guaranteed after either 0, 1, 2, 3, or more executions of S. Thus we conclude that

$$wp(W, s = n*(n + 1)/2)$$
$$\equiv \mathbf{E}(k: k \geqslant 0: i = n - k \text{ and } s = i*(i + 1)/2)$$

which simplifies to $i \leqslant n$ and $s = i*(i + 1)/2$.

You will also have seen a pattern emerging in the general case. Suppose we consider a **while** statement of the form **while** B **do** S with respect to a postcondition Q. Then we can compute in turn the following preconditions:

$P_0 \equiv (\textbf{not } B) \textbf{ and } Q,$	the condition that S is never executed but Q is guaranteed
$P_1 \equiv B \textbf{ and } wp(S, P_0),$	the condition that S is executed once after which Q is guaranteed
$P_2 \equiv B \textbf{ and } wp(S, P_1),$	the condition that S is executed twice after which Q is guaranteed
$P_k \equiv B \textbf{ and } wp(S, P_{k-1}),$	the condition that S is executed k times $(k > 0)$ after which Q is guaranteed.

Having done so we conclude that:

$$wp(\textbf{while } B \textbf{ do } S, Q) \equiv \mathbf{E}(k: k \geqslant 0: P_k).$$

Example

3.32 Suppose S is the program segment

$$j := j*i; \quad k := k + j; \quad n := n + 1$$

and W is

$$\textbf{while } n \neq m \textbf{ do } S.$$

Let Q be

$$k = (i^{m+1} - 1)/(i - 1) \text{ and } j = i^m$$

and assume that $i \neq 0$ and $i \neq 1$.

Then, to compute $wp(W, Q)$, we compute in turn the predicates

$$P_0 \equiv \textbf{not } (n \neq m) \textbf{ and } Q$$
$$P_r \equiv (n \neq m) \textbf{ and } wp(S, P_{r-1}) \text{ for } r = 1, 2, 3, \ldots.$$

Now $P_0 \equiv n = m$ and $k = (i^{m+1} - 1)/(i - 1)$ and $j = i^m$

$P_1 \equiv [n \neq m$ and $(n + 1 = m)$ and

$\qquad k + j*i = (i^{m+1} - 1)/(i - 1)$ and $j*i = i^m]$

$\qquad \equiv n = m - 1$ and $k = (i^m - 1)/(i - 1)$ and $j = i^{m-1}$.

$k + i^m = (i^{m+1} - 1)/(i-1)$

$k = \dfrac{i^{m+1}-1 - i^m(i-1)}{i-1}$

$= \dfrac{i^m - 1}{i-1}$

Similarly,

$\qquad P_2 \equiv n = m - 2$ and $k = (i^{m-1} - 1)/(i - 1)$ and $j = i^{m-2}$.

Thus we see inductively that

$\qquad P_r \equiv n = m - r$ and $k = (i^{m+1-r} - 1)/(i - 1)$ and $j = i^{m-r}$

$\qquad \equiv n = m - r$ and $k = (i^{n+1} - 1)/(i - 1)$ and $j = i^n$.

Thus $wp(W, Q) \equiv \mathbf{E}(r : r \geqslant 0 : n = m - r$ and $k = (i^{n+1} - 1)/(i - 1)$ and $j = i^n)$

$\qquad \equiv n \leqslant m$ and $k = (i^{n+1} - 1)/(i - 1)$ and $j = i^n$.

Exercises

3.35 Verify each of the following:

(a) Let S be

$\qquad i := i + 2; \quad s := s + n*i + k; \quad k := k + i; \quad n := n + 1.$

Let Q be

$\qquad s = m^3$ and $i = 2*m$ and $k = m*(m + 1) + 1.$

Let W be

$$\text{while } n \neq m \text{ do } S.$$

Then $wp(W, Q) \equiv n \leqslant m$ and $s = n^3$ and $i = 2*n$ and $k = n*(n + 1) + 1.$

(b) Let S be

$\qquad n := n + 1; \quad t := a + b; \quad b := a; \quad a := t.$

Let Q be

$\qquad c^2 - c - 1 = 0$ and $c^m = a*c + b.$

Let W be

$$\text{while } n \neq m \text{ do } S.$$

Then $wp(W, Q) \equiv n \leqslant m$ and $c^2 - c - 1 = 0$ and $c^n = a*c + b.$

(*Note*: make use of exercises 3.7 and 3.8 respectively.)

3.36 Compute $wp(W, Q)$ for the following combinations of **while** statement W and postcondition Q.

W	Q

(a) **while** $i \neq n$ **do**
    begin $k := -k; s := s + k; i := i + 1$
    end
	$s = 0$

(b) **while not** $odd(x)$ **do**
    begin $y := 2 * y; x := x$ **div** 2
    end
	$c = x * y$

(c) **while** $x \neq 0$ **do**
    begin $W(b); c := c - y; x := x - 1$
    end
	$c = x * y$

where $W(b)$ is the **while** statement given in (b) above.

3.37 Below is an alternative way of formulating the preconditions P_k in the definition of $wp(\textbf{while } B \textbf{ do } S, Q)$. We begin as in our previous formulation by saying that P_0 is the condition (**not** B) **and** Q. Now, for $k > 0$, P_k is the condition that guarantees Q after exactly k iterations of S. In other words, P_k satisfies the conjunction of the following conditions.

(0) B is initially true,
(1)   after one execution of S, B is still true,
(2)   after two executions of S, B is still true.
.
.
.
$(k-1)$ after $(k-1)$ executions of S, B is still true,
(k) after k executions of S, **not** B **and** Q is true.

Thus, letting S^k denote k iterations of S, we have

$$P_0 \equiv (\textbf{not } B) \textbf{ and } Q$$

and $P_k \equiv B \textbf{ and } wp(S, B) \textbf{ and} \ldots \textbf{and } wp(S^{k-1}, B) \textbf{ and } wp(S^k, \textbf{not } B \textbf{ and } Q)$
            for all $k \geqslant 1$.

This formula can be simplified further. Specifically, let

$$R_0 \equiv B$$

and $R_k \equiv wp(S^k, B)$ for $k \geqslant 1$.

Also, let

$$T_0 \equiv B$$

and $T_k \equiv R_k$ and T_{k-1}.

Then $T_k \equiv B$ and $wp(S, B)$ and $wp(S^2, B)$ and...and $wp(S^k, B)$.

So $P_k \equiv T_{k-1}$ and $wp(S^k, \text{not } B \text{ and } Q)$.

Prove, by induction on k, that

$$P_k \equiv B \text{ and } wp(S, P_{k-1}) \text{ for all } k \geqslant 1.$$

3.4.2   The while Rule

It should now be apparent that the weakest precondition of a **while** loop can be split into the conjunction of two predicates

     (a) the condition for termination of the loop

and   (b) an invariant condition.

In this section our intention is to analyze in more detail the semantics of a **while** statement with the objective of formulating a proof rule for such statements.

First let us use our understanding of weakest preconditions to formulate more precisely concepts (a) and (b) above, beginning with the condition for termination of a loop.

In fact, let us consider an *arbitrary* statement S (not just a **while** statement) and formulate a condition that guarantees its termination. One way to describe the *weakest* such condition is as the condition that will guarantee termination of S in an *arbitrary* state. We already have a notation for that: since **true** describes all states the weakest precondition that will guarantee termination of the statement S in one such state is

$$wp(S, \text{true}) \tag{3.33}$$

Pause a while to check this claim. Try it first on a concrete example such as the statement W: **while** $i \neq n$ **do** $i := i + 1$. You should be able to verify straightforwardly that $wp(W, \text{true}) \equiv i \leqslant n$.

What about an arbitrary **while** statement? In this case too we can reassure ourselves of the correctness of (3.33) by examining the form it takes. Thus, if W is **while** B **do** S, then

$$wp(W, \text{true}) \equiv \mathbf{E}(k: k \geqslant 0: P_k)$$

where $P_0 \equiv (\text{not } B) \text{ and true} \equiv (\text{not } B)$

                     $P_1 \equiv B \text{ and } wp(S, P_0) \equiv B \text{ and } wp(S, \text{not } B)$

and generally $P_k \equiv B \text{ and } wp(S, P_{k-1})$.

This looks right too since P_0 is clearly the condition required for zero iterations, P_1 is the condition required for one iteration and, inductively, P_k is the condition required for k iterations of the loop body.

Another check we can make is to observe that, for the **while** statement W, $wp(W, \textbf{true})$ is identical to $wp(W, \textbf{not } B)$. That is reasonable too because W will not terminate in an arbitrary state but in a state satisfying **not** B. (The formula $wp(W, \textbf{true})$ is the better one, though, because it is valid for all statement types, not just for **while** statements.)

Exercise

3.38 There are several other checks one can make—the preceding ones only checked the validity of (3.33) for **while** statements. What about assignments, conditionals, and sequential composition of statements?

Compute $wp(S, \textbf{true})$ for each of the above types of statement (for example, compute and simplify $wp(\textbf{if } B \textbf{ then } S, \textbf{true})$. Construct a simple example to demonstrate that $wp(S_1; S_2, \textbf{true})$ is not the conjunction of $wp(S_1, \textbf{true})$ and $wp(S_2, \textbf{true})$.

Let us now turn our attention to the invariant condition. When we say that I is an invariant of **while** B **do** S we mean that if S is executed with precondition I and S terminates then I will be a guaranteed postcondition. But $wp(S, I)$ is the weakest precondition that will guarantee postcondition I. So for I to be an invariant we must have:

$$I \textbf{ and } B \textbf{ and } wp(S, \textbf{true}) \Rightarrow wp(S, I) \tag{3.34}$$

That is, the conjunction of I, the condition for executing S and the termination condition for S must be at least as strong as the weakest precondition that will guarantee I after execution of S.

Exercise

3.39 Again you should check this formula against the examples and exercises given in the last section. Doing so will at least give you some confidence in your intuitive grasp of the notion. Other checks are to consider special cases of the invariant I. What about **true** and **false**? Both are invariants of any statement. Check the validity of (3.34) for each of them.

But what about the general case? Formula (3.34) only tells us something about what happens to I under a single execution but intuition tells us that if I is left unchanged after one execution of S it ought therefore to leave it unchanged after two, three, four, or any number of executions of S. Execution of W causes S to be executed an indefinite number of times so we should be able to formulate a theorem to the effect that if I is unchanged by S it is also unchanged by W. This is going to be our proof rule!

Before we can continue we need to establish more formally the connection between $wp(S, Q)$ and $\{P\} S \{Q\}$. We stressed earlier that a proof of $\{P\} S \{Q\}$ is a proof of *conditional* correctness only, that is correctness of S (with respect to

P and Q) assuming termination. We can express this formally as

$$\{P\}\,S\,\{Q\} \equiv [P \textbf{ and } wp(S, \textbf{true}) \Rightarrow wp(S, Q)] \qquad (3.35)$$

Formula (3.35) may be taken as the *definition* of $\{P\}\,S\,\{Q\}$. In words it reads as follows:

S is conditionally correct with respect to precondition P and postcondition Q if and only if the conjunction of P and the weakest precondition guaranteeing termination of S implies the weakest precondition that will guarantee termination of S in a state satisfying predicate Q.

Now we may return to the formulation of a proof rule for **while** statements. The rule, which we stated briefly earlier, is that if I is unchanged by a single execution of S then it is unchanged by the **while** statement W: **while** B **do** S. More precisely, in the notation of inference rules, this is

$$\frac{\{I \textbf{ and } B\}\ S\ \{I\}}{\{I\}\ \textbf{while } B \textbf{ do } S\ \{I \textbf{ and not } B\}}. \qquad (3.36)$$

Since we now have a formal definition of $\{P\}\,S\,\{Q\}$ in terms of weakest preconditions—our formula (3.35)—we ought to be able to derive (3.36) from the rule for computing $wp(\textbf{while } B \textbf{ do } S, Q)$. This we can indeed do as we shown in the next theorem, which Dijkstra has called the *fundamental invariance theorem.*

Theorem Suppose I **and** B **and** $wp(S, \textbf{true}) \Rightarrow wp(S, I)$. Then I **and** $wp(W, \textbf{true}) \Rightarrow wp(W, I \textbf{ and not } B)$ where W is the statement **while** B **do** S.

The statement of this theorem looks nothing like proof rule (3.36) but they are equivalent! All that has been done is to use (3.35) to transform the notation in (3.36) into the wp notation. Thus the supposition I **and** B **and** $wp(S, \textbf{true})$ is equivalent to the premise $\{I \textbf{ and } B\}\,S\,\{I\}$ of (3.36). Also the conclusion I **and** $wp(W, \textbf{true}) \Rightarrow wp(W, I \textbf{ and not } B)$ is equivalent to the conclusion $\{I\}$ **while** B **do** $S\{I \textbf{ and not } B\}$ of (3.36).

Proof We prove by induction on k that

$$I \textbf{ and } P_k(\textbf{true}) \Rightarrow P_k(I \textbf{ and not } B) \qquad (3.37)$$

where $P_0(Q) \equiv Q \textbf{ and not } B$

and $P_k(Q) \equiv B \textbf{ and } wp(S, P_{k-1}(Q))$

Note that, as in the definition of $wp(W, Q)$, $P_k(Q)$ is the weakest precondition guaranteeing termination of W in exactly k iterations in a state satisfying Q. Thus the induction hypothesis is that the conjunction of the invariant I and the weakest precondition guaranteeing termination of W in exactly k steps implies the weakest precondition guaranteeing termination of W in exactly k steps in a state satisfying I and not B.

The basis for the induction is the case $k = 0$. Here we have

I **and** P_0(**true**) $\equiv I$ **and true and not** B (by definition)
                            $\equiv$ **not** B **and** I **and not** B (trivially)
                            $\equiv P_0(I$ **and not** $B)$.

We have thus verified the basis.

Now, for the induction step, assume that the induction hypothesis (3.37) is true of k. Then

I **and** P_{k+1}(**true**)
     $\equiv I$ **and** B **and** $wp(S, P_k$(**true**))   (by definition)
     $\equiv B$ **and** I **and** B **and** $wp(S, P_k$(**true**))   (trivially)
     $\equiv B$ **and** I **and** B **and** $wp(S,$ **true**) **and** $wp(S, P_k$(**true**))
                                                              (**and**-distributivity)
     $\Rightarrow B$ **and** $wp(S, I)$ **and** $wp(S, P_k$(**true**))   (invariant condition on I)
     $\equiv B$ **and** $wp(S, I$ **and** P_k(**true**))   (**and**-distributivity)
     $\Rightarrow B$ **and** $wp(S, P_k(I$ **and not** $B))$
                              (induction hypothesis and $\Rightarrow$-distributivity)
     $\equiv P_{k+1}(I$ **and not** $B)$ (by definition)
i.e. I **and** P_{k+1}(**true**) $\Rightarrow P_{k+1}(I$ **and not** $B)$.

Thus, by induction, I **and** P_k(**true**) $\Rightarrow P_k(I$ **and not** $B)$ for all $k \geqslant 0$.

Hence I **and** $wp(W,$ **true**) $\equiv I$ **and** $\mathsf{E}(k: k \geqslant 0: P_k$(**true**))
                      $\equiv \mathsf{E}(k: k \geqslant 0: I$ **and** P_k(**true**))
                      $\Rightarrow \mathsf{E}(k: k \geqslant 0: P_k(I$ **and not** $B))$
                      $\equiv wp(W, I$ **and not** $B)$
     i.e. I **and** $wp(W,$ **true**) $\Rightarrow wp(W, I$ **and not** $B)$.

Exercises

3.40 The definition of $\{P\}\ S\ \{Q\}$ given by (3.35) can be used to reformulate the proof rule for conditional statements as follows.
Theorem If P **and** B **and** $wp(S_1,$ **true**) $\Rightarrow wp(S_1, Q)$ and P **and not** B **and** $wp(S_2,$ **true**) $\Rightarrow wp(S_2, Q)$ then P **and** $wp(S,$ **true**) $\Rightarrow wp(S, Q)$ where S is the statement **if** B **then** S_1 **else** S_2.
Prove this theorem.

3.41 Reformulate the proof rules for **if** B **then** S and $S_1; S_2$ in the same way and prove their validity.

3.4.3 Binary Search and Its Proof

At this point we return to our very first example algorithm, the search algorithm given in chapter 0. We present a simple implementation of it and then go on to present a formal proof of the correctness of the implementation.

You will recall the statement of the problem—to split an alphabetically ordered deck of cards into two decks in such a way that all of the cards in one deck and none of the cards in the other deck have names preceding a given name X.

Let us suppose that the deck of cards is represented by an array *card*. The declaration of *card* will take the form

card: **array** $[0..n-1]$ **of record**...
　　　　　　　　　name: *integer*
　　　　　　　　　　　...
　　　　　　　end

so that the name on the *j*th card is referenced by *card*$[j]$·*name*. The constant *n* is the number of cards in the deck.

With this implementation we can represent any portion of the deck by just two indices. Thus the (ordered) pair i,j: *cardindex* represents all of the cards in the array segment $i..j-1$. Furthermore this segment is empty if $i \geqslant j$. Consequently, we only need two indices—call them *l* and *u*, say—to represent the left, middle, and right decks. The left deck will be those cards in the array segment $0..l-1$, the middle deck will be those cards in the segment $l..u-1$, and the right deck will be those cards in the segment $u..n-1$.

Initially, the middle deck is the entire deck and the left and right decks are empty. Using our representation this becomes

$$l:=0; u:=n.$$

Subsequently, when we wish to remove all cards up to and including card *i* from the middle deck and place them in the left deck, it suffices to execute the assignment

$$l:=i+1.$$

Equally, when we wish to remove all cards from card *i* onwards (including card *i*) from the middle deck and place them in the right deck, we execute

$$u:=i.$$

In the algorithm on p. 7 we left unspecified the point at which to split the middle deck. As we remarked there, the choice does not affect the correctness of the algorithm although it does have a significant effect on its efficiency. Our representation suggests a simple strategy, namely, to split the middle deck at the point indexed by $i=(l+u-1)$ **div** 2, i.e. the lower deck becomes the array segment from *l* to $i-1$ and the upper deck becomes the array segment from *i* to $u-1$. Moreover, it is not too difficult to convince oneself that this is an efficient strategy since each time a card is inspected at least half of the middle deck will be removed from further consideration. Note, however, that we are now obliged to augment our proof with a proof that the upper deck is nonempty. (Remember that the proof of termination relied on the fact that the first card in the upper deck is always removed from the middle deck.) This amounts to showing that $l \leqslant (l + u - 1)$ **div** $2 < u$ whenever $l < u$—a claim which is certainly not obvious.

It is now straightforward to rewrite the algorithm in the following form.

```
l := 0; u := n;
while l < u do
    begin
    i := (l + u - 1) div 2;
    if card[i]·name < X then l := i + 1
                        else u := i
    end
```

Algorithm 3.2 Binary search.

Let us begin by establishing the conditional correctness of the algorithm using Hoare's proof rules. We must first formalize the output specification for the algorithm, which is that on termination l represents the boundary between those cards which precede X, and those cards which do not precede X in alphabetic order, i.e.

$$0 \leqslant l \leqslant n \text{ and } \mathbf{A}(j : 0 \leqslant j < l : card[j]·name < X)$$
$$\text{and } \mathbf{A}(j : l \leqslant j < n : card[j]·name \geqslant X).$$

Next we formalize the property maintained invariant by the body of the loop. Generally this will contain a clause describing the function of each variable in the algorithm. Here we will have two clauses, one describing l and the other describing u.

The crucial property of l is that the name on all cards inside the region $0 .. l - 1$ precedes X. Denoting this by $L(l)$ we have:

$$L(l) \equiv 0 \leqslant l \leqslant n \text{ and } \mathbf{A}(j : 0 \leqslant j < l : card[j]·name < X).$$

Similarly none of the cards in the region $u .. n - 1$ precedes X. We denote this by $U(u)$:

$$U(u) \equiv 0 \leqslant u \leqslant n \text{ and } \mathbf{A}(j : u \leqslant j < n : card[j]·name \geqslant X).$$

The loop invariant, which we denote by $I(l, u)$, is the conjunction of these two and a further limitation on the range of l and u:

$$I(l, u) \equiv L(l) \text{ and } U(u) \text{ and } l \leqslant u.$$

Given these definitions we can now annotate our algorithm with the most important elements of the proof as shown below.

{**Global Invariant: A**$(j, k: 0 \leqslant j \leqslant k < n: card[j] \cdot name \leqslant card[k] \cdot name)$}
$l := 0; u := n;$
{**Invariant:** $I(l, u)$}
{**Variant:** $u - l$}
while $(l < u)$ **do**
    begin
      {$I(l, u)$ **and** $l < u$}
      $i := (l + u - 1)$ **div** 2;
      if $card[i] \cdot name < X$ **then** $l := i + 1$
                              else $u := i$

    end
{$I(l, u)$ **and** $l \geqslant u$}
{$0 \leqslant l \leqslant n$ **and A**$(j: 0 \leqslant j < l: card[j] \cdot name < X)$
  and A$(j: l \leqslant j < n: card[j] \cdot name \geqslant X)$}

Algorithm 3.3 The main elements of the proof.

The next step is to fill out Algorithm 3.3 with additional assertions so as to form a proof 'tableau'. The requirement here is that every **while** statement, every conditional statement and every complete sequence of statements is parenthesized by a precondition and a postcondition.

The postcondition for the assignment to i is $l \leqslant i < u$. This property is essential both for the proof of conditional correctness and for the proof of termination.

The postcondition for the two assignments $l := i + 1$ and $u := i$ is just the loop invariant, since an aim will be to prove the latter's validity after each iteration of the loop body. The precondition for each of these statements is the conjunction of $I(l, u)$ and the condition under which the statement in question is executed. For instance, the precondition for executing $l := i + 1$ is

$$I(l, u) \text{ \textbf{and} } l < u \text{ \textbf{and} } l \leqslant i < u \text{ \textbf{and} } card[i] \cdot name < X.$$

In this way we arrive at algorithm 3.4.

(Note that it is extremely difficult to highlight additions or modifications in a textbook, particularly when the text being altered is already large and the changes are small. It is much easier to show the changes on a computer as, indeed, it is much easier to perform them. You should compare algorithm 3.3 with algorithm 3.4 and then concentrate your attention on the additions that have been made.)

{**Global Invariant: A**$(j, k: 0 \leqslant j \leqslant k < n: card[j] \cdot name \leqslant card[k] \cdot name)$}
$l := 0; u := n;$
{**Invariant:**$I(l, u)$}
{**Variant:** $u - l$}

```
while l < u do
    begin
    {I(l, u) and l < u}
    i := (l + u − 1) div 2;
    {I(l, u) and l ⩽ i < u}
    if card[i]·name < X
    then {I(l, u) and l ⩽ i < u and card[i]·name < X}
        l := i + 1
        {I(l, u)}
    else {I(l, u) and l ⩽ i < u and card[i]·name ⩾ X}
        u := i
        {I(l, u)}
    end
{I(l, u) and l ⩾ u}
{0 ⩽ l ⩽ n and A(j: 0 ⩽ j < l: card[j]·name < X)
and A(j: l ⩽ j < n: card[j]·name ⩾ X)}
```

Algorithm 3.4 The proof tableau for binary search.

It is now a relatively straightforward matter to write down a formal proof of the algorithm quoting the relevant proof rules. To do this one works from the innermost statements outwards, proving the correctness of each statement relative to the pre- and postconditions appearing in the tableau. Here then is the proof in full.

1. Correctness of **if … then** statement.

(a) By assignment axiom:

$\{I(i + 1, u)\}$

$l := i + 1$

$\{I(l, u)\}$

(b) By input assumption:

$card[i]·name < X \Rightarrow A(j: 0 ⩽ j ⩽ i: card[j]·name < X)$

(c) Hence,

$[card[i]·name < X \text{ and } I(l, u) \text{ and } l ⩽ i < u] \Rightarrow I(i + 1, u)$

(d) By (a), (c), and the consequence rule:

$\{card[i]·name < X \text{ and } I(l, u) \text{ and } l ⩽ i < u\}$

$l := i + 1$

$\{I(l, u)\}$

(e) Similarly,

$\{card[i] \cdot name \geqslant X$ **and** $I(l, u)$ **and** $l \leqslant i \leqslant u\}$

$u := i$

$\{I(l, u)\}$

(f) By (d), (e), and the conditional rule:

$\{I(l, u)$ **and** $l \leqslant i < u\}$

if $card[i] \cdot name < X$ **then** $l := i + 1$ **else** $u := i$

$\{I(l, u)\}$

2. Correctness of body of loop (i.e. $I(l, u)$ is an invariant).

(a) By assignment axiom:

$\{I(l, u)$ **and** $l \leqslant (l + u - 1)$ **div** $2 < u\}$

$i := (l + u - 1)$ **div** 2

$\{I(l, u)$ **and** $l \leqslant i < u\}$

(b) Assuming that $(2 * k)$ **div** $2 = k$ and that k **div** 2 is a monotonically increasing function of k:

$$l < u \Rightarrow l + u - 1 \leqslant u - 1 + u - 1 = 2 * (u - 1)$$
$$\Rightarrow (l + u - 1) \textbf{ div } 2 \leqslant 2 * (u - 1) \textbf{ div } 2 \equiv u - 1$$

and, similarly,

$$l < u \Rightarrow (l + u - 1) \textbf{ div } 2 \geqslant l$$

i.e. $l < u \Rightarrow l \leqslant (l + u - 1)$ **div** $2 < u$

Thus $I(l, u)$ **and** $l < u \Rightarrow I(l, u)$ **and** $l \leqslant (l + u - 1)$ **div** $2 < u$

(c) By (a), (b), and the consequence rule:

$\{I(l, u)$ **and** $l < u\}$

$i := (l + u - 1)$ **div** 2

$\{I(l, u)$ **and** $l \leqslant i < u\}$

(d) By 1(f), 2(c) and the rule of sequential composition:

$\{I(l, u)$ **and** $l < u\}$

$i := (l + u - 1)$ **div** $2;$

if $card[i] \cdot name < X$ **then** ... **else** ...

$\{I(l, u)\}$

(e) By (d) and the **while** rule:

$\{I(l, u)\}$

> **while** $l < u$ **do**
>   **begin** ...
>   **end**
> $\{I(l, u) \textbf{ and } l \geqslant u\}$

3. Correctness of initialization:

By straightforward application of the assignment axiom and the rule of sequential composition:

> $\{0 \leqslant 0 \leqslant n \textbf{ and } \textbf{A}(j: 0 \leqslant j < 0: card[\,j\,] \cdot name < X)$
> $\textbf{and } 0 \leqslant n \leqslant n \textbf{ and } \textbf{A}(j: n \leqslant j < n: card[\,j\,] \cdot name \geqslant X)\}$
> $l := 0; u := n;$
> $\{I(l, u)\}$

i.e. $\{0 \leqslant n\}\, l := 0; u := n \{I(l, u)\}$

4. Conclusion

Applying the rule of sequential composition to 2(e) and 3, we have:

> $\{0 \leqslant n\}$
> $l := 0; u := n;$
> **while** $(l \leqslant u)$ **do**
>   **begin** ...
>   **end**
> $\{I(l, u) \textbf{ and } l \geqslant u\}$

Finally, $I(l, u) \textbf{ and } l \geqslant u$ implies the output specification. So by the consequence rule we have:

> $\{0 \leqslant n\}$
> $l := 0; u := n;$
> **while** $(l \leqslant u)$ **do**
>   **begin** ...
>   **end**
> $\{0 \leqslant l \leqslant n \textbf{ and } \textbf{A}(j: 0 \leqslant j < l: card[\,j\,] \cdot name < X)$
> $\textbf{and } \textbf{A}(j: l \leqslant j < n: card[\,j\,] \cdot name \geqslant X)\}$

3.5   PROOF TABLEAUX AND VERIFICATION CONDITIONS

When we ask for a proof of correctness of a program we do not want the sort of formal step-by-step argument that we have been giving up till now. A clear, well-documented program is more to our taste and much more likely to convince us than a dry, mechanical argument. The art of good documentation is in hitting the right level of detail; too much is boring and swamps the code, too little is confusing.

In this section we discuss proof summaries in the form of proof tableaux. A *proof tableau* is a sequence of intermixed assertions and statements that begins and ends with assertions. A tableau is *valid* if:

1. whenever a triple of the form $\{P\}\ S\ \{Q\}$ occurs in the tableau the triple is a true proposition, and
2. whenever a pair of the form $\{P\}\ \{Q\}$ occurs in the tableau the assertion P implies the assertion Q.

According to this definition a proof tableau may vary considerably in the level of detail it provides. A tableau in which the only assertions are at the beginning and end of the program is simply a statement of conditional correctness of the code it contains. On the other hand, a tableau in which every statement is bracketed by assertions may be tantamount to a complete proof of conditional correctness. Intermediate to these two is a tableau in which assertions are attached to key points in the code, drawing the reader's attention to its most important aspects. We consider all three forms of tableau, beginning our discussion with the two extremes.

3.5.1 Complete Proof Tableaux

For a program consisting solely of the sequential composition of a set of assignment statements a complete proof summary may be generated mechanically from a statement of conditional correctness. For instance, beginning with the specification

$$\{even(k)\ \textbf{and}\ 0 < k\ \textbf{and}\ y * z^k = x^n\}$$
$$k := k\ \textbf{div}\ 2;$$
$$z := z * z$$
$$\{0 \leqslant k\ \textbf{and}\ y * z^k = x^n\}$$

$$(3.38)$$

a *proof summary* may be generated by applying the assignment axiom twice to the postcondition, thus obtaining:

$$\{even(k)\ \textbf{and}\ 0 < k\ \textbf{and}\ y * z^k = x^n\}$$
$$\{0 \leqslant k\ \textbf{div}\ 2\ \textbf{and}\ y * (z * z)^{k\,\text{div}\,2} = x^n\}$$
$$k := k\ \textbf{div}\ 2;$$
$$\{0 \leqslant k\ \textbf{and}\ y * (z * z)^k = x^n\}$$
$$z := z * z$$
$$\{0 \leqslant k\ \textbf{and}\ y * z^k = x^n\}.$$

$$(3.39)$$

We call (3.39) a proof summary because it contains all of the details necessary to construct a proof of conditional correctness of (3.38). Indeed, you are invited to refer back to example 3.18 which was indeed a formal proof of (3.39). The important points to note about that proof are

(a) The first three steps involve the use of substitution only; they do not depend in any way on the properties of the operators **div, ∗** or exponentiation.

(b) The juxtaposition of the two assertions

$$even(k) \text{ and } 0 < k \text{ and } y \ast z^k = x^n$$

and

$$0 \leqslant k \text{ div } 2 \text{ and } y \ast (z \ast z)^{k \text{ div } 2} = x^n$$

in (3.39) corresponds to the use of the consequence rule in steps 4 and 5 of the proof.

We can emphasize the purely *syntactic* nature of the first three steps by rewriting (3.39) using an abbreviation for the postcondition. Specifically, let

$$I(y, z, k) \equiv 0 \leqslant k \text{ and } y \ast z^k = x^n.$$

(The parameter y is unnecessary as yet but we exploit it later.) Then (3.39) becomes:

$$\{even(k) \text{ and } 0 < k \text{ and } I(y, z, k)\}$$
$$\{I(y, z \ast z, k \text{ div } 2)\}$$
$$k := k \text{ div } 2; \hspace{4cm} (3.40)$$
$$\{I(y, z \ast z, k)\}$$
$$z := z \ast z$$
$$\{I(y, z, k)\}.$$

It is abundantly clear from (3.40) that the least obvious part of the proof is the use of the consequence rule, the first three steps being purely mechanical. It is fitting therefore that we abbreviate the tableau to draw attention to this point:

$$\{even(k) \text{ and } 0 < k \text{ and } I(y, z, k)\}$$
$$\{I(y, z \ast z, k \text{ div } 2)\}$$
$$k := k \text{ div } 2; \hspace{4cm} (3.41)$$
$$z := z \ast z$$
$$\{I(y, z, k)\}.$$

When a pair $\{P\}$ $\{Q\}$ appears in a tableau the associated implication is called a *verification condition*. Such conditions form the crux of a proof of conditional correctness, the remainder of the proof being a routine application of the proof rules. Indeed, this is illustrated by our example in which the verification condition is

$$even(k) \text{ and } 0 < k \text{ and } I(y, z, k) \Rightarrow I(y, z \ast z, k \text{ div } 2).$$

This is a formal way of saying that $(z*z)^{k\,\mathbf{div}\,2} = z^k$ when k is an even integer, and is essential to any attempt at understanding the effect of the two assignments in (3.41).

Exercise
3.42 Assuming the above definition of I, generate a proof tableau similar to (3.39) from the following specification. What is the verification condition so generated?

$$
\begin{aligned}
&\{0 \neq k \text{ and } I(y, z, k)\} \\
&k := k - 1; \\
&y := y*z \\
&\{I(y, z, k)\}
\end{aligned}
\tag{3.42}
$$

When a program contains conditional statements it is also routine to generate a complete proof summary from a statement of conditional correctness. In essence, given a specification of the form

$$\{P\} \text{ if } B \text{ then } S_1 \text{ else } S_2 \{Q\}$$

we construct the tableau

$$
\begin{aligned}
&\{P\} \\
&\text{if } B \\
&\text{then } \{P \text{ and } B\} S_1 \{Q\} \\
&\text{else } \{P \text{ and not } B\} S_2 \{Q\}
\end{aligned}
$$

A dummy **else**-part must be introduced when a conditional statement does not already have one, so that the proof summary for the specification

$$\{P\} \text{ if } B \text{ then } S \{Q\}$$

takes the form

$$
\begin{aligned}
&\{P\} \\
&\text{if } B \\
&\text{then } \{P \text{ and } B\} \ S \ \{Q\} \\
&\text{else } \{P \text{ and not } B\} \ \{Q\}
\end{aligned}
$$

Note that, in accordance with our understanding of the juxtaposition of two assertions, the occurrence of

$$\{P \text{ and not } B\} \ \{Q\}$$

in the **else**-part of this specification summarizes that step in the use of the conditional rule that entails verifying

$$P \text{ and not } B \Rightarrow Q.$$

An example of such a proof summary may be obtained by combining the tableau (3.41) with that from the last exercise.

$\{0 < k \text{ and } I(y, z, k)\}$
if *even*(k)
then begin
    $\{even(k) \text{ and } 0 < k \text{ and } I(y, z, k)\}$
    $k := k \text{ div } 2;$
    $z := z * z$
    $\{I(y, z, k)\}$
    end
else begin
    $\{(\textbf{not } even(k)) \text{ and } 0 < k \text{ and } I(y, z, k)\}$
    $k := k - 1;$
    $y := y * z$
    $\{I(y, z, k)\}$
    end

Exercise

3.43 Construct a complete proof summary from the following tableau. What are the verification conditions so generated?

$\{0 \neq k \text{ and } I(y, z, k)\}$
if *odd*(k)
then begin
    $k := k - 1;$
    $y := y * z$
    end;
$\{even(k) \text{ and } I(y, z, k)\}$
$k := k \text{ div } 2;$
$z := z * z$
$\{I(y, z, k)\}$

When a program contains **while** statements it is vital that each be annotated with an invariant property; otherwise it requires considerable ingenuity to construct a proof. However, given the relevant invariants, a proof summary becomes routine once more. For a **while** statement of the form **while** *B* **do** *S* with invariant property *I* equivalent to precondition *P* the proof tableau takes the following form:

$\{\textbf{Invariant: } I\}$
while *B* **do**
    $\{I \text{ and } B\} \, S \, \{I\}$
$\{I \text{ and not } B\}$
$\{Q\}$

The only verification condition generated is

$$I \textbf{ and not } B \Rightarrow Q$$

i.e. the conjunction of the invariant and the termination condition implies the postcondition.

Continuing our example, for the code

```
{0 ≤ n}
y := 1; z := x; k = n;
{Invariant: I(y, z, k)}
while 0 ≠ k do
        begin
            k := k − 1; y := y∗z
        end
{y = xⁿ}
```

we first construct a proof tableau for the initialization and the **while** statement:

```
{0 ≤ n}
{I(1, x, n)}
y := 1;
{I(y, x, n)}
z := x;
{I(y, z, n)}
k := n;
{Invariant: I(y, z, k)}
while 0 ≠ k do
    begin
        {I(y, z, k) and 0 ≠ k}
        k := k − 1; y := y∗z
        {I(y, z, k)}
    end
{I(y, z, k) and 0 = k}
{y = xⁿ}
```

This produces two verification conditions, one for the initialization,

$$0 \leqslant n \Rightarrow I(1, x, n)$$

and one for the termination condition,

$$I(y, z, k) \textbf{ and } 0 = k \Rightarrow y = x^n.$$

Now we use the solution to exercise 3.42 to generate a complete proof tableau:

```
{0 ≤ n}
{I(1, x, n)}
```

$y := 1;$
$\{I(y, x, n)\}$
$z := x;$
$\{I(y, z, n)\}$
$k := n;$
{**Invariant:** $I(y, z, k)$}
while $0 \neq k$ **do**
    begin
        $\{I(y, z, k) \textbf{ and } 0 \neq k\}$
        $\{I(y*z, z, k - 1)\}$
        $k := k - 1;$
        $\{I(y*z, z, k)\}$
        $y := y*z$
        $\{I(y, z, k)\}$
    end
$\{I(y, z, k) \textbf{ and } 0 = k\}$
$\{y = x^n\}$

and a third verification condition

$$I(y, z, k) \textbf{ and } 0 \neq k \Rightarrow I(y*z, z, k - 1)\}$$

Substituting the definition of $I(y, z, k)$, these three verification conditions, which clearly summarize a proof of conditional correctness of the program with respect to the precondition $0 \leq n$ and postcondition $y = x^n$, are as follows.

(Initialization) $0 \leq n \Rightarrow 1*x^n = x^n \textbf{ and } 0 \leq n$
(Loop termination) $y*z^k = x^n \textbf{ and } 0 \leq k \textbf{ and } 0 = k \Rightarrow y = x^n$
(Loop body) $y*z^k = x^n \textbf{ and } 0 \leq k \textbf{ and } 0 \neq k$
                      $\Rightarrow (y*z)*z^{k-1} = x^n \textbf{ and } 0 \leq k - 1$

Exercise

3.44 Construct the complete proof tableau for the following code. (Make use of the preceding material of course.) List the verification conditions.

$\{0 \leq n\}$
$k := n;\ y := 1;\ z := x;$
{**Invariant:** $I(y, z, k) \equiv y*z^k = x^n \textbf{ and } 0 \leq k$}
while $0 \neq k$ **do**
    begin
        if $odd(k)$
        then begin
            $k := k - 1;$
            $y := y*z$
        end;

$$\{even(k) \textbf{ and } I(y, z, k)\}$$
$$k := k \textbf{ div } 2;$$
$$z := z*z$$

end
$$\{y = x^n\}$$

3.5.2 A Minimal Set of Verification Conditions

A complete proof tableau in which every statement is parenthesized by pre-
and postconditions is clearly grossly extravagant in the level of detail it
provides. Indeed, using our knowledge of weakest preconditions of nonloop-
ing statements it is possible to describe an algorithm that generates a
complete Hoare-style proof of conditional correctness of statement S with
respect to precondition P and postcondition Q provided only that an invariant
property is specified for each **while** statement in S. In principle, therefore, a
theorem prover capable of verifying conditions of the form $P \Rightarrow R$ could be
used to completely automate proofs of conditional correctness. Whether such
a theorem prover can be developed or not is beside the point; the main
significance of this remark is that it is the use of the consequence rule and the
invention of invariants which form the crux of a proof of conditional
correctness.

   We refrain from describing the algorithm to generate Hoare-style proofs;
instead, we abstract from it the process of generating a set of verification
conditions. Consider, therefore, an arbitrary program segment S with specified
pre- and postconditions P and Q, respectively. A precondition $pre(S, Q)$ and
two sets of verification conditions $V'(S, Q)$ and $V(P, S, Q)$ are constructed from
P, S and Q as follows.

1. If S is the assignment $x := e$ then $pre(S, Q)$ is $wp(S, Q)$ and $V'(S, Q)$ is empty.
2. If S takes the form $S_1; S_2$ then $pre(S, Q)$ is $pre(S_1, pre(S_2, Q))$ and $V'(S, Q)$ is
   the union of $V'(S_2, Q)$ and $V'(S_1, pre(S_2, Q))$.
3. If S takes the form **if** B **then** S_1 **else** S_2 then $pre(S, Q)$ is $(B \textbf{ and } pre(S_1, Q))$ **or**
   (**not** B **and** $pre(S_2, Q)$) and $V'(S, Q)$ is the union of $V'(S_1, Q)$ and $V'(S_2, Q)$.
4. If S takes the form **while** B **do** S_1 and I is the supplied invariant for S then
   $pre(S, Q)$ is I, and $V'(S, Q)$ is the union of $V(I \textbf{ and } B, S_1, I)$ and the singleton
   set containing the condition

$$I \textbf{ and not } B \Rightarrow Q.$$

5. In all cases $V(P, S, Q)$ is the union of $V'(S, Q)$ and the singleton set
   containing the condition $P \Rightarrow pre(S, Q)$.

The functions of $V'(S, Q)$, $pre(S, Q)$, and $V(P, S, Q)$ in this process are described
by the predicates:

(P1) If all verification conditions in the set $V'(S, Q)$ are valid then S is conditionally correct with respect to precondition $pre(S, Q)$ and postcondition Q.

(P2) If all verification conditions in the set $V(P, S, Q)$ are valid then S is conditionally correct with respect to precondition P and postcondition Q.

Property (P1) may be proved by induction on the 'size' of S, where the size of S is obtained by counting one for every occurrence of the symbols ':=', ';', 'if', and 'while' in S; property (P2) is then an immediate consequence.

Note that $pre(S, Q)$ differs from $wp(S, Q)$ only where **while** statements are involved. This is a recognition of the impossibility, in general, of deriving a closed formula for the weakest precondition for a **while** statement and emphasizes the importance of including invariant properties in the program documentation.

Examples

3.33 For a simple sequential composition, S_1,

$$s := s + a[k]; \; k := k + 1$$

with postcondition $I(k, s) \equiv (s = \mathbf{S}(i: 0 \leqslant i < k: a[i]))$ and precondition $I(k, s)$ **and** $k \neq n$ we find by applying steps 1 and 2 that $V'(S_1, I(k, s))$ is empty, $pre(S_1, I(k, s))$ is $I(k + 1, s + a[k])$ and the set of verification conditions $V(I(k, s)$ **and** $k \neq n, S_1, I(k, s))$ contains the single condition

$$I(k, s) \text{ and } k \neq n \Rightarrow I(k + 1, s + a[k])$$

i.e. $s = \mathbf{S}(i: 0 \leqslant i < k: a[i])$ **and** $k \neq n$

$$\Rightarrow s + a[k] = \mathbf{S}(i: 0 \leqslant i < k + 1: a[i]). \tag{3.43}$$

3.34 Consider the following program for summing the elements of an array.

$$\{0 \leqslant n\}$$
$$k := 0; \; s := 0;$$
$$\{\textbf{Invariant: } I(k, s) \equiv s = \mathbf{S}(i: 0 \leqslant i < k: a[i])\}$$
$$\textbf{while } k \neq n \textbf{ do}$$
$$\quad \textbf{begin}$$
$$\quad\quad s := s + a[k]; \; k := k + 1$$
$$\quad \textbf{end}$$
$$\{s = \mathbf{S}(i: 0 \leqslant i < n: a[i])\}$$

Splitting the program first into the sequential composition, S_0,

$$k := 0; \; s := 0$$

and the **while** statement, W,

> **while** $k \neq n$ **do**
>   **begin**
> $s := s + a[k]; k := k + 1$
>   **end**

we are directed by rule 2 to compute $pre(W, Q)$ and $V'(W, Q)$ where Q is the postcondition

$$s = \mathbf{S}(i: 0 \leqslant i < n: a[i]).$$

Now, by rule 4,

$$pre(W, Q) \equiv I(k, s) \equiv s = \mathbf{S}(i: 0 \leqslant i < k: a[i]).$$

Also $V'(W, Q)$ consists of $V(I(k, s)$ **and** $k \neq n, S_1, I(k, s))$ where S_1 is as defined in example 3.33, and the condition

$$I(k, s) \text{ **and** } k = n \Rightarrow s = \mathbf{S}(i: 0 \leqslant i < n: a[i])$$

i.e. $s = \mathbf{S}(i: 0 \leqslant i < k: a[i]) \text{ **and** } k = n$

$$\Rightarrow s = \mathbf{S}(i: 0 \leqslant i < n: a[i]) \tag{3.44}$$

Finally, as in example 3.33, we find that

$$pre(S_0, I(k, s)) \equiv 0 = \mathbf{S}(i: 0 \leqslant i < 0: a[i])$$

and the set of verification conditions for S_0 consists of the sole condition

$$0 \leqslant n \Rightarrow pre(S_0, I(k, s))$$

i.e. $0 \leqslant n \Rightarrow 0 = \mathbf{S}(i: 0 \leqslant i < 0: a[i]).$ $\qquad$ (3.45)

Thus there are three verification conditions for the program, conditions (3.43), (3.44) and (3.45).

4 PROGRAM CONSTRUCTION

Our method improves by proving

Imre Lakatos

4.1 PROBLEM-SOLVING STRATEGIES

It is now time to alter our view of the proof rules and to begin to regard them not as tools for verifying the correctness of an algorithm once it has been developed but as the principal concepts guiding the actual development.

Let us, for the moment, regard a pair of predicates P, Q as a *problem*, and let us say that a statement S is a *solution* to that problem if $\{P\}$ S $\{Q\}$ and S is guaranteed to terminate. Then we can recognize certain well-known problem-solving strategies embodied in the proof rules.

One of the first problem-solving strategies we all learn is problem decomposition: can the problem be split into two or more simpler problems for which solutions are known? This strategy is apparent in the rule of sequential composition. For, if we can split the problem P, Q into two problems P, R and R, Q and discover solutions S_1 for the first and S_2 for the second, then $S_1; S_2$ is a solution for the original problem P, Q.

Example

4.1   A car is driven for k kilometers and the fuel consumption is l liters. Write a program to assign to y the amount of fuel consumed on a journey of x kilometers.

The solution is first to calculate the liters-per-kilometer (lpk) and then multiply this quantity by the journey length.

$\{l$ liters are consumed every k kilometers$\}$
$lpk := l/k;$

{lpk liters are consumed every 1 kilometer}
$$y := x * lpk$$
{y liters are consumed every x kilometers}

A second problem-solving strategy is case analysis: can the problem be split into particular cases each of which is known to have a solution? The conditional rule embodies this strategy. It says that if one can split the problem P, Q into two cases P **and** B, Q and P **and not** B, Q and discover solutions S_1 and S_2 for these then the statement **if** B **then** S_1 **else** S_2 is a solution to the original problem P, Q.

Example
4.2   The problem is to assign to z the maximum of the two integers x and y. This problem can clearly be solved in the case when $x \geqslant y$ by the assignment $z := x$. Also in the case when $x < y$ the problem is solved by the assignment $z := y$. Thus the solution to the general problem is

$$\textbf{if } x \geqslant y \textbf{ then } z := x \textbf{ else } z := y.$$

A third problem-solving strategy is apparent in the consequence rules, namely, is the given problem a special case of another problem whose solution is known? Formally, the problem P, Q is a special case of the problem P', Q' if $P \Rightarrow P'$ and $Q' \Rightarrow Q$, in which case any solution to P', Q' is a solution to P, Q.

Example
4.3   The problem is to write a program to count the number of lines in a text T. Suppose that we are provided with a function $NoOccurrences(ch: char; T: text): integer$ that counts the number, n, of occurrences of the character ch in the text T. Suppose, also, that every line of T is terminated by an end-of-line character EOL so that

$$n = no. \text{ of } EOL \text{ characters in } T \Rightarrow n = no. \text{ of lines in } T$$

Then $NoOccurrences(EOL, T)$ is a solution to the given problem.

These three strategies are the basis for what is popularly called *structured programming*. But, of course, they are not new to, or exclusive to, programming. Indeed, they are common to all disciplines. What may be claimed to be new to programming is assignment and the formation of loop structures. In this chapter our objective is to elucidate the problem-solving strategies embodied in the proof rules and, in particular, in the proof rule for **while** statements. The concept of an invariant plays a central role.

Because the concept is so new and unfamiliar even to experienced programmers, the question is often asked 'How do I discover an invariant for this problem?' This chapter attempts to give a partial answer to that question by considering a large number of problems and identifying common strands in their solution. But it cannot claim to give a complete answer to the question. Indeed, the same question may be asked of all the problem-solving strategies we have described. How does one split a problem into simpler problems? How does one identify one problem as a special case of another? And, how does one recognize subcases of a problem which are particularly amenable to solution? Ultimately, therefore, the answer must be 'By using your knowledge and experience, and by using your intelligence.'

The chapter is divided into several sections, each addressing problems of a similar nature. Each section begins with a relatively simple problem and then works progressively towards more complex problems. You may find it easier therefore to skip the later subsections of each section, at least on a first reading.

In the first section we begin with some simple arithmetic problems like summing the elements of an array and calculating x^m. These lead on to the discussion of the computation of 'cyclic codes' which are used in data transmission.

The second section is concerned with searching problems. The simplest possible search technique, the 'linear search', is tackled first, following which there are a number of miscellaneous searching problems, each of which imposes its own special conditions.

Sorting problems are discussed in the third section. The first of these, the so-called 'Dutch National Flag Problem', is a subroutine in a well-known sorting technique called 'quicksort'. It is a particularly good example of our development method. The discussions of 'bubblesort' and 'heapsort' that follow illustrate the use of formal predicates in documenting a program.

The problems discussed in the final section are called extremum problems, since they involve minimizing or maximizing some quantity. These problems provide some of the best examples of the use of the properties of quantifiers discussed in chapter 2.

4.2 BASIC ARITHMETIC OPERATIONS

In this section we consider several simple numerical problems, the objective being to illustrate the use of invariants in loop formation in the simplest possible context.

4.2.1 Summing the Elements of an Array

The first problem is to form the sum of the elements of a: **array**$[0..n-1]$ **of** *integer*, i.e. to compute

$$s = \mathbf{S}(i: 0 \leqslant i < n: a[i])$$

This elementary example illustrates one technique for formulating an invariant, namely the *replacement of a constant by a variable*. Specifically, we may replace the constant n by the variable k and rewrite the definition of s as

$$s = \mathbf{S}(i: 0 \leqslant i < k: a[i]) \text{ and } k = n.$$

In so doing we have re-expressed the required postcondition as the conjunction of two conditions, the first of which

$$s = \mathbf{S}(i: 0 \leqslant i < k: a[i])$$

will be our loop invariant, and the second of which

$$k = n$$

will be the termination condition.

The invariant is established by the two assignments

$$s := 0;\ k := 0$$

since then the summation is over the empty set. We make progress towards the termination condition by repeatedly incrementing k by 1 and in the process we maintain the invariant property by adding the next element of the array to s. Thus we obtain the following:

```
{0 ≤ n}
s: = 0; k: = 0;
{Invariant: s = S(i: 0 ≤ i < k: a[i])
 Variant: n − k}
while k ≠ n do
      begin
            s: = s + a[k]; k: = k + 1
      end
{s = S(i: 0 ≤ i < n: a[i])}
```

Note that the variant, $n - k$, is our measure of progress: it is bounded below by zero and is decremented by 1 at each repetition of the loop body.

Of course we could have begun instead by replacing the constant 0 in the postcondition by a variable. Had we done so we would have arrived at the following algorithm:

```
{0 ≤ n}
s: = 0; k: = n;
{Invariant: s = S(i: k ≤ i < n: a[i])
 Variant: k}
while k ≠ 0 do
      begin
            k: = k − 1; s: = s + a[k]
      end
{s = S(i: 0 ≤ i < n: a[i])}
```

4.2.2 Evaluating a Polynomial

A more complicated summation involves evaluating a polynomial. Specifically, suppose a: **array**$[0..n-1]$ **of** *integer*, x: *integer* and we are required to determine

$$s = \mathbf{S}(i\text{: } 0 \leqslant i < n\text{: } a[i] * x^i).$$

It is possible, of course, to regard this problem as a specific instance of the summation problem. An alternative method called *Horner's rule* is preferable because it uses fewer multiplications. Horner's rule involves computing in turn the values

$a[n-1]$
$a[n-1]*x + a[n-2]$
$(a[n-1]*x + a[n-2])*x + a[n-3]$
etc.

Functionally, we can describe Horner's rule as maintaining invariant the property

$$s * x^k = \mathbf{S}(i\text{: } k \leqslant i < n\text{: } a[i] * x^i)$$

The latter property can be established initially by the assignments

$$s := 0; \ k := n$$

and the required postcondition is achieved when

$$k = 0.$$

Making progress towards the termination condition above while maintaining the invariant implies the use of the two assignments

$$k := k - 1; \ s := s * x + a[k].$$

Thus the complete algorithm is as follows:

```
{0 ≤ n}
s := 0; k := n;
{Invariant: s * x^k = S(i: k ≤ i < n: a[i] * x^i)
  Variant: k}
while k ≠ 0 do
    begin
        k := k - 1; s := s * x + a[k]
    end
{s = S(i: 0 ≤ i < n: a[i] * x^i)}
```

4.2.3 Evaluation of Powers

The problem of evaluating x^m, $m \geqslant 0$, seems a trivial one but, in fact, it has been studied for thousands of years. The simplest solution is to replace the constant m in the postcondition

$$y = x^m$$

by the variable k, thus

$$y = x^k \text{ and } k = m.$$

Whence, by a now familiar process, we obtain:

```
{0 ≤ m}
k := 0; y := 1;
{Invariant: y = xᵏ;
 Variant: m − k}
while k ≠ m do
    begin
        y := y∗x; k := k + 1
    end
{y = xᵐ}
```

The obvious alternative is to initialize k to m and to decrement k continually by one. In this case the invariant property is

$$y \ast x^k = x^m$$

and the algorithm takes the following form:

```
{0 ≤ m}
k := m; y := 1;
{Invariant: y∗xᵏ = xᵐ
 Variant: k}
while k ≠ 0 do
    begin
        k := k − 1; y := y∗x
    end
{y = xᵐ}
```

Another method, which is commonly used for large values of m, makes use of Horner's rule. Suppose the binary representation of m is stored in the array a. Thus

$$m = \mathbf{S}(i : 0 \leqslant i < n : a[i] \ast 2^i)$$

Then Horner's rule for evaluating m suggests that x^m be calculated by computing in order

$$x^{a[n-1]}$$
$$x^{a[n-1]*2+a[n-2]}$$
$$x^{(a[n-1]*2+a[n-2])*2+a[n-3]}$$

etc.

Within the algorithm we use y to record the powers of x, and we use the value of k as variant. For the purpose of explaining the algorithm we also employ a variable s which records the exponent of x. To be exact, the functions of y, s, and k are expressed by the invariant properties:

$$y = x^s$$

where $\qquad s*2^k = \mathbf{S}(i: k \leqslant i < n: a[i]*2^i).$

The latter property can be established initially by the assignments

$$y := 1; k := n; s := 0$$

and, when $k = 0$, we have

$$y = x^s$$

where $s = \mathbf{S}(i: 0 \leqslant i < n: a[i]*2^i)$, i.e. $y = x^m$.

To maintain the property of s invariant after decrementing k by 1 we know from our discussion of Horner's rule that we must perform the assignment

$$s := 2*s + a[k].$$

So to maintain the invariance of the property $y = x^s$ we must perform the assignment

$$y := y*y*x^{a[k]}.$$

Thus the algorithm takes the form

```
{0 ≤ m}
y := 1; k := n; s := 0;
{Invariant: y = xˢ where s*2^k = S(i: k ≤ i < n: a[i]*2^i)
 Variant: k}
while k ≠ 0 do
    begin
        k := k - 1; s := 2*s + a[k]; y := y*y*x^a[k]
    end
{y = xᵐ where m = S(i: 0 ≤ i < n: a[i]*2^i)}
```

Two small changes are required before our task is complete. The first is to remove the assignments to s since their only purpose was to explain the operations on y and they have no effect on the latter's value. The second is to take account of the binary value of $a[k]$. Thus when $a[k] = 0$ the assignment to y simplifies to $y := y*y$ and when $a[k] = 1$ it simplifies to $y := y*y*x$. In this way we obtain the algorithm's final version.

$\{0 \leqslant m = \mathbf{S}(i: 0 \leqslant i < n: a[i] * 2^i)\}$
$y := 1; \, k := n;$
$\{$**Invariant:** $y = x^s$ where $s * 2^k = \mathbf{S}(i: k \leqslant i < n: a[i] * 2^i)$
   Variant: $k\}$
while $k \neq 0$ **do**
      begin
            $k := k - 1; \, y := y*y;$
               if $a[k] = 1$ **then** $y := y*x$
      end
$\{y = x^m$ where $m = \mathbf{S}(i: 0 \leqslant i < n: a[i] * 2^i)\}$

The previous algorithm made use of the digits in the binary representation of m in the order $a[n-1]$, $a[n-2]$, ..., $a[0]$. There is an advantage in processing them in the opposite order since they can be computed as the remainders resulting from successive divisions by 2. (Thus $a[0] = m \bmod 2$, $a[1] = (m \operatorname{div} 2) \bmod 2$, $a[2] = (m \operatorname{div} 4) \bmod 2$, etc.) An algorithm that uses this approach is based on maintaining the invariant

$$y * z^k = x^m \text{ and } k \geqslant 0.$$

This property is established by the assignments

$$y := 1; \, z := x; \, k := m$$

and, moreover, when $k = 0$ we obtain

$$y = x^m.$$

To make progress to the latter condition we may perform the operation

$$k := k - 1; \, y := y*z$$

but in the case where k is even we may also perform the operation

$$k := k \operatorname{div} 2; \, z := z*z.$$

The latter operation clearly reduces k by a larger amount and so is preferable to the former. Now, we note that decreasing k by one always changes an odd value to an even value so that the sequential composition

if $odd(k)$ **then begin** $k := k - 1; \, y := y*z$
                        end;
$k := k \operatorname{div} 2; \, z := z*z$

also maintains the invariant. Thus we obtain the following algorithm.

$\{0 \leqslant m\}$
$y := 1;\ z := x;\ k := m;$
$\{$**Invariant:** $y * z^k = x^m$ and $k \geqslant 0$
 Variant: $k\}$
while $k \neq 0$ **do**
      begin
                if $odd(k)$ **then begin** $k := k - 1;\ y := y * z$
                                           end;
                $k := k$ **div** $2;\ z := z * z$
      end
$\{y = x^m\}$

Note: the above algorithm was motivated by requiring that the bits of m be processed in the order $a[0], a[1], \ldots, a[n-1]$. Indeed, we may replace the variable k by a variable j with the property that

$$k = \mathbf{S}(i: j \leqslant i < n: a[i] * 2^i)$$

in which case the test $odd(k)$ is equivalent to the test $a[j] = 1$. In this way the algorithm may be rewritten as follows.

$\{0 \leqslant m = \mathbf{S}(i: 0 \leqslant i < n: a[i] * 2^i)\}$
$y := 1;\ z := x;\ j := 0;$
$\{$**Invariant:** $y * z^k = x^m$ where $k = \mathbf{S}(i: j \leqslant i < n: a[i] * 2^i)$
 Variant: $n - j\}$
while $j \neq n$ **do**
      begin
                if $a[j] = 1$ **then** $y := y * z$
                $j := j + 1;\ z := z * z$
      end
$\{y = x^m\}$

4.2.4 Remainder Computation

The computation of the remainder upon dividing the nonnegative integer p by the strictly positive integer q provides another simple example of invariants. Formally the requirement is that, given

$$0 \leqslant p \text{ and } 0 < q,$$

we are to compute the remainder r where

$$0 \leqslant r < q \text{ and } \mathbf{E}(d:: p = q * d + r). \tag{4.1}$$

For example the remainder on dividing 7 by 3 is 1 since $0 \leqslant 1 < 3$ and $7 = 3 * 2 + 1$.

$$
\begin{array}{ccl}
 & 1 & d_3 \\
 & 20 & d_2 \\
521 & 500 & d_1 \\
\hline
7)3653 & 7)3653 & r_0 \ (=p) \\
35 & 3500 & d_1*q \\
\hline
15 & 153 & r_1 \\
14 & 140 & d_2*q \\
\hline
13 & 13 & r_2 \\
7 & 7 & d_3*q \\
\hline
6 & 6 & r_3 \\
\text{(a)} & \text{(b)} &
\end{array}
$$

Fig. 4.1 Remainder computation in decimal arithmetic ($p = 3653$, $q = 7$). (a) Long-division; (b) filling in details.

The process of long-division, with which we are all familiar, suggests one algorithm. Figure 4.1(a) shows the computation by long-division of the remainder 6 when dividing 3653 by 7. Figure 4.1(b) explains the technique in rather more detail. From it we see that the process begins with the remainder r_0 equal to p (3653). At each subsequent step a multiple $d*q$ of q is subtracted from r thus forming the sequence of remainders r_1, r_2, and r_3. The process is terminated when the remainder is less than q. In Fig. 4.1 all the multiples take the form $a*10^i*q$ for some i. (Thus d_1 is $5*10^2$ and d_2 is $2*10^1$.)

Figure 4.2 shows the same process in binary arithmetic. Here the strategy is identical but the multiples of q subtracted from r all take the form $a*2^i*q$ for some i. Since binary arithmetic is more suited to computer implementation we adopt this approach.

$$
\begin{array}{ccl}
 & 1 & d_2 \\
101 & 100 & d_1 \\
\hline
101)11010 & 101)11010 & r_0 \\
101 & 10100 & d_1*q \\
\hline
110 & 110 & r_1 \\
101 & 101 & d_2*q \\
\hline
1 & 1 & r_2 \\
\text{(a)} & \text{(b)} &
\end{array}
$$

Fig. 4.2 Remainder computation in binary arithmetic ($p = 26$, $q = 5$). (a) Long-division; (b) filling in details.

Abstracting from long-division in binary arithmetic our strategy is to subtract successive multiples m of q from a remainder value r. Each multiple m is of the form 2^i*q for some $i \geqslant 0$. Thus the specification of m is

$$\mathbf{E}(i: i \geqslant 0: m = 2^i*q) \tag{4.2}$$

What about the successive values of r? Our objective here is to identify an invariant property and a termination condition such that their conjunction implies the postcondition (4.1). One such possibility is to postulate the invariant property

$$0 \leqslant r < m \text{ and } \mathsf{E}(d\text{::} p = q*d + r) \tag{4.3}$$

and the termination condition

$$m = q.$$

The skeleton of our algorithm thus takes the following form.

> *Initialize r and m to establish invariant;*
> $\{$**Invariant**: $0 \leqslant r < m$ and $\mathsf{E}(d\text{::} p = q*d + r)$
>   and $\mathsf{E}(i\text{::} i \geqslant 0\text{:} m = 2^i * q))\}$
>   **while** $m \neq q$ **do**
>   *Make progress to termination condition*
>   *whilst maintaining invariant*
> $\{0 \leqslant r < q$ and $\mathsf{E}(d\text{::} p = q*d + r)\}$

The initialization is slightly more complicated than in previous examples. Let us split the required invariant, which is the conjunction of (4.2) and (4.3), into four separate clauses – clause (4.2) and the clauses (4.4), (4.5), and (4.6) below.

$$0 \leqslant r \tag{4.4}$$

$$r < m \tag{4.5}$$

$$\mathsf{E}(d\text{::} p = q*d + r) \tag{4.6}$$

Now (4.6) can be ensured by the assignment

$$r := p$$

since then $p = q*0 + r$. It also has the effect of establishing the inequality (4.4), so we are left with the two properties (4.2) and (4.5). But these may be used as the basis for a loop with (4.2) acting as the invariant and (4.5) as the termination condition. Specifically, the assignment $m := q$ establishes, and the assignment $m := 2*m$ maintains the truth of, property (4.2) so that the sequential composition

> $m := q;$
> **while** $r \geqslant m$ **do** $m := 2*m$

guarantees the conjunction of (4.2) and (4.5).

Summarizing, the initialization of r and m involves executing the following statements.

$r := p;$
$m := q;$
while $r \geqslant m$ **do** $m := 2 * m$

Let us now turn to the loop body. Note that the loop body is only executed when $m \neq q$. Since we have also stipulated that it is to maintain (4.2) invariant we infer that the loop body is only executed when

$$\mathbf{E}(i: i \geqslant 1: m = 2^i * q)$$

We conclude that the assignment

$$m := m \ \mathbf{div} \ 2$$

will always make progress to the termination condition. However, by decreasing m we may violate (4.5). If so, we must also decrease r but at the same time ensure that (4.6) remains invariant. This is achieved by the assignment $r := r - m$, and the loop body therefore takes the following form.

$m := m \ \mathbf{div} \ 2;$
if $r \geqslant m$ **then** $r := r - m$

Exercise
4.1 Did you find the last paragraph convincing? Why not use a loop

$$\mathbf{while} \ r \geqslant m \ \mathbf{do} \ r := r - m$$

rather than the conditional statement? Do both have the same effect? Check the working by proving the invariant property formally, viz.

$\{\mathbf{E}(i: i \geqslant 1: m = 2^i * q) \ \mathbf{and} \ 0 \leqslant r < m \ \mathbf{and} \ \mathbf{E}(d:: p = q * d + r)\}$
$m := m \ \mathbf{div} \ 2;$
if $r \geqslant m$ **then** $r := r - m$
$\{\mathbf{E}(i: i \geqslant 0: m = 2^i * q) \ \mathbf{and} \ 0 \leqslant r < m \ \mathbf{and} \ \mathbf{E}(d:: p = q * d + r)\}$

To conclude, an algorithm for remainder computation is shown below.

$\{0 \leqslant p \ \mathbf{and} \ 0 < q\}$
$r := p;$
$m := q;$
$\{\mathbf{Invariant:} \ \mathbf{E}(i: i \geqslant 0: m = 2^i * q)$
  $\mathbf{Variant:} \ r - m\}$
while $r \geqslant m$ **do** $m := 2 * m;$
$\{\mathbf{Invariant:} \ 0 \leqslant r < m \ \mathbf{and} \ \mathbf{E}(d:: p = q * d + r)$
         $\mathbf{and} \ \mathbf{E}(i: i \geqslant 0: m = 2^i * q)$
  $\mathbf{Variant:} \ m\}$
while $m \neq q$ **do**

```
    begin
        m := m div 2;
        if r ⩾ m then r := r − m
    end
{0 ⩽ r < q and E(d:: p = q∗d + r)}
```

Exercise

4.2 Develop an algorithm that models long-division in base b arithmetic. Use two variables r and m whose function is specified by the following invariant property:

$$0 \leqslant r < m \text{ and } E(d:: p = q\ast d + r)$$
$$\text{and } E(i: 0 \leqslant i: m = b^i \ast q)$$

(*Hint*: the algorithm should be almost identical to the one above, but take note of the last exercise.)

The next algorithm is motivated by hardware rather than software considerations. Suppose that the integer p is stored in binary form as the sequence of bits $p[n-1], p[n-2], \ldots, p[0]$. Thus

$$p = S(i: 0 \leqslant i < n: p[i]\ast 2^i)$$
$$\text{where } A(i: 0 \leqslant i < n: p[i] = 0 \text{ or } p[i] = 1)$$

We envisage a situation where the requirement is to construct a 'black box' into which the bits of p are input one-by-one. When the last bit, bit $p[0]$, has been input it is expected that the remainder r should be ready for output from the black box after at most a constant delay. In other words, the number of operations executed after bit $p[0]$ has been input should be independent of n.

As in section 4.2.3, for the purpose of explanation, we introduce and later discard a variable s to represent an intermediate value of the bit sequence. Specifically, the variable s satisfies the invariant property

$$s\ast 2^k = S(i: k \leqslant i < n: p[i]\ast 2^i)$$

and the process of input into the black box is modeled by the following loop structure.

```
k := n; s := 0;
{Invariant: s∗2^k = S(i: k ⩽ i < n: p[i]∗2^i)
 Variant: k}
while k ≠ 0 do
    begin
        k := k − 1;
        s := 2∗s + p[k]
    end
{s = p where p = S(i: 0 ⩽ i < n: p[i]∗2^i)}
```

The next step is to introduce the variable r with the requirement that r is the remainder after dividing s by q. Formally,

$$0 \leqslant r < q \tag{4.7}$$

and $\mathbf{E}(d:: s = d*q + r)$ \hfill (4.8)

Since s is initially zero, it is clear that the initial value of r is also zero. Let us therefore investigate how the conjunction of (4.7) and (4.8) may be maintained invariant when the assignment $s := 2*s + p[k]$ has been executed. Considering (4.8) and supposing $s = d*q + r$,

$$
\begin{aligned}
2*s + p[k] &= 2*(d*q + r) + p[k] \\
&= (2*d)*q + (2*r + p[k]).
\end{aligned}
$$

Thus (4.8) is maintained invariant by the assignments

$$
\begin{aligned}
s &:= 2*s + p[k]; \\
r &:= 2*r + p[k].
\end{aligned}
$$

The second of these clearly increases r and so maintains invariant the inequality $0 \leqslant r$ appearing in (4.7). But it may violate the inequality $r < q$. Now supposing $r < q$,

$$
\begin{aligned}
2*r + p[k] &\leqslant 2*(q - 1) + 1 \\
&= 2*q - 1.
\end{aligned}
$$

So $2*r + p[k] < 2*q$

and $2*r + p[k] - q < q.$

Since we already know that the subtraction of any multiple of q from r maintains (4.8) invariant we conclude that the three statements

$$
\begin{aligned}
s &:= 2*s + p[k]; \\
r &:= 2*r + p[k]; \\
&\textbf{if } r \geqslant q \textbf{ then } r := r - q
\end{aligned}
$$

maintain invariant the conjunction of (4.7) and (4.8).

Finally, since none of the assignments to r or k involves s, we may discard s except for documentation purposes. The algorithm we have developed is thus as follows.

$\{0 \leqslant p \textbf{ and } 0 < q\}$
$r := 0; k := n;$
$\{\textbf{Invariant: } 0 \leqslant r < q \textbf{ and } \mathbf{E}(d:: s = q*d + r)$
                   where $s*2^k = \mathbf{S}(i: k \leqslant i < n: p[i]*2^i)$
   Variant: $k\}$
while $k \neq 0$ **do**

```
begin
    k:= k − 1;
    r:= 2*r + p[k];
    if r ⩾ q then r:= r − q
end
```
$\{0 \leqslant r < q$ and $\mathbf{E}(d:: p = q*d + r)$
        where $p = \mathbf{S}(i: 0 \leqslant i < n: p[i]*2^i)\}$

Exercises

4.3 Suppose the digits $p[0], p[1], \ldots, p[n-1]$ represent the value of p in base b, where $b \geqslant 2$, i.e.

$$p = p[0] + b*p[1] + b^2*p[2] + \cdots + b^{n-1}*p[n-1].$$

Generalize the algorithm above so that it inputs the digits of p in the order $p[n-1], \ldots, p[0]$, simultaneously computing the remainder r.

4.4 Suppose an algorithm is required which processes integers, each of which has the form 2^m*p for some $m \geqslant 0$ and $p \geqslant 0$. Develop an algorithm requiring n iterations to compute remainders, where n is the number of bits in the binary representation of p. Assume that the value of the remainder on division of 2^m by q is known and stored in the variable rm. In other words, the precondition is $0 \leqslant p$ and $0 \leqslant m$ and $0 \leqslant rm < q$ and $\mathbf{E}(d:: 2^m = d*q + rm)$.
(*Note*: you may choose to process the bits of p in the order $p[n-1], \ldots, p[0]$ or in the opposite order. The former is easier.)

4.2.5 Cyclic Codes

An interesting and practical application of the ideas in this section is to be found in data communication. When communicating information from one site to another, for example by long-distance telephone cable or by satellite, it is usual to *encode* the data in such a way that it is possible for the receiver to detect, and possibly correct, errors that have occurred in the process of transmission. This is achieved by adding redundant information to the message. One of the simplest possible encoding methods is to add a single *parity bit* to the end of a sequence of bits to ensure that the number of unit bits is always even (Fig. 4.3(a)). This method allows a single error in the transmitted data to be *detected*; if there are two or more errors then the transmitted data will be indistinguishable from a message containing zero or one error. Another method is simply to repeat each bit of data some constant number of times. This is called a *repetition code*. The threefold repetition code illustrated in Fig. 4.3(b) permits *correction* of a single error in the transmitted data.

```
000 | 0        0 | 00
001 | 1        1 | 11
010 | 1
011 | 0
100 | 1
101 | 0
110 | 0
111 | 1
  (a)            (b)
```

Fig. 4.3 Two examples of codes. The information bits are to the left of the dotted line. (a) Parity check; (b) threefold repetition code.

Redundancy in the transmitted data results from the fact that only a fraction of all n-bit sequences are ever transmitted. Thus of all 16 possible 4-bit sequences, eight may be transmitted when using a single parity check (Fig. 4.3(a)), and in a threefold repetition code (Fig. 4.3(b)) only two out of eight possible 3-bit sequences are ever transmitted. A *code of length n* is therefore defined as a subset of the 2^n possible n-bit sequences. A *codeword* is an element of the code. If there are k information bits in a code of length n then the *rate* of the code is expressed by the pair (k, n).

A very deep and elegant theory has been developed with the aim of predicting codes which maximize both the ratio k/n and the error detection/correction capability. Among such codes the class of *cyclic codes* has assumed a prominent role, and their use is recommended in several industry standards. In this section we develop encoding and decoding algorithms appropriate to the use of cyclic codes for error detection. Algorithms for error correction are equally fascinating but are beyond the scope of this text.

The idea behind cyclic codes is that a sequence of $n + 1$ binary digits p_0, $p_1, \ldots, p_n$ is regarded as a polynomial in x:

$$p_n x^n + p_{n-1} x^{n-1} + \cdots + p_1 x + p_0.$$

The bits p_0, $p_1, \ldots, p_n$ are called the *coefficients* and the variable x is regarded as a formal symbol having an indeterminate value. Such a polynominal is said to have degree n and leading coefficient p_n if p_n is nonzero. By convention '0', the polynomial whose coefficients are all zero, has degree $-\infty$.

There are many similarities between polynomial and integer arithmetic, arising from their representations as finite power series. Indeed, the fact that x has an indeterminate value in a polynomial but has the determinate value 2 in the binary representation of an integer often makes polynomial arithmetic easier than integer arithmetic. Thus polynomial addition is simply defined as the addition of corresponding coefficients,

$$p(x) + q(x) = r(x)$$

where $r(x) = (p_k + q_k)x^k + (p_{k-1} + q_{k-1})x^{k-1} + \cdots + (p_0 + q_0)$

$\qquad p(x) = p_k x^k + p_{k-1}x^{k-1} + \cdots + p_0$

$\qquad q(x) = q_k x^k + q_{k-1}x^{k-1} + \cdots + q_0$

and $\quad k = max(degree(p(x)), degree(q(x)))$.

(In the latter definition the coefficients p_i and q_j should be treated as zero if $i > degree(p(x))$ or $j > degree(q(x))$.)

In integer arithmetic there is the problem of 'carry'. For instance the computation of $1 + 1$ in binary arithmetic involves 'carrying' 1, since $1 + 1 = 1*2^0 + 1*2^0 = 1*2^1 + 0*2^0$.

A further simplification is also introduced into the addition of polynomials in coding algorithms, and that is to perform addition of coefficients modulo 2. In other words we define

$\qquad 1 + 1 = 0$

$\qquad 1 + 0 = 1$

$\qquad 0 + 1 = 1$

and $\quad 0 + 0 = 0$

so that, in particular,

$$x^m + x^m = 0.$$

This is the same as saying that the addition of polynomials entails **xor**ing corresponding coefficients. Note that it also means that subtraction is identical to addition since

$$x^m = -x^m.$$

Polynomial multiplication is defined by the rule

$\qquad p(x)*q(x) = r(x)$

where $r(x) = r_{m+n}x^{m+n} + r_{m+n-1}x^{m+n-1} + \cdots + r_0$

$\qquad p(x) = p_n x^n + p_{n-1}x^{n-1} + \cdots + p_0$

$\qquad q(x) = q_m x^m + q_{m-1}x^{m-1} + \cdots + q_0$

and $\quad r_i = p_0*q_i + p_1*q_{i-1} + \cdots + p_i*q_0$

(Once again, the coefficients p_j and q_k should be treated as zero if $j > n$ or $k > m$.)

Exact division of polynomials cannot be defined, just as it is impossible to define exact division of integers. Remainder computation can be defined, however, and it is this which is exploited in cyclic codes. To form a sequence of check digits from a *data polynomial* $P(x)$, a so-called *generator polynomial* $q(x)$ is used. Generator polynomials are chosen according to their error

detection/correction capabilities and are published in internationally recognized standards documents. The important thing, however, is that the
transmitter and receiver of the data both agree on which generator polynomial
to use.

The check digits are defined as the coefficients of the remainder polynomial
$r(x)$ after division of the *input polynomial* $p(x) = P(x) * x^m$ by $q(x)$, where m
is the degree of $q(x)$. The coefficients of the data polynomial are then transmitted, followed by the coefficients of the remainder polynomial. In effect
this is equivalent to transmitting $p(x) + r(x)$ which (since addition is equivalent
to negation in modulo 2 arithmetic) is divisible by $q(x)$. Thus the receiver
may check the accuracy of the received data by using the same algorithm
to compute a remainder polynomial, which should have the value zero.

Example
4.4 Using the generator polynomial $q(x) = x^5 + x^4 + x^2 + 1$, the message
1000100101 corresponding to the polynomial $P(x) = x^9 + x^5 + x^2 + 1$
would be encoded as 100010010100011. This corresponds to the polynomial $x^5 * P(x) + r(x) = x^5 * (x^9 + x^5 + x^2 + 1) + (x + 1)$. The remainder
polynomial $r(x)$ is found by determining that

$$x^5 * (x^9 + x^5 + x^2 + 1)$$
$$= (x^5 + x^4 + x^2 + 1) * (x^9 + x^8 + x^7 + x^3 + x^2 + x + 1) + (x + 1).$$

The precise specification of $r(x)$ is

degree$(r(x)) < m$ **and** $\mathbf{E}(d(x):: p(x) = P(x) * x^m = q(x) * d(x) + r(x))$
where $m = degree(q(x))$.

Note the similarity of this definition with the definition of remainders in
integer arithmetic

$$r < q \text{ and } \mathbf{E}(d:: p = q * d + r).$$

The simple parity check illustrated in Fig. 4.3(a) is the cyclic code resulting
from computing the remainder after division of the data polynomial by $x + 1$.
It is easiest to see this from the specification of the remainder polynomial. For
if $q(x)$ is $x + 1$ the remainder $r(x)$ is defined by

$$r(x) = r_0 \text{ and } \mathbf{E}(d(x):: p(x) = d(x) * (x + 1) + r_0).$$

Now suppose we evaluate $p(x) = x * P(x)$ at $x = 1$. Remembering that
$1 + 1 = 0$, $p(1)$ is $P_n + P_{n-1} + \cdots + P_0$ (modulo 2) which is 1 if the number of
nonzero coefficients of $P(x)$ is odd and is zero otherwise. But, again
remembering that $1 + 1 = 0$,

$$\mathbf{E}(d(x):: p(1) = d(x)*(1 + 1) + r_0)$$

i.e. $p(1) = r_0$.

Thus the remainder bit, r_0, is a simple parity check on the coefficients of $P(x)$.

Long-division

The process of long-division can be used just as well to compute polynomial remainders so long as we remember the rules of arithmetic. Figure 4.4 shows one such computation represented in two ways. In the first, the powers of x are made explicit and in the second a more concise form is presented.

Exercises

4.5 Check the calculations in Fig. 4.4 by showing that

$$x^5 + x^4 + x^3 + x = (x^3 + x^2 + 1)*(x^2 + 1) + (x + 1).$$

4.6 Use long-division to compute the remainder after division of the following polynomials by $q(x) = x^4 + x^2 + 1$.

(a) $x^8 + x^6 + x^4 + x^2 + 1$
(b) $x^9 + x^6 + x^3$
(c) $x^{10} + x^9 + x + 1$

Check your solutions as in exercise 4.5.

$$
\begin{array}{r}
1x^3 + 1x^2 + 0x + 1 \\
1x^2 + 0x + 1 \overline{\smash{\big)}\, 1x^5 + 1x^4 + 1x^3 + 0x^2 + 1x + 0} \\
1x^5 + 0x^4 + 1x^3 \\
\hline
1x^4 + 0x^3 + 0x^2 + 1x + 0 \\
1x^4 + 0x^3 + 1x^2 \\
\hline
0x^3 + 1x^2 + 1x + 0 \\
1x^2 + 0x + 1 \\
\hline
\text{Remainder} \quad = \quad 1x + 1
\end{array}
$$

$$
\begin{array}{r}
1101 \\
101 \overline{\smash{\big)}\, 111010} \\
101 \\
\hline
100 \\
101 \\
\hline
110 \\
101 \\
\hline
\text{Remainder} = 11
\end{array}
$$

Fig. 4.4 Long-division of polynomials.

To develop a long-division algorithm formally we introduce a variable k into the specification of $r(x)$.

$$k \leqslant degree(q(x))$$
$$\textbf{and } degree(r(x)) < k \textbf{ and } \mathbf{E}(d(x)::p(x) = q(x)*d(x) + r(x)).$$

The first conjunct will form the termination condition for a loop with the second and third conjuncts being used as invariants.

The invariant property is established by the assignments

$$r(x) := p(x); \; k := degree(r(x)) + 1;$$

and we can make progress to the termination condition by repeatedly decrementing k and then re-establishing the invariant.

> $r(x) := p(x); k := degree(r(x)) + 1;$
> $\{\textbf{Invariant}: degree(r(x)) < k \textbf{ and } \mathbf{E}(d(x)::p(x) = q(x)*d(x) + r(x))$
> $\textbf{Variant}: k - degree(q(x))\}$
> $\textbf{while } k > degree(q(x)) \textbf{ do}$
> $\textbf{begin}$
> $k := k - 1;$
>   *re-establish invariant*
> $\textbf{end}$

Now it is clear that re-establishing the invariant requires no action if the decrementation of k does not violate the inequality, $degree(r(x)) < k$. If the inequality is violated we must reduce the degree of $r(x)$ by adding a multiple of $q(x)$. Since $x^k + x^k = 0$, the addition of $x^{k-m}*q(x)$, where m is the degree of $q(x)$, will have the desired effect and we obtain our algorithm. You should compare this algorithm with the long-division algorithm for integers.

> $r(x) := p(x); k := degree(r(x)) + 1;$
> $\{\textbf{Invariant}: degree(r(x)) < k \textbf{ and } \mathbf{E}(d(x)::p(x) = q(x)*d(x) + r(x))$
> $\textbf{Variant}: k - degree(q(x))\}$
> $\textbf{while } k > degree(q(x)) \textbf{ do}$
> $\textbf{begin}$
> $k := k - 1;$
> $\textbf{if } degree(r(x)) = k$
> $\textbf{then } r(x) := x^{k-m}*q(x) + r(x)$
> $\textbf{where } m = degree(q(x))$
> $\textbf{end}$

Hardware Implementations

We said earlier that polynomial arithmetic is indeed simpler than integer arithmetic although, perhaps, less familiar. Several operations on polynomials

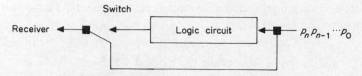

Fig. 4.5 Requirement on the implementation.

are also easily implemented directly in computer hardware. We now investigate the problem of remainder computation using these operations as building blocks.

The requirement on our implementation is to build logic circuitry that inputs the coefficients of the polynomial $p(x)$ one-by-one (Fig. 4.5). Coefficients are transmitted simultaneously to the receiver. When the last coefficient (p_0) has been input we want to throw a switch so that the coefficients of the remainder polynomial may now be transmitted to the receiver.

A shift register (Fig. 4.6(a)) is a fundamental component of computer hardware. It consists of an array of cells each of which is capable of storing one bit of information. On receipt of a signal its basic operation is to simultaneously 'shift' the contents of each cell into the next cell. Suppose we regard the contents $R_{m-1}, R_{m-2}, \ldots, R_0$ of the shift register as a polynomial $R(x) = R_{m-1}x^{m-1} + \cdots + R_1 x + R_0$. Then the shift operation corresponds to the operation

$$R(x) := (x * R(x) + i) \bmod x^m$$

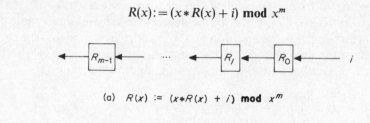

(a) $R(x) := (x*R(x) + i) \bmod x^m$

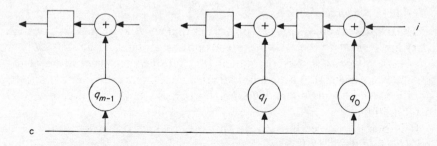

(b) $R(x) := (x*R(x) + i + c*q(x)) \bmod x^m$

Fig. 4.6 Shift register implementation of polynomial operations.

where i is the input bit introduced into the rightmost cell of the register. In this assignment the term $x * R(x)$ represents the shifting process, the addition of i represents the input of i, and the term **mod** x^m represents the loss of the leftmost bit of $R(x)$.

Using a shift register it is easy to implement the combined operation of multiplying a polynomial by x (i.e. shifting) and adding a multiple of a polynomial $q(x)$. Figure 4.6(b) shows the layout of such a circuit. In this figure the circles marked '$+$' represent an **xor** operation and those marked q_j represent the multiplication of q_j by some arbitrary value c. (Since $1 * c = c$ and $0 * c = 0$ the latter operation is in fact realized by a closed circuit if $q_j = 1$ and an open circuit if $q_j = 0$.) Thus the operation of the circuit in Fig. 4.6(b) corresponds to the assignment

$$R(x) := (x * R(x) + i + c * q(x)) \bmod x^m.$$

This assignment and the ability to initialize the register is all we need in the design of our algorithm.

Returning to the specification of the remainder polynomial and bearing in mind the structural requirements of the circuitry (Fig. 4.5) we see that, when the bit p_0 of $p(x)$ has been input, the contents of the shift register $R(x)$ should be the remainder polynomial $r(x)$, i.e.

$\mathbf{E}(d(x):: p(x) = q(x) * d(x) + r(x))$
where $m = degree(q(x))$
and $r(x) = R_{m-1}x^{m-1} + \cdots + R_1 x + R_0.$

Now a suitable invariant property for a loop that inputs the bits of $p(x)$ one at a time is that $R(x)$ should represent the remainder after dividing by $q(x)$ that part of $p(x)$ that has already been input. This can be expressed as

$$I \equiv \mathbf{E}(d(x)::p(x) = q(x) * d(x) + r(x))$$
$$\textbf{and } degree(R(x)) < degree(q(x))$$
$$\textbf{where } r(x) = x^k * R(x) + \mathbf{S}(i: 0 \leqslant i < k: p_i x^i).$$

The invariant I enjoys the two properties that we seek: it can be established by setting k to $n + 1$ ($= 1 + degree(p(x))$) and the contents of the shift register to 0. Also, when $k = 0$, the polynomial $R(x)$ satisfies the specification of the remainder polynomial. We must investigate maintaining I invariant under the operation $k := k - 1$, thus making progress towards the required postcondition.

It is possible to see how to do this by breaking down the terms of I. Consider first the term $x^k * R(x)$. Under a decrease of k by 1 we can maintain this polynomial constant by the operation

$$R(x) := x * R(x),$$

since $x^k * R(x) = x^{k-1} * (x * R(x))$. The value of $r(x)$ can also be maintained constant by the operation

$$R(x) := x * R(x) + p_{k-1},$$

since $r(x) = x^k * R(x) + \mathbf{S}(i: 0 \leqslant i < k: p_i x^i)$

$$= x^k * R(x) + p_{k-1} x^{k-1} + \mathbf{S}(i: 0 \leqslant i < k - 1: p_i x^i)$$

$$= x^{k-1} * (x * R(x) + p_{k-1}) + \mathbf{S}(i: 0 \leqslant i < k - 1: p_i x^i).$$

However, the polynomial $p_{k-1} + x * R(x)$ may have degree equal to m and hence cannot be stored in a shift register of length m. In this case it is necessary to add to it a polynomial that will reduce its degree but that will also maintain invariant the second property of $r(x)$, namely that

$$\mathbf{E}(d(x):: p(x) = q(x) * d(x) + r(x)).$$

We already know that the latter property is maintained invariant by the addition to $r(x)$ of any multiple of $q(x)$; by adding the particular multiple $R_{m-1} * q(x)$ we also guarantee that the degree of $x * R(x) + p_{k-1}$ is reduced to a value less than the degree of $q(x)$. Thus the algorithm takes the following form.

$$\{degree(q(x)) = m\}$$
$$k := 1 + degree(p(x)); R(x) := 0;$$
$$\{\textbf{Invariant: } \mathbf{E}(d(x):: p(x) = q(x) * d(x) + r(x))$$
$$\qquad\qquad \textbf{and } degree(R(x)) < degree(q(x))$$
$$\qquad\qquad\qquad \textbf{where } r(x) = x^k * R(x) + \mathbf{S}(i: 0 \leqslant i < k: p_i x^i)$$
$$\textbf{Variant: } k\}$$
$$\textbf{while } k > 0 \textbf{ do}$$
$$\qquad \textbf{begin}$$
$$\qquad\qquad R(x) := x * R(x) + p_{k-1} + R_{m-1} * q(x);$$
$$\qquad\qquad k := k - 1$$
$$\qquad \textbf{end}$$
$$\{\mathbf{E}(d(x):: p(x) = q(x) * d(x) + R(x)) \textbf{ and } degree(R(x)) < degree(q(x))\}$$

Note that the assignment to $R(x)$ within the loop takes the form of the assignment shown in Fig. 4.6(b) with $c = R_{m-1}$. (Since $R(x)$ is guaranteed to have degree less than m the term $\textbf{mod } x^m$ can be ignored.) The latter coefficient can be obtained using a simple feedback loop. Figure 4.7 illustrates the circuitry for the particular generator polynomial $q(x) = x^5 + x^4 + x^2 + 1$.

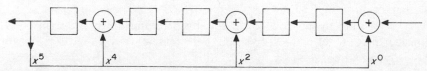

Fig. 4.7 Remainder computation with generator $q(x) = x^5 + x^4 + x^2 + 1$.

Exercises

4.7 Show that the invariant property can also be expressed as

$$E(d(x):: S(i: k \leqslant i < n: p_i x^{i-k}) = q(x) * d[x] + R(x))$$

and $degree(R(x)) < degree(q(x))$

4.8 Early on we said that the input polynomial $p(x)$ is defined to be $P(x) * x^m$ where $P(x)$ is the data polynomial and m is the degree of $q(x)$. The relationship between the coefficients of $p(x)$ and $P(x)$ is clear. We have

$$\begin{aligned} p_i &= 0 & 0 \leqslant i < degree(q(x)) \\ \text{and} \quad p_{i+m} &= P_i & 0 \leqslant i \leqslant degree(P(x)). \end{aligned}$$

But an inefficiency is apparent in our algorithm from these equations, namely, that degree($p(x)$) bits are input to the shift register although it is known that each of the last m bits is zero. It is possible to design an algorithm which inputs only the coefficients of the data polynomial (i.e. degree($P(x)$) bits). Develop such an algorithm based on the invariant property

$$r(x) = x^k * R(x) + x^m * S(i: 0 \leqslant i < k: P_i x^i)$$

and $E(d(x):: x^m * P(x) = q(x) * d(x) + r(x))$
and $degree(R(x)) < m = degree(q(x))$.

4.3   SEARCHING PROBLEMS

Much of computing is concerned with information storage and retrieval and so it is inevitable that searching plays an important role in most computer applications. Efficiency is of course an extremely important aspect of searching, particularly where large amounts of data are involved, so it is vital that search techniques take into account the characteristics of the particular database involved. In this section we consider a variety of searching algorithms.

In general, a searching problem involves determining the truth of a formula of the form:

$$E(i: R_0: P). \tag{4.9}$$

For example, searching an array a for the value x would be expressed as determining the truth of

$$E(i: 0 \leqslant i < n: a[i] = x).$$

When (4.9) is true it is usually required that an instance of i demonstrating its truth be computed.

Typically a solution to such a problem involves a loop structure in which the loop invariant takes the form

$$E(i: R: P) \Leftrightarrow E(i: R_0: P) \qquad (4.10)$$

where the predicate R describes a subrange of R_0, i.e.

$$A(i: R: R_0). \qquad (4.11)$$

(In words, every i in the range R is in the range R_0.) That is, elements of the search space R_0 are eliminated by successive iterations of the loop. Efficiency is achieved by exploiting logical properties of the predicates R_0 and/or P to reduce the range R as much as possible at each iteration.

Termination of a searching algorithm may occur when R is **false** (when the predicate P in (4.9) is unsatisfiable in the range R_0) or a satisfying instance of i has been found. However, there are often reasons why the test for satisfiability is clumsy and why, instead, it is preferable to replace the predicates R_0 and P by predicates R_0' and P' for which the formula

$$E(i: R_0': P')$$

is known to be true. The predicates R_0' and P' are chosen so that a simple test, Q, on any satisfying instance, i, determines whether P **and** R_0 in (4.9) is also satisfiable. More formally, letting $V(i: R: P)$ denote a value of i in the range R satisfying P, the predicates R_0', P', and Q are chosen so that

$$E(i: R_0: P) \equiv Q(V(i: R_0': P')).$$

The binary search algorithm first discussed in chapter 0 and later in chapter 3 illustrates these ideas. The problem as posed was to determine an index l in the range $0..n$ such that the name on $card[i]$ for $0 \leqslant i < l$ is less than X (in alphabetic order) and the name on $card[j]$ for $l \leqslant j < n$ is greater than or equal to X. Such an index is, of course, unique. A typical application of the algorithm would be to determine whether the name X appears on any card in the deck. Having computed l this is straightforward to determine by first testing whether $l < n$ and, if so, comparing the name on $card[l]$ with X. Were one to develop an algorithm to determine directly the truth of the formula

$$E(l: 0 \leqslant l < n: card[l] \cdot name = X)$$

it is inevitable that an extra test would have to be included within the **while** statement, detracting from the algorithm's elegance (and making a negligible improvement—if any—to its efficiency).

The loop invariant for the binary search algorithm took the form (p. 134)

$0 \leqslant l \leqslant u \leqslant n$
and $A(i: 0 \leqslant i < l: card[i] \cdot name < X)$
and $A(i: u \leqslant i < n: card[i] \cdot name \geqslant X)$

which can be written in the form of (4.10) and (4.11) as

$\mathbf{A}(i: l \leqslant i < u: 0 \leqslant i < n)$
and $\mathbf{E}(k: 0 \leqslant k \leqslant n: boundary(k)) \Leftrightarrow \mathbf{E}(k: l \leqslant k \leqslant u: boundary(k))$

where

$boundary(k) \equiv \mathbf{A}(i: 0 \leqslant i < k: card[i] \cdot name < X)$
$\quad\quad\quad\quad$ **and** $\mathbf{A}(i: k \leqslant i < n: card[i] \cdot name \geqslant X)$

4.3.1   Linear Search

The simplest searching problem involves inspecting an unordered array for an occurrence of an item x. Suppose a: **array**$[0 .. n-1]$ **of** *item* and x: *item*. Denoting by $present(l, u)$ the predicate

$$\mathbf{E}(i: l \leqslant i < u: a[i] = x)$$

one solution entails assigning values to an integer variable k and a Boolean variable *found* in such a way that eventually

$$(found \text{ and } 0 \leqslant k < n \text{ and } a[k] = x)$$
$$\text{or } (\text{not } found \text{ and not } present(0, n)).$$

The following loop structure achieves this property:

```
k := 0; found := false;
{Invariant: 0 ≤ k ≤ n and (present(0,n)⇔present(k,n))
           and [not found or (k < n and a[k] = x)]
  Variant: n − k}
  while (k ≠ n) and (not found) do
      begin
          if a[k] = x then found := true
                      else k := k + 1
      end
```

This rather inelegant code can be improved substantially if one adopts the strategy outlined earlier of ensuring that x *is* present in the array. Specifically, by extending the domain of a to include $a[n]$ which is assigned the value x we guarantee $present(0, n + 1)$. The following loop structure will always terminate and, following it, a simple comparison of k with n determines the truth of $present(0, n)$.

```
{0 ≤ n}
a[n] := x; k := 0;
```

{**Invariant**: $0 \leqslant k \leqslant n$ **and** $[present(0, n) \Leftrightarrow present(k, n)]$
            and $a[n] = x$
  Variant: $n - k$}
while $a[k] \neq x$ **do** $k := k + 1$
{$a[k] = x$ **and** $0 \leqslant k \leqslant n$ **and** $[present(0, n) \Leftrightarrow k < n]$}

The original problem of determining whether or not there is an entry in the array equal to x has, thus, been replaced by the problem of determining the unique value of i in the range $0 \leqslant i \leqslant n$ satisfying the predicate *is_first_occurrence* where

$$is\_first\_occurrence(i) \equiv (a'[i] = x) \text{ \textbf{and} (\textbf{not} } present(0, i))$$

and a' is a augmented with the additional element $a[n]$ equal to x.

Exercise

4.9 Suppose b: **array**$[0 .. n - 1]$ **of** *Boolean*. Develop an algorithm to determine whether there is an index i that splits the array into two parts, the first part containing all **true** entries and the second part containing all **false** entries. Specifically, your algorithm should determine whether

$$\mathbf{E}(i{:}0 \leqslant i \leqslant n{:} is\_split(i, n))$$

where $is\_split(i, n) \equiv \mathbf{A}(j{:}0 \leqslant j < i{:} b[j])$
              and $\mathbf{A}(j{:} i \leqslant j < n{:} \textbf{not } b[j])$

(*Hint*: base your solution on two searches, one of which determines the extent of the **true** entries at the beginning of the array and the other of which determines the extent of the **false** entries at the end of the array.)

4.3.2 Saddleback Search

Our next searching problem is an excellent illustration of the importance of invariants in the solution of programming problems. The problem involves a two-dimensional array $a[0 .. m - 1, 0 .. n - 1]$ **of** *integer* with the property that elements of a are strictly increasing both along rows and along columns. That is,

$$a[i, j] < a[i + 1, j]$$
and $a[i, j] < a[i, j + 1]$

whenever the subscripts in these inequalities make sense. Two examples of such an array, one of dimension 5×4 and one of dimension 3×3, are shown below.

9	13	17	21	25
5	8	12	16	20
2	4	7	11	15
0	1	3	6	10

10	11	21
7	10	19
5	9	18

Note that $a[0,0]$ is the bottom left element, that the index i increases from left to right, and that the index j increases from bottom to top (as in conventional Cartesian coordinates).

The task is: given such an array a and an integer x, determine the number of occurrences of x in a. For later use let us define

$$no\_occurrences(p,q,r,s) =$$
$$\mathbf{N}(i,j: p \leqslant i < q \text{ and } r \leqslant j < s: a[i,j] = x)$$

Then we are required to compute $no\_occurrences(0,m,0,n)$. For example, in the 5×4 array above there is one occurrence of 2 and no occurrences of 14. In the 3×3 array there are two occurrences of 10.

When first confronted with this problem many students immediately think that binary search is applicable. This betrays a lack of preliminary investigation into the properties of the supplied data. Rather than trying to bend an existing problem solution to this problem, it is wise to begin by writing down some simple consequences of the problem statement. Two rather obvious properties are the following.

(a) The minimum array element is $a[0,0]$ and, in general, the minimum element of the subarray $a[p..q-1, r..s-1]$ is $a[p,r]$.
(b) Conversely, the maximum element of the array is $a[m-1, n-1]$ and, in general, the maximum element of the subarray $a[p..q-1, r..s-1]$ is $a[q-1, s-1]$.

Special cases of properties (a) and (b) are that $a[p,r]$ is the minimum of the column $a[p,r..s]$ and the row $a[p..q,r]$, and $a[p,r]$ is the maximum of the column $a[p,s..r]$ and the row $a[q..p,r]$.

Of course, the motivation for discovering these properties is to be able to reduce by as much as possible the range of the indices i and j over which we need to search for the given value x. Specifically, we envisage introducing a counter k and a range R such that the number of occurrences of x in $a[0..m-1, 0..n-1]$ is the sum of k and the number of occurrences of x among elements of a indexed by pairs (i,j) in R. An important consideration, however, is that the range R should have a concise representation.

Suppose we investigate what happens if x is compared with an arbitrary element $a[p,q]$ of the array. There are three cases shown in Fig. 4.8 to consider. In each case the shaded area indicates the range of indices that can be eliminated from further consideration. In the case that $a[p,q] < x$ all of those

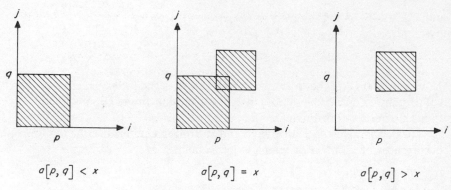

$$a[p, q] < x \qquad a[p, q] = x \qquad a[p, q] > x$$

Fig. 4.8 Reduction of range.

elements below and to the left of $a[p, q]$ (including $a[p, q]$ itself) may be eliminated; in the case that $a[p, q] > x$ all of those elements to the right and above $a[p, q]$ (again including $a[p, q]$ itself) may be eliminated; and in the case that $a[p, q] = x$ both of these areas may be eliminated provided k is incremented by 1.

The problem with choosing an element somewhere 'in the middle' (whatever that means) is that the range left to be searched has either an unattractive L-shape or is split into two separate rectangles. By considering elements on the boundaries of the array it may be possible to maintain a regular search space. Indeed, this is the main clue to the problem's solution; initially the area to be searched is rectangular so why not maintain it so? This is achieved by always comparing x with the bottom right element of the search region R. As shown in Fig. 4.9 this has the effect of always removing a row, or a column, or both, leaving the property of rectangularity invariant.

Generally, a rectangular subarray can be represented by four indices $p, q, r,$

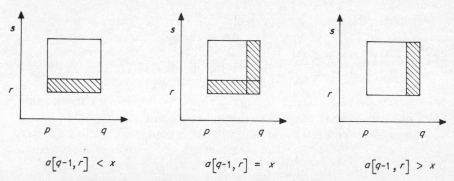

$$a[q\text{-}1, r] < x \qquad a[q\text{-}1, r] = x \qquad a[q\text{-}1, r] > x$$

Fig. 4.9 Reduction of range when a boundary element is chosen.

and s. Using k as the count of occurrences of x we therefore postulate the invariant property:

$0 \leqslant p \leqslant q \leqslant m$ **and** $0 \leqslant r \leqslant s \leqslant n$
and $k + no\_occurrences(p,q,r,s) = no\_occurrences(0,m,0,n)$

The initializations $k:=0$; $p:=0$; $q:=m$; $r:=0$; $s:=n$ clearly establish this property.

We now consider a loop structure that eliminates either a row or a column of the subarray $a[p..q-1, r..s-1]$. The number of rows in such an array is $s-r$ and the number of columns is $q-p$ so we take as variant the sum of these quantities

$$(s-r) + (q-p)$$

and use as termination condition $p = q$ **or** $s = r$ (i.e. the subarray $a[p..q-1, r..s-1]$ is empty). By our earlier analysis, if the bottom right element $a[q-1,r]$ is less than x the entire row $a[p..q-1,r]$ may be eliminated, leaving the subarray $a[p..q-1, r+1..s-1]$. Conversely, if $a[q-1,r]$ is greater than x the entire column $a[q-1, r..s-1]$ may be eliminated. Finally, if $a[q-1,r]$ equals x the addition of 1 to k enables both the row and column to be eliminated. Thus we obtain our solution:

$p:=0$; $q:=m$; $r:=0$; $s:=n$; $k:=0$;
{**Invariant**: $no\_occurrences\ (p,q,r,s) + k = no\_occurrences(0,m,0,n)$
  Variant: $(q-p) + (s-r)$}
while $(p \neq q)$ **and** $(r \neq s)$ **do**
  begin
      if $a[q-1,r] < x$ **then** $r:=r+1$
      else if $a[q-1,r] > x$ **then** $q:=q-1$
      else begin $k:=k+1; r:=r+1; q:=q-1$
          end
  end

Exercises

4.10 The variables p and s remain constant throughout execution of the above algorithm. Construct an algorithm that compares x with the diametrically opposite element $a[p, s-1]$.

4.11 Given an integer $r \geqslant 0$, develop an algorithm that will find the number of nonnegative integers i and j such that $i \leqslant j$ and $i^2 + j^2 = r$.

4.12 Two integer-valued functions f and g defined on the non-negative integers are given. Both functions are monotonically increasing, i.e. $i < j \Rightarrow f(i) \leqslant f(j)$ and $g(i) \leqslant g(j)$. It is known that there are integers i

and j such that $f(i) = g(j)$. Develop an algorithm that will locate the smallest such integers. Generalize your solution to a set $f_0, f_1, \ldots, f_n$ of monotonically increasing functions.

4.3.3   A Majority Voting Algorithm

The following problem may be described as determining the candidate in a ballot receiving more than half the votes, if one exists. We model the problem as follows. Given an array of n items, say,

b b c b d d c c c c d c b c c b c d d c c b e c b c c d

determine whether any item occurs more than n **div** 2 times.

In most ballots there are very few candidates and very many voters. Thus an obvious solution is to create a 'pigeon hole' for each candidate and to put votes one-by-one into the pigeon holes. When all votes have been counted the number of votes gained by the winner can be compared with n **div** 2. However, to make the problem more interesting let us assume that the number of candidates is commensurate with the number of voters, thus making the latter process computationally inefficient. (We shall, in this way, find a solution that is far more elegant than the obvious solution!)

In this problem, as with earlier problems, we are again faced with the task of determining a satisfying instance of a predicate which may not be satisfiable. Letting $no\_of\_occurrences(x, k)$ denote the number of occurrences of x in the array segment $a[0..k-1]$, i.e.

$$no\_of\_occurrences(x, k) = \mathbf{N}(i : 0 \leqslant i < k : a[i] = x)$$

the predicate to be satisfied is

$$majority(x) \equiv no\_of\_occurrences(x, n) > n \ \mathbf{div} \ 2.$$

Our strategy is to replace this predicate by another—*possible_majority*—which is known to be satisfiable. Given a possible majority value it is straightforward to count its occurrences in the array. Thus we consider an algorithm with the following structure.

$\{0 \leqslant n\}$
Compute x;
$\{possible\_majority(x, n)\}$
Count the number of occurrences, c, of x in $a[0..n-1]$
$\{c = no\_of\_occurrences(x, n) \ \textbf{and} \ (c > n \ \textbf{div} \ 2 \Leftrightarrow \mathbf{E}(y :: majority(y)))\}$

But what form should the predicate *possible_majority* take? The answer is a seemingly negative one. To guarantee the correctness of the above outline it suffices that x is a *possible* majority candidate if and only if no other candidate can be a *majority* candidate, i.e.

$$possible\_majority(x,n) \equiv \mathbf{A}(y: y \neq x: no\_of\_occurrences(y,n) \leqslant n \text{ div } 2).$$

(In introducing the parameter n we are anticipating some of the later development.)

Note that, as promised, *possible_majority*(x, n) is always satisfiable since, if there is a majority candidate, then it is also a possible majority candidate, and, if there is no majority candidate, then every candidate is a possible majority candidate. Formally,

$$majority(x) \Rightarrow possible\_majority(x,n)$$

and $\mathbf{A}(x:: \textbf{not } majority(x)) \Rightarrow \mathbf{A}(x:: possible\_majority(x,n)).$

Note also that, as defined, *possible_majority*(x, n) is the *weakest* condition on x that guarantees the validity of the proposed algorithm. There is an obvious alternative, namely that x is the most frequently occurring array value. But this is a much stronger requirement and so may be much harder to satisfy.

The process we envisage for computing a possible majority value is to compute possible majority values for the successive array segments $a[0..k-1]$, starting with $k = 0$ and terminating with $k = n$.

> $k := 0; x := any\_item; \{any \ value \ will \ do \ for \ x\}$
> $\{$**Invariant**: $possible\_majority(x,k) \text{ and } 0 \leqslant k \leqslant n$
> **Variant**: $n - k\}$
> **while** $k \neq n$ **do**
>   **begin**
> $\{possible\_majority(x,k) \text{ and } 0 \leqslant k < n\}$
>   *revise* x;
> $\{possible\_majority(x,k+1) \text{ and } 0 \leqslant k < n\}$
> $k := k + 1$
>   **end**
> $\{possible\_majority(x,n)\}$

The problem we face is how to compute a possible majority value for the array segment $a[0..k]$ given a possible majority value for the array segment $a[0..k-1]$. It is clear that further information is required. But what form should this information take?

Too much information would be the number of occurrences of each value x in the array, since this would take us back to the pigeon-hole algorithm dismissed earlier. Restricting the information to the number of occurrences of just the possible majority value x is no better because we must be prepared to replace x by some other value y on any iteration. Instead we need an 'estimate' of the number of occurrences of the possible majority value.

The information that the estimate must convey is when to *discard* one value and replace it by another. We emphasize 'discard' because the definition of a possible majority value is a negative one. Suppose x is a possible majority value for the array segment $a[0 \,.\, .\, k-1]$. Then it is necessary to discard x as a possible majority value for the array segment $a[0 \,.\, .\, k]$ if the number of occurrences of x in the segment does not guarantee that no other value is a possible majority value. This situation will arise when the number of occurrences of x is at most k **div** 2, and suggests that the estimate we maintain is an upper bound on the number of occurrences of x. Denoting the estimate by e we require that

$$no\_of\_occurrences(x, k) \leqslant e. \tag{4.12}$$

However, this property alone is insufficient. We need to know that it is not a gross overestimate of the number of occurrences of x (the value $e = n$ satisfies the stated property). The value e must also represent some limit on the number of occurrences of other array values which precludes their being majority values. We propose therefore to maintain the invariant property

$$\mathbf{A}(y: y \neq x: no\_of\_occurrences(y, k) \leqslant k - e). \tag{4.13}$$

This property will imply *possible_majority*(x, k) if we also add the requirement

$$2*e \geqslant k. \tag{4.14}$$

(At this stage the development is on less firm ground. Essentially we are conjecturing that it is possible to maintain variables x and e with the properties (4.12), (4.13), and (4.14). However, this may not be so.)

In summary we therefore propose replacing the earlier invariant by the stronger property

$$I(e, k, x) \equiv no\_of\_occurrences(x, k) \leqslant e \text{ and } 2*e \geqslant k$$
$$\text{and } \mathbf{A}(y: y \neq x: no\_of\_occurrences(y, k) \leqslant k - e)$$

and our algorithm now takes the following form.

```
k := 0; x := any_item; e := 0;
{Invariant: I(e, k, x) and 0 ⩽ k ⩽ n
 Variant: n − k}
while k ≠ n do
    begin
            {I(e, k, x) and 0 ⩽ k < n}
            revise e and x;
            {I(e, k + 1, x) and 0 ⩽ k < n}
            k := k + 1
    end
```

Let us now consider what happens when the element $a[k]$ is examined. If $a[k] = x$ then the estimate e of the maximum number of occurrences of x is increased by one and the invariant is thereby preserved.

If, however, $a[k] \neq x$ the estimate e remains constant and the situation is more complicated. One possibility is that incrementing k causes it to exceed $2*e$. This clearly indicates that the number of occurrences of x is certainly not a majority in the new segment $a[0..k]$. Since e is only an upper bound on this number it may be that some other array value occurs a majority of times. The only possible value this could be is $a[k]$, since by the invariant property no value y different from x is a majority value in the smaller segment $a[0..k-1]$ and only the number of occurrences of $a[k]$ has increased in the process of extending the array segment. An upper bound on the number of occurrences of $a[k]$ is k **div** $2 + 1$, since $a[k]$ was certainly not in the majority in the array segment of length k and just one extra occurrence of it has been found. Thus if $a[k] \neq x$ and $2*e = k$ we may replace x by $a[k]$ and e by k **div** $2 + 1$.

The final possibility is that although $a[k] \neq x$ and e remains constant the bound $2*e \geqslant k$ is not violated. In this case $k - e$ increases by *exactly* one and the number of occurrences of each element y increases by *at most* one; so (4.13) remains true and x is retained as the possible majority value. We thus arrive at the complete algorithm.

```
k := 0; x := any_item; e := 0;
{Invariant: no_of_occurrences(x, k) ≤ e and 2*e ≥ k
            and A(y: y ≠ x: no_of_occurrences(y, k) ≤ k - e)
 Variant: n - k}
while k ≠ n do
      begin
            if a[k] = x then e := e + 1
            else if 2*e = k
            then begin
                        x := a[k]; e := e + 1 { = k div 2 + 1}
                  end;
            k := k + 1
      end
{possible_majority(x, n)}
```

Exercise

4.13 Construct a solution to the majority-voting problem that maintains four variables k, x, i, and m with the following properties.

(a) There is no majority element in the array segment $a[0..i-1]$.

(b) $m \geqslant 0$ and the number of occurrences of x in the array segment $a[i..k-1]$ is $(k-i+m)$ **div** 2. In other words, m records by how much x is a majority in the segment $a[i..k-1]$ (doubled to ensure that it is an integer).

You should find that the computation of i is unnecessary and so can be removed, but it may help to retain it when first formulating the solution.

4.3.4 The Longest Prefix Problem

Searching is usually described as the task of finding an exact match, i.e. searching a table for an item *equal* to a given item. When we use a dictionary, however, we are often satisfied with a close match. When searching for 'singing', for example, we would be happy to find the word 'sing'. There are many ways of modeling the problem of finding a word 'close to' but not necessarily equal to a given word; the 'longest prefix' is a particularly simple and idealized model.

Given a dictionary D and a word x the *longest prefix* of x in D is defined to be that word y having the property of being the longest word in the dictionary that is a prefix of x. By a *word x* we mean a sequence $x_0 x_1 \ldots x_{n-1}$ of symbols, examples being 'cat', 'abc', and 'xsgq'. The length of the word is the length of the sequence so that, for example, 'cat' and 'aaa' both have length 3. It is convenient to postulate the existence of the *empty word* which is defined to be a word of length 0. We denote the empty word by λ. The *prefixes* of $x_0 x_1 \ldots x_{n-1}$ are then defined to be $\lambda, x_0, x_0 x_1, \ldots, x_0 x_1 \ldots x_{n-1}$. Thus 'cat' has four prefixes, namely λ, 'c', 'ca', and 'cat'.

An example dictionary is shown in Fig. 4.10. Some examples of longest prefixes are as follows. The longest prefix of 'cat' in the dictionary is 'cat' since the word appears in the dictionary; the longest prefix of 'bdfghi' in the dictionary is 'bdf' and the longest prefix of 'at' is 'λ'.

Given an unordered dictionary there is little alternative but to use a linear search technique. To make our problem more realistic we assume that the dictionary is alphabetically ordered. To be precise we assume that there is an ordering '$<$' on symbols (the conventional ordering being 'a' $<$ 'b' $<$ 'c' $< \ldots$) which is extended to an ordering on words in the conventional way. We also make the simplifying assumption that the empty word, λ, is an entry in the dictionary. This means that every word has at least one prefix in the dictionary.

Within our algorithms we assume that the dictionary D is represented by an array of n words, $d[0], d[1], \ldots, d[n-1]$. The length of the ith word is given by $len(i)$ and the symbols forming the ith word are $d[i][0], d[i][1], \ldots,$ $d[i][len(i)-1]$. We abbreviate $d[i][k]$ to $d[i,k]$. We also use the notation $d[i][k..m-1]$ to denote the word $d[i,k]d[i,k+1] \ldots d[i,m-1]$ formed from the kth to $(m-1)$th symbols of $d[i]$. When $m=k$ the word denoted by $d[i][k..m-1]$ is the empty word, λ.

λ
a a
a b c
a b e
a d
a m
a m t
a z
b
b d e
b d e f
b d f
b h
b k
c
c a
c a r
c a t
c a t a
c a t b
c a t c
c u p

Fig. 4.10 An alphabetically ordered dictionary.

With this notation the predicate $prefix(w, v)$, meaning w is a prefix of v, is specified as

$$prefix(w, v) \equiv len(w) \leqslant len(v) \text{ and } \mathbf{A}(k: 0 \leqslant k < len(w): w[k] = v[k])$$

and we are to construct an algorithm establishing the postcondition

$is\_longest\_prefix(i, x)$
$\equiv 0 \leqslant i < n$ **and** $prefix(d[i], x)$ **and**
$\mathbf{A}(j: 0 \leqslant j < n: prefix(d[j], x) \Rightarrow len(d[j]) \leqslant len(d[i]))$.

That is, we are required to compute an index i in the range $0 .. n - 1$ such that $d[i]$ is a prefix of the given word x and any other prefix of x is no longer than $d[i]$.

Before embarking on the design of an algorithm, it is imperative that the properties of the supplied data are investigated, remembering always that very simple properties often have far-reaching consequences. One such property is that alphabetic ordering on the prefixes of a word x is identical to the ordering on their lengths, i.e.

$$\lambda < x[0] < x[0 .. 1] < \ldots < x[0 .. len(x) - 1]$$

(For example, $\lambda < $ 'c' $ < $ 'ca' $ < $ 'cat'.) This has two important consequences.

(a) The empty word, λ, is the 0th entry in the dictionary.

(b) The longest prefix of x in the dictionary is the last prefix of x in the dictionary. Thus in Fig. 4.10 there are three prefixes of 'bdfg' in the dictionary, λ, 'b' and 'bdf'; the longest 'bdf' is also the last.

From these properties we can immediately construct two algorithms, both of which use linear search. The first begins its search with the last entry and the second begins with the first entry in the dictionary.

$i := n - 1;$
while not $prefix(d[i], x)$ **do** $i := i - 1$

    Algorithm 4.1 Linear search from last dictionary entry.

$j := 0;\ i := 0;$
while $j \neq n$ **do**
    begin
        if $prefix(d[j], x)$ **then** $i := j;$
        $j := j + 1$
    end

    Algorithm 4.2 Linear search from first dictionary entry.

The loop in algorithm 4.1 has the very simple invariant property

$$\mathbf{A}(j : i < j < n : \textbf{not}\ prefix(d[j], x)).$$

Property (a) above guarantees its termination in a state satisfying

$$Prefix(d[i], x)\ \textbf{and}\ \mathbf{A}(j : i < j < n : \textbf{not}\ prefix(d[j], x))$$

which is, of course, the specification of the *last* prefix in the dictionary. The fact that this property implies the required postcondition is one way of formally expressing property (b).

The invariant property for the loop in algorithm 4.2 is that i indexes the longest prefix of x in the array segment $d[0..j-1]$, i.e.

$0 \leqslant i \leqslant j < n$ **and** $prefix(d[i], x)$ **and**
$\mathbf{A}(k : 0 \leqslant k < j : prefix(d[k], x) \Rightarrow len(d[k]) \leqslant len(d[i])).$

Here property (b) is necessary to a proof that this is indeed maintained invariant by the loop body.

Although each is very simple, neither of these algorithms could be described as being efficient. The obvious next step is to consider exploiting binary search in some form. Let us therefore return to an examination of the properties of the dictionary with this in mind.

One way of proceeding is to consider searching in turn for the prefixes, λ, $x[0]$, $x[0..1]$, $x[0..2]$,... of the word x. An important property is the following.

(c) If the word w appears in the dictionary it is the first entry in the dictionary having w as a prefix. For example, in Fig. 4.10 the words 'cat', 'cata', 'catb', and 'catc' all have 'cat' as a prefix and the word 'cat' itself is the first of these entries.

So the prefix $x[0..k-1]$, if it appears in the dictionary, is the first entry in the dictionary that is prefixed by $x[0..k-1]$. (Note that this also applies to the empty word.)

Another important property of all entries in the dictionary having the same prefix is the following. Suppose p and q delimit any portion of the dictionary consisting of words that are all prefixed by w, i.e.

$$\mathbf{A}(j: p \leqslant j < q: prefix(w, d[j])).$$

Consider now the words formed by removing the prefix w from these entries. These are

$$\{d[j, len(w)..len(j) - 1]: p \leqslant j < q\}$$

and they have the important property of being *alphabetically* ordered.

A concrete example should help to clarify the property. Consider all words in Fig. 4.10 that have 'a' as a prefix. These are, in order, 'aa', 'abc', 'abe', 'ad', 'am', 'amt', and 'az'. Removing the common prefix 'a' we obtain the words 'a', 'bc', 'be', 'd', 'm', 'mt', and 'z', which are again alphabetically ordered.

The outline of an algorithm is therefore as follows (see algorithm 4.3, basic structure). We maintain four integer variables i, k, p, and q. The values of p and q delimit the entire set of words in the dictionary that are prefixed by $x[0..k-1]$, i.e.

$$\mathbf{A}(j: 0 \leqslant j < n: prefix(x[0..k-1], d[j]) \Leftrightarrow p \leqslant j < q).$$

Moreover, i is an index to a longest prefix of $x[0..k-1]$ in the dictionary, i.e.

$$is\_longest\_prefix(i, x[0..k-1]).$$

Thus we have the structure shown in Fig. 4.11.

The variables are initialized by assigning i, k, and p the value 0 and q the value n. The termination condition is $k = len(x)$ or the range $p..q-1$ is empty, and progress is made to this condition by continually incrementing k by 1.

The importance of our discussion of the ordering on words with a common prefix is that it is valid to use binary search (section 3.4.3) to compute the

$i := 0;\ k := 0;\ p = 0;\ q := n;$

{**Invariant**: $I(k,\ i,\ p,\ q) \equiv 0 \leqslant p \leqslant q \leqslant n$ and $0 \leqslant i < n$
        and $\mathbf{A}(j: 0 \leqslant j < n:\ prefix(x[0..k-1], d[j]) \Leftrightarrow p \leqslant j < q)$
        and $is\_longest\_prefix(i,\ x[0..k-1])$}
while $(k \neq len(x))$ **and** $p < q$ **do**

```
begin
    'reset p';
    'reset q';
    'reset i';
    {I(k + 1, i, p, q)}
    k := k + 1
end
```

Algorithm 4.3 Basic structure.

```
l := p; u := q;
{Invariant: p ≤ l ≤ u ≤ q
        and A(j: 0 ≤ j < l: d[j] < x[0..k])
        and A(j: u ≤ j < n: d[j] ≥ x[0..k])}
while l < u do
    begin
        m := (l + u − 1) div 2;
        if len(d[m]) = k then l := m + 1
        else if d[m, k] < x[k] then l := m + 1
        else u := m
    end;
p := l
```

Algorithm 4.3 Resetting p.

```
                        λ
                        a a
                        a b c
                        a b e
                        a d
                        a m
                        a m t
                        a z
                        b
                        b d e
                        b d e f
                        b d f
                        b h
                        b k
                        c
            i = p →     c a
                        c a r
                        c a t
                        c a t a
                        c a t b
                        c a t c
                q →     c u p
```

Fig. 4.11 State described by invariant when k = 2 and x = 'cap'.

$l := p; \ u := q;$

{**Invariant**: $p \leqslant l \leqslant u \leqslant q$
          and $\mathbf{A}(j: 0 \leqslant j < l: d[j] \leqslant x[0 .. k])$
          and $\mathbf{A}(j: u \leqslant j < n: d[j] > x[0 .. k])$}
while $l < u$ **do**
    begin
        $m := (l + u - 1)$ **div** $2;$
        if $d[m, k] \leqslant x[k]$ **then** $l := m + 1$ **else** $u := m$
    end;
$q := l$

Algorithm 4.3 Resetting q.

if $p < q$ **then if** $len(d[p]) = k$ **then** $i := p$

Algorithm 4.3 Resetting i.

boundaries p and q. In order to establish the invariant property $I(k + 1, i, p, q)$ defined in algorithm 4.3, the index p must be reset to the boundary between words $d[j]$ that are strictly less than $x[0 .. k]$ and words $d[j]$ that are greater than or equal to $x[0 .. k]$. This is precisely the function of the algorithm in section 3.4.3. Care must be taken, however, when reducing string comparisons to character comparisons. The reason is that some of the words in the segment $p .. q - 1$ may have length k (not $k + 1$) and an attempt to access $d[j, k]$ would therefore be invalid. The code for resetting p shown in Algorithm 4.3 avoids this problem by first testing the length of the string $d[m]$.

The problem of resetting q is similar, but we now have to determine the boundary between those words *less than or equal to* $x[0 .. k]$ and those words *greater than* $x[0 .. k]$. The difference between this and the definition of p is simply the difference between $<$ and $\leqslant$, and between $\geqslant$ and $>$. The code is therefore obtained from section 3.4.3 by making appropriate substitutions. In this case, however, there is no danger of attempting to access a character beyond the end of a word. (Why?)

Finally, we use property (c) to reset i. Having reset p and q to delimit those words prefixed by $x[0 .. k]$, the word $x[0 .. k]$ appears in the dictionary only if it equals $d[p]$. Care must be taken here too because the range $p .. q - 1$ may be empty. Thus the code in algorithm 4.3 first tests for nonemptiness of this range before comparing the length of $d[p]$ with $k + 1$.

Exercises
4.14 The conventional alphabetic ordering is such that 'car' < 'cat' and
     'c' < 'car'. Specify formally the relation ' < ' on words in terms of the

relation '$<$' on symbols. Assume that $len(x)$ denotes the length of the word x and the characters of x are $x_0, x_1, \ldots, x_{len(x)-1}$.

4.15 The code in algorithm 4.3 can be simplified if it can be assumed that no entry in the dictionary occurs more than once. What is this simplification? Is this simplification warranted?

4.16 What is wrong with the following code for resetting i?

$$\textbf{if } p < q \textbf{ and } len(d[p]) = k \textbf{ then } i := p$$

4.17 Another approach is to use binary search to search for in turn $x[0..len(x)-1]$, $x[0..len(x)-2], \ldots, \lambda$. How does an algorithm based on this approach compare with algorithm 4.3?

4.4 SORTING PROBLEMS

Sorting is also a common application of computers and has been extensively studied. Our intention in this section is not to describe all of the many sorting algorithms that have been devised but to show you how their characteristics are neatly captured by formal predicates.

The general idea underlying a solution to a sorting problem is to permute the elements of an array a_0 to form an array a that satisfies some ordering relation on its elements. Thus, if $is\_sorted(a, a_0)$ denotes the relation 'a is the sorted form of a_0', then

$$is\_sorted(a, a_0) \equiv is\_permutation(a, a_0) \textbf{ and } ordered(a).$$

The relation $is\_permutation$ is both symmetric and transitive, and can be succinctly expressed as 'the number of occurrences of each elements $a[i]$ or $a_0[i]$ in the two arrays is identical'. Suppose that a_0 is indexed from 0 to $n-1$; then this is expressed formally as

$is\_permutation(a, a_0)$
$\equiv \mathbf{A}(i:0 \leqslant i < n:$
$\quad no\_occurrences(a, a[i]) = no\_occurrences(a_0, a[i])$
$\quad \textbf{and } no\_occurrences(a, a_0[i]) = no\_occurrences(a_0, a_0[i]))$

where $no\_occurrences(b, x) = \mathbf{N}(j:0 \leqslant j < n: b[j] = x)$.

In chapter 3 we discussed assignment to simple variables but not to subscripted variables, which means that we are unable to formally verify the property $is\_permutation$ in any of the algorithms we discuss. However, in all our algorithms the only changes to array values are effected through a procedure $swap(i, j)$ which swaps the ith and jth array elements. Intuitively, this clearly has the property of permuting the elements of the array, and since the property is transitive and symmetric, $is\_permutation(a, a_0)$ is preserved by an arbitrary number of swaps. For this reason the requirement that a be a permutation of a_0 is not explicitly stated in the ensuing problem formulations.

Our first example is relatively simple. It is called the problem of the Dutch National Flag and was devised by E. W. Dijkstra (who is Dutch). Later we discuss bubblesort and heapsort which, taken together, typify solutions to the conventional sorting problem.

4.4.1   The Problem of the Dutch National Flag

The problem of the Dutch National Flag as originally posed by Dijkstra relates to the control of a robot that has the task of sorting a number of colored pebbles contained in a row of buckets. The buckets are arranged in front of the robot and each contains exactly one pebble colored either red, white, or blue. The robot is equipped with two arms, on the end of each of which is an eye. Using its eyes the robot can determine $color(i)$, the color of the pebble in the ith bucket, and using its arms the robot can perform the action $swap(i, j)$ to swap the pebbles in buckets i and j. We shall assume that $swap(i, i)$ is perfectly valid and has no effect on the state of the buckets.

The motivation for this rather fanciful problem statement is partly to prohibit some rather obvious solutions and partly to emphasize certain aspects of an efficient solution to the problem. In simple terms, we are given $b: \mathbf{array}[0..n-1] \mathbf{of} \{red, white, blue\}$ and we are required to sort the array into segments $b[0..r-1], b[r..w-1]$, and $b[w..n-1]$ so that all elements in the first segment are red, all elements in the second segment are white, and all elements in the last segment are blue. However, the only way to change the values in the array b is by use of the statement $swap(i, j)$, and the only way to inspect their values is by use of the function $color(i)$. These requirements prohibit solutions that simply count the number of red, white, and blue pebbles and then create a new array by assigning the appropriate numbers of elements of b to red, white, and blue. It may also be assumed that the swap operation is cumbersome and that a good solution will be one that minimizes the number of times it is performed.

In summary, the given precondition is that all of the elements of the array b are either red, white, or blue, i.e.

$0 \leqslant n$ **and**
$\mathbf{A}(i: 0 \leqslant i < n: color(i) = red \textbf{ or } color(i) = white \textbf{ or } color(i) = blue)$

and we are required to rearrange the elements of b, using only swap, so that eventually for some indices r and w all of the elements in the segments $b[0..r-1], b[r..w-1], b[w..n-1]$ are, respectively, red, white, and blue, i.e.

$0 \leqslant r \leqslant w \leqslant n$
and $A(i: 0 \leqslant i < r: color(i) = red)$
and $A(i: r \leqslant i < w: color(i) = white)$
and $A(i: w \leqslant i < n: color(i) = blue)$.

Note that we do not assume that there is at least one pebble of each color. Indeed, our specification would allow the case $r = 0$ which would indicate the absence of red pebbles. Similarly, $r = w$ and $w = n$ indicate the absence, respectively, of white and blue pebbles.

The Two-color Problem

One way of tackling this problem is to decompose it into simpler problems. An obvious simplification is to consider the case where there are pebbles of two colors to be sorted. (We might also consider the one-color problem but this is clearly trivial!) Indeed, it is clear that the three-color problem can be solved by first extracting the reds and then separating the blues from the whites. This is expressed as a sequential composition of two two-color solutions.

$\{A(i: 0 \leqslant i < n: color(i) = red$ **or** $color(i) = white$
$\qquad\qquad\qquad\qquad$ **or** $color(i) = blue)\}$

'extract reds';
$\{A(i: 0 \leqslant i < r: color(i) = red)$
 and $A(i: r \leqslant i < n: color(i) = blue$ **or** $color(i) = white)\}$
'separate blues and whites'
$\{0 \leqslant r \leqslant w \leqslant n$
and $A(i: 0 \leqslant i < r: color(i) = red)$
and $A(i: r \leqslant i < w: color(i) = white)$
and $A(i: w \leqslant i < n: color(i) = blue)\}$

We begin, therefore, by considering the two-color problem. The experience we gain will help us later to tackle the three-color problem directly and we leave the reader to fill in the details of the decomposition outlined above.

Let us consider, therefore, an array b in which the colors are white or black. The symmetry of the problem suggests that we accumulate the black elements at one end, and the white elements at the other end of the array as shown below

	m		w	
black		mixed		white

Introducing variables m and w to represent the beginning of the mixed and white segments, respectively, we therefore consider an iterative process with the following invariant property.

$0 \leqslant m \leqslant w \leqslant n$

and $A(i: 0 \leqslant i < m: color(i) = black)$
and $A(i: w \leqslant i < n: color(i) = white)$

Three aspects of this property need to be considered:

(a) How should the variables m and w be initialized so that the property is established?
(b) What termination condition for the iterative process will guarantee that the array is completely sorted into black and white segments?
(c) How is progress to be made towards the termination condition whilst maintaining the invariant property?

Establishing the invariant property is straightforward once it is realized that all of the elements of the array are mixed initially, so that the boundaries of the mixed portion are $m = 0$ and $w = n$. (Note that these values ensure the ranges $0 \leqslant i < m$ and $w \leqslant i < n$ are identically **false** so that both universal quantifications are **true**.)

The appropriate termination condition is $w = m$ since, if w is substituted for m in the invariant, we obtain

$$A(i: 0 \leqslant i < w: color(i) = black)$$
and $A(i: w \leqslant i < n: color(i) = white)$

i.e. w is the boundary between the black and white segments.

Finally, it is clear that progress towards termination is achieved by reducing the number of elements in the mixed portion of the array. The number of such elements is $w - m$, so we take this expression as the variant.

Note that $w - m$ is decreased either by decreasing w or by increasing m. These correspond to discovering a new white element and ensuring that it occupies the $(w - 1)$th element of the array, or to discovering a new black element and ensuring that it occupies the mth element of the array. To discover one or the other it is necessary to examine at least one of the elements in the 'mixed' segment. We could choose to examine any such element, but a little thought should convince you that it is preferable to examine either the mth or the $(w - 1)$th element. Choosing arbitrarily the mth element, there are two cases to consider. In the first case, when the mth element is already black, it suffices to increment the black boundary. In the second case, when the mth element is white, it may be swapped with the $(w - 1)$th and the white boundary decremented. We thus arrive at a complete solution.

$$\{A(i: 0 \leqslant i < n: color(i) = black \textbf{ or } color(i) = white)\}$$
$m := 0; \ w := n;$
$\{\textbf{Invariant: } 0 \leqslant m \leqslant w \leqslant n$
                     and $A(i: 0 \leqslant i < m: color(i) = black)$
                     and $A(i: w \leqslant i < n: color(i) = white)$
    Variant: $w - m\}$

```
while m ≠ w do
    if color(m) = black then m: = m + 1
    else {color(m) = white}
        begin w: = w − 1; swap(m, w)
        end
{0 ≤ w ≤ n
and A(i: 0 ≤ i < w: color(i) = black)
and A(i: w ≤ i < n: color(i) = white)}
```

Exercises

4.18 What would the body of the loop look like if the $(w - 1)$th element had been chosen for examination?

4.19 A more complicated loop body is obtained if both the mth and the $(w - 1)$th elements of the array are examined. Suggest suitable code.

4.20 Complete the details of the outlined solution of first extracting the reds and then separating the whites from the blues.

A Direct Solution to the Three-color Problem

The solution to the two-color problem suggests a more direct solution to the three-color problem. The idea is to partition the array into four segments containing only red elements, only white elements, only blue elements, and a mixture of colors. Four possible ways of arranging the boundaries are shown below.

mixed	red	white	blue
red	mixed	white	blue
red	white	mixed	blue
red	white	blue	mixed

Any solutions based on the first and the last of these figures would be entirely symmetrical, as would solutions based on the two inner figures. The real choice is therefore between maintaining the 'mixed' section at one end of the array or in the interior of the array. With foresight we take the latter option because it is simpler and it reduces the number of swaps that need to be performed. You are invited, however, to consider the former option and see for yourself why it is indeed more complex. The important point is always to be aware of the alternatives so that, should you choose one that is inefficient or unsuccessful, you can always try another.

Adopting the second of the figures as the framework for a solution we introduce the variables r, m, and w with the following functional specifications:

$$0 \leqslant r \leqslant m \leqslant w \leqslant n$$
and $\mathbf{A}(i: 0 \leqslant i < r: color(i) = red)$
and $\mathbf{A}(i: m \leqslant i < w: color(i) = white)$
and $\mathbf{A}(i: w \leqslant i < n: color(i) = blue)$

The appropriate initial values are $r = 0$ and $m = w = n$ thus ensuring that all of the conjuncts are vacuously true.

Again, progress is made towards satisfaction of the termination condition—when $r = m$—by always decreasing the size, $m - r$, of the 'mixed' segment. When the 'mixed' segment is nonempty we have a choice between examining the color of the rth element, the color of the $(m - 1)$th element, or both; but now there is not the symmetry of the two-color problem and so the choice may affect the simplicity or efficiency of the algorithm. (Indeed, it does!)

Whichever choice is made, if the color of the examined element is red or white the action taken will be as in the two-color solution. The hardest case, however, arises when the color of the examined element is blue, because, in this case, it is clear that the $(w - 1)$th element must be moved to make room for the newly discovered blue element. Further investigation reveals that two swaps are necessary if the rth element is examined, but only one is necessary if the $(m - 1)$th is examined. We therefore take the latter choice.

More precisely, if the color of the $(m - 1)$th element is found to be white it suffices to decrement m.

if $color(m - 1) = white$ **then** $m := m - 1$

On the other hand, if it is red the rth and $(m - 1)$th elements are swapped and r is incremented.

if $color(m - 1) = red$ **then begin** $swap(m - 1, r)$; $r := r + 1$
$\qquad\qquad\qquad\qquad\qquad\qquad$ **end**

Finally, if its color is blue the $(m - 1)$th element is swapped with the $(w - 1)$th element and *both* w and m are decremented.

if $color(m - 1) = blue$ **then begin** $w := w - 1$; $m := m - 1$;
$\qquad\qquad\qquad\qquad\qquad\qquad$ $swap(m, w)$
$\qquad\qquad\qquad\qquad\qquad\qquad$ **end**

Note that simultaneously decrementing m and w has no effect on the size of the white segment $w - m$. When the white segment is nonempty, i.e. $m < w$, the last code segment does indeed swap a white element with the newly discovered blue element. But, if the white segment is empty, then $m = w$ and the effect is to swap the newly discovered blue element with itself.

The complete solution to this problem is shown below.

{**Global invariant**: $0 \leqslant n$
$\qquad\qquad$ **and** $A(i: 0 \leqslant i < n: color(i) = red$
$\qquad\qquad\qquad\qquad$ **or** $color(i) = white$
$\qquad\qquad\qquad\qquad$ **or** $color(i) = blue)$}

$r := 0;\ m := n;\ w := n;$

{**Invariant**: $0 \leqslant r \leqslant m \leqslant w \leqslant n$
$\qquad$ **and** $A(i: 0 \leqslant i < r: color(i) = red)$
$\qquad$ **and** $A(i: m \leqslant i < w: color(i) = white)$
$\qquad$ **and** $A(i: w \leqslant i < n: color(i) = blue)$
Variant: $m - r$}

while $r \neq m$ **do**
$\quad$ **if** $color(m - 1) = white$ **then** $m := m - 1$
$\quad$ **else if** $color(m - 1) = red$ **then begin** $swap(m - 1, r);$
$\qquad\qquad\qquad\qquad\qquad\qquad\qquad\qquad\qquad r := r + 1$
$\qquad\qquad\qquad\qquad\qquad\qquad\qquad$ **end**
$\quad$ **else begin** $m := m - 1;\ w := w - 1;\ swap(m, w)$
$\qquad\qquad$ **end**

{$0 \leqslant r \leqslant w \leqslant n$
$\quad$ **and** $A(i: 0 \leqslant i < r: color(i) = red)$
$\quad$ **and** $A(i: r \leqslant i < w: color(i) = white)$
$\quad$ **and** $A(i: w \leqslant i < n: color(i) = blue)$}

4.4.2 Bubblesort

The standard 'sorting problem' is to permute the elements of the array a so that $a[0] \leqslant a[1] \leqslant a[2]$, etc. In this and the next section two solutions to this problem are discussed. The one in this section is one of the more elementary but less efficient solutions; the one in the next section is a truly ingenious solution.

'Bubblesort' is so named because it is based on the idea of the largest values in the array 'bubbling' to the top. Consider, for example, an array consisting of the elements 5, 3, 6, 2, 1. Then in a first 'bubble' the first and second elements are compared and swapped if (as in this case) the first is larger than the second, then the second and third elements are compared and if necessary swapped and so on. Figure 4.12 shows the effect of this first bubble on the array elements of our example. (The array elements are displayed vertically to suggest bubbles rising; the elements being compared are boxed.)

Note that, after the first 'bubble', the largest value occupies the last entry in the array. Thus, by repeating the process, it is possible to foresee a situation in

```
a[4]   1   1   1  |1|  6
a[3]   2   2  |2| |6|  1
a[2]   6  |6| |6|  2   2
a[1]  |3| |5|  5   5   5
a[0]  |5| |3|  3   3   3
(a)

       6   6   6   6
       1   1  |1|  5
       2  |2| |5|  1
      |5| |5|  2   2
      |3| |3|  3   3
         (b)
```

Fig. 4.12 Bubblesort: (a) first and (b) second iteration of bubble.

which after $n - q$ 'bubbles' the last $n - q$ entries in the array are ordered and none is smaller than any of the first q entries of the array. This property is captured by the predicate *bubble_ordered* where we define

$bubble\_ordered(q, n)$
$\quad \equiv 1 \leqslant q \leqslant n$ **and** $\mathbf{A}(i, j: 0 \leqslant i < j$ **and** $q \leqslant j < n: a[i] \leqslant a[j])$

and $ordered(r, s) \equiv \mathbf{A}(i, j: r \leqslant i \leqslant j < s: a[i] \leqslant a[j])$.

Note that

$\quad bubble\_ordered(q, n) \Rightarrow partitioned(q, n)$ **and** $ordered(q, n)$

where $partitioned(q, n)$

$\quad \equiv \mathbf{A}(i, j: 0 \leqslant i < q$ **and** $q \leqslant j < n: a[i] \leqslant a[j])$

expresses the property that every element in the array segment $a[0 .. q - 1]$ is smaller than every element in the segment $a[q .. n - 1]$.

Note also that

$\quad bubble\_ordered(q, n) \Rightarrow ordered(q - 1, n)$.

In particular,

$\quad bubble\_ordered(1, n) \Rightarrow ordered(0, n)$.

The framework of bubblesort is a simple loop that maintains invariant the property $bubble\_ordered(q, n)$.

```
q := n;
{Invariant: bubble_ordered(q, n)
  Variant: q - 1}
while q ≠ 1 do
```

```
begin
    q := q − 1;
    bubble
end
```
$\{bubble\_ordered(1,n)\}$
$\{ordered(0, n)\}$

Algorithm 4.4 Bubblesort.

The function of bubble, to guarantee postcondition $bubble\_ordered(q,n)$ given precondition $bubble\_ordered(q + 1,n)$, can be achieved by 'bubbling' the maximum of the array segment $a[0..q]$ to the qth position.

$\{bubble\_ordered(q + 1,n)\}$
$r := 0;$
$\{$**Invariant**: $bubble\_ordered(q + 1,n)$
        and $a[r] = $ **MAX**$(i: 0 \leqslant i \leqslant r: a[i])$
        and $0 \leqslant r \leqslant q$
  Variant: $q − r\}$
while $r \neq q$ **do**
    begin
        $r := r + 1;$
        if $a[r] < a[r − 1]$
        then $swap(r, r − 1)$
    end
$\{bubble\_ordered(q + 1,n)$ **and** $a[q] = $ **MAX**$(i: 0 \leqslant i \leqslant q: a[i])\}$
$\{bubble\_ordered(q,n)\}$

Algorithm 4.5 Bubble.

4.4.3 Heapsort

A major disadvantage of bubblesort is that the ith bubble makes $n − i$ comparisons so that, in total, $(n − 1) + (n − 2) + \cdots + 2 + 1 = n*(n − 1)/2$ comparisons are made. Although perfectly adequate for small arrays, the method becomes increasingly unacceptable for large arrays, particularly where a comparison may involve determining, for example, the alphabetic ordering between two strings. Heapsort is more complicated than bubblesort but is superior in performance for large arrays.

Heapsort exploits the binary heap structure discussed in section 2.2.3. That is, the elements of the array are to be considered as forming a tree structure in which the children of node i are nodes $2*(i + 1) − 1$ and $2*(i + 2) − 2$ (see Fig. 4.13(a)). More generally the kth generation of children of node i are those nodes j satisfying the inequalities

$$2^k*(i + 1) − 1 \leqslant j \leqslant 2^k*(i + 2) − 2.$$

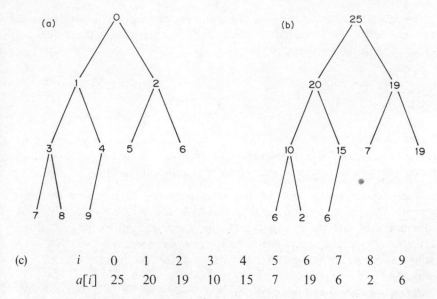

Fig. 4.13 A *heap_ordered* array: (a) indices *i*; (b) values, $a[i]$; (c) table of values.

Thus the descendants of node *i* are those nodes *j* satisfying the predicate

$$is\_descendant(j,i) \equiv \mathbf{E}(k: 0 \leqslant k: 2^k*(i+1)-1 \leqslant j \leqslant 2^k*(i+2)-2).$$

(Note that *i* is a descendant of itself according to this definition.)

Heapsort proceeds in two phases which, for want of better names, we call *phase_1* and *phase_2*. *Phase_1* has the task of sorting the array elements to the extent that, along any path from the root of the tree to a leaf, their values are ordered. We call this property *heap_ordered*$(0,n)$, the two parameters being introduced now for later convenience. Figure 4.13 provides an example of a '*heap_ordered*' array. The precise definition of *heap_ordered* is:

$$heap\_ordered(p,q) \equiv \mathbf{A}(i,j: p \leqslant i \leqslant j < q:$$
$$is\_descendant(j,i) \Rightarrow a[i] \geqslant a[j]).$$

As in bubblesort, the relation *ordered* is defined by

$$ordered(p,q) \equiv \mathbf{A}(i,j: p \leqslant i \leqslant j < q: a[i] \leqslant a[j]).$$

(Note the reversal of inequalities in the definitions of *heap_ordered* and *ordered*.)

The maximum element of a *heap_ordered* array *a* is $a[0]$ since every element is a descendant of the 0th element. Moreover, the predicate *heap_ordered*$(n \mathbf{\,div\,} 2, n)$ is vacuously **true** since no node in the range $(n \mathbf{\,div\,} 2)..n-1$ has a descendant in the range $0..n-1$.

The second phase has the task of sorting the elements of a *heap_ordered* array into order. Thus the basic structure of the algorithm is the sequential composition of the two phases:

$\{0 \leqslant n\}$
phase_1;
$\{heap\_ordered(0, n)\}$
phase_2
$\{ordered(0, n)\}$

Algorithm 4.6 Heapsort.

The beauty of heapsort is that it, too, uses a 'bubbling' process, in both its first and second phases, to order the array elements. However, in this case elements are bubbled along paths through the tree structure. It is a consequence of the fact that such paths have length at most $\log_2 n$ that the number of comparisons required by heapsort is proportional to $n * \log_2 n$. To distinguish between the two algorithms we call the 'bubbling' process *sift* in heapsort.

Phase_1 establishes postcondition *heap_ordered*$(0, n)$ using a loop with invariant *heap_ordered*(p, n).

$p := n$ **div** 2;
$\{$**Invariant**: *heap_ordered*(p, n)
  Variant: $p\}$
while $p \neq 0$ **do**
    begin
        $p := p - 1$;
        sift
    end
$\{heap\_ordered(0, n)\}$

Algorithm 4.7 Phase_1.

Phase_1 thus has the task of building up the heap structure beginning with a state in which only the leaves (those nodes with no descendants) are (vacuously) *heap_ordered* (Fig. 4.14). Here the procedure *sift* has to satisfy the specification

$$\{heap\_ordered(p + 1, q)\} \; sift \; \{heap\_ordered(p, q)\}$$

where q has the constant value n. (The parameter, q, anticipates the use of *sift* in the second phase.)

Sift satisfies this specification by bubbling the wth element, where initially $w = p$, down a path in the tree until a leaf node is reached. At each step the wth element is made equal to the largest value among itself and its two children, possibly by swapping it with the larger of its children. Figure 4.14(b) illustrates

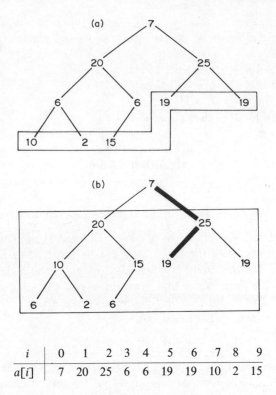

i	0	1	2	3	4	5	6	7	8	9
$a[i]$	7	20	25	6	6	19	19	10	2	15

Fig. 4.14 The first phase. *Heap_ordered* elements are boxed. (a) Initially; the leaves of the tree are (vacuously) *heap_ordered*. (b) Prior to final sift; path taken by the value 7 is indicated by a heavy line.

the path taken by the value 7 when constructing the heap in Fig. 4.13. Formally, *sift* maintains invariant the property I where

$$I \equiv p \leqslant w < q \text{ and } \mathbf{A}(i, j: p \leqslant i \leqslant j < q:$$
$$is\_descendant(j, i) \Rightarrow (a[i] \geqslant a[j] \text{ or } w = i))$$

Note that w has at least one child in the heap if $2*w + 1 < q$, and two children if $2*(w + 1) < q$. When w has no children we find

$$I \text{ and } 2*w + 1 \geqslant q \Rightarrow heap\_ordered(p, q).$$

So *sift* takes the following form.

```
w := p;
{Invariant: I;
 Variant: q − w}
while 2*w + 1 < q do
```

begin
  {make a[w] the largest of itself and its two children}
  $v := 2*w + 1$; *{1st child}*
  if $v + 1 < q$ *{2nd child exists}*
  then if $a[v] < a[v + 1]$ **then** $v := v + 1$;
  {a[v] is largest child}
  if $a[w] < a[v]$ **then** *swap(w, v)*;
  $w := v$
end

Algorithm 4.8 Sift.

Phase_2 maintains invariant the property

$$heap\_ordered(0, q) \textbf{ and } bubble\_ordered(q, n)$$

i.e. the first q elements of the array are *heap_ordered*, the remaining elements are *ordered*, and none of the first q elements is larger than any of the last $n - q$ elements. This invariant is established by assigning q the value n after completion of the first phase. Making progress to the state *ordered*$(0, n)$ is achieved by exploiting the fact that the maximum element in a heap is at the root. Thus the sequential composition

$$q := q - 1; swap(0, q)$$

will add an extra element ($a[0]$) to the ordered elements as well as preserving the partitioning. The new value of $a[0]$ may not, however, be *heap_ordered* and so it must be sifted down the tree.

  $q := n$;
  *{**Invariant:** heap_ordered(0, q) **and** bubble_ordered(q, n)*
   Variant: q}
  while $q \neq 1$ **do**
    begin $q := q - 1$; *swap*$(0, q)$;
      *{heap_ordered(1, q) **and** bubble_ordered(q, n)}*
      sift
      *{heap_ordered(0, q) **and** bubble_ordered(q, n)}*
    end
  *{heap_ordered(0, 1) **and** bubble_ordered(1, n)}*
  {ordered(0, n)}

Algorithm 4.9 Phase_2.

Exercise

4.21 (Swapping sections) Suppose the array a has length $m + n$. It is required to swap the first m elements of the array with the last n elements, as shown diagrammatically below, using as little extra storage as possible.

| $a_0[0 \ldots m - 1]$ | $a_0[m \ldots m + n - 1]$ | Initial state |

| $a_0[m \ldots m + n - 1]$ | $a_0[0 \ldots m - 1]$ | Final state |

Formally, the precondition is

$$\mathbf{A}(i: 0 \leqslant i < m + n: a[i] = a_0[i])$$

and the postcondition is

$$\mathbf{A}(i: 0 \leqslant i < n: a[i] = a_0[m + i])$$
$$\mathbf{and} \quad \mathbf{A}(i: 0 \leqslant i < m: a_0[i] = a[n + i])$$

(a) Prove that the postcondition can be expressed more succinctly as either

$$\mathbf{A}(i: 0 \leqslant i < m + n: a[i] = a_0[(i + m) \bmod (m + n)])$$

or $\quad \mathbf{A}(i: 0 \leqslant i < m + n: a_0[i] = a[(i + n) \bmod (m + n)])$

(b) Develop two algorithms to solve this problem, one using the invariant property

$$0 \leqslant k \leqslant m \text{ and } \mathbf{A}(i: 0 \leqslant i < m + n: a[i] = a_0[(i + k) \bmod (m + n)])$$

and the second using the invariant property

$$0 \leqslant k \leqslant n \text{ and } \mathbf{A}(i: 0 \leqslant i < m + n: a_0[i] = a[(i + k) \bmod (m + n)]).$$

4.5 EXTREMUM PROBLEMS

The final class of problems we consider involves minimizing or maximizing some quantity; we call the members of the class *extremum problems*.

All of our solutions exploit the so-called *optimality principle of dynamic programming*. Dynamic programming is a technique often used in operations research for determining optimal solutions to multi-stage decision problems. An example is the determination of when to scrap one's current computer equipment in order to replace it with the latest technology, taking into account factors such as annual maintenance costs, the expected depreciation in value of one's current equipment, the expected inflation in the cost of new equipment, etc. (The term 'programming' was coined in the fifties and may be misleading—a better name nowadays would be dynamic planning.)

The principle of optimality is very simply stated: 'Any optimal solution to a problem comprises only optimal subsolutions.' An example will illustrate the principle. Suppose you are planning an overland trip from Paris to Delhi. To minimize costs you wish to minimize the total journey length. Suppose that the shortest route takes you through Istanbul. Then your route will comprise the *shortest* route from Paris to Istanbul and the *shortest* route from Istanbul to Delhi. This simple observation can have a dramatic effect on the efficiency of algorithms for route planning and other extremum problems because it drastically reduces the initial solution space.

Algebraically, an important characteristic of extremum problems is that they involve quantification with respect to an idempotent operator **q** (e.g. *min* is idempotent since $min(a, a) = a$). Indeed, it is generally true that an idempotent operator **q** defines an ordering $\leqslant_q$ as follows (see exercise 2.30)

$$a \leqslant_q b \equiv a\,\mathbf{q}\,b = a$$

Thus, since **or** is idempotent, it defines the ordering relation **false** > **true** on the truth values and, therefore, all the searching problems in section 4.3 can be viewed as extremum problems—determining whether E(*i*: R(*i*): P(*i*)) is **true** or **false** is equivalent to minimizing the truth value of *P(i)* where *i* ranges over *R(i)*. The optimality principle is also evident in those problems. For instance, *x* occurs in the array segment $a[i..j-1]$ if it occurs in the array segment $a[i..k-1]$ for some *k*, $i < k \leqslant j$.

Typically, extremum problems involve operators in addition to the minimization operator. For example, shortest distances involve summation as well as minimization. Here the important algebraic characteristic to look out for is distributivity. For instance, conjunction (**and**) distributes over disjunction (**or**), i.e. *a* **and** (*b* **or** *c*) ≡ (*a* **and** *b*) **or** (*a* **and** *c*), and, in addition, summation distributes over minimization, i.e. $i + min(j, k) = min(i + j, i + k)$. The significance of these remarks will become evident in the ensuing examples.

4.5.1 The Longest Ascending Segment Problem

An elementary extremum problem is to determine the length of a longest ascending segment in an array *a*. An *ascending segment* is defined to be a segment $a[i..j-1]$ such that consecutive values are ascending. Denoting this property by *as(i, j)* we define

$$as(i, j) \equiv \mathbf{A}(r: i < r < j: a[r-1] \leqslant a[r]).$$

The problem is to compute the length of a longest ascending segment in *a*: **array**$[0..n-1]$ **of** *integer*, i.e.

$$las(n) = \mathbf{MAX}(i, j: 0 \leqslant i < j \leqslant n \text{ and } as(i, j): j - i).$$

Obviously, $las(1) = 1$. The principle of optimality suggests that $las(k + 1)$ is composed from the values $las(1)$, $las(2), \ldots, las(k)$. Optimistically, let us conjecture that $las(k + 1)$ can be computed from $las(k)$ alone. We therefore introduce a variable *m* to record successive values of *las(k)* and consider a loop with the following structure.

$\{n \geqslant 1\}$
$k := 1; m := 1;$

{**Invariant**: $0 < k \leqslant n$ and $m = las(k)$
 Variant: $n - k$}
while $k \neq n$ **do**
  begin
   {$m = las(k)$ and $0 < k < n$}
   revise m;
   {$m = las(k + 1)$}
   $k := k + 1$
  end
{$m = las(n)$}

To see how to compute $las(k + 1)$ from $las(k)$ we write

$$las(k + 1) = \textbf{MAX}(j: 0 < j \leqslant k + 1: las\_at(j))$$
$$= max(\textbf{MAX}(j: 0 < j \leqslant k: las\_at(j)), las\_at(k + 1))$$
$$= max(las(k), las\_at(k + 1))$$

where

$$las\_at(j) = \textbf{MAX}(i: 0 \leqslant i < j \text{ and } as(i, j): j - i)$$

is the length of the longest ascending segment ending at $a[j - 1]$. This suggests that we introduce another variable, m', with the invariant property

$$m' = las\_at(k).$$

Then the process of revising m decomposes into revising m' and assigning to m the maximum of its old value and the new value of m'.

 {$m = las(k)$ and $m' = las\ at(k)$}
 revise m';
 $m := max(m, m')$
 {$m = las(k + 1)$ and $m' = las\_at(k + 1)$}.

Now, examining the definition of $las\_at(k + 1)$, we have two cases to consider. In the first case suppose $a[k - 1] \leqslant a[k]$. Then $as(i, k + 1) \equiv as(i, k)$ for all $i < k$ and so

$$las\_at(k + 1) = max(\textbf{MAX}(i: 0 \leqslant i < k \text{ and } as(i, k): k + 1 - i),$$
$$\textbf{MAX}(i: i = k \text{ and } as(i, k + 1): k + 1 - i))$$
$$= max(las\_at(k) + 1, 1)$$
$$= las\_at(k) + 1.$$

In the second case, suppose $a[k - 1] > a[k]$. Then $as(i, k + 1)$ is **false** for all $i < k$ and so, by similar argument,

$$las\_at(k + 1) = max(\textbf{MAX}(i: \textbf{false}: k + 1 - i), 1)$$
$$= 1.$$

Thus the revision of m' is achieved by the statement

$$\textbf{if } a[k-1] \leqslant a[k] \textbf{ then } m' := m' + 1 \textbf{ else } m' := 1$$

and we obtain the following algorithm.

```
k := 1; m := 1; m' := 1;
{Invariant: 0 < k ≤ n and m = las(k) and m' = las_at(k)
 Variant: n − k}
while k ≠ n do
      begin
          if a[k − 1] ≤ a[k] then m' := m' + 1 else m' := 1;
          m := max(m, m');
          k := k + 1
      end
{m = las(n)}
```

Exercises

4.22 (Plateau problem) A plateau of a: **array**$[0 .. n-1]$ **of** *integer* is a segment $a[i..j-1]$ in which all values are equal. (See example 2.23 for a precise definition and an example.) It is clear that computing the length of a longest plateau in an array is identical to computing $las(n)$ provided only that the relation '$\leqslant$' in the test $a[k-1] \leqslant a[k]$ is replaced by '$=$'. However, suppose that the array a is ascending, i.e. $\textbf{A}(k: 0 < k < n: a[k-1] \leqslant a[k])$. In this case one can dispense with the variable m'. What is the appropriate simplification?

4.23 (Boolean split) Consider again exercise 4.9. The problem was to determine whether the Boolean array b satisfies $split(n)$ where

$$split(n) \equiv \textbf{E}(i: 0 \leqslant i \leqslant n: is\_split(i, n))$$

and $is\_split(i, n) \equiv \textbf{A}(j: 0 \leqslant j < i: b[j])$ **and** $\textbf{A}(j: i \leqslant j < n: \textbf{not } b[j])$.

Develop a solution that computes $split(k)$ for successive k, beginning with $k = 0$.

4.24 (Almost ascending segment problem) An *almost ascending segment* in an array a is a segment $a[i..j-1]$ of the array such that at most one pair of consecutive elements is not ascending, i.e.

$$aas(i, j) \equiv \textbf{N}(r: i < r < j: a[r-1] > a[r]) \leqslant 1.$$

Develop an algorithm to compute the length of the longest almost ascending segment of a: **array**$[0..n-1]$ **of** *integer*.

4.25 (Minsum problem) Given a: **array**$[0..n-1]$ **of** *integer*, develop an algorithm to compute the minimum sum of consecutive elements of a, i.e.

$$minsum(n) = \textbf{MIN}(i, j: 0 \leqslant i \leqslant j \leqslant n: sum(i, j))$$
where $sum(i, j) = \textbf{S}(k: i \leqslant k < j: a[k])$.

See example 2.11 for further clarification of the problem statement. Make use of examples 2.14, 2.18, and 2.34.

4.5.2   The Largest True Square Problem

Section 4.5.1 was restricted to instances of problems in which the computation of an extremum value necessitated the introduction of one or two additional scalar variables. The *largest* **true** *square problem* discussed in this section illustrates a situation where an additional *array* of values is required.

The problem is, given b: **array**$[0 .. m - 1, 0 .. n - 1]$ **of** *Boolean*, to compute the size, s, of the largest square subarray of b all of whose elements are **true**. (You are referred to example 2.12 for an example of a largest **true** square.) Formally, 'there is a **true** square at (p, q) of size d' is defined by

$$true\_square(p, q, d) \equiv 0 \leqslant d \leqslant min(m - p, n - q) \textbf{ and } alltrue(p, q, d)$$

where $alltrue(p, q, d) \equiv \textbf{A}(i, j: p \leqslant i < p + d \textbf{ and } q \leqslant j < q + d: b[i, j])$

The size of the largest **true** square at (p, q) is then defined to be

$$t(p, q) = \textbf{MAX}(d: true\_square(p, q, d): d)$$

and the required postcondition is that the value of s satisfy (see example 2.26)

$$s = \textbf{MAX}(p, q: 0 \leqslant p < m \textbf{ and } 0 \leqslant q < n: t(p, q)).$$

As in the longest ascending segment problem we use a simple linear search of the array; the search is begun at $b[m - 1, n - 1]$ and terminates at $b[0, 0]$. The variable k counts the number of elements yet to be examined so that initially k is set to $m*n$ and termination occurs when $k = 0$; the coordinates of the examined array element $b[p, q]$ are given by $p = k$ **div** n and $q = k$ **mod** n (so that the array elements are examined in the order $b[m - 1, n - 1]$, $b[m - 1, n - 2], \ldots, b[m - 1, 0]$, $b[m - 2, n - 1], \ldots, b[0, 0]$). To begin our development we propose as invariant the property $S(k, s)$ where

$$S(k, s) \equiv s = \textbf{MAX}(i, j: (p < i < m \textbf{ and } 0 \leqslant j < n) \textbf{ or } (p = i \textbf{ and } q \leqslant j < n): t(i, j)).$$

Thus the basic loop structure is as follows.

```
{0 ≤ m and 0 ≤ n}
k:= m*n; {0 ≤ k ≤ m*n}
s:= 0;
{Invariant: S(k, s) and 0 ≤ k ≤ m*n
 Variant: k}
while 0 < k do
```

begin
    $k := k - 1$; $p := k$ **div** n; $q := k$ **mod** n;
    $\{S(k + 1, s)$ **and** $p = k$ **div** n **and** $q = k$ **mod** $n\}$
    '*revise s*'
    $\{S(k, s)\}$
end
$\{S(k, s)$ **and** $k = 0\}$
$\{s = \textbf{MAX}(i, j: 0 \leqslant i < m$ **and** $0 \leqslant j < n : t(i, j))\}$

Our problem has now become one of determining what additional information is required to establish $S(k, s)$ knowing the truth of $S(k + 1, s)$.

Figure 4.15 illustrates the problem. It is assumed that s is the size of the largest **true** square in the shaded area and we are required to determine the new value of s when the element $b[p, q]$ is added to this area. The analysis so far suggests that we record the value of $t(p, q)$ as each array element is examined. We shall see later that this amount of additional information is unnecessary but, for the moment, let us pursue this approach.

There are several solutions to this problem, but the best known is the following. For points (p, q) exterior to the array, i.e. $p = m$ and $0 \leqslant q \leqslant n$, or $q = n$ and $0 \leqslant p \leqslant m$, *true_square*$(p, q, d)$ equals **true** when $d = 0$ and equals **false** otherwise. So, for such points, $t(p, q) = 0$.

For interior points we argue that there is a **true** square of size $d + 1$ at the position (p, q) if and only if (i) $b[p, q]$ is **true**, (ii) there are **true** squares of size d at

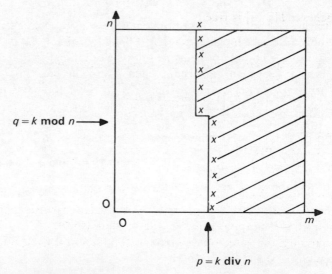

Fig. 4.15 Bottom left corner of squares of size $M[j]$.

$(p, q + 1)$ and $(p + 1, q)$, and (iii) $b[p + d, q + d]$ is **true**. Formally (see example 2.25),

$\quad alltrue(p, q, d + 1)$
$\quad\quad \equiv alltrue(p + 1, q, d)$ **and** $alltrue(p, q + 1, d)$
$\quad\quad\quad$ **and** $b[p, q]$ **and** $b[p + d, q + d]$

and hence, also,

$\quad true\_square(p, q, d + 1)$
$\quad\quad \equiv true\_square(p + 1, q, d)$ **and** $true\_square(p, q + 1, d)$ $\hfill (4.15)$
$\quad\quad\quad$ **and** $b[p, q]$ **and** $b[p + d, q + d]$.

Using the properties of range disjunction (see in particular exercise 2.30) and distributivity of summation over *max*, two consequences of (4.15) are

$$t(p, q) \leqslant t(p, q + 1) + 1$$
and $\quad t(p, q) \leqslant t(p + 1, q) + 1$.
Thus $\quad t(p, q) \leqslant min(t(p, q + 1), t(p + 1, q)) + 1$. $\hfill (4.16)$

A property of **true** squares that can be proved similarly to (4.15) is

$\quad true\_square(p, q + 1, d)$ **and** $true\_square(p + 1, q, d)$ **and** $b[p, q]$
$\quad\quad \Rightarrow true\_square(p, q, d)$

from which we deduce that, whenever $b[p, q]$ is **true**,

$$t(p, q + 1) \leqslant t(p, q)$$
and $\quad t(p + 1, q) \leqslant t(p, q)$.

Thus, whenever $b[p, q]$ is **true**,

$$min(t(p + 1, q), t(p, q + 1)) \leqslant t(p, q). \hfill (4.17)$$

We now consider two cases. The easy case occurs when $b[p, q]$ is **false** because it is then clear from (4.15) that $true\_square(p, q, d + 1)$ is also **false** for all $d \geqslant 0$. Thus, when $b[p, q]$ is **false**, $t(p, q) = 0$.

The harder case occurs when $b[p, q]$ is **true**. However, from (4.16) and (4.17) it follows that

$$r \leqslant t(p, q) \leqslant r + 1$$

where $\quad r = min(t(p + 1, q), t(p, q + 1))$.

So, we have only to decide whether $t(p, q) = r + 1$. But from (4.15) this decision is determined by the value of $b[p + r, q + r]$. If the latter is **true** there is a **true** square of size $r + 1$ at (p, q) and if it is **false** there is not.

Summarizing, the value of $t(p, q)$ for $0 \leqslant p \leqslant m$ and $0 \leqslant q \leqslant n$ is given by

$$t(p, q) = 0,$$

when $p = m$ or $q = n$,

and $t(p, q) = $ **if not** $b[p, q]$ **then** 0
                 else if $b[p + r, q + r]$ **then** $r + 1$
                 else r,
otherwise,
where $r = min(t(p + 1, q), t(p, q + 1))$.

One final observation needs to be made before we present the algorithm. We hinted earlier that it is unnecessary to record the value of $t(p, q)$ for every point (p, q) that has been examined. Indeed, the value of $t(p, q)$ is used just twice, the first time to compute $t(p, q - 1)$ and the second time to compute $t(p - 1, q)$. After the second usage its value is not required, with the implication that a one-dimensional array will suffice. Specifically, we store M: **array**$[0 .. n]$ **of** *integer*, where the elements of M are the values of $t(p, q)$ at the points marked 'x' in Fig. 4.15. Formally, M satisfies the property $T(k, M)$ where

$$T(k, M) \equiv \mathbf{A}(j: q \leqslant j \leqslant n: M[j] = t(p, j))$$
$$\text{and } \mathbf{A}(j: 0 \leqslant j < q: M[j] = t(p + 1, j)).$$

The invariant property is the conjunction of the properties S and T and the range limitation on k,

$$I(k, s, M) \equiv S(k, s) \text{ and } T(k, M) \text{ and } 0 \leqslant k \leqslant m*n$$

and the completed algorithm is as follows.

```
{0 ⩽ m and 0 ⩽ n}
k:= m*n; {0 ⩽ k ⩽ m*n}
s:= 0; {S(k, s)}
for j:= 0 to n do M[j]:= 0; {T(k, M)}
{Invariant: I(k, s, M)
 Variant: k}
while 0 < k do
    begin
        k:= k − 1; p:= k div n; q:= k mod n;
        r:= min(M[q], M[q + 1]); { = min(t(p + 1, q), t(p, q + 1))}
        if not b[p, q]
        then M[q]:= 0
        else if b[p + r, q + r] then M[q]:= r + 1
                           else M[q]:= r;
        {S(k + 1, s) and T(k, M)}
        s:= max(s, M[q])
    end
{I(k, s, M) and k = 0}
{s = MAX(i, j: 0 ⩽ i < m and 0 ⩽ j < n: t(p, q))}
```

Exercises

4.26 Suppose the calculations of the coordinates i and j are achieved using $i := k$ **mod** m and $j = k$ **div** m (so that the array elements are accessed in the order $b[m-1, n-1]$, $b[m-2, n-1]$, ..., $b[0, n-1]$, $b[m-1, n-2]$, ..., $b[0,0]$). What changes should be made to the algorithm?

4.27 (Minimax of an array) Given a: **array**$[0..m-1, 0..n-1]$ **of** *integer* the maximum element in row j is

$$M(j) = \mathbf{MAX}(i: 0 \leqslant i < m: a[i,j])$$

and the minimum row maximum is

$$\mathbf{MIN}(j: 0 \leqslant j < n: M(j)).$$

An example is the array below in which the boxed elements are the row maxima. The value 9 is the minimum row maximum.

5	$\boxed{10}$	1	1	3
2	3	$\boxed{9}$	7	6
6	12	13	15	$\boxed{16}$

Develop an algorithm to compute the coordinates (p, q) of the minimum row maximum in a. (*Note*: this problem does not necessitate the introduction of any additional arrays.)

4.5.3 Shortest Paths

The final extremum problem in our list is more abstract than any of the earlier ones but it is a very important problem, having wide-ranging applications. The problem is to find the shortest distance from a given start node to every other node in a graph. The solutions presented are at a relatively high level, and not at the level of detailed implementations; the bibliographic notes direct you to discussions of such implementations.

A *directed graph H* is defined to be a pair consisting of a finite set, X, of *nodes* and a finite set, A, of *arcs* (or edges). Two mappings are defined from A into X, the first called the *from* component and the second called the *into* component. If a is an arc these are denoted, respectively, by $a \cdot from$ and $a \cdot into$. If $a \cdot from = x$ and $a \cdot into = y$ the arc a is said to be *directed from x to y*. A *labeled directed graph* is a directed graph that has, in addition, a mapping defined from the arc set A to the natural numbers (the set of nonnegative integers). This mapping is called the *length* function, the length of arc a being denoted by $a \cdot length$. (*Note*: the assumption that the arc labels are nonnegative is crucial to several observations we make later.)

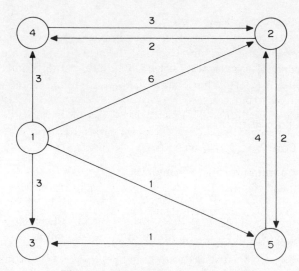

Fig. 4.16 A labeled directed graph.

Figure 4.16 is a diagrammatic representation of a directed graph. The set X of nodes in the graph may be identified with the set of integers $\{1, 2, 3, 4, 5\}$. The arcs are the lines connecting nodes, the arrow head pointing to the *into* component. The arc lengths are indicated by the labels attached to the arcs. Thus, there is an arc from 1 to 2 of length 6 and an arc from 2 to 5 of length 2.

The problem we consider is this. Given a *start node* s, determine the *shortest distance* from s to each node z in the graph. A *path from the node x to the node y* is defined to be a sequence of arcs $a_1, a_2, \ldots, a_t$ where $x = a_1 \cdot from$, $y = a_t \cdot into$ and $a_i \cdot into = a_{i+1} \cdot from$ $(1 \leqslant i < t)$. The path is said to be of *arc-count* t and *length* $\mathbf{S}(i: 1 \leqslant i < t: a_i \cdot length)$. Additionally, there is a path from each node x to itself of zero arc-count and length. This path is denoted by λ_x.

Yet more formally, the predicate *path* and the functions *from* and *into* are defined as follows.

$$path(p) \equiv \mathbf{E}(t: 0 \leqslant t: P(p, t))$$

where

$$P(p, 0) \equiv \mathbf{E}(x :: p = \lambda_x)$$
$$P(p, t + 1) \equiv \mathbf{E}(p', a: P(p', t): p = p'a \textbf{ and } p' \cdot into = a \cdot from)$$
$$\lambda_x \cdot from = \lambda_x \cdot into = x$$
$$(pa) \cdot from = p \cdot from$$
$$(pa) \cdot into = a \cdot into$$

In these definitions and elsewhere p and p' denote sequences of arcs, a denotes an arc, and x denotes a node. The notation $p'a$ simply means the sequence obtained by adding a to the end of p'. The definition of $P(p, t)$, which should be verbalized as 'p is a path of arc-count t', is called an *inductive definition* because it has a basis, the statement that p is a path of arc-count zero if and only if

$p = \lambda_x$ for some node x, and an inductive step, the statement that p is a path of arc-count $t + 1$ if and only if it consists of a path p' of arc-count t concatenated with an arc a such that $p' \cdot into = a \cdot from$. Note that the mappings *from* and *into* on paths are also defined inductively. The length of a path p is likewise defined inductively as follows.

$\lambda_x \cdot length = 0$

$(pa) \cdot length = p \cdot length + a \cdot length.$

The problem we have is to tabulate a function *distance* that, for a given graph H and a given start node s, computes the length of the shortest path from s to each node x in the graph, i.e.

$$distance(x) = \mathbf{MIN}(p: path(p) \text{ and } p \cdot from = s \text{ and } p \cdot into = x:$$
$$p \cdot length). \tag{4.18}$$

The principle of optimality suggests a first step in this problem's solution. Suppose that a shortest path p from s to x consists of the path p' from s to y followed by the arc a from y to x. Then the distance from s to x is the distance from s to y plus the length of arc a. Generally, therefore, for nodes $x \neq s$ the distance from s to x is the minimum over all arcs a into x of the distance to $a \cdot from$ added to the length of arc a. Formally, this claim is verified by taking the definition of distance and splitting its range into two cases, the first in which the path p has zero arc length and the second in which p has nonzero arc length.

$$distance(x) = min(\mathbf{MIN}(p: path(p)$$
$$\text{and } p \cdot from = s \text{ and } p \cdot into = x$$
$$\text{and } \mathbf{E}(y:: p = \lambda_y):$$
$$p \cdot length),$$
$$\mathbf{MIN}(p: path(p)$$
$$\text{and } p \cdot from = s \text{ and } p \cdot into = x$$
$$\text{and } \mathbf{E}(p', a:: p = p'a \text{ and } p' \cdot into = a \cdot from):$$
$$p \cdot length))$$

Using distributivity of **and** over **or** the two existential quantifications can be substantially simplified. For example,

$\mathbf{E}(y:: p = \lambda_y)$ **and** $p \cdot from = s$ **and** $p \cdot into = x$
$\equiv \mathbf{E}(y:: p = \lambda_y$ **and** $p \cdot from = s$ **and** $p \cdot into = x)$

                                                      (distributivity)

$\equiv \mathbf{E}(y:: p = \lambda_y$ **and** $\lambda_y \cdot from = s$ **and** $\lambda_y \cdot into = x)$

                                                      (substitutivity)

$\equiv \mathbf{E}(y:: p = \lambda_y$ **and** $y = s$ **and** $y = x)$

                                              (definition of *from* and *into*)

$\equiv p = \lambda_s$ **and** $s = x$

Thus the definition of *distance* splits into two cases:

$$distance(s) = min(\lambda_s \cdot length,$$
$$\mathbf{MIN}(p', a: path(p') \textbf{ and } p' \cdot into = a \cdot from$$
$$\textbf{and } p' \cdot from = s \textbf{ and } a \cdot into = s:$$
$$p' \cdot length + a \cdot length) \tag{4.19}$$

and, for $x \neq s$,

$$distance(x) = \mathbf{MIN}(p', a: path(p') \textbf{ and } p' \cdot into = a \cdot from$$
$$\textbf{and } p' \cdot from = s \textbf{ and } a \cdot into = x:$$
$$p' \cdot length + a \cdot length) \tag{4.20}$$

Now it is obvious that if all *arc* lengths are nonnegative then all *path* lengths are also nonnegative. Thus, since $\lambda_s \cdot length = 0$, the empty path λ_s is the shortest path from s to itself, i.e. equation (4.19) simplifies to:

$$distance(s) = 0. \tag{4.21}$$

Equation (4.20) can also be simplified by exploiting the distributivity of $+$ over *min*. Specifically,

$$distance(x) = \mathbf{MIN}(a: a \cdot into = x:$$
$$\mathbf{MIN}(p': path(p') \textbf{ and } p' \cdot into = a \cdot from \textbf{ and } p' \cdot from = s:$$
$$p' \cdot length) + a \cdot length)$$

$$\text{(distributivity)}$$
$$= \mathbf{MIN}(a: a \cdot into = x: distance(a \cdot from) + a \cdot length) \tag{4.22}$$

Equations (4.21) and (4.22) are crucial to all solutions to the shortest path problem; other texts often taken them as the problem specification. For the graph shown in Fig. 4.16, taking $s = 1$, we obtain

$$distance(1) = 0$$
$$distance(2) = min(distance(1) + 6, distance(5) + 4, distance(4) + 3)$$
$$distance(3) = min(distance(5) + 1, distance(1) + 3) \tag{4.23}$$
$$distance(4) = min(distance(1) + 3, distance(2) + 2)$$
$$distance(5) = min(distance(1) + 1, distance(2) + 2)$$

Solution by Successive Approximations

One way of solving a system of simultaneous equations is by successive approximations. For our example graph this method would proceed as follows. Introducing the notation $d(x)$ for an 'approximation' to *distance*(x) we begin by setting

$$d(1) = 0, d(2) = d(3) = d(4) = d(5) = \infty.$$

Then, substituting these approximations into the right sides of (4.23), we obtain new approximations for the left sides:

$$d(2) = min(0 + 6, \infty + 4, \infty + 3) = 6$$

and

$$d(3) = min(\infty + 1, 0 + 3) = 3.$$

Similarly, using the best available approximations,

$$d(4) = min(0 + 3, 6 + 2) = 3$$

and

$$d(5) = min(0 + 1, 6 + 2) = 1.$$

This process is repeated until an equality is observed between all corresponding left and right sides.

Two conditions are crucial to this technique. The first is that the iterative process does indeed *converge*, i.e. terminate, after a finite number of iterations. Fortunately, this is not a problem for us since a variant is $\mathbf{S}(x{::}\ d(x))$. This variant is bounded below by zero and we shall construct our code so that the idempotency of *min* clearly demonstrates that its value decreases on each iteration except the last.

The second condition is to ensure that any solution we obtain to the equations (4.21) and (4.22) is also a solution to equation (4.18). The problem is that simultaneous equations like (4.21) and (4.22) need not have a unique solution and our calculations may determine the wrong one! (In fact equations (4.21) and (4.22) can be shown to have a unique solution but the next exercise illustrates a similar problem analysis in which a system of simultaneous equations with a nonunique solution may be obtained.)

To formulate the method we introduce a variable *unequal* to determine when equality between the left and right sides is achieved. The property maintaind by *unequal* is

    unequal **or** $\mathbf{A}(x{:}\ x \neq s{:}\ d(x) = \mathbf{MIN}(a{:}\ a\cdot into = x{:}\ d(a\cdot from) + a\cdot length)).$

The notion of $d(x)$ approximating *distance*(x) is made precise by the statement that, whenever $d(x)$ is finite, it is the length of a path to the node x, i.e.

    $\mathbf{A}(x{:}\ d(x) < \infty{:}$
        $\mathbf{E}(p{::}\ p\cdot from = s$ **and** $p\cdot into = x$ **and** $p\cdot length = d(x))).$

The algorithm then takes the form

unequal$:=$ **true**; $d(s):= 0$; **for each** $x \neq s$ **do** $d(x):= \infty$;
{**Invariant**: [*unequal* **or**
        $\mathbf{A}(x{:}\ x \neq s{:}\ d(x) = \mathbf{MIN}(a{:}\ a\cdot into = x{:}\ d(a\cdot from) + a\cdot length))]$

and $A(x: d(x) < \infty$:

$E(p:: p \cdot from = s$ **and** $p \cdot into = x$ **and** $p \cdot length = d(x)))$

Variant: $S(x:: d(x)) + $ **if** $unequal$ **then** 1 **else** $0\}$

while $unequal$ **do**

    begin

        $unequal := $ **false**;

        for each a **do**

           begin

               if $d(a \cdot into) > d(a \cdot from) + a \cdot length$

               then begin

                     $d(a \cdot into) := d(a \cdot from) + a \cdot length;$

                     $unequal := $ **true**

               end

           end

    end

$\{$ **not** $unequal$ **and** $A(x: x \neq s$:

               $d(x) = MIN(a: a \cdot into = x: d(a \cdot from) + a \cdot length))$

        and $A(x: d(x) < \infty$:

               $E(p:: p \cdot from = s$ **and** $p \cdot into = x$ **and** $p \cdot length = d(x)))\}$

$\{A(x:: d(x) = distance(x))\}$

Note that the algorithm terminates in a state in which each finite $d(x)$ is the length of a path from s to x and in which a solution to (4.21) and (4.22) has been found. Were $d(x)$ not equal to $distance(x)$, for each node x, we could consider a node y closest to s for which $d(y) \neq distance(y)$. (If there are two or more nodes equidistant from s for which the latter inequality holds, choose one for which the shortest path also has least arc-count). Clearly $y \neq s$ and so a shortest path to y must take the form pa where

$$p \cdot into = a \cdot from$$

and $distance(y) = distance(p \cdot into) + a \cdot length.$

But by the choice of y,

$$d(p \cdot into) = distance(p \cdot into)$$

and, since $d(y)$ is infinite or is the length of a path to y,

$$d(y) > distance(y).$$

But then $d(y) > d(a \cdot from) + a \cdot length$

which contradicts the invariant property of $unequal$. We conclude, therefore, that the algorithm terminates in a state satisfying $d(x) = distance(x)$ for all nodes x.

Fig. 4.17 Example for exercise 4.28.

Exercise
4.28 Consider the simpler problem of determining for each node x whether there is a path p from s to x. Define

$$is\_path(x) \equiv \mathbf{E}(p::p \cdot from = s \text{ and } p \cdot into = x).$$

(a) Show that

$$is\_path(s) \equiv \mathbf{true} \tag{4.24}$$

and, for all $x \neq s$,

$$is\_path(x) \equiv \mathbf{E}(a:a \cdot into = x: is\_path(a \cdot from)). \tag{4.25}$$

(b) Figure 4.17 shows a particularly simple graph having two nodes a and b. Taking a as the start node use (4.24) and (4.25) to construct equations for $is\_path(a)$ and $is\_path(b)$. Show that the equations you obtain do not have a unique solution.

(c) Develop an algorithm similar to the one above for computing $is\_path(x)$ for each node x in a graph. Provide a convincing argument that the termination condition for your algorithm is indeed correct.

Dijkstra's Algorithm

The method of successive approximations has the (severe) disadvantage that it may require n complete iterations before it terminates, where n is the number of nodes in the graph; moreover, the last iteration serves no useful purpose except to determine that a solution to equations (4.21) and (4.22) has been found. There is some merit, therefore, in investigating a particular order for accessing arcs, a, in the '**for each** a' statement in order that convergence may be guaranteed after exactly one complete iteration.

Consider again the graph of Fig. 4.16. Starting with the initial approximations $d(1) = 0$, $d(2) = d(3) = d(4) = d(5) = \infty$, it is obvious that the arcs from node 1 should first be used to reset $d(2)$ to $min(\infty, 0 + 6) = 6$, $d(3)$ to $min(\infty, 0 + 3) = 3$, $d(4)$ to $min(\infty, 0 + 3) = 3$, and $d(5)$ to $min(\infty, 0 + 1) = 1$. This gives us the approximations

$$d(1) = 0, \ d(2) = 6, \ d(3) = 3, \ d(4) = 3, \ d(5) = 1.$$

Which arcs should be chosen next? It seems reasonable to *conjecture* that $d(5) = distance(5)$, since node 5 is apparently the closest to s, and hence the arcs from node 5 should be used to update the distances d. Thus, using the arcs from 5 to 2 and 3, $d(2)$ is reset to $min(6, 1 + 4) = 5$ and $d(3)$ is reset to $min(3, 1 + 1) = 2$. At this stage we have the approximations

$$d(1) = 0, \ d(2) = 5, \ d(3) = 2, \ d(4) = 3, \ d(5) = 1.$$

Apart from nodes 1 and 5, which have already been considered, node 3 is now the closest to s. We *conjecture* therefore that $d(3) = distance(3)$. Since there are no arcs from node 3, its choice causes no change to the distances d. Now, node 4 is chosen. The only arc from node 4 has no effect on the known distance to node 2. Finally, choosing the arcs from node 2 also has no effect on the known distances. In this way, after accessing each arc once only we obtain

$$d(1) = 0, \ d(2) = 5, \ d(3) = 2, \ d(4) = 3, \ d(5) = 1$$

which are easily verified to be the shortest distances to each of the nodes.

Verifying a solution strategy on one particular example is highly unreliable, but choosing the node closest to s does appear to be plausible. We must now try to prove or disprove the conjecture.

We recall that a graph consists of a pair (X, A) where X is the set of nodes and A is the set of arcs. The method just outlined processes arcs in A one-by-one in a certain order. Let us, therefore, call the pair (X, B) a *subgraph* of (X, A) whenever B is a subset of A, and conjecture that a solution exists with the property that $d(x)$ is the distance to node x in the graph (X, B) where B is the set of arcs that have been processed. More precisely, letting $distance_B(x)$ denote the distance to node x in the subgraph (X, B) we consider an algorithm with the following structure.

$d(s) := 0;$ **for each** $x \neq s$ **do** $d(x) := \infty;$
$B := \emptyset;$
{**Invariant**: $B \subseteq A$ **and** $\mathbf{A}(x :: d(x) = distance_B(x))$
  Variant: *number of nodes not already chosen*}
while $B \neq A$ **do**
    begin *choose a node* $y;$
        for each *arc* a *from* y **do**
            begin
                $d(a \cdot into) := min(d(a \cdot into), \ d(y) + a \cdot length);$
                $B := B \cup \{a\}$
            end
    end

The choice of node y within the loop body is, of course, crucial to the success of this algorithm. For our conjecture to be valid it must be the case that $d(y) = distance_A(y)$ otherwise the assignment to $d(a \cdot into)$ uses an inaccurate estimate of $distance_A(y)$. Also, for progress to be made to the termination condition it is necessary that no node y is chosen more than once. We therefore introduce a new variable *chosen* that records all of the nodes already chosen, and strengthen the invariant to include the clause

$$\mathbf{A}(x: x \ \textbf{in} \ chosen: d(x) = distance_A(x)).$$

The remaining details of our conjecture are that the node chosen at each iteration should be a node not already chosen which is estimated to be closest to s.

$d(s): = 0; \ \textbf{for each} \ x \neq s \ \textbf{do} \ d(x): = \infty;$
$B: = \emptyset; \ chosen: = \emptyset;$
$\{\textbf{Invariant}: B \subseteq A \ \textbf{and} \ \mathbf{A}(x::d(x) = distance_B(x))$
$\qquad\qquad \ \ \textbf{and} \ \mathbf{A}(x: x \ \textbf{in} \ chosen: d(x) = distance_A(x))$
$\quad \textbf{Variant}: \ |X| - |chosen| \ (|C| \ denotes \ number \ of \ nodes \ in \ C)\}$
$\textbf{while} \ B \neq A \ \textbf{do}$
$\quad \textbf{begin}$
$\qquad choose \ a \ node \ y \ not \ in \ chosen \ such \ that$
$\qquad\quad d(y) = \mathbf{MIN}(x: \textbf{not} \ (x \ \textbf{in} \ chosen): d(x))$
$\qquad chosen: = chosen \cup \{y\};$
$\qquad \textbf{for each} \ arc \ a \ from \ y \ \textbf{do}$
$\qquad\quad \textbf{begin}$
$\qquad\qquad d(a \cdot into): = min(d(a \cdot into), \ d(y) + a \cdot length);$
$\qquad\qquad B: = B \cup \{a\}$
$\qquad\quad \textbf{end}$
$\quad \textbf{end}$

In order to verify the correctness of this solution we make three further observations.

(a) At the beginning of each execution of the loop body every path in the graph (X, A) is either also a path in (X, B) or is prefixed by a path in (X, B) to a nonchosen node z. (This is true initially because λ_s is a path in the graph $(X, \emptyset)$. It is true subsequently because each execution of the loop body adds *all* the arcs from the chosen node y to B.)

(b) Every path in the graph (X, B), except for the empty path from s to itself, consists of a sequence of arcs each of which is from a chosen node. Thus only the last arc can be into a nonchosen node.

(c) Since $B \subseteq A$

$$distance_B(x) \geqslant distance_{B \cup \{a\}}(x) \geqslant distance_A(x)$$

for all nodes x and all arcs a.

Now, clearly, the initial statements establish the invariant property, and on termination the conjunction of the invariant and the condition $B = A$ imply that $distance_A(x) = d(x)$ for all x. It remains for us to establish that the invariant is maintained by the loop body.

Consider first the choice of a node y. We have to prove that the mechanism for making the choice guarantees that $d(y) = distance_A(y)$ under the inductive hypothesis that the invariant is true. The argument we use is to divide paths in the graph into two sets:

(i) paths that are in the graph (X, B);
(ii) paths that are not in the graph (X, B).

By the first of our observations we can assert that any path p of type (ii) from s to y consists of a path in (X, B) to a nonchosen node, z, followed by a path from z to y. Hence

$$p \cdot length \geqslant distance_B(z), \text{ since all arc lengths are nonnegative.}$$

But $distance_B(z) = d(z)$, by the invariant property, and $d(z) \geqslant d(y)$, by the choice of y.
Thus $p \cdot length \geqslant d(y)$.

Since $distance_A(y)$ is the minimum over paths into y of types (i) and (ii) and $d(y) = distance_B(y)$ it follows that $d(y) = distance_A(y)$.

We have just verified that the assignment $chosen := chosen \cup \{y\}$ maintains the invariant property. We now have to prove that the sequence of assignments

$$d(a \cdot into) := min(d(a \cdot into), d(y) + a \cdot length);$$
$$B := B \cup \{a\}$$

also maintains the invariant, for each arc a from y. It suffices to show that

$$\mathbf{A}(x :: d(x) = distance_B(x))$$

is maintained. This may be established by dividing the nodes into two sets, those in $chosen$ and those not in $chosen$. For those nodes x in $chosen$ the invariant property asserts that

$$distance_B(x) = distance_A(x).$$

Thus, by observation (c),

$$d(x) = distance_B(x) = distance_{B \cup \{a\}}(x).$$

For nodes x not in $chosen$ we appeal to observation (b). Any path in the graph $(X, B \cup \{a\})$ to a nonchosen node x that is not also a path in the graph (X, B) must terminate with the arc a, i.e. $x = a \cdot into$ and

$$distance_{B \cup \{a\}}(x) = min(distance_B(x), \ distance_B(a \cdot from) + a \cdot length)$$
$$= min(d(x), \ d(a \cdot from) + a \cdot length)$$
$$= min(d(x), \ d(y) + a \cdot length)$$

thus confirming the validity of the assignment to $d(a \cdot into)$.

Exercises

4.29 (Bridge problem) A high load has to be driven from x to y and on each possible route several low bridges have to be negotiated. The problem is to compute a route that maximizes the height of the lowest bridge on the route.

This problem is modeled as a graph-searching problem in which the graph (X, A) represents the various routes that can be taken and the arc labels represent the bridge heights, a label of ∞ signifying no bridge. Thus, if the labels in Fig. 4.16 are interpreted as bridge heights, the best route from node 1 to node 5 involves negotiating the bridge of height 2 between nodes 2 and 5. Either the path from 1 to 2 to 5, or the path from 1 to 4 to 2 to 5 achieve the specification of maximizing the lowest bridge height.

Formulate the problem as we did for shortest paths and develop solutions, along the same lines.

4.30 Consider graphs in which all of the arc lengths are $+1$ or -1. Define the length of a path to be the *product* of the arc lengths. (Note that path lengths are also either $+1$ or -1.) What implications does this change in definition of the length of a path have on solutions to the shortest path problem? Develop an algorithm to solve the shortest path problem in this case.

BIBLIOGRAPHIC NOTES

Writing this book has been a great pleasure for me if only because I have had to read a large number of other authors' works. These notes describe a selection of texts and papers that have particularly influenced the presentation.

Although not directly related to programming, George Polya's books [24, 25] have been a particular source of inspiration. Polya's concern is with the process of problem-solving, including the formulation of conjectures and their subsequent verification or refutation. He illustrates his ideas with a tremendous collection of examples taken from many branches of mathematics. I first saw the algorithm for computing powers of n, described in chapter 0, in [24]; it was originally discovered by A. Moessner [22] and proved by O. Perron [23]. The quotation at the head of section 0.2 is from [25] and exercise 0.2 is from [24] (though not its solution). The idea for Fig. 1.2 and exercise 1.2 came from [25] and the quotations at the heads of sections 3.3.2 and 3.3.3 came from [24].

Texts on logic are traditionally concerned with studying logical systems, rather than using logic—logicians do not appear to have had the need to apply logic as much as computing scientists. Two of the best texts on logic are those by Raymond Smullyan [29, 30], the first of these being the source of the examples and exercises in sections 1.8 and 1.9. Smullyan's approach to presenting logic is highly entertaining and educational. Another, more traditional, account of logic has been given by Copi [4]. The argument about the nonexistence of Superman in chapter 1 was adapted from an argument about the nonexistence of God in [9]. The rules of inference in section 1.9 are from [11].

A very large part of the text has been directly influenced by the work of E. W. Dijkstra. The quotation attributed to Dijkstra in chapter 0 appears in [3], which is also the source of Hopkins' remarks. The notation for quantifiers introduced in chapter 2 was invented by Dijkstra and presented along with the wp-rules of chapter 3 in his book *A Discipline of Programming* [6], to which the reader is referred for many more examples of program development. Dijkstra's philosophy on computing is well represented by a collection of trip reports, technical reports, and essays [7]; the article entitled 'Craftsman or Scientist' is particularly recommended. Dijkstra has also written an introductory text on program development with W. H. J. Feijen [8]. The text was originally in Dutch but is also available in other languages, although not, as yet, in English. A number of the problems discussed in chapter 4 are due to Dijkstra or his colleagues at the Technische Hogeschool Eindhoven. One of them, M. Rem, has a regular column in the journal *The Science of Computer Programming* [26] devoted to such problems and their solutions. The longest almost ascending segment problem is one of those posed by Rem. The presentation of sorting problems in section 4.4, particularly those of bubblesort and heapsort, follows closely Dijkstra's presentation of the algorithms. An account of the shortest path algorithm in section 4.5.3 first appeared in [5]. The solution to the Boolean split problem in exercise 4.23 is due to W. H. J. Feijen, and was shown to me by Rudolf Mak.

A companion text to this is one written by David Gries [12]. I have deliberately avoided using the same programming examples as Gries, although his are particularly well chosen, so that the texts do not compete, and so that the reader may profit by studying both. Nevertheless, I owe to David Gries several of the examples I have used. The minsum and largest true square problems were the subject of a lecture given by Gries at the University of Essex; his own account of their solution appears in [13]; the development of the majority voting algorithm is based on a summary of the algorithm given by Misra and Gries [21]—they attribute the algorithm to R. Boyer and J. Moore—and the longest prefix problem and its solution were sent to me by Gries.

Although Dijkstra invented the quantifier notation in chapter 2, I had never seen a detailed investigation of its properties when preparing the text. My formulation of the properties was partly influenced by D. E. Knuth's account of quantification [18]. The warning about their use with infinite ranges concerns problems with convergence of series. For example, the summation $\mathbf{S}(i: 0 \leqslant i: (-1)^i)$ is not well defined since the finite summation $\mathbf{S}(i: 0 \leqslant i < n: (-1)^i)$ evaluates alternately to 1 and 0 as n is incremented by 1. Distributivity properties also rely on notions of so-called 'continuity' of the operators. See Apostol [1] for a detailed analysis of infinite series. Knuth's books [18, 19] are a mine of historical information on the development of algorithms. For a history of methods of calculating powers (briefly mentioned in section 4.2.3) see [19, pp. 398–422].

Hoare's proof rules were first published in 1969 [15]. Binary search is an old chestnut. The idea of using a deck of cards to illustrate its solution was given to me by Stuart Anderson.

There is a rich and growing amount of literature that will take the reader further. David Gries's textbook [12] has already been mentioned. Other recommended texts are those by Hehner [14], Jones [17], and Reynolds [27]. For further information on cyclic codes and error-control coding in general see [2].

Finally, I acknowledge the source of some of my exercises and quotations. Exercise 0.1 is from [28], where it is attributed to the great American puzzle maker, Sam Loyd. The problem of the amorous beetles (exercise 3.19) is from [10]. The quotation at the head of section 3.3.1 is from [16], and the quotation at the head of chapter 4 is from [20].

[1] T. M. Apostol, *Mathematical Analysis*, Addison-Wesley, Reading, Mass. (1957).
[2] Richard E. Blahut, *Theory and Practice of Error Control Codes*, Addison-Wesley, Reading, Mass. (1983).
[3] J. N. Buxton and B. Randell, *Software Engineering Techniques*, Report on a Conference sponsored by the NATO Science Committee, Rome, Italy, 27–31 October, 1969. NATO Science Committee (April 1970).
[4] Irving M. Copi, *Symbolic Logic*, Fourth Edition, Macmillan Publ., New York (1973).
[5] Edsger W. Dijkstra, 'A note on two problems in connexion with graphs', *Numerische Mathematik* 1, 269–271 (1959).

[6] Edsger W. Dijkstra, *A Discipline of Programming*, Prentice-Hall Series in Automatic Computation, Prentice-Hall, Englewood Cliffs, N.J. (1976).

[7] Edsger W. Dijkstra, *Selected Writings on Computing: A Personal Perspective*, Springer-Verlag Texts and Monographs in Computer Science, Springer-Verlag, New York (1982).

[8] E. W. Dijkstra and W. H. J. Feijen, *Een Methode van Programmeren*, Academic Service, Den Haag (1984).

[9] Alan Foster and Graham Shute, 'Propositional logic: a student introduction', *Aston Educational Enquiry Monograph No. 4*, University of Aston in Birmingham (1976).

[10] Martin Gardner, *Mathematical Puzzles and Diversions*, Penguin Books, Harmondsworth, Middlesex (1959).

[11] Gerhard Gentzen, 'Investigations into logical deduction', in *The Collected Papers of Gerhard Gentzen*, 68–213, ed. M. E. Szabo, North-Holland, Amsterdam (1969).

[12] David Gries, *The Science of Programming*, Springer-Verlag, New York (1981).

[13] David Gries, 'A note on a standard strategy for developing loop invariants and loops, *Science of Computer Programming* 2, 207–214 (1982).

[14] Eric C. R. Hehner, *The Logic of Programming*, Prentice-Hall International Series in Computer Science, Prentice-Hall, Englewood Cliffs, N.J. (1984).

[15] C. A. R. Hoare, 'An axiomatic basis for computer programming', *Comm. ACM* 12 (10), 576–580, 583 (Oct. 1969).

[16] D. R. Hofstadter, *Gödel, Escher, Bach: An Eternal Golden Braid*, Penguin Books, Harmondsworth, Middlesex (1979).

[17] Cliff B. Jones, *Software Development: A Rigorous Approach*, Prentice-Hall International Series in Computer Science, Prentice-Hall, Englewood Cliffs, N.J. (1980).

[18] D. E. Knuth, *The Art of Computer Programming Vol. I: Fundamental Algorithms*, Addison-Wesley, Reading, Mass. (1968).

[19] D. E. Knuth, *The Art of Computer Programming Vol. II: Seminumerical Algorithms*, Addison-Wesley, Reading, Mass. (1969).

[20] Imre Lakatos, *Proofs and Refutations*, Cambridge University Press, Cambridge (1976).

[21] J. Misra and D. Gries, 'Finding repeated elements', *Science of Computer Programming* 2, 143–152 (1982).

[22] A. Moessner, 'Eine Bemerkung über die Potenzen der natürlichen Zahlen', *Sitzungsberichte der Bayerische Akademie der Wissenschaften, Math.—naturwissenschaftliche Klasse*, 29 (1951).

[23] O. Perron, 'Beweis der Moessnerschen Satzes', *Sitzungsberichte der Bayerische Akademie der Wissenschaften, Math.—naturwissenschaftliche Klasse*, 31–34 (1951).

[24] George Polya, *Induction and Analogy in Mathematics*, Volume I of Mathematics and Plausible Reasoning, Princeton University Press, Princeton, N.J. (1954).

[25] George Polya, *Mathematical Discovery. On Understanding, Learning and Teaching Problem Solving*, Combined Edition, John Wiley & Sons, New York (1981).

[26] M. Rem, 'Small programming exercises', *Science of Computer Programming* 3, 217–222, 313–319 (1983), 4, 87–94, 205–210, 323–333 (1984), 5, 97–106 (1985).

[27] John C. Reynolds, *The Craft of Programming*, Prentice-Hall International Series in Computer Science, Prentice-Hall, Englewood Cliffs, N.J. (1981).

[28] T. Rice, *Mathematical Games and Puzzles*, B. T. Batsford, London (1973).
[29] Raymond Smullyan, *What is the Name of This Book?*, Prentice-Hall, Englewood Cliffs, N.J. (1978).
[30] Raymond Smullyan, *The Lady or the Tiger? and Other Logical Puzzles*, Penguin Books, Harmondsworth, Middlesex (1983).

SOLUTIONS

CHAPTER 0

0.1 The second player always wins. The second player's first move is to 'copy' the first player's first move by removing the petals diametrically opposite to those taken by the first player. This initial sequence of moves divides the remaining petals into two halves and enforces the constraint that each subsequent move may not remove two petals from different halves. The second player's strategy is therefore to maintain the symmetry of the daisy by always copying the first player's moves.

0.2 This problem is similar to the daisy problem although this time it is the first player who wins. Imagine x, y axes drawn through the center of the table as shown below.

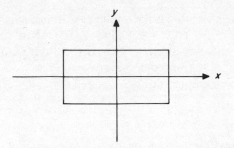

The first player begins by putting a coin at the center of the table, i.e. at the coordinates $(0, 0)$. Subsequently, whenever the second player places a coin at coordinates (a, b) the first player copies the move by placing an identical coin at the point $(-a, -b)$. The property being maintained invariant by the first player is that whenever there is a coin covering the coordinates (x, y) there is a coin covering the coordinates $(-x, -y)$.

0.3 The key property in this problem is that any rectangle must have an upper-right corner, i.e. to form a rectangle player A must always draw two lines in the shape. ⌐.

Player B wins by ensuring that this shape never appears on the grid. So whenever A draws a vertical line, B reponds by adding a horizontal dashed line forming the shape ⌐.

And if A draws a horizontal line B draws a vertical dashed line forming the shape ⌐.

If A's move already forms either of these shapes B may make an arbitrary move.

CHAPTER 1

1.1 Two basic properties that are assumed are that the sum of the angles of a triangle is 180° and that, for example, IJ is a straight line only if $I\hat{B}J$ is 180°. These properties are necessary to show that IJ, JK, KL, and LT are indeed straight lines, and to show that the inner square is indeed a square. Other properties that are assumed are the formulae for the area of a triangle or square, and basic properties of arithmetic.

1.2 The flaw in the algorithm is the implicit assumption in steps 3 and 4 that if $l > r$ then $l^2 > r^2$. This is not always true when r is negative. (For example, $0 > -1$ but $0^2 < (-1)^2$) and the subtraction in step 2 may cause the right side to become negative.

An example demonstrating the bug is $a = 1, b = 3, c = 1$, and $d = 2$. Clearly

$$\sqrt{1} + \sqrt{3} > \sqrt{1} + \sqrt{2}.$$

However, following through the algorithm, we obtain:

Step 1. left side simplifies to $4 + 2\sqrt{3}$
right side simplifies to $3 + 2\sqrt{2}$
Step 2. left side simplifies to $2\sqrt{3}$
right side simplifies to $-1 + 2\sqrt{2}$

Step 3.   left side simplifies to 12
            right side simplifies to $9 - 4\sqrt{2}$
Step 4.   left side simplifies to 9
            right side simplifies to 32
Hence $\sqrt{1 + \sqrt{3}} < \sqrt{1 + \sqrt{2}}$!

Think carefully about the construction of this example. It certainly was not constructed by random testing!

1.3   (a) Yes,   (b) No,   (c) Yes,   (d) No,   (e) No.

1.4   (a) Premises are 'each new student brings a little knowledge in' and 'the graduates do not take any away'. The conclusion is 'knowledge in universities grows and grows'. Decide for yourself whether it is logical or not!
(b) The conclusion is 'if a student submits no project work whatsoever he/she must achieve a mark of at least 60 in the examination questions in order to pass'. The remaining sentences are the premises. This is a logical argument.
(c) The conclusion is 'the President's mother is either an elephant or a whale' and the first two sentences are the premises. The argument is clearly illogical.

1.5 $[(\text{not } T \text{ or } N) \text{ and } (N \Rightarrow M) \text{ and } T] \Rightarrow M$.

1.6 $[(\text{not } A) \text{ and } (A \Rightarrow B \text{ and } C)] \Rightarrow (\text{not } B \text{ or not } C)$.
(*Note*: this is not valid.)

1.7   (b), (d), (e), (g), (l), (m), (n), (o), (p), (q) are the true propositions.

1.8   (a)

A is lying	B is lying	At least one of A and B is lying
T	T	T
T	F	T
F	T	T
F	F	F

'At least one of p or q' is equivalent to 'p or q'.

(b)

A is lying	B is lying	Exactly one of A and B is lying
T	T	F
T	F	T
F	T	T
F	F	F

'Exactly one of p and q' is equivalent to p **xor** q.

(c)

A is lying	B is lying	Either both are lying or both are telling the truth
T	T	T
T	F	F
F	T	F
F	F	T

'Either both p and q or both not p and not q' is equivalent to '$p \Leftrightarrow q$'.

(d)

x is positive	y is zero	x is positive unless y is zero
T	T	F
T	F	T
F	T	T
F	F	T

'p unless q' is equivalent to $q \Rightarrow$ **not** p.

The truth tables have been omitted in the remainder of these solutions.

(e) 'From the fact that p one can infer q' is equivalent to '$p \Rightarrow q$'.
(f) 'p provided that q' is equivalent to '$q \Rightarrow p$'.
(g) 'Were p we would know q' is equivalent to '$p \Rightarrow q$'.
(h) 'p because q' is equivalent to 'p **and** q'. (It may be read as 'q, and q implies p' which is the same as 'p **and** q'.)
(i) 'p contradicts q' is equivalent to '**not** (p **and** q)'.

1.9 L_1 and L_3 satisfy (a). L_2 and L_3 satisfy (b).

1.10   (a) $[(X$ **and** (**not** Y)) **or** $Z] \Rightarrow X$.
(b) $X \Leftrightarrow [($**not** $Y)$ **and** $Z]$.
(c) $(X$ **and** $Y) \Rightarrow ($**not** $Z)$.
(d) $[X$ **or** $(Y$ **and** $Z)$ **or** $($**not** $Z)] \Leftrightarrow X$.
(e) $X \Leftrightarrow ((Y$ **and** $Z) \Leftrightarrow X)$.

1.11   (a) F,   (b) F,   (c) F,   (d) F,   (e) T.

1.12   When 'or' is interpreted as '**or**' we obtain the following truth table:

P R	$(R \Rightarrow P)$	$\Rightarrow$	$(P$ **or not** $R)$
T T	T	T	T F
T F	T	T	T T
F T	F	T	F F
F F	T	T	T T

However, when 'or' is interpreted as '**xor**' we obtain the following:

P R	$(R \Rightarrow P)$	$\Rightarrow$	$(P$ **xor not** $R)$	
T T	T	T	T	F
T F	T	F	F	T
F T	F	T	F	F
F F	T	T	T	T

The first proposition is thus a tautology whereas the second is not. The moral is beware the ambiguities of English!

1.13 (a)

X Y Z	$[(X \Rightarrow Y$ **or** $Z)$ **and** $Z]$			$\Rightarrow$	$[Y \Rightarrow$ **not** $X]$	
T T T	T	T	T	F	F	F
F T T	T	T	T	T	T	T
T F T	T	T	T	T	T	F
F F T	T	T	T	T	T	T
T T F	T	T	F	T	F	F
F T F	T	T	F	T	T	T
T F F	F	F	F	T	T	F
F F F	T	F	F	T	T	T

The argument is invalid. A counterexample is when x equals 0, y is positive and z is negative.

(b)

X Y Z	$[(X \Rightarrow (Y \Rightarrow Z))$ **and** $Y]$			$\Rightarrow$	$[X$ **or** $Z]$
T T T	T	T	T	T	T
F T T	T	T	T	T	T
T F T	T	T	F	T	T
F F T	T	T	F	T	T
T T F	F	F	F	T	T
F T F	T	F	T	F	F
T F F	T	T	F	T	T
F F F	T	T	F	T	F

The argument is invalid.

(c)

I T P	$[(I$ **and** $T \Rightarrow P)$ **and** $P]$			$\Rightarrow$	$(I \Rightarrow T)$
T T T	T	T	T	T	T
F T T	F	T	T	T	T
T F T	F	T	T	F	F
F F T	F	T	T	T	T
T T F	T	F	F	T	T
F T F	F	T	F	T	T
T F F	F	T	F	T	F
F F F	F	T	F	T	T

the argument is invalid.

(d) A B C $\quad\{[(A\Rightarrow B)\text{ and }(B\Rightarrow C)]\text{ and }(\text{not }A\text{ or not }B)\}\Rightarrow(\text{not }B\text{ or }C)$

A	B	C									
T	T	T	T	T	T	F	F	F	F	T	F	T
F	T	T	T	T	T	T	T	T	F	T	F	T
T	F	T	F	F	T	F	F	T	T	T	T	T
F	F	T	T	T	T	T	T	T	T	T	T	T
T	T	F	T	F	F	F	F	F	F	T	F	F
F	T	F	T	F	F	F	T	T	F	T	F	F
T	F	F	F	F	T	F	F	T	T	T	T	T
F	F	F	T	T	T	T	T	T	T	T	T	T

The argument is valid.

1.14 (a) p or $(q$ and $p)\equiv(p$ and **true**$)$ or $(p$ and $q)$

                (constants and commutativity)

        $\equiv p$ and $(\textbf{true}$ or $q)$ (distributivity)

        $\equiv p$ and **true** (constants)

        $\equiv p$ (constants)

(b) $(p$ or $q)$ and $q\equiv(p$ and $q)$ or $(q$ and $q)$ (distributivity)

        $\equiv(p$ and $q)$ or q (idempotency)

        $\equiv q$ (exercise (a))

(c) $(p$ and $q)$ or $(\text{not }p$ and $q)$ or $(p$ and not $q)$

        $\equiv(p$ and $q)$ or $(p$ and $q)$ or $(\text{not }p$ and $q)$ or $(p$ and not $q)$

                (idempotency)

        $\equiv(p$ and $q)$ or $(\text{not }p$ and $q)$ or $(p$ and $q)$ or $(p$ and not $q)$

                (commutativity)

        $\equiv[(p$ or not $p)$ and $q]$ or $[p$ and $(q$ or not $q)]$

                (distributivity)

        $\equiv(\textbf{true}$ and $q)$ or $(p$ and **true**$)$ (excluded middle)

        $\equiv p$ or q (constants and commutativity)

(d) $(p\Rightarrow q)$ and $(p\Rightarrow\text{not }q)$

        $\equiv p\Rightarrow(q$ and not $q)$ (distributivity)

        $\equiv p\Rightarrow\textbf{false}$ (contradiction)

        $\equiv\text{not }p$ (constants)

(e) $(p$ and $q)\Leftrightarrow p$

        $\equiv[(p$ and $q)\Rightarrow p]$ and $[p\Rightarrow(p$ and $q)]$ (equivalence)

        $\equiv[q\Rightarrow(p\Rightarrow p)]$ and $(p\Rightarrow p)$ and $(p\Rightarrow q)$

                (implication and distributivity)

Now, $p\Rightarrow p\equiv\text{not }p$ or p (implication)

        $\equiv\textbf{true}$ (excluded middle)

Hence, $(p$ and $q)\Leftrightarrow p$

        $\equiv(q\Rightarrow\textbf{true})$ and **true** and $(p\Rightarrow q)$ (substitution)

        $\equiv p\Rightarrow q$ (constants)

(f) **not** $(p \Rightarrow q)$

$\equiv$ **not** $[(p$ **and** $q)$ **or** (**not** p **and not** $q)]$ (equivalence)

$\equiv$ (**not** p **or not** q) **and** (**not not** p **or not not** q)

(De Morgan—twice)

$\equiv$ (**not** p **or not** q) **and** (p **or** q)   (negation)

$\equiv$ (**not** p **and** p) **or** (**not** q **and** p) **or** (**not** p **and** q) **or** (q **and not** q)

(distributivity—twice)

$\equiv$ **false or** (**not** q **and** p) **or** (**not** p **and** q) **or false**

(contradiction)

$\equiv$ (**not** q **and** p) **or** (**not** p **and** q)   (constants)

$\equiv (p \Leftrightarrow$ **not** q)   (equivalence)

(g) (p **and** $q \Rightarrow r$) **and** (p **and not** $q \Rightarrow$ **not** r)

$\equiv (p \Rightarrow (q \Rightarrow r))$ **and** $(p \Rightarrow ($**not** $q \Rightarrow$ **not** $r))$ (implication)

$\equiv p \Rightarrow [(q \Rightarrow r)$ **and** (**not** $q \Rightarrow$ **not** $r)]$ (distributivity)

$\equiv p \Rightarrow (q \Leftrightarrow r)$ (equivalence)

(h) (**not** p **and** q) **or** (p **and not** q)

$\equiv$ **not** $p \Leftrightarrow q$ (equivalence)

$\equiv$ (**not** $p \Rightarrow q$) **and** ($p \Rightarrow$ **not** q)   (equivalence & negation)

$\equiv (p$ **or** q) **and** (**not** p **or not** q) (implication & negation)

$\equiv (p$ **or** q) **and not** (p **and** q)   (De Morgan)

(i) (p **and** $q \Rightarrow r$) **and** (p **and not** $q \Rightarrow s$)

$\equiv (p \Rightarrow (q \Rightarrow r))$ **and** $(p \Rightarrow ($**not** $q \Rightarrow s))$ (implication)

$\equiv p \Rightarrow [(q \Rightarrow r)$ **and** (**not** $q \Rightarrow s)]$ (distributivity)

(j) $(p \Rightarrow q)$ **and** (**not** $p \Rightarrow r$)

$\equiv$ (**not** p **or** q) **and** (p **or** r)   (implication & negation)

$\equiv$ **not** p **and** p **or not** p **and** r **or** q **and** p **or** q **and** r

(distributivity)

$\equiv$ **not** p **and** r **or** q **and** p **or** q **and** r (contradiction)

$\equiv (p$ **and** q) **or** q **and** r **and** (p **or not** p) **or** (**not** p **and** r)

(commutativity and excluded middle)

$\equiv (p$ **and** q) **or** (p **and** q **and** r) **or** (**not** p **and** q **and** r) **or** (**not** p **and** r)   (distributivity)

$\equiv [p$ **and** (q **or** q **and** r)] **or** [**not** p **and** (q **and** r **or** r)]

(distributivity)

$\equiv (p$ **and** q) **or** (**not** p **and** r)   (exercise (a))

1.15 (a) and (c) are false, (b) is true. Because (a) is false you should never write $p \Rightarrow q \Rightarrow r$ without parentheses since its meaning is unclear. For a quite different reason you should avoid writing $p \Leftrightarrow q \Leftrightarrow r$ without parentheses (or if you do you should make the meaning very clear). The reason is that $p \Leftrightarrow q \Leftrightarrow r$ is likely to be interpreted conjunctively as $(p \Leftrightarrow q)$ **and** $(q \Leftrightarrow r)$ which, by (c), is not the same as $(p \Leftrightarrow q) \Leftrightarrow r$.

1.16 See text for solution.

1.17 A's statement can be expressed as $B \Rightarrow \textbf{not } A$. So we begin with the premise

$$A \Leftrightarrow (B \Rightarrow \textbf{not } A).$$

The truth table for this proposition (below) shows that it is true only when A is true and B is false. We conclude that A is a knight and B is a knave.

A	B	$A \Leftrightarrow (B \Rightarrow \textbf{not } A)$		
T	T	F	F	F
F	T	F	T	T
T	F	T	T	F
F	F	F	T	T

Alternatively,

$A \Leftrightarrow (B \Rightarrow \textbf{not } A)$
  $\equiv [A \Leftrightarrow (\textbf{not } B \textbf{ or not } A)]$
  $\equiv [A \textbf{ and } (\textbf{not } B \textbf{ or not } A)] \textbf{ or } [\textbf{not } A \textbf{ and not } (\textbf{not } B \textbf{ or not } A)]$
  $\equiv [A \textbf{ and not } B] \textbf{ or } [\textbf{not } A \textbf{ and } B \textbf{ and } A]$
  $\equiv A \textbf{ and not } B.$

1.18 Let G denote the proposition 'there is gold on this island'. Then the problem can be reformulated as simplifying the proposition

$$A \Leftrightarrow (G \Leftrightarrow A).$$

The truth table for this proposition (below) shows that it is only true when G is true but when either A or $\textbf{not } A$ is true. Thus the conclusion is that there is gold on the island but A may be a knight or a knave.

A	G	$A \Leftrightarrow (G \Leftrightarrow A)$	
T	T	T	T
F	T	T	F
T	F	F	F
F	F	F	T

1.19 C's statement 'Don't believe B, he's lying!' is equivalent to 'B is a knave', and so we infer the premise.

$$C \Leftrightarrow \textbf{not } B$$

which simply says that B and C are of different types—either C is a knight and B is a knave or C is a knave and B is a knight.

   B's statement is a little more difficult to handle. Let us introduce S as an abbreviation for '*A* said that he is a knave'. Using the basic rule we can then assert:

$$B \Leftrightarrow S.$$

Now consider *S*. If it is true we know that *A* made a statement, namely 'I (*A*) am a knave'. If it is false we know that *A* said something, but we do not know what. Thus from *S* we only have a one-way implication, viz.

$$S \Rightarrow (A \Leftrightarrow \text{not } A).$$

In summary, the problem involves simplifying the expression

$$[C \Leftrightarrow \text{not } B] \text{ and } [B \Leftrightarrow S] \text{ and } [S \Rightarrow (A \Leftrightarrow \text{not } A)].$$

In outline this simplification proceeds as follows:

$[C \Leftrightarrow \textbf{not } B] \textbf{ and } [B \Leftrightarrow S] \textbf{ and } [S \Rightarrow (A \Leftrightarrow \textbf{not } A)]$
$\equiv [C \Leftrightarrow \textbf{not } B] \textbf{ and } [B \Leftrightarrow S] \textbf{ and } [S \Rightarrow \textbf{false}]$
$\equiv [C \Leftrightarrow \textbf{not } B] \textbf{ and } [B \Leftrightarrow S] \textbf{ and not } S$
$\equiv [C \Leftrightarrow \textbf{not } B] \textbf{ and not } B \textbf{ and not } S$
$\equiv C \textbf{ and not } B \textbf{ and not } S.$

We conclude that *C* is a knight, *B* is a knave, and *A* did not say that he was a knave.

1.20 Again, we shall begin with *C'*s statement which, as in the previous question, gives us

$$C \Leftrightarrow \textbf{not } B$$

The proposition 'there is one knight among us' can be formulated as

$((A \textbf{ and not } B \textbf{ and not } C)$
$\textbf{or } (\textbf{not } A \textbf{ and } B \textbf{ and not } C)$
$\textbf{or } (\textbf{not } A \textbf{ and not } B \textbf{ and } C))$

which we shall denote by 1.
   So if *B'*s statement is true then

$$A \Leftrightarrow 1$$
i.e. $B \Leftrightarrow S$
where $S \Rightarrow (A \Leftrightarrow 1).$

Thus the proposition to be simplified is

$$[C \Leftrightarrow \textbf{not } B] \textbf{ and } [B \Leftrightarrow S] \textbf{ and } [S \Rightarrow (A \Leftrightarrow 1)]$$

where 1 is as defined above.

Now $[C \Leftrightarrow \textbf{not } B] \textbf{ and } [S \Rightarrow (A \Leftrightarrow 1)]$
$\equiv [C \Leftrightarrow \textbf{not } B] \textbf{ and } [S \Rightarrow (A \Leftrightarrow \textbf{not } A)].$

So, by substitutivity, we get as in exercise 1.19

$[C \Leftrightarrow \text{not } B]$ and $[B \Leftrightarrow S]$ and $[S \Rightarrow (A \Leftrightarrow 1)]$
$\equiv [C \Leftrightarrow \text{not } B]$ and $[B \Leftrightarrow S]$ and **not** S
$\equiv [C \Leftrightarrow \text{not } B]$ and **not** B and **not** S
$\equiv C$ and **not** B and **not** S.

The conclusion is thus identical to the conclusion of exercise 1.19.

1.21 In this question we begin with the premise

$[A \Leftrightarrow (\text{not } A$ and **not** B and **not** $C)]$
and $[B \Leftrightarrow ((A$ and **not** B and **not** $C)$ **or**
$(\text{not } A$ and B and **not** $C)$ **or**
$(\text{not } A$ and **not** B and $C))]$

Now, intuitively, it is clear that a knight cannot make A's statement. Indeed the first conjunct in this expression can be simplified to

not A and $(B$ **or** $C)$.

The second conjunct can also be simplified to

$(B$ and **not** A and **not** $C)$ **or**
$(\text{not } B$ and **not** A and **not** $C)$ **or**
$(\text{not } B$ and A and $C)$.

Thus the entire expression simplifies to

not A and B and **not** C

i.e. A and C are knaves and B is a knight.

1.22 We use B to denote the proposition 'there is gold on island B' and H to denote the proposition 'the native who is asked the question is a knight (i.e. is Honest)'.

Our question 'Is Q true?' should be designed to meet the following four criteria:

 (i) If the native is a knight and his answer is yes then there is gold on island B.
 (ii) If the native is a knave and his answer is yes then there is gold on island B.
 (iii) If the native is a knight and his answer is no then there is no gold on island B.
 (iv) If the native is a knave and his answer is no then there is no gold on island B.

To symbolize these four requirements we need only understand the meaning of 'the answer is yes' and 'the answer is no'. Consider requirement (i). If a knight says 'yes' to the question 'Is Q true?' then we know that Q is true. Requirement (i) is therefore just

(i) H and $Q \Rightarrow B$.

Now consider the requirement (ii). If a knave says 'yes' to the question 'Is Q true?' then we know that Q is false, i.e, we know **not** Q. Thus requirement (ii) is equivalent to

(ii) **not** H and **not** $Q \Rightarrow B$.

Similarly we have for requirement (iii) and (iv)

(iii) H and **not** $Q \Rightarrow$ **not** B,
(iv) **not** H and $Q \Rightarrow$ **not** B.

In total, Q must meet the specification:

$(H$ and $Q \Rightarrow B)$ and (**not** H and **not** $Q \Rightarrow B)$
and $(H$ and **not** $Q \Rightarrow$ **not** $B)$ and (**not** H and $Q \Rightarrow$ **not** $B)$.

From now on it is straightforward to use the equivalences of section 1.7.3 to deduce Q.
Firstly, we replace p **and** $q \Rightarrow r$ everywhere by $q \Rightarrow (p \Rightarrow r)$ to obtain:

$[Q \Rightarrow (H \Rightarrow B)]$ and $[$**not** $Q \Rightarrow ($**not** $H \Rightarrow B)]$
and $[$**not** $Q \Rightarrow (H \Rightarrow$ **not** $B)]$ and $[Q \Rightarrow ($**not** $H \Rightarrow$ **not** $B)]$.

Now, we note that $\Rightarrow$ distributes over **and** so that we can combine the two terms involving Q and the two terms involving **not** Q:

$\{Q \Rightarrow [(H \Rightarrow B)$ and (**not** $H \Rightarrow$ **not** $B)]\}$
and $\{$**not** $Q \Rightarrow [($**not** $H \Rightarrow B)$ and $(H \Rightarrow$ **not** $B)]\}$.

Thus, recalling that if and only if is the conjunction of two if's:

$\{Q \Rightarrow (H \Leftrightarrow B)\}$ and $\{$**not** $Q \Rightarrow ($**not** $H \Leftrightarrow B)\}$

i.e. $\{Q \Rightarrow (H \Leftrightarrow B)\}$ and $\{$**not** $Q \Rightarrow$ **not** $(H \Leftrightarrow B)\}$
hence $Q \Leftrightarrow (H \Leftrightarrow B)$.

The last proposition defines Q for us. Thus the question to ask is 'Is $H \Leftrightarrow B$ true?' Or, in full,

'Is the statement that you are a knight equivalent to the statement that there is gold on island B?'

1.23 (a) Assume 1. (**not** A **or** B) and A
　　　　　　　　2. **not** A **or** B　　　　　　　　　(1, **and**-E)
　　　　　　　　3. A　　　　　　　　　　　　　　　　(1, **and**-E)
　　　　　　　　Assume 4. B

Assume 5. **not** A
      6. **false**   (3 and 5, **not**-E)
      7. B (6, **not**-I)
   8. B (2, 4 and 7, **or**-E)
9. $[(\text{**not** } A \text{ **or** } B) \text{ **and** } A] \Rightarrow B$ (1 and 8, $\Rightarrow$-I)

(b) Assume 1. $(A \text{ **or** } B) \text{ **and** } (A \Rightarrow C) \text{ **and** } (B \Rightarrow D)$
      2. $A \text{ **or** } B$ (1, **and**-E)
      3. $A \Rightarrow C$ (1, **and**-E)
      4. $B \Rightarrow D$ (1, **and**-E)
    Assume 5. A
          6. C (3 and 5, $\Rightarrow$-E)
          7. $C \text{ **or** } D$ (6, **or**-I)
    Assume 8. B
          9. D (4 and 8, $\Rightarrow$-E)
        10. $C \text{ **or** } D$ (9, **or**-I)
      11. $C \text{ **or** } D$ (2, 7 and 10, **or**-E)
   12. $[(A \text{ **or** } B) \text{ **and** } (A \Rightarrow C) \text{ **and** } (B \Rightarrow D)] \Rightarrow (C \text{ **or** } D)$
                                (1 and 11, $\Rightarrow$-I)

(c) Assume   1. $A \Rightarrow (B \text{ **and** } C)$
     Assume 2. A
         3. $B \text{ **and** } C$ (1 and 2, $\Rightarrow$-E)
         4. B (3, **and**-E)
     5. $A \Rightarrow B$ (2 and 4, $\Rightarrow$-I)
     Assume 6. A
         7. $B \text{ **and** } C$ (1 and 6, $\Rightarrow$-E)
         8. C (7, **and**-E)
     9. $A \Rightarrow C$ (6 and 8, $\Rightarrow$-I)
    10. $(A \Rightarrow B) \text{ **and** } (A \Rightarrow C)$ (5 and 9, **and**-I)
   11. $[A \Rightarrow (B \text{ **and** } C)] \Rightarrow [(A \Rightarrow B) \text{ **and** } (A \Rightarrow C)]$ (1 and 10, $\Rightarrow$I)

1.24 (a) Assume 1. $(A \Rightarrow B) \text{ **and** } (A \Rightarrow C)$
      2. $A \Rightarrow B$ (1, **and**-E)
      3. $A \Rightarrow C$ (1, **and**-E)
    Assume 4. A
         5. B (2 and 4, $\Rightarrow$-E)
         6. C (3 and 4, $\Rightarrow$-E)
         7. $B \text{ **and** } C$ (5 and 6, **and**-I)
     8. $A \Rightarrow (B \text{ **and** } C)$ (4 and 7, $\Rightarrow$-I)
   9. $[(A \Rightarrow B) \text{ **and** } (A \Rightarrow C)] \Rightarrow [A \Rightarrow (B \text{ **and** } C)]$ (1 and 8, $\Rightarrow$-I)

(b) Assume 1. $(A \Rightarrow B) \text{ **and** } (C \Rightarrow D) \text{ **and** } (\text{**not** } B \text{ **or** **not** } D)$
      2. $A \Rightarrow B$ (1, **and**-E)

3. $C \Rightarrow D$	(1, **and**-E)
4. **not** B **or not** D	(1, **and**-E)

Assume   5. **not** B

        Assume   6. A

7. B	(2 and 6, $\Rightarrow$-E)
8. **false**	(5 and 7, **not**-E)
9. **not** A	(6 and 8, **not**-I)
10. **not** A **or not** C	(9, **or**-I)

Assume   11. **not** D

        Assume   12. C

13. D	(3 and 12, $\Rightarrow$-E)
14. **false**	(11 and 13, **not**-E)
15. **not** C	(12 and 14, **not**-I)
16. **not** A **or not** C	(15, **or**-I)
17. **not** A **or not** C	(4, 10 and 16, **or**-E)
18. $[(A \Rightarrow B)$ **and** $(C \Rightarrow D)$ **and** $($**not** B **or not** $D)] \Rightarrow ($**not** A **or not** $C)$	
	(1 and 17, $\Rightarrow$-I)

(c) Assume   1. $($**not** $A \Rightarrow (B \Rightarrow C))$ **and** $($**not** $D \Rightarrow (C \Rightarrow E))$
                 and $(A \Rightarrow D)$ **and** $($**not** $D)$

2. **not** $A \Rightarrow (B \Rightarrow C)$	(1, **and**-E)
3. **not** $D \Rightarrow (C \Rightarrow E)$	(1, **and**-E)
4. $A \Rightarrow D$	(1, **and**-E)
5. **not** D	(1, **and**-E)
6. $C \Rightarrow E$	(3 and 5, $\Rightarrow$-E)

Assume   7. A

8. D	(4 and 7, $\Rightarrow$-E)
9. **false**	5 and 8, **not**-E)
10. **not** A	(7 and 9, **not**-I)
11. $B \Rightarrow C$	(2 and 10, $\Rightarrow$-E)

Assume   12. B

13. C	(11 and 12, $\Rightarrow$-E)
14. E	(6 and 13, $\Rightarrow$-E)
15. $B \Rightarrow E$	(12 and 14, $\Rightarrow$-I)
16. $[($**not** $A \Rightarrow (B \Rightarrow C))$ **and** $($**not** $D \Rightarrow (C \Rightarrow E))$	
and $(A \Rightarrow D)$ **and** $($**not** $D)] \Rightarrow (B \Rightarrow E)$	(1 and 15, $\Rightarrow$-I)

1.25 The suitor should choose the lead casket. The argument goes as follows.

Suppose   1. The inscription on the lead casket is false.

Then   2. It is the only false inscription and the inscriptions on the gold and silver caskets are both true.

           3. By 2, the portrait is in both the gold and silver caskets. This is a contradiction.

    4. We conclude that the inscription on the lead casket is true.

5. Hence both the inscriptions on the gold and silver caskets are false.

6. Hence the portrait is in the lead casket.

The premises are

(a) (*G* **and not** *S* **and not** *L*)
    or (**not** *G* **and** *S* **and not** *L*)
    or (**not** *G* **and not** *S* **and** *L*)
       (the portrait is in exactly one casket)

(b) $g \Leftrightarrow G$ (gold casket)

(c) $s \Leftrightarrow S$ (silver casket)

(d) $l \Leftrightarrow$(**not** *g* **and not** *s*) **or** (**not** *g* **and not** *l*) **or** (**not** *s* **and not** *l*)
       (lead casket)

1.26 The suitor should choose the lead casket. An informal argument for this proceeds as follows.

1. The dagger is in exactly one of the caskets.

2. If the inscription on the lead casket is true then the inscriptions on the gold and silver caskets are false.

3. If the inscription on the lead casket is false then the inscriptions on the gold and silver caskets are true.

4. The inscription on the gold casket is true if and only if the dagger is in the gold casket.

5. The inscription on the silver casket is true if and only if the dagger is not in the silver casket.

6. From 2, 4 and 5, if the inscription on the lead casket is true then the dagger is in the silver casket and not in the gold casket.

7. From 3, 4 and 5, if the inscription on the lead casket is false then the dagger is in the gold casket and not in the silver casket.

8. Combining 6 and 7, the dagger is either in the gold or the silver casket.

9. Thus, from 1 and 8, the dagger cannot be in the lead casket and this is the one the suitor should choose.

The premises are

(a) (*G* **and not** *S* **and not** *L*) **or** (**not** *G* **and** *S* **and not** *L*) **or** (**not** *G* **and not** *S* **and** *L*)

(b) $g \Leftrightarrow G$

(c) $s \Leftrightarrow$ **not** *S*

(d) $l \Leftrightarrow$ **not** [(*g* **and** *s*) **or** (*g* **and** *l*) **or** (*s* **and** *l*)]

CHAPTER 2

2.1   (a) and (c) are valid, (e) is unsatisfiable. For (b), (d), and (f) the following states satisfy the predicate

(b) $(m = 1, n = 0)$
(d) $(n = 0, k = 1, j = 1)$
(f) $(i = 0, j = 0)$
and the following do not
(b) $(m = 1, n = 1)$
(d) $(n = 0, k = 0, j = 1)$
(f) $(i = 1, j = 1)$.
(There are, of course, lots of other possibilities.)

2.2 (a) $\leqslant$, (b) $\leqslant$, (c) $\geqslant$, (d) $\geqslant$.

2.3 $i | j \equiv i \neq 0$ **and** $i * (j \text{ div } i) = j$
$even(i) \equiv 2 * (i \text{ div } 2) = i$.

2.4 (a) $i = j$.
(b) A trick question! This does not simplify any further than $z^{2(k \text{ div } 2)}$. The answer z^k is definitely wrong.
(c) This simplifies to **true** since it is valid.

2.5 $\{i: P(i)\} \div \{i: Q(i)\}$
$= \{i: (P(i) \text{ and not } Q(i)) \text{ or } (Q(i) \text{ and not } P(i))\}$.

2.6 (a) $\{i, j: p - m < i \leqslant p \text{ and } q - m < j \leqslant q\}$.
(b) $\{i, j: p \leqslant i < p + m \text{ and } q - m < j \leqslant q\}$.
(c) $\{i, j: (i = q \text{ and } p \leqslant j < n) \text{ or } (q < i < m \text{ and } 0 \leqslant j < n)\}$.
(d) $\{i, j: 0 \leqslant j \leqslant i < m\}$.

2.7 $\{i, j: (0 \leqslant i < q \text{ and } 0 \leqslant j \leqslant p) \text{ or } (q \leqslant i < m \text{ and } 0 \leqslant j < p)\}$.

2.8 $\{i, j: 0 < i \text{ and } 0 < j \text{ and } i + j \leqslant m\}$.

2.9 $greatgrandchildren(i) = \{j: 8 * i + 7 \leqslant j \leqslant 8 * i + 14\}$.

2.10 $children(i) = \{j: 3 * i + 1 \leqslant j \leqslant 3 * i + 3\}$,
$grandchildren(i) = \{j: 9 * i + 4 \leqslant j \leqslant 9 * i + 12\}$.
In a k-ary heap
$children(i) = \{j: k * i + 1 \leqslant j \leqslant k * (i + 1)\}$,
$grandchildren(i) = \{j: k^2 * i + k + 1 \leqslant j \leqslant k^2 * i + k^2 + k\}$.

2.11 The parent of node i in a binary heap is $(i - 1) \text{ div } 2$.
The parent of node i in a k-ary heap is $(i - 1) \text{ div } k$.

2.12 (a), (c), (d) all satisfy the proposition. The proposition is satisfied by all $q \geqslant 4$, so $q = 4$ is the minimum and there is no maximum.

2.13 (a) $\mathbf{A}(i: 0 \leqslant i < n: a[i] = b[i])$.
(b) $\mathbf{A}(i: 0 \leqslant i < n: a[i] < b[i])$.
(c) $\mathbf{A}(i, j: 0 \leqslant i < n \text{ and } 0 \leqslant j < n: a[i] < b[j])$.
(d) $\mathbf{A}(i: 0 < i < n: a[i - 1] \leqslant a[i])$
$\Rightarrow \mathbf{A}(i: 0 < i < n: b[i - 1] \leqslant b[i])$.
(e) $\mathbf{A}(i, j: 0 \leqslant i < n \text{ and } 0 \leqslant j < n: a[i] \leqslant a[j] \Rightarrow b[i] \leqslant b[j])$.
(f) $\mathbf{A}(i, j: 0 \leqslant i < n \text{ and } 0 \leqslant j < n: i \neq j \Rightarrow a[i] \neq a[j])$.

(g) $\mathbf{A}(i, j: 0 \leqslant i < n$ and $0 \leqslant j < n: a[i] \neq b[j])$.

2.14 (b) $\mathbf{E}(v: R: P) \equiv \mathbf{E}(v:: R$ and $P)$.

(d) $\mathbf{A}(v: R: P) \equiv \mathbf{A}(v:: R \Rightarrow P)$.

2.15 We formalize the predicate *nonredundant_copy* as 'every element of a is included at least once in b, and vice versa' and 'all the elements of b are distinct'.

$nonredundant\_copy(a, b, m, n)$
$\quad = \mathbf{A}(k:: \mathbf{E}(i: 0 \leqslant i < m: a[i] = k) \Leftrightarrow \mathbf{E}(j: 0 \leqslant j < n: b[j] = k))$
$\quad$ **and** $\mathbf{A}(i, j: 0 \leqslant i < n$ **and** $0 \leqslant j < n: i \neq j \Rightarrow b[i] \neq b[j])$.

2.16 (c) Some British cars are well made.

2.17 Consider the jth element of b. Its defining property is that it is an index to the array a, and $a[b[j]]$ is the smallest element of a after disregarding the elements $a[b[0]], \ldots, a[b[j-1]]$. The former property is expressed by

$0 \leqslant b[j] < n$

and the latter by

$\mathbf{A}(i: 0 \leqslant i < n: \mathbf{E}(k: 0 \leqslant k < j: b[k] = i)$ **or** $a[b[j]] \leqslant a[i])$.

Thus the predicate *ordering* is defined by

$ordering(a, b, n)$
$\quad \equiv \mathbf{A}(j: 0 \leqslant j < n:$
$\qquad \mathbf{A}(i: 0 \leqslant i < n:$
$\qquad\quad \mathbf{E}(k: 0 \leqslant k < j: b[k] = i)$
$\qquad\qquad$ **or** $a[b[j]] \leqslant a[i]$
$\qquad)$
$\quad)$

2.18 (a), (d), (f), and (h) are valid. The remainder are invalid.

2.19 $\mathbf{LEAST}(i: r(i): p(i)) = \mathbf{MIN}(i: r(i)$ **and** $p(i): i)$.

2.20 $is\_rank \equiv \mathbf{A}(j: 0 \leqslant j < n: b[j] = \mathbf{N}(i: 0 \leqslant i < n: a[i] < a[j]))$.

2.21 Several definitions of *allequal* can be given, all of which are equivalent. Three of them are

$allequal(j, len) \equiv \mathbf{A}(i: j - len < i < j: a[i-1] = a[i])$,
$allequal(j, len) \equiv \mathbf{A}(k: 0 < k < len: a[j - len] = a[j - k])$,
$allequal(j, len) \equiv \mathbf{A}(k: 0 < k < len: a[j - 1] = a[j - k])$.

The definitions of *plateau* and *longest_plateau_length* are then

$plateau(len, n) \equiv \mathbf{E}(j: 0 < j \leqslant n: 0 < len \leqslant j$ **and** $allequal(j, len))$,
$longest\_plateau\_length(n) = \mathbf{MAX}(len: plateau(len, n): len)$.

2.22 A maximal plateau is a plateau that cannot be extended either at its lower or its upper boundary. Thus

$maximal\_plateau(i, len, n)$
$\equiv allequal(i, len)$ (a plateau)
    and $(i = n$ **or** $a[i] \neq a[i-1])$
    and $(i = len$ **or** $a[i - len - 1] \neq a[i - len])$

The number of maximal plateaus can be obtained by counting their end points.

$no\_maximal\_plateaus\ (n) = \mathbf{N}(i{:}0 \leqslant i < n{:}$
$\mathbf{E}(len{:}\ len \geqslant 0{:}\ maximal\_plateau(i, len, n)))$

2.23 Two possible definitions are

$adjacent\_equal\_values(n)$
$\equiv \mathbf{A}(i, k{:}0 \leqslant i \leqslant k < n{:}(a[i] = a[k])$
$\Leftrightarrow \mathbf{A}(j{:}i \leqslant j \leqslant k{:}a[i] = a[j]))$

(This says that $a[i]$ and $a[j]$ are equal if and only if every element $a[k]$ between $a[i]$ and $a[j]$ is also equal to $a[i]$.)

$adjacent\_equal\_values(n)$
$\equiv \mathbf{A}(i, j, k{:}\ 0 \leqslant i < j < k < n{:}$
$a[i] = a[j]$ **or** $a[i] \neq a[k])$

2.24 $\mathbf{S}(i{:}\ 0 \leqslant i < n{:}\ \mathbf{S}(j{:}\ 0 \leqslant j < i{:}\ a[i, j]))$
$= \mathbf{S}(i, j{:}\ 0 \leqslant i < n$ **and** $0 \leqslant j < i{:}\ a[i, j])$ (Cartesian product)
$= \mathbf{S}(i, j{:}\ 0 \leqslant j < n$ **and** $j < i < n{:}\ a[i, j])$ (inequalities)
$= \mathbf{S}(j{:}\ 0 \leqslant j < n{:}\ \mathbf{S}(i{:}\ j < i < n{:}\ a[i, j]))$ (Cartesian product)

2.25 $\mathbf{Q}(i{:}\ r(i){:}\ \mathbf{Q}(j{:}\ s(i, j){:}\ f(i, j))$
$= \mathbf{Q}(i, j{:}\ r(i)$ **and** $s(i, j){:}\ f(i, j))$ (Cartesian product)
$= \mathbf{Q}(i, j{:}\ r(i)$ **and** $s(i, j)$ **and** $\mathbf{E}(k{:}\ r(k){:}\ s(k, j)){:}\ f(i, j))$ (exercise 2.27)
$= \mathbf{Q}(j{:}\ \mathbf{E}(k{:}\ r(k){:}\ s(k, j)){:}$
$\mathbf{Q}(i{:}\ r(i)$ **and** $s(i, j){:}\ f(i, j)))$ (Cartesian product)
$= \mathbf{Q}(j{:}\ \mathbf{E}(i{:}\ r(i){:}\ s(i, j)){:}$
$\mathbf{Q}(i{:}\ r(i)$ **and** $s(i, j){:}\ f(i, j)))$ (change of variable)

2.26 $minsum = \mathbf{MIN}(i, j{:}\ 0 \leqslant i < j \leqslant n{:}\ sum(i, j))$
$= \mathbf{MIN}(i, j{:}\ 0 \leqslant i < n$ **and** $i < j \leqslant n{:}\ sum(i, j))$ (inequalities)
$= \mathbf{MIN}(i, j{:}\ 0 \leqslant i < n$ **and** $i < j + 1 \leqslant n{:}\ sum(i, j + 1))$
                                                        (range translation, $g{:}\ j \mapsto j + 1$)
$= \mathbf{MIN}(i, j{:}\ 0 \leqslant i < n$ **and** $i \leqslant j < n{:}\ sum(i, j + 1))$ (inequalities)
$= \mathbf{MIN}(i, j{:}\ 0 \leqslant i \leqslant j < n{:}\ s(i, j))$
where $s(i, j) = sum(i, j + 1)$
$= \mathbf{S}(k{:}\ i \leqslant k < j + 1{:}\ b[k])$
$= \mathbf{S}(k{:}\ i \leqslant k \leqslant j{:}\ b[k])$ (inequalities)
2.27 $r(i)$ **and** $\mathbf{E}(k{::}\ r(k))$
$\equiv r(i)$ **and** $[\mathbf{E}(k{:}\ k = i{:}\ r(k))$ **or** $\mathbf{E}(k{:}\ k \neq i{:}\ r(k))]$ (range splitting)

$\equiv r(i)$ **and** $[r(i)$ **or** $\mathbf{E}(k: k \neq i: r(k))]$ (singleton range)
$\equiv r(i)$ (propositional calculus)

2.28 $\mathbf{Q}(i: [r(i)$ **and** $s(i)]$ **or** $[$**not** $r(i)$ **and** $t(i)]: f(i))$
$\quad = \mathbf{Q}(i: \{[r(i)$ **and** $s(i)]$ **or** $[$**not** $r(i)$ **and** $t(i)]\}$ **and** $r(i): f(i))$
$\quad\quad$ **q** $\mathbf{Q}(i: \{[r(i)$ **and** $s(i)]$ **or** $[$**not** $r(i)$ **and** $t(i)]\}$ **and not** $r(i): f(i))$
    (range splitting)
$\quad = \mathbf{Q}(i: r(i)$ **and** $s(i): f(i))$ **q** $\mathbf{Q}(i:$ **not** $r(i)$ **and** $t(i): f(i))$
    (propositional calculus)

2.29 $\mathbf{Q}(i: r(i): f(i))$ **q** $\mathbf{Q}(i: s(i): f(i))$
$\quad = \mathbf{Q}(i: r(i): f(i))$ **q**
$\quad\quad [\mathbf{Q}(i:$ **not** $r(i)$ **and** $s(i): f(i))$ **q** $\mathbf{Q}(i: r(i)$ **and** $s(i): f(i))]$
    (range splitting)
$\quad = [\mathbf{Q}(i: r(i): f(i))$ **q** $\mathbf{Q}(i:$ **not** $r(i)$ **and** $s(i): f(i))]$
$\quad\quad$ **q** $\mathbf{Q}(i: r(i)$ **and** $s(i): f(i))$ (associativity of **q**)
$\quad = \mathbf{Q}(i: r(i)$ **or** $s(i): f(i))$ **q** $\mathbf{Q}(i: r(i)$ **and** $s(i): f(i))$
    (range splitting and
    propositional calculus)

2.30 (a) Reflexivity: a **q** $a \equiv a$ (idempotency). Hence $a \leqslant a$.
   (b) Transitivity: $a \leqslant b$ **and** $b \leqslant c$
$\quad\quad\quad \equiv a$ **q** $b = a$ **and** b **q** $c = b$
$\quad\quad\quad \Rightarrow a$ **q** $b = a$ **and** a **q** $(b$ **q** $c) = a$
$\quad\quad\quad \Rightarrow a$ **q** $b = a$ **and** $(a$ **q** $b)$ **q** $c = a$
$\quad\quad\quad \Rightarrow a$ **q** $c = a$
$\quad\quad\quad \equiv a \leqslant c$.
   (c) Antisymmetry: $a \leqslant b$ **and** $b \leqslant a$
$\quad\quad\quad \equiv a$ **q** $b = a$ **and** b **q** $a = b$
$\quad\quad\quad \equiv a$ **q** $b = a$ **and** a **q** $b = b$
$\quad\quad\quad \equiv a = b$.
Since $a \equiv a$ **or** a **and** b,
$\mathbf{Q}(i: r(i): f(i))$
$\quad = \mathbf{Q}(i: r(i)$ **or** $r(i)$ **and** $s(i): f(i))$
$\quad = \mathbf{Q}(i: r(i): f(i))$ **q** $\mathbf{Q}(i: r(i)$ **and** $s(i): f(i))$ (range disjunction)
i.e. $\mathbf{Q}(i: r(i): f(i)) \leqslant_{\mathbf{q}} \mathbf{Q}(i: r(i)$ **and** $s(i): f(i))$

2.31 $c * \mathbf{MAX}(i: r(i): f(i))$.

2.32 $\mathbf{A}(i: r(i): \mathbf{true}) \equiv \mathbf{A}(i: r(i): \mathbf{true}$ **or** **true**$)$
$\quad\quad\quad\quad\quad\quad\quad\quad \equiv \mathbf{true}$ **or** $\mathbf{A}(i: r(i): \mathbf{true})$ (distributivity)
$\quad\quad\quad\quad\quad\quad\quad\quad \equiv \mathbf{true}$ (propositional calculus)

2.33 $\mathbf{S}(i: 0 \leqslant i < n: x^i)$
$\quad = x^0 + \mathbf{S}(i: 1 \leqslant i < n: x^i)$ (range splitting and
    singleton range)
$\quad = 1 + x * \mathbf{S}(i: 1 \leqslant i < n: x^{i-1})$ (distributivity)

$$= 1 + x*S(i: 0 \leqslant i < n - 1: x^i) \qquad \text{(range translation)}$$
$$= 1 + x*[S(i: 0 \leqslant i < n: x^i) - x^{n-1}] \qquad \text{(range splitting and}$$
$$\text{singleton range)}$$

$$= 1 - x^n + x*S(i: 0 \leqslant i < n: x^i)$$
Hence $(1 - x)*S(i: 0 \leqslant i < n: x^i) = 1 - x^n$
i.e. $S(i: 0 \leqslant i < n: x^i) = (1 - x^n)/(1 - x)$

2.34 $E(i: r(i): \textbf{false})$
$\equiv \textbf{not } A(i: r(i): \textbf{true}) \qquad \text{(De Morgan)}$
$\equiv \textbf{not true} \qquad \text{(exercise 2.32)}$
$\equiv \textbf{false}$

2.35 $E(i: r(i): p(i)) \Rightarrow E(j: s(j): q(j))$
$\equiv \textbf{not } E(i: r(i): p(i)) \textbf{ or } E(j: s(j): q(j)) \qquad \text{(implication)}$
$\equiv A(i: r(i): \textbf{not } p(i)) \textbf{ or } E(j: s(j): q(j)) \qquad \text{(De Morgan)}$
$\equiv A(i: r(i): \textbf{not } p(i) \textbf{ or } E(j: s(j): q(j))) \qquad \text{(generalized distributivity)}$
$\equiv A(i: r(i): p(i) \Rightarrow E(j: s(j): q(j))) \qquad \text{(implication)}$

2.36 $A(i: r(i): \textbf{false})$
$\equiv \textbf{not } E(i: r(i): \textbf{true}) \qquad \text{(De Morgan)}$
$\equiv \textbf{not } E(i: r(i) \textbf{ and true}: \textbf{true}) \qquad \text{(propositional calculus)}$
$\equiv \textbf{not } E(i: \textbf{true}: r(i) \textbf{ and true}) \qquad \text{(\textbf{E}-rule)}$
$\equiv \textbf{not } E(i: \textbf{true}: r(i)) \qquad \text{(propositional calculus)}$

2.37 $A(i: p \leqslant i < q: r(i) \Rightarrow (s(i) \textbf{ or } i = p))$
$\equiv A(i: p \leqslant i < q \textbf{ and } r(i): s(i) \textbf{ or } i = p) \qquad \text{(\textbf{A}-rule)}$
$\equiv A(i: p \leqslant i < q \textbf{ and } r(i) \textbf{ and } i \neq p: s(i)) \qquad \text{(\textbf{A}-rule and}$
$\text{propositional calculus)}$
$\equiv A(i: p < i < q \textbf{ and } r(i): s(i)) \qquad \text{(propositional calculus)}$
$\equiv A(i: p < i < q: r(i) \Rightarrow s(i)) \qquad \text{(\textbf{A}-rule)}$

2.38 $E(i: 0 \leqslant i: m = 2^i*q) \textbf{ and } E(d:: p = q*d + r - m)$
$\equiv E(i: 0 \leqslant i: m = 2^i*q \textbf{ and } E(d:: p = q*d + r - m)) \qquad \text{(distributivity)}$
$\equiv E(i: 0 \leqslant i: E(d:: m = 2^i*q \textbf{ and } p = q*d + r - m)) \qquad \text{(distributivity)}$
$\equiv E(i: 0 \leqslant i: E(d:: m = 2^i*q \textbf{ and } p = q*d + r))$
$\qquad \text{(range translation, } g: d \mapsto d - 2^i)$
$\equiv E(i: 0 \leqslant i: m = 2^i*q \textbf{ and } E(d:: p = q*d + r)) \qquad \text{(distributivity)}$
$\equiv E(i: 0 \leqslant i: m = 2^i*q) \textbf{ and } E(d:: p = q*d + r) \qquad \text{(distributivity)}$

CHAPTER 3

3.1 (a) $i \geqslant 0$
(b) $i + j = 0.$
(c) $i = -1 \textbf{ or } j = 1.$
(d) $z*j^i = c.$
(e) $a[i] = i.$

3.2 (a) This is valid; for,

$wp(S, \textbf{not } Q) \textbf{ and } wp(S, Q) \equiv wp(S, \textbf{false})$ (**and**-distributivity)

$\equiv \textbf{false}$ (excluded miracle)

i.e. $wp(S, \textbf{not } Q) \Rightarrow \textbf{not } wp(S, Q)$ (propositional calculus)

(b) Invalid. A state satisfying **not** $wp(S, Q)$ is one that either (i) causes S to not terminate or (ii) guarantees termination of S in a state satisfying **not** Q. A state satisfying $wp(S, \textbf{not } Q)$ is one satisfying (ii) and the disjunction (i) or (ii) does not imply (ii). Indeed, substituting $Q \equiv \textbf{false}$ in (b) we would obtain

$$\textbf{true} \Rightarrow wp(S, \textbf{true})$$

hence $\textbf{true} \equiv wp(S, \textbf{true})$

Thus (b) is equivalent to the claim that S always terminates.

(c) Valid; for,

$wp(S, Q \Rightarrow R) \Rightarrow [wp(S, Q) \Rightarrow wp(S, R)]$

$\equiv [wp(S, Q \Rightarrow R) \textbf{ and } wp(S, Q)] \Rightarrow wp(S, R)$ (propositional calculus)

$\equiv wp(S, (Q \Rightarrow R) \textbf{ and } Q) \Rightarrow wp(S, R)$ (**and**-distributivity)

$\equiv wp(S, Q \textbf{ and } R) \Rightarrow wp(S, R)$ (propositional calculus)

$\equiv \textbf{true}$

(d) Invalid. Taking $Q \equiv \textbf{false}$ and $R \equiv \textbf{true}$ we obtain

$(wp(S, \textbf{true}) \Rightarrow \textbf{false}) \Rightarrow wp(S, \textbf{true})$

(using the law of the excluded miracle). Thus

$\textbf{not } wp(S, \textbf{true}) \Rightarrow wp(S, \textbf{true})$

which (as in (b)) is clearly invalid.

3.3 $\{P\}$ S $\{\textbf{false}\}$ is valid if and only if P guarantees nontermination of S. $\{\textbf{true}\}$ S $\{\textbf{true}\}$ is always valid. Since $P \Rightarrow \textbf{true}$ is valid for any predicate P it therefore follows that $\{P\}$ S $\{\textbf{true}\}$ is valid for all P and S.

3.4 1. $\{i*j = j^k\} i := i*j \{i = j^k\}$ (assignment axiom)

2. $\{i*j = j^{k+1}\} k := k+1 \{i*j = j^k\}$ (assignment axiom)

3. $i = j^k \Rightarrow i*j = j^{k+1}$

4. $\{i = j^k\} k := k+1 \{i*j = j^k\}$ (2 and 3, consequence rule)

5. $\{i = j^k\} k := k+1; i := i*j \{i = j^k\}$ (1 and 4, sequential composition)

3.5 1. $\{s+j = i*(i+1)*(2*i+1)/6 \textbf{ and } j = i^2\}$

$s := s+j$

$\{s = i*(i+1)*(2*i+1)/6 \textbf{ and } j = i^2\}$ (assignment axiom)

2. $\{s+j+2*i-1 = i*(i+1)*(2*i+1)/6 \textbf{ and } j+2*i-1 = i^2\}$

$j := j+2*i-1$

$\{s+j = i*(i+1)*(2*i+1)/6 \textbf{ and } j = i^2\}$ (assignment axiom)

3. $\{s+j+2*(i+1)-1 = (i+1)*(i+2)*(2*i+3)/6$

$\textbf{and } j+2*i+1 = (i+1)^2\}$

$i := i+1$

$\{s + j + 2*i - 1 = i*(i + 1)*(2*i + 1)/6 \text{ and } j + 2*i - 1 = i^2\}$

(assignment axiom)

4. $\{s + j + 2*(i + 1) - 1 = (i + 1)*(i + 2)*(2*i + 3)/6$
   $\text{and } j + 2*i + 1 = (i + 1)^2\}$
   $i := i + 1; j := j + 2*i - 1$
   $\{s + j = i*(i + 1)*(2*i + 1)/6 \text{ and } j = i^2\}$

(2 and 3, sequential composition)

5. $\{s + j + 2*(i + 1) - 1 = (i + 1)*(i + 2)*(2*i + 3)/6$
   $\text{and } j + 2*i + 1 = (i + 1)^2\}$
   $i := i + 1; j := j + 2*i - 1; s := s + j$
   $\{s = i*(i + 1)*(2*i + 1)/6 \text{ and } j = i^2\}$

(1 and 4, sequential composition)

6. $s = i*(i + 1)*(2*i + 1)/6 \text{ and } j = i^2$
   $\Rightarrow s + j + 2*(i + 1) - 1 = i*(i + 1)*(2*i + 1)/6 + i^2 + 2*(i + 1) - 1$
   $\qquad\qquad\qquad = (i + 1)*(i + 2)*(2*i + 3)/6$

7. $j = i^2 \Rightarrow j + 2*i + 1 = i^2 + 2*i + 1 = (i + 1)^2$

8. $s = i*(i + 1)*(2*i + 1)/6 \text{ and } j = i^2$
   $\Rightarrow s + j + 2*(i + 1) - 1 = (i + 1)*(i + 2)*(2*i + 3)/6$
   $\text{and } j + 2*i + 1 = (i + 1)^2$

(6 and 7, propositional calculus)

9. $\{s = i*(i + 1)*(2*i + 1)/6 \text{ and } j = i^2\}$
   $i := i + 1; j := j + 2*i - 1; s := s + j$
   $\{s = i*(i + 1)*(2*i + 1)/6 \text{ and } j = i^2\}$

(5 and 8, consequence rule)

3.6   1. $\{j = i^{n+1} \text{ and } k = (i^{n+2} - 1)/(i - 1)\}$
   $n := n + 1$
   $\{j = i^n \text{ and } k = (i^{n+1} - 1)/(i - 1)\}$

(assignment axiom)

2. $\{j = i^{n+1} \text{ and } k + j = (i^{n+2} - 1)/(i - 1)\}$
   $k := k + j$
   $\{j = i^{n+1} \text{ and } k = (i^{n+2} - 1)/(i - 1)\}$

(assignment axiom)

3. $\{j = i^{n+1} \text{ and } k + j = (i^{n+2} - 1)/(i - 1)\}$
   $k := k + j; n := n + 1$
   $\{j = i^n \text{ and } k = (i^{n+1} - 1)/(i - 1)\}$

(1 and 2, sequential composition)

4. $\{j*i = i^{n+1} \text{ and } k + j*i = (i^{n+2} - 1)/(i - 1)\}$
   $j := j*i$
   $\{j = i^{n+1} \text{ and } k + j = (i^{n+2} - 1)/(i - 1)\}$

(assignment axiom)

5. $\{j*i = i^{n+1} \text{ and } k + j*i = (i^{n+2} - 1)/(i - 1)\}$
   $j := j*i; k := k + j; n := n + 1$

$\{j = i^n$ and $k = (i^{n+1} - 1)/(i - 1)\}$

(3 and 4, sequential composition)

6. $j = i^n$ and $k = (i^{n+1} - 1)/(i - 1)$

$\Rightarrow j*i = i^{n+1}$ and $k + j*i = (i^{n+1} - 1)/(i - 1) + i^{n+1}$

$= (i^{n+1} - 1 + i^{n+2} - i^{n+1})/(i - 1)$

$= (i^{n+2} - 1)/(i - 1)$

7. $\{j = i^n$ and $k = (i^{n+1} - 1)/(i - 1)\}$

$j := j*i; k := k + j; n := n + 1$

$\{j = i^n$ and $k = (i^{n+1} - 1)/(i - 1)\}$

(5 and 6, consequence rule)

3.7   1. $wp(n := n + 1, s = n^3$ and $i = 2*n$ and $k = n*(n + 1) + 1)$

$\equiv s = (n + 1)^3$ and $i = 2*(n + 1)$ and $k = (n + 1)*(n + 2) + 1$

(assignment axiom)

2. $wp(k := k + i,$

$s = (n + 1)^3$ and $i = 2*(n + 1)$ and $k = (n + 1)*(n + 2) + 1)$

$\equiv s = (n + 1)^3$ and $i = 2*(n + 1)$ and $k + i = (n + 1)*(n + 2) + 1$

(assignment axiom)

3. $wp(k := k + i; n := n + 1,$

$s = n^3$ and $i = 2*n$ and $k = n*(n + 1) + 1)$

$\equiv s = (n + 1)^3$ and $i = 2*(n + 1)$ and $k + i = (n + 1)*(n + 2) + 1$

(1 and 2, sequential composition)

4. $wp(s := s + n*i + k,$

$s = (n + 1)^3$ and $i = 2*(n + 1)$ and $k + i = (n + 1)*(n + 2) + 1)$

$\equiv s + n*i + k = (n + 1)^3$ and $i = 2*(n + 1)$

and $k + i = (n + 1)*(n + 2) + 1$

(assignment axiom)

5. $wp(s := s + n*i + k; k := k + i; n := n + 1,$

$s = n^3$ and $i = 2*n$ and $k = n*(n + 1) + 1)$

$\equiv s + n*i + k = (n + 1)^3$ and $i = 2*(n + 1)$

and $k + i = (n + 1)*(n + 2) + 1$

(3 and 4, sequential composition)

6. $wp(i := i + 2,$

$s + n*i + k = (n + 1)^3$ and $i = 2*(n + 1)$

and $k + i = (n + 1)*(n + 2) + 1)$

$\equiv s + n*(i + 2) + k = (n + 1)^3$ and $i + 2 = 2*(n + 1)$

and $k + i + 2 = (n + 1)*(n + 2) + 1$

(assignment axiom)

7. $wp(i := i + 2; s := s + n*i + k; k := k + i; n := n + 1,$

$s = n^3$ and $i = 2*n$ and $k = n*(n + 1) + 1)$

$\equiv s + n*(i + 2) + k = (n + 1)^3$ and $i + 2 = 2*(n + 1)$

and $k + i + 2 = (n + 1)*(n + 2) + 1$

(5 and 6, sequential composition)

8. $s = n^3$ and $i = 2*n$ and $k = n*(n+1)+1$
$\Rightarrow s + n*(i+2) + k = n^3 + n*(2*n+2) + n*(n+1)+1$
$\qquad = n^3 + 3*n^2 + 3*n + 1$
$\qquad = (n+1)^3$

9. $s = n^3$ and $i = 2*n$ and $k = n*(n+1)+1$
$\Rightarrow i + 2 = 2*(n+1)$

10. $s = n^3$ and $i = 2*n$ and $k = n*(n+1)+1$
$\Rightarrow k + i + 2 = n*(n+1) + 1 + 2*n + 2$
$\qquad = (n+1)*(n+2) + 1$

11. $s = n^3$ and $i = 2*n$ and $k = n*(n+1)+1$
$\Rightarrow s + n*(i+2) + k = (n+1)^3$ and $i + 2 = 2*(n+1)$
and $k + i + 2 = (n+1)*(n+2) + 1$

(8, 9, 10, propositional calculus)

12. $\{s = n^3$ and $i = 2*n$ and $k = n*(n+1)+1\}$
$i := i + 2; s := s + n*i + k; k := k + i; n := n + 1$
$\{s = n^3$ and $i = 2*n$ and $k = n*(n+1)+1\}$

(7 and 11, definition of wp and $\{P\}\ S\ \{Q\}$)

3.8
1. $wp(a := t, c^n = a*c + b) \equiv c^n = t*c + b$ (assignment axiom)
2. $wp(b := a, c^n = t*c + b) \equiv c^n = t*c + a$ (assignment axiom)
3. $wp(t := a + b, c^n = t*c + a) \equiv c^n = (a+b)*c + a$ (assignment axiom)
4. $wp(n := n + 1, c^n = (a+b)*c + a) \equiv c^{n+1} = (a+b)*c + a$
(assignment axiom)
5. $wp(n := n + 1;\ t := a + b;\ b := a;\ a := t,\ c^n = a*c + b)$
$\equiv c^{n+1} = (a+b)*c + a$ (1 to 4, sequential composition)
6. $c^2 - c - 1 = 0$ and $c^n = a*c + b$
$\Rightarrow c^{n+1} = a*c^2 + b*c = a*c^2 - a*c - a + a*c + a + b*c$
$\qquad = (a+b)*c + a$
i.e. $c^2 - c - 1 = 0$ and $c^n = a*c + b \Rightarrow c^{n+1} = (a+b)*c + a$
7. $\{c^2 - c - 1 = 0$ and $c^n = a*c + b\}$
$n := n + 1;$
$t := a + b;$
$b := a;$
$a := t;$
$\{c^n = a*c + b\}$ (5 and 6, definitions of wp and $\{P\}\ S\ \{Q\}$)

3.9
1. $1 \leqslant t \leqslant n$ and $q \geqslant 0$ and $p = q + 1$ and $s = p*(t-1) + q*(n-t)$
$\equiv 1 \leqslant t \leqslant n$ and $q \geqslant 0$ and $p = q + 1$ and $s = t - 1 + q*(n-1)$
(substitutivity and arithmetic)

2. $wp(t := s + 1 - q*(n-1), s = t - 1 + q*(n-1))$
$\equiv s = s + 1 - q*(n-1) - 1 + q*(n-1)$ (assignment axiom)
$\equiv$ **true** (arithmetic)

3. Hence,
$wp(q := s$ **div** $(n-1); p := q + 1; t := s + 1 - q*(n-1),$

$$s = t - 1 + q*(n-1))$$
$$\equiv \textbf{true} \qquad\qquad\qquad \text{(substitutivity)}$$
4. $wp(p:= q+1; t:= s+1-q*(n-1), p=q+1)$
$$\equiv q+1 = q+1 \quad \text{(assignment axiom and sequential composition)}$$
$$\equiv \textbf{true}$$
5. Hence,
$$wp(q:= s \,\textbf{div}\,(n-1); p:= q+1; t:= s+1-q*(n-1), p=q+1)$$
$$\equiv \textbf{true}$$
6. $wp(q:= s\,\textbf{div}\,(n-1); p:= q+1; t:= s+1-q*(n-1), q\geqslant 0)$
$$\equiv s\,\textbf{div}\,(n-1) \geqslant 0$$
$$\qquad\qquad\qquad \text{(assignment axiom and sequential composition)}$$
7. $wp(q:= s\,\textbf{div}\,(n-1); p:= q+1; t:= s+1-q*(n-1), 1\leqslant t\leqslant n)$
$$\equiv 1 \leqslant s+1 - [s\,\textbf{div}\,(n-1)] \leqslant n$$
$$\qquad\qquad\qquad \text{(assignment axiom and sequential composition)}$$
$$\equiv 0 \leqslant s - [s\,\textbf{div}\,(n-1)] < n \qquad\qquad \text{(arithmetic)}$$
8. $wp(q:= s\,\textbf{div}\,(n-1); p:= q+1; t:= s+1-q*(n-1),$
$$1\leqslant t\leqslant n \,\textbf{and}\, q\geqslant 0 \,\textbf{and}\, p=q+1 \,\textbf{and}\, s=p*(t-1)+q*(n-t))$$
$$\equiv s\,\textbf{div}\,(n-1)\geqslant 0 \,\textbf{and}\, 0\leqslant s-[s\,\textbf{div}\,(n-1)] < n$$
$$\qquad\qquad\qquad \textbf{(and-distributivity)}$$
9. $0\leqslant s < n$
$$\Rightarrow s\,\textbf{div}\,(n-1)\geqslant 0 \,\textbf{and}\, 0\leqslant s-[s\,\textbf{div}\,(n-1)] < n$$
$$\qquad\qquad\qquad \text{(properties of \textbf{div})}$$
10. $\{0\leqslant s < n\}$
$$q:= s\,\textbf{div}\,(n-1); p:= q+1; t:= s+1-q*(n-1)$$
$$\{1\leqslant t\leqslant n \,\textbf{and}\, q\geqslant 0 \,\textbf{and}\, p=q+1 \,\textbf{and}\, s=p*(t-1)+q*(n-t)\}$$
$$\qquad\qquad\qquad \text{(9, definition of } \{P\}\,S\,\{Q\})$$

3.10 The equivalence of (3.16) and (3.17) follows from exercise 1.14(j) by substituting B for $p, wp(S_1, Q)$ for q and $wp(S_2, Q)$ for r.

3.11 (a) $[odd(x)\Rightarrow even(x+1)]$ and $[\textbf{not}\ odd(x)\Rightarrow even(x)]$
which simplifies to **true**.
(b) $[even(i)\Rightarrow (y*y)^{i\,\textbf{div}\,2} = c]$ and $[\textbf{not}\ even(i)\Rightarrow y^i = c]$
which simplifies to $y^i = c$.
(c) $[x>y\Rightarrow x-y\geqslant 0$ and $y\geqslant 0]$ and $[x\leqslant y\Rightarrow x\geqslant 0$ and $y-x\geqslant 0]$
which simplifies to $x\geqslant 0$ and $y\geqslant 0$.
(d) $[x=y\Rightarrow(\textbf{true}\Leftrightarrow x=y)]$ and $[x\neq y\Rightarrow(equal\Leftrightarrow x=y)]$
which simplifies to $x\neq y\Rightarrow \textbf{not}\ equal$.
(e) $[(i+k)^2\leqslant n\Rightarrow(i+k)^2\leqslant n$ and $j^2 > n]$
and $[(i+k)^2 > n\Rightarrow\{(j-k)^2 > n\Rightarrow i^2\leqslant n$ and $(j-k)^2 > n\}$
and $\{(j-k)^2\leqslant n\Rightarrow i^2\leqslant n$ and $j^2 > n\}]$.
This does not simplify significantly.
(f) $[j=k+1\Rightarrow m=(i+1)*j]$ and $[j\neq k+1\Rightarrow m=i*j+k+1]$
which simplifies to $m=i*j+k+1$.

3.12 $wp(\text{if } B \text{ then } S, Q)$
   $\equiv (B \text{ and } wp(S,Q)) \text{ or } (\text{not } B \text{ and } Q)$

3.13   If one can prove that

{P and B}   (a) if **P and B** describes the state before
S   S is executed
{Q}   then Q will describe the state afterwards
                  and also that

P and not B   (b) if **P and not B** describes the state
⇒   then
Q   Q is automatically true
──────────   then one can infer that
{P}   if **P** describes the state before
if B then S   if **B then S** is executed
{Q}   then Q will describe the state afterwards.

3.14 Theorem Let P denote $[(B \Rightarrow wp(S,Q)) \text{ and } (\text{not } B \Rightarrow Q)]$.
Then   (a) {P} **if B then** S{Q}
and   (b) {R} **if B then** S {Q} implies $R \Rightarrow P$.
Proof
(a) By definition of *wp*, if $R \Rightarrow wp(S,Q)$ then {R} S {Q}.
    But **P and** $B \Leftrightarrow B$ **and** $wp(S,Q)$
              $\Rightarrow wp(S,Q)$
    Therefore {**P and B**} S {Q}   (1)
    Also **P and not** $B \equiv$ **not** B **and** Q
              $\Rightarrow Q$ (2)
    So, by (1) and (2) and the conditional rule,
          {P} **if B then** S{Q}
(b) Suppose {R} **if B then** S{Q}
    Then   {**R and B**} S {Q}
    and   **R and not** $B \Rightarrow Q$ (3)
    Hence, by definition of *wp*,
          R and $B \Rightarrow wp(S,Q)$ (4)
    So, by (3) and (4),
          $R \Rightarrow (B \Rightarrow wp(S,Q)) \text{ and } (\text{not } B \Rightarrow Q)$
    i.e. $R \Rightarrow P$.

3.15 (Example 3.27)
  1. $wp(m := k, m \geq i \text{ and } m \geq j \text{ and } m \geq k)$
     $\equiv k \geq i \text{ and } k \geq j$ (assignment axiom)
  2. $wp(m := j, m \geq i \text{ and } m \geq j \text{ and } m \geq k)$
     $\equiv j \geq i \text{ and } j \geq k$ (assignment axiom)
  3. $wp(S_1, m \geq i \text{ and } m \geq j \text{ and } m \geq k)$
     $\equiv j < k \Rightarrow (k \geq i \text{ and } k \geq j) \text{ and } j \geq k \Rightarrow (j \geq i \text{ and } j \geq k)$
                                              (2 and 3, conditional rule)
     $\equiv max(j, k) \geq i$

4. $wp(S_2, m \geqslant i$ **and** $m \geqslant j$ **and** $m \geqslant k)$
$\qquad \equiv max(i, k) \geqslant j$
The last step is proved similarly to step 3. Equally, 4 is 3 with the roles of i
and j reversed.

5. $wp(\textbf{if } i \leqslant j \textbf{ then } S_1 \textbf{ else } S_2, m \geqslant i$ **and** $m \geqslant j$ **and** $m \geqslant k)$
$\qquad \equiv [i \leqslant j \Rightarrow max(j, k) \geqslant i]$ **and** $[i > j \Rightarrow max(i, k) \geqslant j]$
$\qquad\qquad\qquad\qquad\qquad\qquad\qquad$ (3 and 4, conditional rule)

$\qquad \equiv$ **true**

(Example 3.28)
1. $\{j \geqslant i \geqslant k\}$ $interchange(i, j)\{i \geqslant j \geqslant k\}$ $\qquad$ (interchange rule)
2. $i < j$ **and** $[i \geqslant k$ **and** $j \geqslant k] \Rightarrow j \geqslant i \geqslant k$
3. $\{i < j$ **and** $[i \geqslant k$ **and** $j \geqslant k]\}$ $interchange(i, j)\{i \geqslant j \geqslant k\}$
$\qquad\qquad\qquad\qquad\qquad\qquad$ (1 and 2, consequence rule)
4. $i \geqslant j$ **and** $[i \geqslant k$ **and** $j \geqslant k] \Rightarrow i \geqslant j \geqslant k$
5. $\{i \geqslant k$ **and** $j \geqslant k\}S_3\{i \geqslant j \geqslant k\}$ $\qquad$ (3 and 4, conditional rule)

Note that the motivation for introducing the predicate $i \geqslant k$ **and** $j \geqslant k$ in
steps 2 to 5 is our earlier calculation that $wp(S_3, i \geqslant j \geqslant k) \equiv i \geqslant k$ **and**
$j \geqslant k$.

6. $\{i \geqslant j$ **and** $k \geqslant j\}$ $interchange(j, k)\{i \geqslant k$ **and** $j \geqslant k\}$
$\qquad\qquad\qquad\qquad\qquad\qquad$ (interchange rule)
7. $j < k$ **and** $i \geqslant j \Rightarrow i \geqslant j$ **and** $k \geqslant j$
8. $\{j < k$ **and** $i \geqslant j\}$ $interchange(j, k)$ $\{i \geqslant k$ **and** $j \geqslant k\}$
$\qquad\qquad\qquad\qquad\qquad\qquad$ (6 and 7, consequence rule)
9. $j \geqslant k$ **and** $i \geqslant j \Rightarrow i \geqslant k$ **and** $j \geqslant k$
10. $\{i \geqslant j\}S_2\{i \geqslant k$ **and** $j \geqslant k\}$ $\qquad$ (8 and 9, conditional rule)

In steps 6 to 10 the motivation for introducing $i \geqslant j$ is our earlier
calculation of $wp(S_2, i \geqslant k$ **and** $j \geqslant k)$.

11. $\{j \geqslant i\}$ $interchange(i, j)\{i \geqslant j\}$ $\qquad$ (interchange rule)
12. $i < j$ **and true** $\Rightarrow j \geqslant i$
13. $\{i < j$ **and true**$\}$ $interchange(i, j)\{i \leqslant j\}$
$\qquad\qquad\qquad\qquad\qquad\qquad$ (11 and 12, consequence rule)
14. $i \geqslant j$ **and true** $\Rightarrow i \geqslant j$ $\qquad\qquad\qquad$ (obviously!)
15. $\{$**true**$\}S_1\{i \geqslant j\}$ $\qquad\qquad$ (13 and 14, conditional rule)
16. $\{i \geqslant j\}S_2; S_3\{i \geqslant j \geqslant k\}$
$\qquad\qquad\qquad$ (5 and 10, rule of sequential composition)
17. $\{$**true**$\}S_1; S_2; S_3\{i \geqslant j \geqslant k\}$
$\qquad\qquad\qquad$ (15 and 16, rule of sequential composition)

3.16 1. $\{1 = x*y\}z := 1\{z = x*y\}$ $\qquad$ (assignment axiom)
2. $\{0 = x*y\}z := 0\{z = x*y\}$ $\qquad$ (assignment axiom)
3. $(x = y = 1)$ **and** $odd(p) \Rightarrow 1 = x*y$
4. $\{(x = y = 1)$ **and** $odd(p)\}z := 1\{z = x*y\}$
$\qquad\qquad\qquad\qquad\qquad\qquad$ (1 and 3, consequence rule)
5. $\{(x = 0$ **or** $y = 0)$ **and not** $odd(p)\}z := 0\{z = x*y\}$ $\quad$ (similar to 4)

Let P denote $[odd(p) \Rightarrow x = y = 1]$ and $[\textbf{not } odd(p) \Rightarrow x = 0 \textbf{ or } y = 0]$

6. $odd(p)$ **and** $P \equiv odd(p)$ **and** $x = y = 1$

7. **not** $odd(p)$ **and** $P \equiv$ **not** $odd(p)$ **and** $(x = 0 \textbf{ or } y = 0)$

8. $\{P\}$ **if** $odd(p)$ **then** $z := 1$ **else** $z := 0 \{z = x * y\}$

$\qquad\qquad\qquad\qquad\qquad\qquad$ (4, 5, 6, 7, conditional rule)

9. $p = m * n$ **and** $odd(p) \Rightarrow odd(m)$ **and** $odd(n)$

10. $p = m * n$ **and not** $odd(p) \Rightarrow$ **not** $odd(m)$ **or not** $odd(n)$

Hence

11. $[p = m * n$ **and** $(odd(m) \Leftrightarrow x = 1)$ **and** (**not** $odd(m) \Leftrightarrow x = 0)$
$\qquad$ **and** $(odd(n) \Leftrightarrow y = 1)$ **and** (**not** $odd(n) \Leftrightarrow y = 0)]$
$\qquad \Rightarrow [(odd(p) \Rightarrow x = y = 1)$ **and** (**not** $odd(p) \Rightarrow x = 0$ **or** $y = 0)]$

12. $\{p = m * n$ **and** $(odd(m) \Leftrightarrow x = 1)$ **and** (**not** $odd(m) \Leftrightarrow x = 0)$
$\qquad$ **and** $(odd(n) \Leftrightarrow y = 1)$ **and** (**not** $odd(n) \Leftrightarrow y = 0)\}$
if $odd(p)$ **then** $z := 1$ **else** $z := 0$
$\{z = x * y\}$ $\qquad\qquad\qquad\qquad$ (8 and 11, consequence rule)

Let Q denote $[p = m * n$ **and** $(odd(m) \Leftrightarrow x = 1)$ **and** (**not** $odd(m) \Leftrightarrow x = 0)$
$\qquad\qquad\qquad$ **and** $(odd(n) \Leftrightarrow y = 1)$ **and** (**not** $odd(n) \Leftrightarrow y = 0)]$

13. $\{p = m * n$ **and** $(odd(m) \Leftrightarrow x = 1)$ **and** (**not** $odd(m) \Leftrightarrow x = 0)$ **and not** $odd(n)\}$
$y := 0$
$\{Q\}$ $\qquad\qquad\qquad$ (assignment axiom and propositional calculus)

14. $\{p = m * n$ **and** $(odd(m) \Leftrightarrow x = 1)$ **and** (**not** $odd(m) \Leftrightarrow x = 0)$ **and** $odd(n)\}$
$y := 1$
$\{Q\}$ $\qquad\qquad\qquad$ (assignment axiom and propositional calculus)

15. $\{p = m * n$ **and** $(odd(m) \Leftrightarrow x = 1)$ **and** (**not** $odd(m) \Leftrightarrow x = 0)\}$
if $odd(n)$ **then** $y := 1$ **else** $y := 0$
$\{Q\}$ $\qquad\qquad\qquad\qquad\qquad$ (13 and 14, conditional rule)

16. $\{p = m * n$ **and not** $odd(m)\}$
$x := 0$
$\{p = m * n$ **and** $(odd(m) \Leftrightarrow x = 1)$ **and** (**not** $odd(m) \Leftrightarrow x = 0)\}$
$\qquad\qquad\qquad$ (assignment axiom and propositional calculus)

17. $\{p = m * n$ **and** $odd(m)\}$
$x := 1$
$\{p = m * n$ **and** $(odd(m) \Leftrightarrow x = 1)$ **and** (**not** $odd(m) \Leftrightarrow x = 0)\}$
$\qquad\qquad\qquad$ (assignment axiom and propositional calculus)

18. $\{p = m * n\}$
if $odd(m)$ **then** $x := 1$ **else** $x := 0$
$\{p = m * n$ **and** $(odd(m) \Leftrightarrow x = 1)$ **and** (**not** $odd(m) \Leftrightarrow x = 0)\}$
$\qquad\qquad\qquad\qquad\qquad$ (16 and 17, conditional rule)

19. $\{p = m * n\}$
if $odd(m)$ **then** $x := 1$ **else** $x := 0;$
if $odd(n)$ **then** $y := 1$ **else** $y := 0;$
$\{Q\}$ $\qquad\qquad\qquad$ (15 and 18, rule of sequential composition)

20. $\{p = m*n\}$
    if $odd(m)$ **then** $x := 1$ **else** $x := 0$;
    if $odd(n)$ **then** $y := 1$ **else** $y := 0$;
    if $odd(p)$ **then** $z := 1$ **else** $z := 0$
    $\{z = x*y\}$ (12 and 19, rule of sequential composition)

3.17 (a) N N

(b) ε S

(c) m ∀

3.18 (a) One possible answer is ○|○ because it is the only one with circles on both sides of the line.

(b) ◇ The line is opposite the marked angle. In all other cases the marked angle is adjacent to the line.

(c) ◁ The marked angle is not a right angle.

3.19 At all times the four beetles occupy the corners of a square. Thus at no time does any beetle have a component of its velocity away from its pursuer. The distance traveled by any one beetle is therefore identical to the distance it would travel were the pursued beetle to remain stationary i.e. 10 cm.

3.20 The operations preserve the parity of the white balls. Thus a white ball remains if and only if there were originally an odd number of white balls in the bag.

3.21 There are, respectively, 1, 3, and 7 **true** entries in the truth tables of p_0, $p_0 \Rightarrow p_1$, and $p_0 \Rightarrow (p_1 \Rightarrow p_2)$. The conjecture is therefore that there are $2^n - 1$ **true** entries in the truth table for $p_0 \Rightarrow (p_1 \Rightarrow (p_2 \Rightarrow \cdots (p_{n-2} \Rightarrow p_{n-1}) \cdots))$.

3.22 Let k denote the number of indices i for which a_i is **true**. Then $((\cdots((a_0 \Leftrightarrow a_1) \Leftrightarrow a_2) \cdots) \Leftrightarrow a_{n-1})$ is **true** if and only if k **div** 2 $= n$ **div** 2 (i.e. k is even if and only if n is even). Thus $a \Leftrightarrow b$ is **true** if and only if neither of or both of a and b are **true**; $(a \Leftrightarrow b) \Leftrightarrow c$ is **true** if and only if all three of or just one of a, b, and c is **true**, and $((a \Leftrightarrow b) \Leftrightarrow c) \Leftrightarrow d$ is **true** if and only if none of, exactly two of or all four of a, b, c, and d are **true**.

In these solutions we shall use the abbreviations lhs and rhs for the left-hand side and right-hand side of the equations, respectively.

3.23 Basis. When $n = 1$, lhs $= 1^2 = 1$, rhs $= 1*2*3/6 = 1$.
Induction step. Assume that

$$1^2 + 2^2 + \cdots + n^2 = n*(n+1)*(2*n+1)/6.$$

Then

$$1^2 + 2^2 + \cdots + n^2 + (n+1)^2$$
$$= n*(n+1)*(2*n+1)/6 + (n+1)^2$$

$$= (n+1)*[2*n^2 + n + 6*n + 6]/6$$
$$= (n+1)*(n+2)*(2*n+3)/6$$
$$= (n+1)*((n+1)+1)*(2*(n+1)+1)/6.$$

Hence, by induction,

$$1^2 + 2^2 + \cdots + n^2 = n*(n+1)*(2*n+1)/6 \quad \text{for all } n \geqslant 1.$$

3.24 Basis. When $n = 1$, lhs $= 1^3 = 1$, rhs $= 1^2*(1+1)^2/4 = 1$.
Induction step. Assume that

$$1^3 + 2^3 + \cdots + n^3 = n^2*(n+1)^2/4.$$

Then

$$1^3 + 2^3 + \cdots + n^3 + (n+1)^3$$
$$= n^2*(n+1)^2/4 + (n+1)^3$$
$$= (n+1)^2*(n^2 + 4*(n+1))/4$$
$$= (n+1)^2*(n+2)^2/4.$$
$$= (n+1)^2*((n+1)+1)^2/4.$$

Hence, by induction,
$$1^3 + 2^3 + 3^3 + \cdots + n^3 = n^2*(n+1)^2/4 \quad \text{for all } n \geqslant 1.$$

3.25 Assume $x \neq 1$.
Basis. When $n = 0$, lhs $= x^0 = 1$, rhs $= (x-1)/(x-1) = 1$.
Induction step. Assume that

$$x^0 + x^1 + x^2 + \cdots + x^n = (x^{n+1} - 1)/(x-1).$$

Then

$$x^0 + x^1 + x^2 + \cdots + x^n + x^{n+1}$$
$$= (x^{n+1} - 1)/(x-1) + x^{n+1}$$
$$= (x^{n+1} - 1 + x^{n+2} - x^{n+1})/(x-1)$$
$$= (x^{n+2} - 1)/(x-1)$$
$$= (x^{(n+1)+1} - 1)/(x-1).$$

Hence, by induction,

$$x^0 + x^1 + x^2 + \cdots + x^n = (x^{n+1} - 1)/(x-1)$$
$$\text{for all } n \geqslant 0 \text{ and } x \neq 1.$$

3.26 Assume $p > -1$
Basis. When $n = 1$, lhs $= 1 + p$, rhs $= 1 + p$ and clearly $1 + p \geqslant 1 + p$.
Induction step. Assume that

$$(1+p)^n \geqslant 1 + n*p.$$

Then, since $1 + p > 0$ by assumption,

$$(1+p)^{n+1} = (1+p)^n*(1+p)$$
$$\geqslant 1 + n*p + p + n*p^2$$

$$\geqslant 1 + n*p + p, \text{ since } p^2 \geqslant 0 \text{ and } n \geqslant 0$$
$$= 1 + (n+1)*p.$$

Hence, by induction,

$$(1+p)^n \geqslant 1 + n*p \text{ for all } n \geqslant 1 \text{ and } p > -1.$$

3.27 Basis. When $n = 1$, lhs $= 1/2$, rhs $= 1/2$.
Induction step. Assume that

$$1/(1*2) + 1/(2*3) + \cdots + 1/(n*(n+1)) = n/(n+1).$$

Then

$$1/(1*2) + 1/(2*3) + \cdots + 1/(n*(n+1)) + 1/((n+1)*(n+2))$$
$$= n/(n+1) + 1/((n+1)*(n+2))$$
$$= (n^2 + 2*n + 1)/((n+1)*(n+2))$$
$$= (n+1)^2/((n+1)*(n+2))$$
$$= (n+1)/(n+2)$$
$$= (n+1)/((n+1)+1).$$

Hence, by induction,

$$1/(1*2) + 1/(2*3) + \cdots + 1/(n*(n+1)) = n/(n+1) \text{ for all } n \geqslant 1.$$

3.28 Basis. When $n = 1$, lhs $= 1/2$, rhs $= 2 - 3/2 = 1/2$.
Induction step. Assume that

$$1/2 + 2/2^2 + 3/2^3 + \cdots + n/2^n = 2 - (n+2)/2^n.$$

Then

$$1/2 + 2/2^2 + 3/2^3 + \cdots + n/2^n + (n+1)/2^{n+1}$$
$$= 2 - (n+2)/2^n + (n+1)/2^{n+1}$$
$$= 2 - (2*n + 4 - (n+1))/2^{n+1}$$
$$= 2 - (n+3)/2^{n+1}$$
$$= 2 - ((n+1)+2)/2^{n+1}.$$

Hence, by induction,

$$1/2 + 2/2^2 + 3/2^3 + \cdots + n/2^n = 2 - (n+2)/2^n \text{ for all } n \geqslant 1.$$

3.29 Assume $q \neq 1$.
Basis. When $n = 1$, lhs $= 1$, rhs $= (1 - 2*q + q^2)/(1-q)^2 = 1$.
Induction step. Assume that

$$1 + 2*q + 3*q^2 + \cdots + n*q^{n-1}$$
$$= [1 - (n+1)*q^n + n*q^{n+1}]/(1-q)^2.$$

Then

$$1 + 2*q + 3*q^2 + \cdots + n*q^{n-1} + (n+1)*q^n$$
$$= [1 - (n+1)*q^n + n*q^{n+1}]/(1-q)^2 + (n+1)*q^n$$

$$= [1 - (n+1)*q^n + n*q^{n+1} + (n+1)*q^n$$
$$- 2*(n+1)q^{n+1} + (n+1)*q^{n+2}]/(1-q)^2$$
$$= [1 - (n+2)*q^{n+1} + (n+1)*q^{n+2}]/(1-q)^2$$
$$= [1 - ((n+1)+1)*q^{n+1} + (n+1)*q^{(n+1)+1}]/(1-q)^2.$$

Hence, by induction,

$$1 + 2*q + 3*q^2 + \cdots + n*q^{n-1}$$
$$= [1 - (n+1)*q^n + n*q^{n+1}]/(1-q)^2$$

for all $n \geqslant 1$ and $q \neq 1$.

3.30 (Exercise 3.21)

We begin by proving that

$$[p_0 \Rightarrow (p_1 \Rightarrow (p_2 \Rightarrow \cdots \Rightarrow (p_{n-2} \Rightarrow p_{n-1}) \cdots))]$$
$$\equiv [\mathbf{E}(i: 0 \leqslant i < n - 1: \mathbf{not}\ p_i)\ \mathbf{or}\ p_{n-1}]$$

Proof For $n = 1$ the right-hand side $\equiv p_0 \equiv$ the left-hand side. Suppose the proposition is **true** for n.

Then $p_0 \Rightarrow [p_1 \Rightarrow (p_2 \Rightarrow (p_3 \Rightarrow \cdots \Rightarrow (p_{n-1} \Rightarrow p_n) \cdots))]$
$$\equiv p_0 \Rightarrow [\mathbf{E}(i: 1 \leqslant i < n: \mathbf{not}\ p_i)\ \mathbf{or}\ p_n]$$
$$\equiv \mathbf{not}\ p_0\ \mathbf{or}\ [\mathbf{E}(i: 1 \leqslant i < n: \mathbf{not}\ p_i)\ \mathbf{or}\ p_n]$$
$$\equiv \mathbf{E}(i: 0 \leqslant i < n: \mathbf{not}\ p_i)\ \mathbf{or}\ p_n$$

Hence, by De Morgan's laws,

$$[p_0 \Rightarrow (p_1 \Rightarrow (p_2 \Rightarrow \cdots \Rightarrow (p_{n-2} \Rightarrow p_{n-1}) \cdots))]$$
$$\equiv \mathbf{not}\ (\mathbf{A}(i: 0 \leqslant i < n - 1: p_i)\ \mathbf{and}\ \mathbf{not}\ p_{n-1}).$$

There is exactly one combination of **true/false** values which satisfies $\mathbf{A}(i: 0 \leqslant i < n - 1: p_i)\ \mathbf{and}\ (\mathbf{not}\ p_{n-1})$ and so there are $2^n - 1$ combinations of **true/false** values for which

$$p_0 \Rightarrow (p_1 \Rightarrow (p_2 \Rightarrow \cdots (p_{n-2} \Rightarrow p_{n-1}) \cdots))\ \text{is}\ \textbf{true}.$$

(Exercise 3.22)

$a_0 \Leftrightarrow a_1 \Leftrightarrow \cdots \Leftrightarrow a_{n-1}$ is **true** if and only if the number k of indices i for which a_i is **true** satisfies $n\ \mathbf{div}\ 2 = k\ \mathbf{div}\ 2$.

Proof The basis is $n = 2$, in which case it is easily verified that $a_0 \Leftrightarrow a_1$ is **true** if and only if both of or neither of a_0 and a_1 is **true**.

Induction step. Suppose the proposition is true of n. Let k denote the number of **true** values among $a_0, a_1, \ldots, a_{n-1}$.

Then $(a_0 \Leftrightarrow a_1 \Leftrightarrow \cdots \Leftrightarrow a_{n-1}) \equiv k\ \mathbf{div}\ 2 = n\ \mathbf{div}\ 2$
So $a_0 \Leftrightarrow a_1 \Leftrightarrow \cdots \Leftrightarrow a_{n-1} \Leftrightarrow a_n$

$$\equiv [(k \ \textbf{div} \ 2 = n \ \textbf{div} \ 2) \ \textbf{and} \ a_n]$$
$$\textbf{or} \ [(k \ \textbf{div} \ 2 \neq n \ \textbf{div} \ 2) \ \textbf{and not} \ a_n]$$

Let k' denote the number of **true** entries among $a_0, \ldots, a_n$. Then $k' = k + 1$ if a_n is **true** and $k' = k$ if a_n is **false**. So $(k' \ \textbf{div} \ 2 = (n + 1) \ \textbf{div} \ 2) \Leftrightarrow (k \ \textbf{div} \ 2 = n \ \textbf{div} \ 2)$ if a_n is **true**, and $(k' \ \textbf{div} \ 2 \neq (n + 1) \ \textbf{div} \ 2) \Leftrightarrow (k \ \textbf{div} \ 2 = n \ \textbf{div} \ 2)$ if a_n is **false**.

Hence

$$a_0 \Leftrightarrow a_1 \Leftrightarrow \cdots \Leftrightarrow a_{n-1} \Leftrightarrow a_n$$
$$\equiv (k' \ \textbf{div} \ 2 = (n + 1) \ \textbf{div} \ 2).$$

3.31 We have $T(1) = 1$

and $\quad T(n) = 1 + T(1) + T(2) + \cdots + T(n - 1), \quad n \geqslant 2.$

So $\quad T(n) = 2 * T(n - 1).$

Basis. $\quad T(1) = 1 = 2^{1-1}.$
Induction step. Assume that $T(n) = 2^{n-1}$.
Then $T(n + 1) = 2 * T(n) = 2 * 2^{n-1} = 2^n = 2^{(n+1)-1}$.
Hence, by induction, $T(n) = 2^{n-1}$ for all $n \geqslant 1$.

3.32 Basis. When $n = 1$, lhs $= F_2 * F_0 - F_1^2$

$$= (F_1 + F_0) * F_0 - F_1^2$$
$$= 1 * 0 - 1^2 = -1$$
$$= \text{rhs}$$

Induction step. Suppose $n \geqslant 1$ and $F_{n+1} * F_{n-1} - F_n^2 = (-1)^n$.
Then $F_{n+2} * F_n - (F_{n+1})^2$

$$= (F_{n+1} + F_n) * F_n - (F_n + F_{n-1}) * F_{n+1}$$
$$= F_n^2 - F_{n-1} * F_{n+1}$$
$$= -(F_{n+1} * F_{n-1} - F_n^2)$$
$$= (-1) * (-1)^n$$
$$= (-1)^{n+1}$$

Hence, by (simple) induction, $F_{n+1} * F_{n-1} - (F_n)^2 = (-1)^n$ for all $n \geqslant 1$.

3.33 In the induction step it is stated that $F_{n+1} = F_n + F_{n-1}$. But this is false when $n = 0$.

3.34 Q_{n+1} is **true** if p_n is **true** or p_n and Q_n are both **false**. There are 2^n combinations of **true/false** values of $p_0, p_1, \ldots, p_{n-1}$ and so

$$T_{n+1} = 2^n + (2^n - T_n)$$

Hence $T_{n+1} + T_n = 2^{n+1}$ \hfill (1)

Now, from (1)

$$T_{n+2} = 2^{n+2} - T_{n+1}$$
$$= 2^{n+2} - 2^{n+1} + T_n$$
$$= 2^{n+1} + T_n$$ \hfill (2)

It is straightforward to use (2) to prove by induction on n that

$$T_{2n} = (2^{2n+1} + 1)/3 \qquad \text{for } n \geqslant 1$$

Whence from (1) we deduce that

$$T_{2n+1} = (2^{2n+1} - 1)/3 \quad \text{for } n \geqslant 1.$$

3.35 (a) $P_0 \equiv n = m$ **and** $s = m^3$ **and** $i = 2*m$ **and** $k = m*(m+1)+1$
$\equiv n = m$ **and** $s = n^3$ **and** $i = 2*n$ **and** $k = n*(n+1)+1$

Now, $wp(S, s = n^3$ **and** $i = 2*n$ **and** $k = n*(n+1)+1)$
$\equiv wp(i := i+2; s := s+n*i+k; k := k+i,$
$\quad s = (n+1)^3$ **and** $i = 2*(n+1)$ **and**
$\quad k = (n+1)*(n+2)+1)$
$\equiv wp(i := i+2; s := s+n*i+k,$
$\quad s = (n+1)^3$ **and** $i = 2*(n+1)$ **and**
$\quad k+i = (n+1)*(n+2)+1)$
$\equiv wp(i := i+2; s := s+n*i+k,$
$\quad s = (n+1)^3$ **and** $i = 2*(n+1)$ **and**
$\quad k = n*(n+1)+1)$
$\equiv wp(i := i+2,$
$\quad s+n*i+k = (n+1)^3$ **and** $i = 2*(n+1)$ **and**
$\quad k = n*(n+1)+1)$
$\equiv wp(i := i+2,$
$\quad s+2*n*(n+1)+n*(n+1)+1 = (n+1)^3$ **and**
$\quad i = 2*(n+1)$ **and** $k = n*(n+1)+1)$
$\equiv wp(i := i+2,$
$\quad s = n^3$ **and** $i = 2*(n+1)$ **and** $k = n*(n+1)+1)$
$\equiv s = n^3$ **and** $i+2 = 2*(n+1)$ **and** $k = n*(n+1)+1$
$\equiv s = n^3$ **and** $i = 2*n$ **and** $k = n*(n+1)+1$

(i.e. the latter formula is an invariant of S).

Thus $P_1 \equiv n \neq m$ **and** $wp(S, P_0)$
$\equiv n \neq m$ **and** $wp(S, n = m)$
$\qquad$ **and** $wp(S, s = n^3$ **and** $i = 2*n$ **and** $k = n*(n+1)+1)$
$\equiv n \neq m$ **and** $n+1 = m$
$\qquad$ **and** $s = n^3$ **and** $i = 2*n$ **and** $k = n*(n+1)+1)$

Similarly, by induction,

$P_k \equiv n \neq m$ **and** $n+k = m$
$\qquad$ **and** $s = n^3$ **and** $i = 2*n$ **and** $k = n*(n+1)+1$
$\equiv n = m-k$ **and** $s = n^3$ **and** $i = 2*n$ **and** $k = n*(n+1)+1$

Thus $wp(W, Q) \equiv n \leqslant m$ **and** $s = n^3$ **and** $i = 2*n$ **and** $k = n*(n+1)+1$.

(b) $P_0 \equiv n = m$ **and** $c^2 - c - 1 = 0$ **and** $c^m = a*c+b$
$\equiv n = m$ **and** $c^2 - c - 1 = 0$ **and** $c^n = a*c+b$
$\equiv n = m$ **and** $I(n, a, b)$

where $I(n, a, b) \equiv c^2 - c - 1 = 0$ and $c^n = a*c + b$.

Now $wp(S, I(n, a, b)) \equiv wp(n := n + 1; t := a + b; b := a, I(n, t, b))$
$\equiv wp(n := n + 1; t := a + b, I(n, t, a))$
$\equiv wp(n := n + 1, I(n, a + b, a))$
$\equiv I(n + 1, a + b, a)$
$\equiv c^2 - c - 1 = 0$ and $c^{n+1} = (a + b)*c + a$
$\equiv c^2 - c - 1 = 0$ and $c^{n+1} = a*(c + 1) + b*c$
$\equiv c^2 - c - 1 = 0$ and $c^{n+1} = a*c^2 + b*c$
$\equiv c^2 - c - 1 = 0$ and $c^n = a*c + b$
$\equiv I(n, a, b)$

(i.e. $I(n, a, b)$ is an invariant of S).

Thus $P_1 \equiv n \neq m$ and $wp(S, n = m$ and $I(n, a, b))$
$\equiv n \neq m$ and $wp(S, n = m)$ and $wp(S, I(n, a, b))$
$\equiv n + 1 = m$ and $I(n, a, b)$.

And, by induction,

$$P_k \equiv n + k = m \text{ and } I(n, a, b).$$

Hence $wp(W, Q) \equiv n \leqslant m$ and $I(n, a, b)$
$\equiv n \leqslant m$ and $c^2 - c - 1 = 0$ and $c^n = a*c + b$.

3.36 (a) Let S be $k := -k; s := s + k; i := i + 1$.
Then $wp(S, s = 0) \equiv s - k = 0 \equiv s = k$.
Also $wp(S, s = k) \equiv s - k = -k \equiv s = 0$
(i.e. $s = 0$ is left invariant by two executions of S).

Thus $P_0 \equiv i = n$ and $s = 0$
$P_1 \equiv i \neq n$ and $wp(S, i = n)$ and $wp(S, s = 0)$
$\equiv i = n - 1$ and $s = k$
$P_2 \equiv i \neq n$ and $wp(S, i = n - 1)$ and $wp(S, s = k)$
$\equiv i = n - 2$ and $s = 0$

Inductively, therefore,

$$P_{2k} \equiv i = n - 2*k \text{ and } s = 0 \qquad (k \geqslant 0)$$
$$P_{2k+1} \equiv i = n - 2*k - 1 \text{ and } s = k \qquad (k \geqslant 0)$$

Hence $wp(W, s = 0) \equiv \mathbf{E}(k: k \geqslant 0: i = n - 2*k$ and $s = 0)$
or $\mathbf{E}(k: k \geqslant 0: i = n - 2*k - 1$ and $s = k)$

(b) Let S be $y := 2*y; x := x$ **div** 2
Then $wp(S, c = x*y) \equiv c = (x$ **div** $2)*2*y$
(*Note*: this cannot be simplified further.)

So, $P_0 \equiv odd(x)$ and $c = x*y$
$P_1 \equiv \mathbf{not}\ odd(x)$ and $wp(S, odd(x)$ and $c = x*y)$
$\equiv \mathbf{not}\ odd(x)$ and $odd(x$ **div** $2)$ and $c = (x$ **div** $2)*2*y$
$\equiv \mathbf{not}\ odd(x)$ and $odd(x$ **div** $2)$ and $c = x*y$
(since $\mathbf{not}\ odd(x) \Rightarrow (x$ **div** $2)*2 = x$).

Similarly, $P_2 \equiv$ **not** $odd(x)$ **and not** $odd(x \textbf{ div } 2)$
$$\textbf{and } odd(x \textbf{ div } 4) \textbf{ and } c = x * y$$

and, by induction,

$$P_k \equiv [\textbf{A}(i: 0 \leqslant i < k: \textbf{ not } odd(x \textbf{ div } 2^i))]$$
$$\textbf{and } odd(x \textbf{ div } 2^k) \textbf{ and } c = x * y.$$

Hence $wp(W, Q) \equiv \textbf{E}(k: k \geqslant 0:$
$$[\textbf{A}(i: 0 \leqslant i < k: \textbf{ not } odd(x \textbf{ div } 2^i))]$$
$$\textbf{and } odd(x \textbf{ div } 2^k))$$
$$\textbf{and } c = x * y.$$

But, for any integer x, successive division by 2 will always yield an odd value. Formally,

$\textbf{E}(k: k \geqslant 0:$
$\quad [\textbf{A}(i: 0 \leqslant i < k: \textbf{ not } odd(x \textbf{ div } 2^i))]$
$\quad \textbf{and } odd(x \textbf{ div } 2^k))$
$\equiv \textbf{true}$

So $wp(W, Q) \equiv c = x * y$.

(c) Let S be $W(b); c := c - y; x := x - 1$
Then $wp(S, c = x * y) \equiv wp(W(b), c - y = (x - 1) * y)$
$$\equiv wp(W(b), c = x * y)$$
$$\equiv c = x * y$$

So, $P_0 \equiv x = 0$ **and** $c = x * y$
$P_1 \equiv x \neq 0$ **and** $wp(S, P_0)$
$\quad \equiv x = 1$ **and** $c = x * y$

and, by induction,

$$P_k \equiv x = k \textbf{ and } c = x * y$$

Thus $wp(W, Q) \equiv x \geqslant 0$ **and** $c = x * y$.

3.37 We are given that

$P_0 \equiv (\textbf{not } B) \textbf{ and } Q$
$R_0 \equiv B$
$T_0 \equiv B$
$P_k \equiv T_{k-1} \textbf{ and } wp(S^k, \textbf{not } B \textbf{ and } Q)$
$R_k \equiv wp(S^k, B)$ $\qquad\qquad k \geqslant 1.$
$T_k \equiv R_k \textbf{ and } T_{k-1}$

and we are to prove that

$$P_k \equiv B \textbf{ and } wp(S, P_{k-1}) \text{ for all } k \geqslant 1.$$

We begin by proving, by induction on k, that

$$T_k \equiv B \text{ and } wp(S, T_{k-1}) \text{ for all } k \geqslant 1.$$

Basis. $T_1 \equiv R_1 \text{ and } T_0$ (definition)
       $\equiv wp(S, B) \text{ and } B$ (definition)
       $\equiv B \text{ and } wp(S, T_0)$

Induction step. Assume that $T_k \equiv B \text{ and } wp(S, T_{k-1})$.

Then $T_{k+1} \equiv R_{k+1} \text{ and } T_k$ (definition)
          $\equiv wp(S^{k+1}, B) \text{ and } T_k$
          $\equiv wp(S, wp(S^k, B)) \text{ and } B \text{ and } wp(S, T_{k-1})$
          $\equiv B \text{ and } wp(S, wp(S^k, B) \text{ and } T_{k-1})$
          $\equiv B \text{ and } wp(S, T_k)$.   (induction hypothesis)

Thus, by induction,

$$T_k \equiv B \text{ and } wp(S, T_{k-1}). \qquad \text{(for all } k \geqslant 1)$$

Now we prove, by induction on k, that

$$P_k \equiv B \text{ and } wp(S, P_{k-1}) \text{ for all } k \geqslant 1.$$

Basis. $P_1 \equiv T_0 \text{ and } wp(S, \text{not } B \text{ and } Q)$
       $\equiv B \text{ and } wp(S, P_0)$.

Induction step. Assume that $P_k \equiv B \text{ and } wp(S, P_{k-1})$.
  Then $P_{k+1} \equiv T_k \text{ and } wp(S^{k+1}, \text{not } B \text{ and } Q)$
             $\equiv B \text{ and } wp(S, T_{k-1}) \text{ and } wp(S, wp(S^k, \text{not } B \text{ and } Q))$
             $\equiv B \text{ and } wp(S, T_{k-1} \text{ and } wp(S^k, \text{not } B \text{ and } Q))$
             $\equiv B \text{ and } wp(S, P_k)$.

So, by induction, $P_k \equiv B \text{ and } wp(S, P_{k-1})$ for all $k \geqslant 1$.

3.38 $wp(x := e, \textbf{true}) \equiv \textbf{true}$
(An assignment always terminates.)
$wp(\textbf{if } B \textbf{ then } S, \textbf{true}) \equiv B \Rightarrow wp(S, \textbf{true})$
                           $\equiv \textbf{not } B \textbf{ or } wp(S, \textbf{true})$
(**if** B **then** S terminates if B is **false** or S terminates.)
$wp(\textbf{if } B \textbf{ then } S_1 \textbf{ else } S_2, \textbf{true})$
       $\equiv [B \text{ and } wp(S_1, \textbf{true})] \text{ or } [\textbf{not } B \text{ and } wp(S_2, \textbf{true})]$
(**if** B **then** S_1 **else** S_2 terminates if either B is **true** and S_1 terminates or B is **false** and S_2 terminates.)
$wp(S_1; S_2, \textbf{true}) \equiv wp(S_1, wp(S_2, \textbf{true}))$

This does not simplify any further. The sequential composition

$i := 1;$
while $i > 0$ **do** $i := i + 1$

shows that $wp(S_1; S_2, \textbf{true}) \not\equiv wp(S_1, \textbf{true})$ and $wp(S_2, \textbf{true})$.
For $wp(S_1; S_2, \textbf{true})$ is **false**, whereas $wp(S_1, \textbf{true})$ and $wp(S_2, \textbf{true})$
is **true and** $i \leqslant 0$.

3.39 For **true** and **false** we have to verify that

$$\textbf{true and } B \textbf{ and } wp(S, \textbf{true}) \Rightarrow wp(S, \textbf{true})$$
$$\text{and } \textbf{false and } B \textbf{ and } wp(S, \textbf{false}) \Rightarrow wp(S, \textbf{false})$$

Both of these implications are simple consequences of the propositional
calculus.

3.40 We have to prove

$\{ [P \textbf{ and } B \textbf{ and } wp(S_1, \textbf{true}) \Rightarrow wp(S_1, Q)]$
and $[P \textbf{ and not } B \textbf{ and } wp(S_2, \textbf{true}) \Rightarrow wp(S_2, Q)] \}$
$\Rightarrow \{ [P \textbf{ and } (B \Rightarrow wp(S_1, \textbf{true})) \textbf{ and } (\textbf{not } B \Rightarrow wp(S_2, \textbf{true}))]$
$\Rightarrow [(B \Rightarrow wp(S_1, Q)) \textbf{ and } (\textbf{not } B \Rightarrow wp(S_2, Q))] \}.$

Letting T_1, T_2, Q_1, Q_2 denote $wp(S_1, \textbf{true})$, $wp(S_2, \textbf{true})$, $wp(S_1, Q)$, and
$wp(S_2, Q)$, respectively, the problem becomes one of showing that

$[(P \textbf{ and } B \textbf{ and } T_1 \Rightarrow Q_1) \textbf{ and } (P \textbf{ and not } B \textbf{ and } T_2 \Rightarrow Q_2)]$
$\Rightarrow \{ [P \textbf{ and } (B \Rightarrow T_1) \textbf{ and } (\textbf{not } B \Rightarrow T_2)] \Rightarrow [(B \Rightarrow Q_1) \textbf{ and } (\textbf{not } B \Rightarrow Q_2)] \}$
$\equiv \textbf{true}.$

This is a straightforward, although long, application of the equivalences
in section 1.7.3. Alternatively, it may be proved using the rules of
inference in 1.9.1.

3.41 The rule for **if** B **then** S is as follows:

If $P \textbf{ and } B \textbf{ and } wp(S, \textbf{true}) \Rightarrow wp(S, Q)$
and $P \textbf{ and not } B \Rightarrow Q$
then $P \textbf{ and } wp(\textbf{if } B \textbf{ then } S, \textbf{true}) \Rightarrow wp(\textbf{if } B \textbf{ then } S, Q).$

The rule for $S_1; S_2$ is as follows:

If $P \textbf{ and } wp(S_1, \textbf{true}) \Rightarrow wp(S_1, Q)$
and $Q \textbf{ and } wp(S_2, \textbf{true}) \Rightarrow wp(S_2, R)$
then $P \textbf{ and } wp(S_1; S_2, \textbf{true}) \Rightarrow wp(S_1; S_2, R).$

As in exercise 3.40, verifying the rule for **if** B **then** S involves
straightforward application of the equivalences in section 1.7.3. Verifying
the rule for sequential composition is not so straightforward since it
requires the use of Dijkstra's healthiness conditions (section 3.1.4). An

outline of a natural deduction style proof (section 1.9.2) is as follows.

First note that, since $wp(S_2, \textbf{true}) \Rightarrow \textbf{true}$ is a tautology, $wp(S_1, wp(S_2, \textbf{true})) \Rightarrow wp(S_1, \textbf{true})$, by Dijkstra's healthiness conditions,

i.e.   1. $wp(S_1; S_2, \textbf{true}) \Rightarrow wp(S_1, \textbf{true})$

Now, assume 2. $P \textbf{ and } wp(S_1, \textbf{true}) \Rightarrow wp(S_1, Q)$

and   3. $Q \textbf{ and } wp(S_2, \textbf{true}) \Rightarrow wp(S_2, R)$

Then, from 3 and Dijkstra's healthiness conditions,

           4. $wp(S_1, Q) \textbf{ and } wp(S_1; S_2, \textbf{true}) \Rightarrow wp(S_1; S_2, R)$

Now, make the further assumption,

           5. $P \textbf{ and } wp(S_1; S_2, \textbf{true})$

Then, by 1 and 2,

           6. $wp(S_1, Q)$

So, by 4, 5, and 6,

           7. $wp(S_1; S_2, R)$

Discharging the assumptions 2, 3, and 5, we have proved that

If $P \textbf{ and } wp(S_1, \textbf{true}) \Rightarrow wp(S_1, Q)$

and $Q \textbf{ and } wp(S_2, \textbf{true}) \Rightarrow wp(S_2, R)$

Then $P \textbf{ and } wp(S_1; S_2, \textbf{true}) \Rightarrow wp(S_1; S_2, R)$

3.42 $\{0 \neq k \textbf{ and } I(y, z, k)\}$
$\{I(y*z, z, k-1)\}$
$k := k - 1$
$y := y*z$
$\{I(y, z, k)\}$

The verification condition is

$$0 \neq k \textbf{ and } I(y, z, k) \Rightarrow I(y*z, z, k-1)$$

i.e. $0 \neq k \textbf{ and } 0 \leqslant k \textbf{ and } y*z^k = x^n$

$$\Rightarrow 0 \leqslant k - 1 \textbf{ and } (y*z)*z^{k-1} = x^n$$

3.43 $\{0 \neq k \textbf{ and } I(y, z, k)\}$
if $odd(k)$
then begin
     $\{odd(k) \textbf{ and } 0 \neq k \textbf{ and } I(y, z, k)\}$
     $\{even(k-1) \textbf{ and } I(y*z, z, k-1)\}$
     $k := k - 1;$

$y := y * z$
$\{even(k) \text{ and } I(y, z, k)\}$
end
else $\{\textbf{not } odd(k) \textbf{ and } 0 \neq k \textbf{ and } I(y,z,k)\} \{even(k) \textbf{ and } I(y,z,k)\}$
$\{even(k) \text{ and } I(y, z, k)\}$
$\{I(y, z*z, k \textbf{ div } 2)\}$
$k := k \textbf{ div } 2;$
$z := z * z$
$\{I(y, z, k)\}$

The verification conditions are

$odd(k) \textbf{ and } 0 \neq k \textbf{ and } I(y,z,k) \Rightarrow even(k-1) \textbf{ and } I(y*z,z,k-1)$
$\textbf{not } odd(k) \textbf{ and } 0 \neq k \textbf{ and } I(y,z,k) \Rightarrow even(k) \textbf{ and } I(y,z,k)$
$even(k) \textbf{ and } I(y, z, k) \Rightarrow I(y, z*z, k \textbf{ div } 2)$

3.44 $\{0 \leqslant n\}$
$\{1 * x^n = x^n \text{ and } 0 \leqslant n\}$
$k := n; \; y := 1; \; z := x;$
$\{\textbf{Invariant: } I(y, z, k)\}$
while $0 \neq k$ **do**
    begin
        (solution to exercise 3.43)
    end
$\{I(y, z, k) \text{ and } 0 = k\}$
$\{y = x^n\}$

The verification conditions are those obtained in exercise 3.43 together with

$0 \leqslant n \Rightarrow 1 * x^n = x^n \text{ and } 0 \leqslant n$

and

$y * z^k = x^n \text{ and } k = 0 \Rightarrow y = x^n.$

CHAPTER 4

4.1 1. $\{\textbf{E}(i: i \geqslant 0: m = 2^i * q) \text{ and } 0 \leqslant r < 2*m$
        $\text{and } \textbf{E}(d:: p = q*d + r)\}$
    if $r \geqslant m$ **then** $r := r - m$
    $\{\textbf{E}(i: i \geqslant 0: m = 2^i * q) \text{ and } 0 \leqslant r < m$
        $\text{and } \textbf{E}(d:: p = q*d + r)\}$
        (assignment axiom, conditional rule, and some simplification)
  2. $\{\textbf{E}(i: i \geqslant 0: m \textbf{ div } 2 = 2^i * q) \text{ and } 0 \leqslant r < 2*(m \textbf{ div } 2)$
        $\text{and } \textbf{E}(d:: p = q*d + r)\}$
    $m := m \textbf{ div } 2;$

if $r \geqslant m$ **then** $r := r - m$
$\{\mathbf{E}(i: i \geqslant 0: m = 2^i * q)$ **and** $0 \leqslant r < m$ **and** $\mathbf{E}(d:: p = q*d + r)\}$
              (assignment axiom and rule of sequential composition)

3. $\mathbf{E}(i: i \geqslant 1: m = 2^i * q) \Rightarrow \mathbf{E}(i: i \geqslant 0: (m \ \mathbf{div} \ 2) = 2^i * q)$
   Also, $m - 1 \leqslant 2*(m \ \mathbf{div} \ 2)$
   So $0 \leqslant r < m \equiv 0 \leqslant r \leqslant m - 1$
   $\Rightarrow 0 \leqslant r \leqslant 2*(m \ \mathbf{div} \ 2)$
   Hence $\mathbf{E}(i: i \geqslant 1: m = 2^i * q)$ **and** $0 \leqslant r < m$
         and $\mathbf{E}(d:: p = q*d + r)$
   $\Rightarrow \mathbf{E}(i: i \geqslant 0: (m \ \mathbf{div} \ 2) = 2^i * q)$ **and** $0 \leqslant r < 2*(m \ \mathbf{div} \ 2)$
         and $\mathbf{E}(d:: p = q*d + r)$

4.2 $\{0 \leqslant p$ **and** $0 < q\}$
$r := p;$
$m := q;$
$\{$**Invariant:** $\mathbf{E}(i: i \geqslant 0: m = b^i * q)$
 Variant: $r - m\}$
while $r \geqslant m$ **do** $m := b*m;$
$\{$**Invariant:** $0 \leqslant r < m$ **and** $\mathbf{E}(d:: p = q*d + r)$
        and $\mathbf{E}(i: i \geqslant 0: m = b^i * q)$
 Variant: $m - q\}$
while $m \neq q$ **do**
    begin
        $m := m \ \mathbf{div} \ b;$
        $\{$**Invariant:** $0 \leqslant r < b*m$ **and** $\mathbf{E}(d:: p = q*d + r)$
                 and $\mathbf{E}(i: i \geqslant 0: m = b^i * q)$
         Variant: $r - m\}$
        while $r \geqslant m$ **do** $r := r - m$
    end
$\{0 \leqslant r < q$ **and** $\mathbf{E}(d:: p = q*d + r)\}$

4.3 $\{0 \leqslant p$ **and** $0 < q\}$
$r := 0; k := n;$
$\{$**Invariant:** $0 \leqslant r < q$ **and** $\mathbf{E}(d:: s = q*d + r)$
        where $s*b^k = \mathbf{S}(i: k \leqslant i < n: p[i] * b^i)$
 Variant: $k\}$
while $k \neq 0$ **do**
    begin
        $k := k - 1;$
        $r := b*r + p[k];$
        while $r \geqslant q$ **do** $r := r - q$
    end
$\{0 \leqslant r < q$ **and** $\mathbf{E}(d:: p = q*d + r)$
    where $p = \mathbf{S}(i: 0 \leqslant i < n: p[i] * b^i)\}$

4.4 $\{0 \leqslant p = \mathbf{S}(i: 0 \leqslant i < n: p[i] * 2^i)\}$
$r:= 0;\ k:= n;$
$\{$Invariant: $0 \leqslant r < q$ and $\mathbf{E}(d:: s = q * d + r)$
        where $s * 2^k = 2^m * \mathbf{S}(i: k \leqslant i < n: p[i] * 2^i)$
  Variant: $k\}$
while $k \neq 0$ **do**
     begin
          $k:= k - 1;$
          $r:= 2 * r + p[k] * rm;$
          while $r \geqslant q$ **do** $r:= r - q\{at\ most\ two\ iterations\}$
     end
$\{0 \leqslant r < q$ and $\mathbf{E}(d:: p = q * d + r)\}$

Alternative solution that processes the bits of p in the order $p[0]$, $p[1], \ldots$.

$\{0 \leqslant p$ and $0 \leqslant rm < q$ and $\mathbf{E}(d:: 2^m = q * d + rm)\}$
$r:= 0;\ s:= rm;\ pp:= p;$
$\{$Invariant: $0 \leqslant r < q$ and $0 \leqslant s < q$ and $0 \leqslant pp$
        and $\mathbf{E}(k: k \geqslant 0: \mathbf{E}(d:: 2^m * p = q * d + 2^{m+k} * pp + r)$
        and $\mathbf{E}(d:: 2^{m+k} = q * d + s)$
  Variant: $pp\}$
while $pp \neq 0$ **do**
     begin
          if $odd(p)$
          then begin $r:= r + s;$ **if** $r \geqslant q$ **then** $r:= r - q$
               end;
          $pp:= pp$ **div** 2;
          $r:= 2 * r;$ **if** $r \geqslant q$ **then** $r:= r - q;$
          $s:= 2 * s;$ **if** $s \geqslant q$ **then** $s:= s - q$
     end
$\{0 \leqslant r < q$ and $\mathbf{E}(d:: 2^m * p = q * d + r)\}$

4.5 $(x^3 + x^2 + 1)*(x^2 + 1) + x + 1$
    $= (x^5 + x^4 + x^2) + (x^3 + x^2 + 1) + (x + 1)$
    $= x^5 + x^4 + x^3 + (x^2 + x^2) + x + (1 + 1)$
    $= x^5 + x^4 + x^3 + x$

4.6 (a) $x^2 + 1$
    (b) 1
    (c) $x^3 + x^2 + x$

4.7 $\mathbf{E}(d(x):: \mathbf{S}(i: k \leqslant i < n: p_i x^{i-k}) = q(x) * d(x) + R(x))$
    $\equiv \mathbf{E}(d(x):: x^k * \mathbf{S}(i: k \leqslant i < n: p_i x^{i-k}) = x^k * q(x) * d(x) + x^k * R(x))$
    $\equiv \mathbf{E}(d(x):: p(x) = q(x) * x^k * d(x) + x^k * R(x) + \mathbf{S}(i: 0 \leqslant i < k: p_i x^i))$

$$\equiv \mathbf{E}(d(x)\text{::}\, p(x) = q(x) * x^k * d(x) + r(x))$$
$$\Rightarrow \mathbf{E}(d(x)\text{::}\, p(x) = q(x) * d(x) + r(x))$$

4.8 $\{degree(q(x)) = m\}$
$k := degree(p(x)) + 1;\ R(x) := 0;$
$\{$**Invariant**: $\mathbf{E}(d(x)\text{::}\, x^m * P(x) = q(x) * d(x) + r(x))$
  and $degree(R(x)) < m$
  where $r(x) = x^k * R(x) + x^m * \mathbf{S}(i\text{:}\, 0 \leqslant i < k\text{:}\, P_i x^i)$
 Variant: $k\}$
while $k > 0$ **do begin**
$$k := k - 1;$$
$$R(x) := x * R(x) + (R_{m-1} + P_k) * q(x)$$
    end
$\{\mathbf{E}(d(x)\text{::}\, x^m * P(x) = q(x) * d(x) + R(x))$ **and** $degree(R(x)) < m\}$

4.9 The index t delimiting the extent of the **true** entries at the beginning of the array can be defined by

$0 \leqslant t \leqslant n$ **and** $\mathbf{A}(i\text{:}\, 0 \leqslant i < t\text{:}\, b[i])$ **and** $(t = n$ **or not** $b[t])$.

The value of t can be computed by adding a **false** entry at the end of the array and searching for the first **false** entry.

$b[n] := \mathbf{false};\ t := 0;$
$\{$**Invariant**: $0 \leqslant t \leqslant n$ **and** $\mathbf{A}(i\text{:}\, 0 \leqslant i < t\text{:}\, b[i])$
 Variant: $n - t\}$
while $b[t]$ **do** $t := t + 1$
$\{0 \leqslant t \leqslant n$ **and** $\mathbf{A}(i\text{:}\, 0 \leqslant i < t\text{:}\, b[i])$ **and not** $b[t]\}$

Similarly by setting $b[-1]$ to **true** and searching from the end of the array for the first **true** entry we determine f where

$-1 \leqslant f < n$ **and** $\mathbf{A}(i\text{:}\, f < i \leqslant n\text{:}\, \mathbf{not}\ b[i])$ **and** $b[f]$.

Then is_*split* is determined by

is_*split* $\equiv f = t - 1$.

4.10 $p := 0;\ s := n;\ k := 0;$
$\{$**Invariant**: $no\_occurrences(p, m, 0, s) + k = no\_occurrences(0, m, 0, n)$
 Variant: $s - p\}$
while $(p \neq m)$ **and** $(s \neq 0)$ **do**
   begin
    if $a[p, s-1] < x$ **then** $p := p + 1$
    else if $a[p, s-1] > x$ **then** $s := s - 1$
    else begin $k := k + 1;\ p := p + 1;\ s := s - 1$
      end
   end

4.11 Imagine an array of infinite extent such that the value at location (i, j) is $i^2 + j^2$. This array satisfies the ordering relation on rows and columns required by Saddleback Search and so it suffices first to delimit the area of search and then to apply one of the solutions to Saddleback Search.

Noting that $0 \leqslant i \leqslant j$ and $i^2 + j^2 = r \Rightarrow 0 \leqslant i \leqslant j \leqslant r$ we begin with the assignments $p := 0$ and $q := r$ and terminate the search when $p > q$.

$p := 0;\ q := r;\ k := 0;$
{**Invariant**: $\mathbf{N}(i, j: 0 \leqslant i \leqslant j: i^2 + j^2 = r)$
$\qquad\qquad = k + \mathbf{N}(i, j: p \leqslant i \leqslant j \leqslant q: i^2 + j^2 = r)$
   Variant: $q - p$}
while $p \leqslant q$ **do**
      begin
            if $p^2 + q^2 < r$ **then** $p := p + 1$
            else if $p^2 + q^2 > r$ **then** $q := q - 1$
            else begin $k := k + 1;\ p := p + 1;\ q := q - 1$
                 end
      end

4.12 Consider the array $a[i, j] = f(i) - g(j)$. This *increases* along rows and *decreases* along columns. Thus with a little bit of rethinking of Saddleback Search one obtains the following.

{$\mathbf{E}(i, j :: f(i) = g(j))$}
$p := 0;\ q := 0;$
{**Invariant**: $\mathbf{A}(i, j: 0 \leqslant i < p\ \text{or}\ 0 \leqslant j < q: f(i) \neq g(j))$}
while $f(p) \neq g(q)$ **do**
      begin
            if $f(p) < g(q)$ **then** $p := p + 1$
            else {$f(p) > g(q)$}$q := q + 1$
      end

4.13 {$0 \leqslant n$}
$k := 0;\ x := any\_item;\ i := 0;\ m := 0;$
{**Invariant**: $\mathbf{A}(y :: no\_occurrences(y, i) \leqslant i\ \mathbf{div}\ 2$
               and $\mathbf{N}(j: i \leqslant j < k: a[j] = x) = (k - i + m)\ \mathbf{div}\ 2$
   Variant: $n - k$}
while $k \neq n$ **do**
      begin
            if $a[k] = x$ **then** $m := m + 1$
            else if $m = 0$ **then begin** $x := a[k];$
                              $i := k;$
                              $m := 1$
                     end
            else $m := m - 1;$

$k := k + 1$
end
$\{possible\_majority(x, n)\}$

4.14 $x < y \equiv \mathbf{E}(i: 0 \leqslant i$ and $i < len(x) - 1$ and $i < len(y) - 1:$
$\mathbf{A}(j: 0 \leqslant j < i: x_j = y_j)$ and $x_i < y_i)$
or $(len(x) < len(y)$ and $\mathbf{A}(i: 0 \leqslant i < len(x): x_i = y_i)).$

4.15 The complication in resetting p (comparing $len(d[m])$ with k) can be removed from the loop by first testing whether $len(d[p]) = k$ and if so incrementing p by 1. The simplification is *not* warranted because there are lots of words in the English dictionary that have many entries. (Look up the word 'set' next time you have a dictionary to hand.)

4.16 The boundaries p and q may both take the value n, in which case the array access $d[p]$ would give a runtime error.

4.17 The problem with this approach is that information gleaned from searching for $x[0..k]$ cannot be utilized in searching for $x[0..k-1]$. Such an algorithm would therefore require a much larger number of character comparisons.

4.18 **if** $color(w - 1) = white$ **then** $w := w - 1$
else begin $swap(m, w - 1); m := m + 1$
end

4.19 **if** $color(m) = black$ **then** $m := m + 1$
else if $color(w - 1) = white$ **then** $w := w - 1$
else begin $swap(m, w - 1);$
$m := m + 1; w := w - 1$
end
This code is marginally more efficient since it reduces the number of swaps. In particular, it will never swap two white elements or two black elements.

4.20 $\{$**Global invariant**: $\mathbf{A}(i: 0 \leqslant i < n: color(i) = red$
or $color(i) = white$ **or** $color(i) = blue)\}$
$r := 0; w := n;$
$\{$**Invariant**: $0 \leqslant r \leqslant w \leqslant n$
and $\mathbf{A}(i: 0 \leqslant i < r: color(i) = red)$
and $\mathbf{A}(i: w \leqslant i < n: color(i) = white$ **or** $color(i) = blue)$
Variant: $w - r\}$
while $r \neq w$ **do**
begin
if $color(r) = red$ **then** $r := r + 1$
else begin $w := w - 1; swap(r, w)$
end
end
$\{0 \leqslant r = w \leqslant n$

and $A(i: 0 \leqslant i < r: color(i) = red)$
and $A(i: r \leqslant i < n: color(i) = white$ or $color(i) = blue)\}$
$b := n;$
$\{$**Invariant:** $0 \leqslant r \leqslant w \leqslant b \leqslant n$
      and $A(i: 0 \leqslant i < r: color(i) = red)$
      and $A(i: r \leqslant i < w: color(i) = white)$
      and $A(i: b \leqslant i < n: color(i) = blue)$
      and $A(i: w \leqslant i < b: color(i) = white$ or $color(i) = blue)$
Variant: $b - w\}$
while $w \neq b$ **do**
  if $color(w) = white$ **then** $w := w + 1$
  else begin $b := b - 1; swap(w, b)$
        end
$\{A(i: 0 < i < r: color(i) = red)$
and $A(i: r \leqslant i < w: color(i) = white)$
and $A(i: w \leqslant i < n: color(i) = blue)\}$

4.21 (a)
$$A(i: 0 \leqslant i < m: a_0[i] = a[n + i])$$
$$\equiv A(i: n \leqslant i < m + n: a_0[i - n] = a[i])$$
$$\equiv A(i: n \leqslant i < m + n:$$
$$a_0[(i - n + (m + n)) \bmod (m + n)] = a[i])$$
$$\equiv A(i: n \leqslant i < m + n: a_0[(i + m) \bmod (m + n)] = a[i])$$

Also,
$$A(i: 0 \leqslant i < n: a[i] = a_0[m + i])$$
$$\equiv A(i: 0 \leqslant i < n: a[i] = a_0[(m + i) \bmod (m + n)])$$

Hence
$$A(i: 0 \leqslant i < m: a_0[i] = a[n + i])$$
$$\text{and } A(i: 0 \leqslant i < n: a[i] = a_0[m + i])$$
$$\equiv A(i: 0 \leqslant i < n: a[i] = a_0[(m + i) \bmod (m + n)])$$
$$\text{and } A(i: n \leqslant i < m + n: a[i] = a_0[(m + i) \bmod (m + n)])$$
$$\equiv A(i: 0 \leqslant i < m + n: a[i] = a_0[(m + i) \bmod (m + n)])$$

Similarly, by translating the range of

$$A(i: 0 \leqslant i < n: a[i] = a_0[m + i])$$

to $m \leqslant i < m + n$, one proves the second part of this question.

(b) $\{0 \leqslant m$ and $A(i: 0 \leqslant i < m + n: a[i] = a_0[i])\}$
$k := 0;$
$\{$**Invariant:** $0 \leqslant k \leqslant m$ **and**
      $A(i: 0 \leqslant i < m + n: a[i] = a_0[(i + k) \bmod (m + n)])$
Variant: $m - k\}$
while $k \neq m$ **do**
  begin $j := 0; t := a[0]$
    $\{$**Invariant:** $0 \leqslant j < m + n$
    and $A(i: 0 \leqslant i < j: a[i] = a_0[(i + k + 1) \bmod (m + n)])$
    and $A(i: j \leqslant i < m + n: a[i] = a_0[(i + k) \bmod (m + n)])$

and $t = a_0[k]$
Variant: $m + n - 1 - j$}
while $j < m + n - 1$ **do**
    begin $a[j] := a[j + 1]; j := j + 1$
    end
{$\mathbf{A}(i: 0 \leqslant i < m + n - 1: a[i] = a_0[(i + k + 1) \bmod (m + n)])$
and $t = a_0[k]$}
$a[m + n - 1] := t;$
$k := k + 1$
  end
{$\mathbf{A}(i: 0 \leqslant i < m + n: a[i] = a_0[(i + m) \bmod (m + n)])$}

A similar algorithm with invariant property $0 \leqslant k \leqslant n$ **and**
$\mathbf{A}(i: 0 \leqslant i < m + n: a_0[i] = a[(i + k) \bmod (m + n)])$ can be derived as
follows:
(a) decrease k from n to 0, (b) decrease j from $m + n$ to 1, (c) record
$a[m + n - 1]$ in t.

4.22 The simplification is that there is a plateau of length $m + 1$ ending at $a[k]$
if $a[k - m] = a[k]$. If, however, $a[k - m] \neq a[k]$ then the length of the
longest plateau ending at $a[k]$ is at most m. Thus, m' is unnecessary, and
the statement to reset m is

if $a[k - m] = a[k]$ **then** $m := m + 1$

4.23 Consider expressing $split(k + 1)$ in terms of $split(k)$

$split(k + 1) \equiv \mathbf{E}(i: 0 \leqslant i \leqslant k: is\_split(i, k + 1))$
             and $is\_split(k + 1, k + 1)$.   (range splitting)

The predicate $is\_split(k + 1, k + 1)$ expresses the assertion that all the
elements of the array segment $b[0..k]$ are **true**. This suggests that we
introduce a variable *alltrue*, say, into our program with the property
  $alltrue \equiv is\_split(k, k)$

Clearly the following code will suffice to compute *alltrue*

  $alltrue :=$ **true**; $k := 0;$
  while $k \neq n$ **do**
    begin $alltrue := alltrue$ **and** $b[k]; k := k + 1$
    end

Now $\mathbf{E}(i: 0 \leqslant i \leqslant k: is\_split(i, k + 1))$
  $\equiv \mathbf{E}(i: 0 \leqslant i \leqslant k: \mathbf{A}(j: 0 \leqslant j < i: b[j])$
    and $\mathbf{A}(j: i \leqslant j < k + 1: \mathbf{not}\ b[j]))$
  $\equiv \mathbf{E}(i: 0 \leqslant i \leqslant k: \mathbf{A}(j: 0 \leqslant j < i: b[j])$
    and $\mathbf{A}(j: i \leqslant j < k: \mathbf{not}\ b[j]))$ **and not** $b[k]$ (distributivity)

  $\equiv split(k)$ **and not** $b[k]$

Thus we obtain the following code:

```
alltrue:= true; split:= true; k:= 0
{Invariant: 0 ⩽ k ⩽ n
            and alltrue ≡ A(i: 0 ⩽ i < k: b[i])
            and split ≡ split(k)
   Variant: n − k}
while k ≠ n do
   begin
      alltrue:= alltrue and b[k];
      split:= (split and not b[k]) or alltrue;
      k:= k + 1
   end
```

4.24 Taking our cue from the solution to the longest ascending segment problem, let

$$laas(n) = \textbf{MAX}(i, j: 0 \leqslant i < j \leqslant n \text{ and } aas(i, j): j − i)$$

and $laas\_at(j) = \textbf{MAX}(i: 0 \leqslant i < j \text{ and } aas(i, j): j − i).$

Then $laas(1) = laas\_at(1) = 1$

and $laas(k + 1) = \textbf{MAX}(j: 0 < j \leqslant k + 1: laas\_at(j))$
$$= max(laas(k), laas\_at(k + 1))$$

Now, $laas\_at(k + 1) = laas\_at(k) + 1$ if $a[k − 1] \leqslant a[k]$

and, $laas\_at(k + 1) = las\_at(k) + 1$ if $a[k − 1] > a[k].$

Thus, adding two extra variables $p = laas(k)$ and $p' = laas\_at(k)$ to the solution to the longest ascending segment problem we obtain the following (the variable m is no longer necessary):

```
{1 ⩽ n}
k:= 1; m':= 1; p:= 1; p':= 1;
{Invariant: 0 < k ⩽ n and m' = las_at(k)
            and p = laas(k) and p' = laas_at(k)
   Variant: n − k}
while k ≠ n do
   begin
      if a[k − 1] ⩽ a[k]
      then begin m':= m' + 1; p':= p' + 1
           end
      else begin p':= m' + 1; m':= 1
           end;
      p:= max(p, p');
      k:= k + 1
   end
{p = laas(n)}
```

4.25 (Minsum problem) We consider a loop that computes $minsum(k)$ for successive values of k

$k := 0;\ m := 0;$
{**Invariant:** $0 \leqslant k \leqslant n$ **and** $m = minsum(k)$
 Variant: $n - k$}
while $k \neq n$ **do**
    begin
        {$m = minsum(k)$ **and** $0 \leqslant k < n$}
        revise m;
        {$m = minsum(k + 1)$}
        $k := k + 1$
    end
{$m = minsum(n)$}

What further information is required to compute $minsum(k + 1)$ from $minsum(k)$? Examples 2.14 and 2.18 suggest we introduce a variable m' with the invariant property

$$m' = ms(k)$$
where $ms(j) = \textbf{MIN}(i: 0 \leqslant i \leqslant j: sum(i, j))$

is the minimum sum of a sequence of array elements ending with $a[j - 1]$. Then (example 2.34)

    $minsum(k + 1) = min(minsum(k), ms(k + 1))$
and $ms(k + 1) = min(a[k], ms(k) + a[k])$

so we obtain

$k := 0;\ m := 0;\ m' := 0;$
{**Invariant:** $m = minsum(k)$ **and** $m' = ms(k)$ **and** $0 \leqslant k \leqslant n$
 Variant: $n - k$}
while $k \neq n$ **do**
    begin
        $m' := min(a[k], m' + a[k]);$
        $m := min(m, m')$
        $k := k + 1$
    end

4.26 The array M would need to be indexed from 0 to m, and the invariant property $T(k, M)$ replaced by

$\textbf{A}(i: p \leqslant i < m: M[j] = t(i, q))$
and $\textbf{A}(i: 0 \leqslant i < p: M[i] = t(i, q + 1))$.

A similar change in the roles of p and q needs to be made to the property

$S(k, s)$, and, within the algorithm itself, references to $M[q]$ would be changed to $M[p]$.

4.27 $\{1 \leqslant m \text{ and } 1 < n\}$
$i := 1; \ p := 0;$
$\{$**Invariant**: $a[p, 0] = \mathbf{MAX}(i': 0 \leqslant i' < i: a[i', 0])$
  Variant: $m - i\}$
while $i \neq m$ **do**
    begin if $a[i, 0] > a[p, 0]$ **then** $p := i;$
        $i := i + 1$
    end
$k := 1; \ q := 0;$
$\{$**Invariant**: $0 < k \leqslant n$ and $0 \leqslant p < m$ and $0 \leqslant q < n$
        and $a[p, q] = M(p) = \mathbf{MIN}(j: 0 \leqslant j < k: M(j))$
Variant: $n - k\}$
while $k \neq n$ **do**
    begin
        if $a[0, k] < a[p, q]$
        then begin $r := 0; \ i := 1; \ a[m, k] := a[p, q];$
               $\{$**Invariant**: $0 < i \leqslant m$ and $0 \leqslant r < m$
                 and $a[r, k] = \mathbf{MAX}(i': 0 \leqslant i' < i: a[i, k]) < a[p, q]$
                 and $a[m, k] = a[p, q]$
               Variant: $m - i\}$
               while $a[i, k] < a[p, q)$ **do**
                 begin
                     if $a[i, k] > a[r, k]$ **then** $r := i;$
                     $i := i + 1$
                 end
               if $i = m$ **then begin** $p := r; \ q := k$
                                     end
        end;
           $k := k + 1$
    end
$\{a[p, q] = M(p) = \mathbf{MIN}(j: 0 < j < n: M(j))\}$

4.28 (a) $is\_path(s) \equiv \mathbf{E}(p:: \mathbf{E}(x:: p = \lambda_x)$ and $p \cdot from = s$ and $p \cdot into = x)$
                     or $\mathbf{E}(p', a: path(p')$ and $p' \cdot into = a \cdot from: p' \cdot from = s$
                       and $a \cdot into = s)$
           $\equiv$ **true**
    For $x \neq s$
    $is\_path(x) \equiv \mathbf{E}(p', a: path(p')$ and $p' \cdot into = a \cdot from: p' \cdot from = s$
                and $a \cdot into = x)$

$$\equiv \mathbf{E}(a\colon a \cdot into = x\colon$$
$$\mathbf{E}(p'\colon path(p') \textbf{ and } p' \cdot from = s \textbf{ and } p' \cdot into = a \cdot from))$$
$$\equiv \mathbf{E}(a\colon a \cdot into = x\colon is\_path(a \cdot from))$$

(b) $is\_path(a) \equiv \textbf{true}$
   $is\_path(b) \equiv is\_path(b)$

Both $is\_path(b) \equiv \textbf{true}$ and $is\_path(b) \equiv \textbf{false}$ are solutions to the second equation.

(c) $unequal\colon = \textbf{true}; ip(s)\colon = \textbf{true}; \textbf{for each } x \neq s \textbf{ do } ip(x)\colon = \textbf{false};$
   {**Invariant**: [*unequal* or $\mathbf{A}(x\colon x \neq s\colon$
$$ip(x) \equiv \mathbf{E}(a\colon a \cdot into = x\colon ip(a \cdot from)))]$$
     and $\mathbf{A}(x\colon ip(x)\colon \mathbf{E}(p\colon p \cdot from = s \textbf{ and } p \cdot into = x))$
   Variant: $\mathbf{N}(x\colon\colon ip(x)) + \textbf{if } unequal \textbf{ then } 1 \textbf{ else } 0\}$
   while *unequal* **do**
      begin
         $unequal\colon = \textbf{false};$
         for each a **do**
            begin
               if (**not** $ip(a \cdot into)$) **and** $ip(a \cdot from)$
               then begin
                     $ip(a \cdot into)\colon = \textbf{true};$
                     $unequal\colon = \textbf{true}$
                  end
            end
      end

The algorithm terminates in a state in which $ip(s) \equiv \textbf{true}$ and, for all $x \neq s$, $ip(x) \equiv \mathbf{E}(a\colon a \cdot into = x\colon ip(a \cdot from))$. Moreover, whenever $ip(x)$ is **true** there is a path from s to x. Thus if $ip(x) \not\equiv is\_path(x)$ on termination it must be the case that $x \neq s$, $ip(x) \equiv \textbf{false}$ and $is\_path(x) \equiv \textbf{true}$. Consider such a node y that is closest to s (where now distance is measured by arc_count). Then a path to y must take the form $p\ a$ where $p \cdot into = a \cdot from$ and, by the choice of y, $ip(p \cdot into) \equiv \textbf{true}$. But then $ip(y) \not\equiv \mathbf{E}(a\colon a \cdot into = y\colon ip(a \cdot from))$, which is a contradiction.

4.29 The least bridge height on a path p is defined inductively as follows.

$$\lambda_x \cdot height = \infty$$
$$(p\ a) \cdot height = min(p \cdot height, a \cdot height)$$

The minimum bridge height on a route from s to x that maximises the minimum bridge height is then

$$h(x) = \mathbf{MAX}(p\colon path(p) \textbf{ and } p \cdot from = s \textbf{ and } p \cdot into = x\colon p \cdot height)$$

Noting that min distributes over max, we can then prove

$$h(s) = \infty$$

and $h(x) = \mathbf{MAX}(a: a \cdot into = x: min(h(a \cdot from), a \cdot height))$

when $x \neq s$.

Using $d(x)$ to denote an approximation to $h(x)$, both the solution by successive approximations and Dijkstra's algorithm can be converted by changing occurrences of $+$ to min, occurrences of min to max and the initial assignments to $d(s) := \infty$ and $d(x) := -\infty$, for all $x \neq s$. (The important observation is that max and min obey the same algebraic properties as those of min and $+$ that are used in the derivation of the two solutions.) Thus Dijkstra's algorithm for the bridge problem takes the following form.

$d(s) := \infty$; **for each** $x \neq s$ **do** $d(x) := -\infty$;
$B := \emptyset$; $chosen := \emptyset$;
{**Invariant**: $B \subseteq A$ and $\mathbf{A}(x::d(x) = h_B(x))$
         and $\mathbf{A}(x: x$ **in** $chosen: d(x) = h_A(x))$
  Variant: $|X| - |chosen|$}
  while $B \neq A$ **do**
    begin
        choose a node y not in chosen such that
            $d(y) = \mathbf{MAX}(x: \mathbf{not}(x$ **in** $chosen): d(x))$
        $chosen := chosen \cup \{y\}$;
        for each *arc a from y* **do**
            begin
                $d(a \cdot into) := max(d(a \cdot into), min(d(y), a \cdot height))$;
                $B := B \cup \{a\}$
            end
    end

4.30 The significance of this exercise is that the change from sum to product in the definition of the length of a path destroys the essential distributivity property, namely that summation distributes over min, but product does not distribute over min.

The solution by successive approximations can be retrieved by defining the *measure* of a path to be a pair of Booleans $(u, \mathbf{not}\ u)$ where u is **true** if and only if the path has length 1. The measure of an arc is defined similarly. Defining summation on measures by

$(u, v) + (u', v') = ((u$ **and** $u')$ **or** $(v$ **and** $v')$,
$\qquad\qquad\qquad\qquad (u$ **and** $v')$ **or** $(u'$ **and** $v))$

ensures   that $(pa) \cdot measure = p \cdot measure + a \cdot measure$. Also,   defining minimization on measures by

$$min((u, v), (u', v')) = (u \text{ or } u', v \text{ or } v'),$$

the distance to node x is obtained from

$$(u, v) = \text{MIN}(p: p \cdot from = s \text{ and } p \cdot into = x: p \cdot measure)$$

as follows. If v is **true** then the distance to x is -1; if v is **false** the distance to x is 1 if u is **true**; otherwise, there is no path to x in the graph. Moreover, with these definitions, min does indeed distribute over $+$.

Dijkstra's algorithm is not applicable. Were it so the distance to the start node, s, would be known at the outset. But it is clearly possible for there to be a path of length -1 from s to itself. Such a path would necessarily have nonzero arc-length.

Index